Also by Jane Stern

TRUCKER:
A Portrait of the Last American Cowboy

Also by Jane and Michael Stern

ROADFOOD

AMAZING

David Obst Books

Random House New York

JANE & MICHAEL STERN

Manufactured in the United States of America

to FLORENCE, HARRY, and TEDDY

ACKNOWLEDGMENTS

Without the efforts and interest of others,
the task of writing *Amazing America*
would have been considerably more difficult.
In acknowledgment, we want to establish
THE JANE AND MICHAEL STERN HALL OF FAME.

Charter Members:

KATHY MATTHEWS—For singular editorial acumen,
an inspiration and a joy to work with.

DAVID OBST—For his enthusiasm,
which served as a foundation for our energies.

BETTY ANNE CLARKE—For careful guidance and good advice.

PREFACE

It is possible—especially if you are an urban dweller—that some of the addresses to specific sights in *Amazing America* will seem skimpy. In every case we have tried to be as specific as possible. An attraction that bears a route number and a town name but no street address is listed that way because the town is so small they don't use street names or numbers. There are a few sights so far from main roads that they may be hard to find, and for these we have tried to indicate as clearly as possible just how to get there. If you have trouble, don't hesitate to ask local people to point the way. We have found postmen and police to be the most valuable sources for directions.

We hope you enjoy the sights that we have selected for this book as much as we have. If you find any new ones you feel are terrific, too, we would love to hear about them for future editions.

Jane and Michael Stern
c/o Random House / Obst Books
201 East 50th Street
New York, N.Y., 10022

CONTENTS

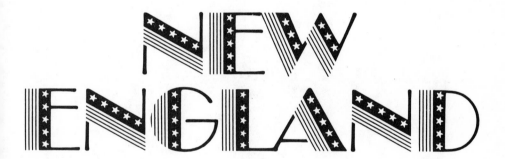

CONNECTICUT

BLOOMFIELD

COPACO FOOD CENTER

335 Cottage Grove Rd., Bloomfield, Conn.;
Mon–Sat 8 AM–6 PM;
Free; tours available to interested groups (203) 242–5521

Copaco Food Center is a complete meat-processing house. Live animals come in one end, and steaks and chops leave in customers' shopping bags from the other. This means that Copaco has for sale some of the most unusual cuts of beef you will see, and many parts of the steer you'd rather not see. One item they've got here is "Steamship Rounds," which is the slaughterhouse term for a huge roast, about one hundred pounds worth, or one-eighth of a steer. If that's a bit much for your oven, Copaco has a stock of suckling pigs. Of course, they always have a good supply of brains, sweetbreads, mountain oysters and beef blood, as well as dressed baby goats, lamb and veal heads, and pork casings.

Among the nonedible by-products are steer hides, sheepskins, raw wool for spinning, and assorted eyes, hearts, etc. "for school science projects."

Almost all of this stuff is on display, just like the T-bones and ground chuck in a usual supermarket. Copaco offers tours of their enormous facility to university groups, consumer organizations, and other organized sightseers. How much of the processing plant you get to see on a tour "depends on the maturity of the group," a Copaco spokesman said. "The slaughterhouse isn't for everyone."

BRIDGEPORT

THE BARNUM MUSEUM

820 Main St., Bridgeport, Conn.;
Tues–Sat noon–5 PM, Sun 2 PM–5 PM; donation

Aside from being the hometown of Bob Mitchum, Bridgeport's primary claim to fame is that it was P. T. Barnum's favorite city. This perhaps explains why Bridgeport, like Podunk and Paducah, is usually mentioned at the butt end of a joke. It was once the original Circus City, and it was here that Phineas Taylor Barnum decided to build "The Barnum Institute of Science and Industry." It was built as a cultural center, Barnum-style, and among P. T.'s coups were an appearance by the Wright Brothers to explain their flying machine and a lecture by Thomas Edison explaining the electric light. Eventually the Barnum Institute went broke. The gaudy Victorian building served as the Bridgeport City Hall until 1965, when the City moved out, the building was restored, and the Barnum Museum was opened.

The vestibule of the museum contains figures of clowns, trapeze artists, and a ringmaster. Past them, you can view "Baby Bridgeport," the stuffed skin of a three-year-old elephant that was part of Barnum's circus. The museum contains what it says is the most extensive collection of clown props and costumes in any museum. Glass cases contain costumes worn by Barnum, Jenny Lind, and "General" Tom Thumb. Among the Victorian furniture scattered throughout the building is "General" Thumb's pint-sized bed. Other exhibits include an unwrapped mummy, an unbelievably elaborate animated Swiss village, and a coat that Charles Dickens left behind him in the United States. The *pièce de résistance* is the $100,000 hand-carved, fully animated miniature five-ring circus, "the only complete hand-carved circus in the world." It is forty by sixty feet, a five-ring tent with moving acts, lights, and a small railroad.

You can't travel around the United States without stumbling over evidence of Barnum's outrageously inflated showmanship. On a recent trip to Franconia Notch in New Hampshire, we learned that he once had plans to scrape the "Great Stone Face" off Profile Mountain and take the multiton natural visage around the country on exhibition. Had he succeeded, the Old Man of the Mountain might now reside here in the Barnum Museum, alongside the other grandiose schemes and artifacts that made Barnum "the Prince of Showmen."

THE EEL INSTITUTE

Milford Hall, University of Bridgeport,
Linden Ave. & Myrtle Ave., Bridgeport, Conn.;
Always viewable; free

Dr. Michael Somers, the man in charge of eel research at the University of Bridgeport, feels that eels are victims of a bad press. To promote the slimy creatures' image, the University of Bridgeport Anguilliform Research Department has published an eel cookbook listing recipes from eel soufflé to a robust eel served with peppers and onions. On the drawing board are eel swizzle sticks and an eel calendar.

Eels are a popular delicacy in Japan and parts of Europe, and Dr. Somers believes that if their PR were a little better here, we too could take advantage of their high-protein meat. Weiners have already been supplemented with "chicken franks." Why not "eel dogs," too?

The Eel Farm at the Eel Institute is located under a geodesic dome, and is open for public viewing any time. The resident "farmers" throw sewer sludge into the dome along with bucketfuls of worms. The worms get fat and are in turn fed to the eels, which range in size from elvers (barely visible) to big boys like Elmer, the official mascot, who is shown to visitors and children's groups. There are up to 1000 head of eel on hand at some times, but once they are sold the population dwindles down to just Elmer. It seems that all eels must spawn in a particular area of the Atlantic Ocean. Scientists have not yet developed the capability of breeding them in captivity, but once they do, eels are sure to become an important staple. Yum yum.

BRISTOL

AMERICAN CLOCK AND WATCH MUSEUM

100 Maple St., Bristol, Conn.;
April–Oct Tues–Sun 1 PM–5 PM;
Adults: $2, 8–15: $1, family: $4

A recent study indicated that along with modern art and old cameras, antique clocks were the best place to invest your money if you wanted to double and quadruple your savings. Of course, this isn't very helpful, since it means that prices are already out of sight. The reason is simple. They don't make clocks the way they used to. Craftsmanship like that displayed at the American Clock and Watch Museum is gone forever.

This is the premier clock and watch museum in the country, containing tools once used by New England's best clockmakers, a complete library and archives of horological material, and beautiful clocks of every shape and size. The museum is housed in the Miles Lewis House, built in 1801, and still boasts its original chestnut and oak furnishings. Clocks are displayed everywhere, on mantels and tables and against the walls. They have clocks here by all the great American craftsmen: Seth Thomas, Eli and Samuel Terry of Plymouth, Simon Willard, and Alexander Willard. As in those other venerable New England crafts, locksmithing and gunsmithing, the names of the "greats" are few, and the apprentice system that taught these men their craft has all but disappeared.

In addition to the grand clocks on display in the Museum, there are hundreds of watches and unusual movements displayed in cases—everything from the most elaborate jeweled timepiece to an original "Mickey Mouse."

THE WITCH'S DUNGEON

Battle St., Bristol, Conn.;
Oct only weekends 7 PM–midnight;
Call ahead (203) 583-8306; 50¢

Adjacent to the Hull family home in Bristol, Connecticut is an attraction that is practically guaranteed to scare visitors to death. It is a "haunted house" built by Mr. and Mrs. Hull and their son Cortlandt. It began as a hobby, but soon became too horrible to keep to themselves, and so they have opened it to the public on weekends during Halloween month.

Cortlandt has made thirteen monsters to populate the "dungeon." His mom sews the costumes, and his dad helps with the special effects. Cortlandt's monsters are mostly the classical menaces: Frankenstein's Monster, the Mummy, the Phantom of the Opera, the Fly, the Werewolf, and the Mole Man. More modern repulsive creatures are represented by Dr. Phibes (from the Vincent Price movie). Cortlandt has been a monsterologist since high-school days, and has personally studied the behind-the-scenes techniques of make-up and special-effects departments in Hollywood. A trip through the Witch's Dungeon includes thirteen specially designed set pieces in which lighting, sound, and electronic effects combine to scare the pants off visitors.

Cortlandt says he has two major problems at the Dungeon. Occasionally vandals have tried stunts like setting the Wolfman's hair on fire. And sometimes when children visit they get freaked out. "I try to make sure that any kids entering the Dungeon have at least seen the Munsters," he mused.

What exactly does one experience in the dungeon? It is far too horrific to tell.

CANAAN

THE POST-CARD MUSEUM

Church Street, Canaan, Conn.;
June, July & Aug weekends noon–4 PM; other times,
summer only, by appointment (P.O. Box 73); 99¢ donation

Mr. and Mrs. George MacCallum specialize in post cards printed between 1890 and 1910, a period considered by collectors to be the zenith of picture-post-card lithography. Mrs. MacCallum estimates that they have 50,000 cards altogether, most of them printed in France and Germany. About 6,000 cards can be displayed at one time in the two-story red barn that serves as their museum. The cards are arranged thematically in categories. There are sets of "Leap-Year cards," "Mardi Gras cards," "Meet-Me-at-the-Fair cards," "Loch and Glen cards," and a huge section of "American Landmarks," subdivided into Dams, Canals, Statues, Buildings, etc. There are groups showing "Cuba of Yesteryear," "Land of the Pyramids," and "Pompeii."

One of Mrs. MacCallum's favorite categories is patriotic cards, which people used to send to each other on holidays. She has cards of twenty-six presidents and their homes. Patriotic cards faded out about the time of World War I, she explains. That's when pictures of music-hall girls were becoming popular.

Some of the cards themselves are unusually designed. There is a "fan card" made in 1906 that says "Greetings from New York." It contains six smaller cards that can be pulled out and opened like a fan to show six scenes of city life. There are other cards made of velvet or satin, some with real fur pasted onto drawings of bears, real hair affixed to pictures of young women, and feathers onto birds.

Mrs. MacCullum thinks that her museum is a real bargain. "Where else can you go and see so many pictures in such a small space?"

COVENTRY

CAPRILANDS HERB FARM

Silver St. off 44A, Coventry, Conn.,
Tours Tues–Fri at 12:30 by reservation only (203) 742–7244;
$6.50; gift shop open daily 9 AM–5 PM

Visiting Caprilands is a favorite ritual for many who tour New England during the spectacular fall foliage season, but it is a lovely place to visit at any time of year. It is run by herbalist Adelma Simmons, who has turned the quaint old house and surrounding barns and sheds into a model herb farm.

Tours through Caprilands begin at 12:30 PM; one first walks through the gardens, where one learns about the varieties of herbs grown and their purposes. There are herbs growing, herbs drying to be used for wreaths and decoration, herbs that taste good, herbs that cure illness, and some herbs that are merely—and wonderfully—odoriferous. From the sheds and outdoor gardens, tours proceed into the comfortable and cozy house, where a "herbal meal" is served. There are casseroles, biscuits, cakes, and punch—all highlighted by Ms. Simmons's home-grown seasonings.

In the Caprilands gift shop (which is open even if you don't take the tour), you can purchase pomander balls (oranges pierced with dozens of cloves), sachets, necklaces made of herbs, frankincense and myrrh for Christmas, books, charts, and recipes. Caprilands exudes a particularily New England charm. A visit here can be a delight for all senses.

EAST HAVEN

THE TROLLEY MUSEUM

River St., East Haven, Conn.;
Sundays April–Nov; Sat, Sun & Holidays May 28–Oct 31;
daily June 27–Labor Day 11 AM–5 PM;
Adults: $2, 5–11: $1 (unlimited rides)

Trolleys were once so popular that the Brooklyn Dodgers were named after them; or rather, after the Brooklynites who had to dodge trolleys as they walked along the street. Today, one of the few places in America where you still have to look out for trolleys is a beautiful stretch of track along the

Connecticut shoreline that runs from the Trolley Museum in East Haven to Short Beach. The ride curves through a salt marsh and over a creek, past swans and mallards, past woods, meadows, and cliffs. It is a real trip into the past, not so much because of what you see but because of the sounds and smells and feel of the Trolley Museum's restored electric streetcars and rapid-transit cars.

Admission to the Museum includes not only unlimited rides back and forth to Short Beach (some people come here and ride all day), but a tour of the car barn and shop area. Here you see approximately one hundred cars, from workaday subways and snowplows to the plushest wood-and-brass parlor cars. The automobile has virtually expunged the memory of trolley transportation from most people's minds. Here is a place where its popularity, efficiency, and pleasures are brought back to life.

GREENWICH

U. S. TOBACCO MUSEUM

100 W. Putnam Ave., Greenwich, Conn.;
Tues–Sat 1 PM–5 PM; free

It is thanks to the Indians that tobacco became a vital part of western culture, and whether you think they were getting even or being friendly when they gave Christopher Columbus the world's first cigar in 1492, there is no denying the importance of the aromatic leaf. The U. S. Tobacco Museum is a small, white frame building in front of the U. S. Tobacco Company that tells all about tobacco—all, that is, except in the form of cigarettes, which are considered "too modern" and best kept in low profile for health reasons.

At the desk as you enter there are cans of Copenhagen Snuff, "the oldest packaged goods item in existence." You can take a pinch as a free sample and then sneeze your way through the exhibits. Along the walls are displays of pipe-carving, the original tobacco vending machine, and all kinds of tobacco art, including a fetching French lithograph from 1924 showing a group of bleary-eyed women taking snuff and proclaiming *"Ah, qu'il est bon!"* Display cases are filled with Indian pipes, clay pipes, meerschaum pipes, porcelain pipes, water pipes, and African hemp pipes. One learns that the "church-warden" clay pipe was made with an extremely long stem because in seventeenth-century England, churchwardens were kept in taverns for customers' use. After each customer had his smoke, a portion of the stem was broken off, thus making the pipe hygienically safe for the next smoker.

Some of the pipes and other objects on display are handmade and beautifully decorated and carved. There is one Austrian meerschaum three feet long and a foot high depicting Napoleon's retreat from Moscow. Another carved pipe is called "pipe dream," and has the figure of a seminude woman wrapped around the bowl. There are tobacco figures everywhere—Highland Laddies with their snuff, and, of course, a whole tribe of wooden Indians. Even some of the cuspidors are decoratively designed—especially those made from blown glass and porcelain for use by ladies who chew or take an occasional pinch.

It is said that Indians believed tobacco to be divine, and that smoking it lifted their thoughts into the cosmic realm. There is a large collection of Indian calumets (better known as peace pipes) here, as well as Oriental opium pipes made from ivory, jade, and cane.

Even if you don't smoke, chew, sniff, or pinch, you'll find the U. S. Tobacco Museum a heady place, where nicotine and its attendant paraphernalia can be appreciated for its aesthetic as well as its addictive properties.

GUILFORD

THE WORLD'S LARGEST GREENHOUSE (MAYBE)

William Pinchbeck, Inc., 929 Boston Post Rd., Guilford, Conn.;
Call for tour (203) 453–2186

Until recently there was no doubt that William Pinchbeck, Inc., had the largest greenhouse in the world. It peeks through the trees along Route 1 in Guilford for what seems like half a mile. Employees of Pinchbeck's have recently informed us that they believe a longer greenhouse has been built. Where and by whom they will not say.

Even if it is in fact the second-largest, Pinchbeck's is worth a trip. It is filled with roses. Like a romantic Garden of Eden, the fragrant blooms are everywhere, interspersed with a few hanging plants and other flowers. Roses are the main "crop" here. Pinchbeck is one of the country's major suppliers.

There are no regular tours, but curious rose-lovers can call up and schedule one. You will be shown the inside of the spectacular glass house, the area where roses are sorted and graded, and a large refrigerated "holding tank," where fully grown blooms are kept until they are ready to be sold.

HAMDEN

THE GHOST PARKING LOT

Hamden Plaza Shopping Center, Dixwell Ave., Hamden, Conn.;
Always viewable; free

The Ghost Parking Lot is an endeavor on the part of an architectural group called SITE (an acronym for Sculpture in the Environment) to comment on the two most important elements of a suburban mall—cars and asphalt. They have taken twenty-seven discarded automobiles and paved over them just enough to leave undulating asphalt skins, enveloping the car bodies in their shallow graves. The result is a "Ghost Parking Lot" in which you can make out the shapes of cars pushing up through (or being suppressed by) a thick layer of asphalt. It is a startling piece of art, worth a detour off the nearby Merritt Parkway even if you don't need to go shopping.

MIDDLETOWN

THE SUBMARINE MUSEUM

440 Washington St., Middletown, Conn.;
Mon–Fri 10 AM–1 PM, Sat & Sun 10 AM–5 PM; free

The Submarine Museum looks just like every other home on this residential block in Middletown except for two signs outside: "Submarine Museum," and "Visitor Parking." It is, in fact, Bernie Bastura's home. He is a submarine veteran who began collecting sub mementos and memorabilia back in 1954. As you look at his collection, you can't help but get a good glimpse of Bernie's own homey life style, and a whiff of what he's cooking for dinner. There is nothing sleek or awesome here as in Groton, Connecticut, where the real subs are stationed. This is home-style museum-going at its best.

A number of rooms in Bernie's home are cordoned off for museum use. He has the largest private collection of submarine plaques and patches, all displayed in glass cases or tacked to the wall along with the original name board from the U.S.S. *Sarda,* the commissioning pennant from the U.S.S. *S–38,* and the original ensign from the U.S.S. *Hake.* There are logbooks, photos, and files on every submarine commissioned, as well as on tenders, sub rescues, and oceanography. There are sub models from six inches to five feet long, and records tracing the history of the submarine from the earliest model called the Turtle to nuclear-powered vessels.

The expressed purpose of the museum is to give the public an understanding of "the true facts of the long arm of the U. S. Navy known as the 'Silent Service.' " Bernie believes that "the heart and soul of every sub vet, past and present," is expressed by his collection.

NAUGATUCK

PETER PAUL FACTORY

New Haven Rd. (Rt. 63), Naugatuck, Conn.;
Mon–Weds 10:30 AM & 1:30 PM by appointment only (203) 729–0221 ext. 271;
Free; no children under 6

It is fascinating as an adult to view the manufacture of those junk foods one consumed in mass quantities as a child. It forces you to confront the fact that Mounds and Almond Joys—the products manufactured here—do not grow on trees or on the glass shelves of movie theater concession stands. Somebody has to mix up the coconut and sugar, add enough thickening agent to form it into flattened ovals, drop on the nuts (if an Almond Joy), pour on the chocolate, and wrap it up. In some ways this is a sensuous, appetizing tour. But in another way the mystery, the tantalizing lure of the unknown sweet, evaporates in the industrial light of the Peter Paul factory. Seeing them made here is like learning Puffed Rice isn't really shot from Civil War–style cannons, and M&M's, if held long and hard enough, really will melt in your hand. It's a sad but necessary part of growing up.

NEW HAVEN

HANDSOME DAN

Payne Whitney Gymnasium, Yale U., Tower Parkway at the end of Grove St.,
New Haven, Conn.;
Mon–Fri 10 AM–8:30 PM, Sat 10 AM–5:30 PM, Sun 2 PM–5:30 PM
During school vacations Mon–Sat noon–6:30 PM; free

You can't move in New Haven without running into the Yale Bulldog. Pizzerias and dry cleaners are named after him, and trucks from Yale's dining service and maintenance crew bear the likeness of a bulldog, the former in a chef's toque, the latter in a hard-hat. Among the gargoyles that embellish the University's buildings, bulldog faces sprout everywhere.

Handsome Dan is the granddaddy of them all (figuratively speaking). Found in a New Haven blacksmith's shop by the class of 1892, he became Yale's symbol and has been followed by at least a dozen bulldogs, all named "Handsome Dan" in his honor. The original "sourmug" is stuffed and on display in the Payne Whitney Gymnasium (known as the Cathedral of Muscle for its Gothic design). He is kept in a glass box in the center of a room filled with loving cups, plaques, and souvenir footballs from famous Harvard–Yale games. Since the enclosed trophies—and indeed Handsome Dan himself—are such likely targets for prankster thieves from rival universities, the room is kept locked, and the famous dog may be viewed only through a glass partition, darkly.

Dan is—let us be kind—a slim dog. Modern standards of the breed declare that the bulldog should be the most dog in the least space. By contrast to recent beefcakes that have served as Handsome Dan XII and XIII, Dan I is positively skeletal. This long, tall Dan has what is known as a "bitchy" (small) head and a less-than-magnificent "front" (the expanse between the shoulders). But what he lacks in pulchritude is made up for by a most stalwart expression. He is seated, looking up, ears perked, with the expression of tenacity and determination that is unique to the breed. He is wearing a fantastic leather-studded collar, worthy of the progenitor of at least a dozen mascots.

OLD LYME

THE NUT MUSEUM

Ferry Road, Old Lyme, Conn.; May–Nov Weds, Sat & Sun 2 PM–5 PM; Admission: one nut and $1 donation

Elizabeth Tashjian, curator of the Nut Museum, recently wrote us, "A week ago, a nutworthy news item came to my attention. Namely, Nut, according to Egyptian mythology, was the sky goddess." Ms. Tashjian referred to her dictionary of non-Christian religions: " 'Nut was a lady of Heaven. Heaven was feminine and Nut was stretched out over her husband, the earth god.' Doubtless," she concluded, "this is the first association of Nut to person—the personification of Nut."

Enter the Nut Museum–which is one wing of a vast nineteenth-century mansion named Elya—and meet Elizabeth Tashjian. You see her through the eight-foot nutcracker that hangs from the branch of a tree. She is dressed in a purple silk Armenian robe that was once her grandmother's. (The robe is a reminder that most popular nuts come from Asia Minor.) She wears raspberry-red lipstick. Her manner is sharp and whimsical. She accepts one nut as ticket of admission to the museum. The tour begins.

The Nut Museum is in fact one of the most scholarly and erudite specialized collections anywhere. The history of the nut predates Adam and Eve. Look at the thirty-five pound Coco de Mer nut. Elizabeth Tashjian points out its resemblance to the human form. "All nuts have a heart," she says. "Each nut is an idea."

The main room of her collection includes specimens of nuts from around the world, nut masks, and her own nut paintings and collages. There is also an extensive display of nutcrackers, which have been, your hostess explains, "the companion pieces—not the historical enemies—of nuts."

Elizabeth Tashjian is an expert on the subject. A tour includes a description of how the betel nut is used as a gesture of hospitality on the Malay Peninsula, how the beach nut is believed to bring good luck in Cuba, and how, according to the Song of Solomon, King Solomon's garden was filled with walnuts. The Queen of Sheba favored the pistachio.

But Elizabeth Tashjian is not just a nut pedant, and there is more to a visit here than goober scholarship. There are songs about nuts, one, "The March of the Nuts," especially for children, and a nut anthem called "Nuts Are Beautiful." The highlight of a visit is her a cappella rendition of her original compositions. She is an exuberant artist and curator whose enthusiasm for nuts is contagious. Hundreds of people have sent her nut jewelry and unusual nuts from around the world.

The only dark cloud hanging over this delightful place is the presence of chipmunks and squirrels. They have carried off over fifty of Elizabeth Tashjian's prized exhibits.

STAMFORD

UNITED HOUSE WRECKING

328 Selleck St., Stamford, Conn.;
Tues–Sat 9 AM–5 PM; free

United House Wrecking is five acres of junk, antiques, pseudoantiques, curios, knickknacks, and more junk. Its several barns and buildings are crammed with items as diverse as "Tiffany-style" imitation lamps, real copper cookware, stuffed moose heads, pianos, ships' mastheads, crockery, street signs, stoves, oxen yokes and Naugahyde couches. On a recent visit we found a wet bar that had been made from a coffin that still opened up to show a wax "corpse."

Everything here has its price; few things are bargains; but if wading through five acres of the most diverse merchandise imaginable is your idea of fun, then you couldn't do better than United House Wrecking, "the junkyard with a personality."

STONINGTON

THE PULLMAN MUSEUM

2 Bayview Heights, Stonington, Conn.;
Any time, by appointment only, call James E. Bradley (203) 535–1021;
Free, "donations welcome"

James Bradley has six beautiful old railroad cars parked on tracks not far from his home. Each has been tenderly restored; each looks and smells as if you've just boarded the "20th Century" or the "Chief" and are about to travel first class. Of course, these cars are from the days when "first class" meant more than just a wider seat, free drinks, and an abundance of airline "food." The six cars are Pullman Heavyweights from the New Haven Railroad, "Staghound," "Great Republic," "Forest Hills," "Philinda," "Breslin Tower," and "Fox Point," all manufactured between 1914 and 1930.

This is a private museum, open by appointment, so Mr. Bradley can open up and air out the cars in advance. Like all railroad buffs, he loves his collection, and is happy to show it to appreciative visitors.

TERRYVILLE

LOCK MUSEUM OF AMERICA

114 Main St., Terryville, Conn.;
May–Oct Tues–Sun 1:30 PM–4 PM or other times by appointment (203) 582–4751;
free

Terryville has been the "Lock Town of America" since 1834, when Lewis McKee & Co. opened one of the first of forty lock companies that made Connecticut into the country's lock-producing capital. The Lock Museum of America is the only place we know devoted exclusively to the display of locks, keys, and related hardware. There are more than 18,000 items on exhibit in the small building on Main Street, including chest locks, skeleton keys, padlocks, doorknobs, and elaborate tumblers. The walls are lined with pictures of some of the lock manufacturing plants, and there are cabinets containing lock catalogs and photographs of locks in action. It is all a mind-boggling array of ways to keep things secure inside other things.

WATERBURY

HOLY LAND, U.S.A.

Slocum St., Waterbury, Conn.;
Dawn–dusk; donation

Holy Land U.S.A. is a mystery. The religious order that tends the miniature village says that the person or persons who built it must remain anonymous. It is perched on a hillside overlooking the busy town of Waterbury. From this tiny community of over two hundred buildings, you can look out over the real city, which itself looks miniaturized from the elevated perspective of the Holy Land. Distant sounds of traffic on the Waterbury Expressway provide a surreal audio backdrop for a visit to this Land of the Lord.

Whoever built Holy Land was moved by a passion that exceeded their artistic abilities. Its audacious cosmology is written on plaques, signs, and stones everywhere. Psalms, prayers and exclamations are spelled out in paint, bas-relief, or stick-on, glow-in-the-dark letters. Buildings appear to be made from clay or tin siding. Circling the villages of Bethlehem and Jerusalem that cap the hilltop are glass-fronted sheds containing "actual photographs" of Jesus Christ, replicas of the Dead Sea Scrolls, mock-ups of the catacombs, and jars containing ashes of the ancients. The inn that turned Joseph and Mary away has a "no vacancy" sign tacked to the door.

Visitors are free to walk about the Holy Land to learn from and be inspired by the exhibits. There is no "hard sell" here, no souvenirs, no slick promotion. It is an environment of spiritual sincerity and naïve craft. Even if you are not religiously exalted, it is hard not to be affected by the sentimental fervor of this tattered but high-minded Holy Land.

SEGRE'S IRON WORKS

116 Reidville Dr., Waterbury, Conn.;
Always viewable; free

The people at Segre's remember when a somewhat eccentric man used to come to them, asking that they cut or weld a certain piece of iron in a certain way. He'd throw the iron in the back of his car and drive off, and come back a few days later with requests for another shape, or a particular weld. The man was Alexander Calder, whose mobiles and monumental iron pieces made him famous as one of the masters of twentieth-century sculpture. You can see his work on display at the Guggenheim Museum and other notable art galleries around the country, or you can see it at Segre's Iron Works.

What you see here are models, one-fifth the size of the finished works but looking exactly like the originals. In fact, these are more original than the originals, since it was from these models that the "real" works were made. There are two full-size Calders on display at Segre's, along with about eight scale models.

WOODBRIDGE

JACQUES MILLER'S PLACE

8 Dillon Rd., Woodbridge, Conn.;
Always viewable; free

"I used to be known as an innovative architect," Jacques Miller told us. "Now they call me an eccentric." Mr. Miller's change of status is due to the environment he has created on his property. Woodbridge is a fashionable suburb of New Haven, a land of bland ranch homes and family dwellings. Here Jacques Miller has created an environment of barely controlled chaos, an acre of architectural experiments and massive iron sculpture. The land around an artificial lake and among several grand, drooping willow trees is crowded with "junk sculpture" and just plain junk. There are old boilers, huge pieces of scrap metal, cement truck tanks, oil drums, and half-laid concrete pathways. There is a 1790 barn undergoing complete, radical renovation. If somehow this acre of experimentation were put within four walls and called a studio, it would seem much more logical, and perhaps the neighbors wouldn't complain. Some of them hate Jacques Miller's place. "I'm building this driveway twenty-two inches thick," he said. "You know what for? So the Concorde can land here. *That* will give them something to complain about."

Miller's place is an intriguing compendium of architectural achievements, monumental sculpture, and piles of material awaiting use. At first glance, it does resemble a junkyard, but the more one looks, the more logic and invention there is to see. Miller lucidly explains what each project is going to be, and uses complicated architectural jargon to describe the construction methods he employs. What looks like a messy slab of concrete turns out to be the suspended roof of a mushroom cellar. He points out a cement-mixer tank that he has turned into a wood-burning stove. There are reversible construction panels that may be turned according to the weather. All of his construction materials are recycled. The use of old things, he contends, creates an atmosphere of renewal, like the phoenix rising out of ashes. All around the yard are sculptures reminiscent of the work of Alexander Calder's, made entirely from old and discarded materials.

Miller is now seventy-one years old; his career as an architect includes decorating the Officer's Club at the U.S. Military Academy at West Point. He now concentrates exclusively on his property in Woodbridge, working up to sixteen hours a day, doing everything himself. "I love this damn place," he said. And yet there is a "for sale" sign out front. We asked him why, and he spoke of a desire to "hit the road" and get away from his neighbors. But we doubt if he'll ever tear himself away from his project. The "for sale" sign has been up for over a year, and Jacques Miller is the first to admit his asking price is way too high. "Who would be crazy enough to buy this place?" he asks, knowing full well that there is nobody on earth who could be happy living in the very personal universe he has created for himself by the side of the road.

MAINE

THE EARTH STATION

Rt. 120, Andover, Maine;
Memorial Day–Labor Day daily 9 AM–5 PM; free

Nestled in the midst of the heady inland woods of Maine are "The Big Ear" and "The Big Bubble," components of the Andover Ground Station for satellite control. It is an eerie environment, with the scientific "hum" of the instruments providing a background for natural sounds and conversations.

The Big Bubble is as tall as a thirteen-story building. It is a giant dacron-polyester globe that houses the elaborate horned antenna called The Big Ear. You can walk inside The Big Bubble and gaze up at the intricacies of the mobile antenna through a pane of glass. The bubble weighs 20 tons, the antenna 380. It can amplify signals from outer space 500,000 times, which means it is capable of receiving one trillionth of a watt.

There are two giant dish antennae outside The Bubble and Ear. The whole complex forms the key facility for earth stations and satellite communication all over the world. While lectures and movies are available in the adjacent building to explain all about the way these colossal machines work, you might consider appreciating them as a sheer visual statement—a giant white polyester balloon and two dish shapes surrounded by acres of nature.

BAR HARBOR

THE JACKSON LABORATORY

Bar Harbor, Mount Desert Island, Maine;
mid-June–mid-Sept. Tues, Weds & Fri at 3 PM; free (207) 288–3373

Most people think of Mount Desert Island as a vacation paradise, the quintessential rockbound coast of towering pines and crashing surf. It is surely that, but how many people realize that Mount Desert Island is also the breeding ground for millions of mice? Before you yell "eeek!" or jump on a chair, we should explain that the mice are bred in a controlled environment, the Jackson Laboratory, which is the largest center for mammalian genetics research in the world.

Here at "Jax," as the natives call it, over three million mice are bred each year. Many are supplied to scientists and institutions around the world. Most are used for experiments here—by geneticists, immunogeneticists, biochemists, cytologists, embryologists, radiobiologists, and psychologists. If you wonder about some of these specialties, you ought to visit the Jackson Laboratory. The hour-long tour explains the work of Jax's scientists through lectures and films, and gives you a look at the facilities.

Most of the lab's research focuses on cancer, muscular dystrophy, and neuromuscular disorders, although work is also done on diabetes, anemia, tissue grafting, radiation exposure, and aging. There are more than one hundred mutant mouse strains here, from the completely bald "nude streaker" to the runty rickets carriers. All of these fancy-bred strains trace their roots back to the *Mus musculus,* or common house mouse.

BATH

THE BATH MARINE MUSEUM

Percy & Small Shipyard: 263 Washington St., Winter St. Center:
880 Washington St., Sewall House: 963 Washington St.,
Apprenticeshop: 375 Front St., Bath, Maine;
Mid-May–Mid-Sept, daily 10 AM–5 PM;
adults $2.75–$3.50, children: 75¢–$1.00 (seasonal)

The Bath Marine Museum is composed of four exhibit buildings in the city with the longest continuing history of shipbuilding in America. The best place to begin is the Percy & Small Shipyard, the only surviving yard that once built the heroic wooden vessels of long ago. The original buildings are restored and now house small boats, tools, machinery, and exhibits describing construction techniques. Leaving the shipyard, you walk to the Kennebec River for a ride on the M/V *Sasanoa,* from which you get a ship's-eye-view of the modern freighters and naval vessels being constructed or in for repair at Bath's Iron Works. After your ride you can look into the Winter Street Center, a classic white-spired building filled with displays of maritime history, the story of the shipworker's life, and ships' carpenters' art. At the Sewell House there are exhibits on lobstering and fishing, as well as models, dioramas and paintings of every kind of ship from a yacht to a naval destroyer. There is a "please touch" room here for kids, with ships' wheels and nautical gear to play with.

Our favorite part of the Bath Marine Museum is the Apprenticeshop, where you can see the skills of boat builders in action. Students still work in this building, drawing on the old skills and updating them to build "dories," "pinkies," "peapods," "skiffs," and "Muscongus Bay sloops."

This is the complete Marine Museum—a full day's worth of basking in all the maritime crafts that represent the essence of the coastal Maine personality. Bring your copy of *Moby Dick,* and you may never go inland again.

BELFAST

FRED BURNS'S HOUSE

End of Commercial St. (on the water), Belfast, Maine;
always viewable; free

Fred Burns is a very old man who lives alone with a dozen tailless Maine coon cats and a gimpy dog inside a handmade house nestled against the edge of industrial Belfast. There are just a couple of rooms to the tiny house, which in shape and size is what most people call a shack. But what a spectacular shack it is!

To the exterior walls of his home Fred Burns has affixed hundreds of pieces of wood. Moldings, one-by-twos, elaborate curlicues cover the house, painted in more colors than come in a large-size Crayola set. Some panels are covered with irregular-sized lengths of wood that run parallel to the ground, others are perpendicular, a few form cross-hatching. Hundreds of vivid colors create an abstract pointillistic pattern, a festive explosion of hues by the side of an otherwise drab waterfront.

Mr. Burns is a little deaf, and you might have to holler a few times before he knows you're there. But finding his home and meeting him is worth the effort. He is an original, a man who has made beauty out of very little.

PERRY'S TROPICAL NUT HOUSE

Rt. 1, Belfast, Maine;
daily April–May 8:30 AM–6 PM, June–Dec 8:30 AM–9 PM, Jan–March 8 AM–5 PM; free

Perry's started in 1926 when a local merchant received a mountain of Georgia pecans as a gift to his store. He piled them high on his wooden building as a special attraction to customers. Around the nuts he placed some unusual curios, and pretty soon people started making special trips to see the unusual (for Maine) nuts and oddities. He added to the exhibit, bringing in parrots, monkeys, stuffed alligators, and a whole menagerie. Pretty soon there were fun-house mirrors, nut candy, and souvenirs. Perry's Nut House was born.

It is now called Perry's Tropical Nut House and is one of the primary sources for gimcrackery and bric-a-brac on the east coast. Tourists flock to see the delapidated sloth, manatee, a bear in boxing gloves, a lowland gorilla, and several alligators (all stuffed). Perry's sells every kind of souvenir you can think of, and they have some nice plaster bears outside to pose next to for gag photos. It is unrestrained and unashamedly commercial, yet lovable for its disheveled sprawl and naïve showmanship. Personal touches abound, like the paper bag we saw on our last visit tacked to the wall next to the candy counter. On it was a handwritten pledge by a Perry's worker that she would not eat another piece of candy for six months, lest she become "big as a house." Her words were witnessed by the local sheriff.

Among the nuts on display is "the largest nut in the world," from the Seychelles Islands in the Indian Ocean, a specimen that appears to be coming apart at the seams. There are dozens of other shapes, sizes, and mutations of nuts from around the world. For serious nut study, we would recommend Elizabeth Tashjian's more learned and witty Nut Museum in Old Lyme, Connecticut (see p. 13). But for a rough-and-tumble display of nutdom's treasures amidst a charmingly tatty bit of roadside hullabaloo, Perry's Tropical Nut House cannot be beat.

BRUNSWICK

THE PEARY–MACMILLAN ARCTIC MUSEUM

1st floor of Hubbard Hall, Bowdoin College, Brunswick, Maine;
weekday hours vary, Sat 10 AM–5 PM, Sun 2 PM–5 PM; free

Admiral Robert E. Peary graduated from Bowdoin College in 1877. Donald B. MacMillan was a member of the class of '98. Together they made the first expedition to the North Pole. To honor these famous alumni Bowdoin has established an arctic museum on the first floor of Hubbard Hall, the former college library. The museum is divided into three sections, each of which presents a chapter in the story of arctic exploration.

Greeting visitors in the first section are life-size painted cut-out figures showing the fur-clad explorers Peary and MacMillan. Beyond them you see etchings, engravings, and photographs that tell the history of arctic exploration from Pytheas the Greek through the Vikings to Henry Hudson and to Peary's first expedition. The last exhibit here is the odometer Peary used to measure his mileage as he crossed the Greenland ice cap in 1895.

Section Two shows details of Peary's successful expedition. It contains his North Pole log and one of the five sledges he used to get to the Pole. Also shown are the heavy fur suits Perry adapted for his own use from those worn by the Eskimos of Greenland. A small panorama shows the sun traveling parallel to the horizon—which is the way it looked as the explorer advanced on the Pole.

Section three tells of the arctic after Peary's first successful expedition. There are eskimo carvings and hunting implements, costumes and primitive paintings, as well as MacMillan's cameras and arctic bird and egg collections.

Bowdoin's interest in all things northern is evident in the name of the college's athletic teams—The Polar Bears.

BRYANT POND

HOME OF THE CRANK PHONE CALL

Bryant Pond, Maine (Rt. 26)

If you get a crank phone call from Bryant Pond, it probably won't be obscene.

Every call from here is a crank call because Bryant Pond is one of the last places in the country that still has hand-cranked telephones. It's in a lovely scenic area, an ideal setting for a weekend trip away from city things.

BUCKSPORT

COLONEL JONATHAN BUCK'S ACCURSED TOMB

Buck Cemetery, Main St. near Hinks St., Bucksport, Maine;
always viewable; free

Colonel Buck died in 1795, but not before he had condemned an alleged witch to the stake. She vowed revenge on him, and on his tomb there is a blot in the shape of a woman's leg. Rumor has it that the Buck family has replaced the tombstone numerous times, as well as cleaned it with every possible bleach over the ages, but the shapely gam keeps coming back. It does look like someone's leg symbolically kicking an enemy in the rump.

Next door to the accursed tomb, modern-day Bucksport teen-agers nonchalantly play pinball.

DOVER-FOXCROFT

THE BLACKSMITH SHOP MUSEUM

Park St. 2 mi. N. of Post Office, Dover-Foxcroft, Maine;
April–Oct daily, hours vary; donation

This tiny blacksmith shop was built in the community of Dover-Foxcroft during the Civil War. What you see inside are not reproductions or antiques gathered from the area, but the shop's original equipment, including the great anvil, bellows, and tacks. The most interesting artifact is a gizmo called "Joseph M. Bachelor's patented invention of an Ox-Lifter, by use of which any ox, however stubborn, can be shod, without any of the hard labor usually attending the raising of the feet . . . The worst cases can be handled by the shoer with perfect ease." Names of neighboring farmers are chalked up on the rafters, where sample horseshoes were once kept on hand for their individual work horses.

This is a charming, informal museum that authentically conveys a sense of history without hoopla or fanfare. It is a simple shingle-style building last used as a blacksmith shop in 1905.

FREEPORT

THE DESERT OF MAINE

Desert Rd., 1 1/2 mi. S. of Freeport, Maine;
April 15–Nov daily 8 AM–8 PM,
adults: $1.50, 6–12: 50¢

The last thing you would expect to find in Maine, the Pine Tree State, is a full-fledged desert. But in Freeport, south of the venerable down-east bastion L. L. Bean, is The Desert of Maine, one of the most incongruous tourist attractions in the northeast.

It began in 1797 when the Tuttle Family moved to a three-hundred-acre farm in Freeport. Tuttle was a potato farmer who had a small herd of cattle and some vegetable gardens. The farm passed from Tuttle to Tuttle, Jr., and as the son continued to graze the cattle on the fertile land, he noticed that the grass was growing shorter and sparser. Soon the sod started pulling up by the roots. Gradually the soil became a thin layer of dry dirt, and lo!—sand appeared, acres of sand, endless dunes and drifts of sand that completely covered the Tuttle farm, crops, and even the Tuttle home. All that was left was the present-day mini-Sahara, three hundred acres of fine desert sand.

All this is dramatically explained to you by your desert guide, who also somewhat disconcertingly points out the coincidental similarity between the name "Tuttle" and "King Tut," that ancient denizen of the desert. One is asked to ponder the question, "Coincidence?" Perhaps . . . perhaps not.

KENNEBUNKPORT

NATIONAL DUMP WEEK

Kennebunkport, Maine;
1st full weekend in July, beginning at the Shawmut Inn; free

We have always noticed a certain fascination among New Englanders for their trash. We once passed a dump in New Hampshire called "The Disposal Gardens." Our own dump in Weston, Connecticut is itself beautifully land-scaped with trash—tires piled up in one area, heavy metal somewhere else, and a display of choice throwaways always shown in a rotating exhibit near the dumpmaster's cabin—an aesthetic environment that is anything but a mere pile of trash. In Kennebunkport every year they set aside a week to celebrate the town dump.

During Dump Week, garbage is turned into "dump art" and displayed on the city streets, a "Miss Dumpy" is selected from among the town's beautiful girls, and dump credit cards are given out—allegedly entitling the bearer to throw away his trash in any dump in the country. The reason for all this is to promote cleanliness. The founders of the Kennebunkport Dump Associa-tion say "A society that lives by its obsolescence need not necessarily perish of its own junk."

The Miss Dumpy Pageant is staged on Friday night at the Shawmut Inn on the ocean. The next day, the trash parade begins at Dock Square and travels to the dump. Garbage art is displayed everywhere. The Kennebunkport Dump Association tells us they have won the National Trash Pile Trophy, and that their "beloved trash pile" has become "America's Number One."

KINGFIELD

HEAVYWEIGHT SKI CONTEST

Sugarloaf Mtn. Ski Resort, Maine 16 & 27, Kingfield, Maine;
April—1st week, call (207) 237-2000

Don't bother to strap on a pair of skis for this contest unless you have eaten a double order of pancakes and can easily tip the scales at 250. In some years a total poundage of over 20,000 has descended the beautiful slopes of this northern ski resort in competition at the Heavyweight Ski Contest.

Competition for skiing "chubbies" and "chubbettes" begins with a banquet, where contestants fill up before the run. We are not sure if the resort keeps a winch on hand in case of slope accidents, but we do know that ski runs are cleared of fragile-boned folks before the heavyweights tumble down.

Entry fees at the Heavyweight Ski Contest are determined at a cost-per-pound rate. The proceeds go to charity, and winners are determined by a handicap system that gives the really big fellows (over 400 pounds) a break.

LYNCHVILLE

THE MOST EXOTIC SIGNPOST IN AMERICA

Junction of Rts. 35 & 5, Lynchville, Maine

In the middle of Lynchville is the all-time hokey but true guidepost. It points in all directions, giving mileage to the towns of Paris, Naples, Poland, Peru, Mexico, China, Norway, Denmark, and Sweden, Maine—all authentic down-easter hamlets.

OXFORD

THE WORLD'S LARGEST LOBSTER TRAP

Pinewood Products, Inc., Rt. 121, Oxford, Maine;
always viewable; free

Pinewood Products is one of Maine's major builders of lobster traps. A few years back, the company was inspired to build what they believe to be the world's largest. It is a flat-topped model, rigged with two compartments just like the conventionally sized ones, with a net cone that allows the lobster to enter the "parlor" but not get out. The cage is sixteen feet long, and is occasionally used in local parades.

It is said that lobsters are an ancient species, going back to prehistoric times. No doubt if ever a *Homarus tyrannosaurus* appears, Pinewood Products are the people to notify.

PATTEN

THE LUMBERMAN'S MUSEUM

The Shin Pond Road, Patten, Maine;
Memorial Day—2nd week in Oct, Tues–Sat 9 AM–4 PM, Sun 1 PM–4 PM;
adults: $1, 6–12: 50¢

The Shin Pond Road off Highway 159 has been the main highway for lumber traffic out of the upper valley of the East Branch Penobscot for the last hundred years. From oxcarts and horse-drawn logging sleds to modern trucks, vehicles have been hauling pine and spruce out of the forests of northern Maine. The Lumberman's Museum consists of seven buildings that tell the whole story of the industry that has thrived in The Pine Tree State.

One building is a log structure made with hewn timber salvaged from two log houses built in the mid-nineteenth century. It contains models and dioramas of lumber camps, utensils used to feed the lumberjacks, and examples of equipment and tools used to chop down the trees. There are working models of sawmills, and tools used by carpenters and coopers. Two other buildings house the heavy equipment, including logging sleds, wagons, and bateaux. Another building, which is an exact replica of an 1820 logging camp, is made entirely of wood, without a single nail. There is a blacksmith's shop that contains farriers', wheelwrights', and smiths' tools, a building housing a portable sawmill and shingle machine, and a replica of a camp office.

The museum takes you back to a rugged and rustic profession that is now the stuff of legend. The trucks still roll out of Patten, Maine carrying the pulp and hardwoods south, but the world described in the Lumberman's Museum has disappeared.

PITTSFIELD

THE WORLD'S LARGEST NONSTICK FRY PAN

The Central Maine Egg Festival in Pittsfield, Maine;
1st weekend July; free (contact Chamber of Commerce)

This may, in fact, be the world's largest frying pan, stick or nonstick. Presumably this pan was coated with Teflon to save a wee bit on the amount of cholesterol ingested by the town of Pittsfield every year when they get together to honor the egg. Fifty dozen eggs can be cooked at once—with minimal butter —in this pan that measures ten feet across. The spatulas used are certainly among the world's longest.

Aside from viewing the pan and participating in a few egg-cooking, eating, and throwing contests, the Central Maine Egg Festival affords visitors the opportunity to view a fireworks display, the main attraction of which is a pyrotechnical image of a hen laying an egg.

SEDGWICK

GRAY'S DREAM

Rt. 15 N. of Sedgwick, Maine;
always viewable; free

Along the narrow road north of Sedgwick sits a green-and-gray mobile home. It belongs to L. J. Gray. We never met Mr. Gray personally, but we couldn't resist pulling to the side of the road to look at his "Dream." The expansive yard in front of his mobile home is covered with more lawn ornaments, gewgaws, doodads and gizmos than you'll find on most miniature golf courses. Some appear to be storebought, others handmade. Most are stationary, but some twirl in the seacoast breeze. There are roosters, gulls, birds, lighthouses, lobsters, flowers, ships, ducks, and odd shapes. A sign in front labels it all as "Gray's Dream"—and what a spectacle of a dream it is!

SKOWHEGAN

THE SKOWHEGAN INDIAN

Pleasant St. & Madison Ave, behind the Bowl-o-drome, Skowhegan, Maine;
always viewable; free

The Indians of Maine are honored as "The first people to use these lands in a peaceful way" by a 62-foot tall statue, sculpted of native pine by Bernard Langlais during Maine's 150th anniversary in 1969. Langlais is an alumnus of the well-known Skowhegan School of Painting and Sculpture, and now lives in Cushing, Maine.

The Indian, which is called "The Largest Wooden Indian in the World," holds a giant fishing spear and wooden weir or fish trap. He is dressed in wooden "buckskin" and feathers, and his angular Maine face and body are suitably and traditionally painted in earthy tones.

SOUTHWEST HARBOR

THE MOUNT DESERT OCEANARIUM

Route 102 into Southwest Harbor, Maine, left at flashing yellow light;
May–Oct Mon–Sat 9 AM–5 PM;
adults: $1.50, children: 75¢

Ralph Phippen, a 78-year-old retired lobsterman, is a regular fixture at the Mount Desert Oceanarium. He holds court in the "Lobster Room," a small space devoted to explaining the lobster life cycle. Ralph shows how traps are built and nets are woven, and uses live lobsters to show how the crushing claws are pegged.

Learning about lobsters from this archetypal Maine Old Salt is but one joy of the Oceanarium. There is a "touch tank" for children, which affords them the opportunity to hold a starfish, feel a sea urchin, a sea cucumber, a sea potato, and other undersea creatures able to survive the grip of a tiny fist. In the fisherman's gallery you can see the thirty-three species of fish harvested from Maine's waters, as well as displays of fishing gear from the simplest lines to the electronic apparatus used by modern professional fisherman. Children can have fun with a boat tank and small model boats they can haul around, and there is an old sea chest filled with boots and fishermen's clothing for them to dress up in.

Just about anything you want to know about the ocean around Maine will be explained here. The idea behind this small and personal museum is to get visitors close to the sea, through exhibits and chatty personnel. There are also games that challenge your knowledge of seafood, and dare you to guess what sea creature you are touching without looking at it. Of course, the Oceanarium is perfectly located to help visitors get a sense of the seacoast. There are few places with as salty a feel about them as Mount Desert Island.

STONINGTON

EVERETT KNOWLTON'S TOWN

Rt. 15 N. of Stonington, Maine;
always viewable; free; no dogs

As you head toward Stonington on Route 15, you top a small hill and see a village on the left side of the road. It could be Stonington. But as you approach, your sense of perspective goes awry. This picture-perfect Maine village looks like many other Maine towns, except that it is all on a miniature scale and occupies one portion of Everett Knowlton's front yard.

Knowlton has spent over twenty years constructing the tiny town. He has worked without benefit of urban planning, erecting the structures one by one, landscaping as he went along. There are several dozen homes in town, each inhabited by dolls wearing crocheted dresses, hats, or suits. Organdy and calico curtains hang in the miniature windows. Each home is well appointed with furniture, wallpaper, and modern appliances. There is a church—a tall-spired New England beauty—at which a wedding is taking place. The bride and groom are about to depart, no doubt to spend the night at the miniature "Rock Hill Motel." There is a barber shop and a one-room kiddie school—integrated, thanks to the presence of one dark-complexioned doll among the others. There is a bridge leading into town; there are telephone poles and wires, trees, bushes, garden terraces, and lovely lawns.

Mr. Knowlton's fame as a minibuilder is acknowledged for miles around. On our way to Stonington we stopped by a house about thirty miles away where an old man was working on a single scaled-down home in his front yard. "Yup, it's a nice one," he said. "But nothing like that fellow down in Stonington. That's a real sight." We couldn't agree with him more.

THOMASTON

THE MAINE STATE PRISON STORE

Wadsworth & Main St. (Rt. 1), Thomaston, Maine;
daily April–Sept 9 AM–5 PM, Oct–March 9 AM–4 PM;
free (207) 354–2535

We have visited the Maine State Prison Store over a period of many years, and have seen the peaks and valleys of craftsmanship and artistry in the goods displayed—all depending, of course, on who is locked up at the time. The rate of recidivism is rather low here, so that once a particular lamp design, chair model, or knickknack disappears from the shelves—indicating the con has been sprung—it may never be available again. The moral of this is—don't hesitate. If you see something you like, buy it.

Unlike the few larger stores in pens around the country, the Maine State Prison Store is staffed by an all-convict crew, except for the man who handles the money. But convicts are everywhere inside to help you with your purchase, tell you about the man who crafted a particular item, and assist you in taking your goods out to the car.

The items sold here are mostly home furnishings. The coffee tables, end tables, lamps, and desks all have a similar look—pine that has been shellacked to a mirror finish, sort of glassy Colonial. Our favorite items have always been the lamps and bric-a-brac. We have gotten lamps in the shape of bucking broncs and happy faces, and one that has an entire farm scene carved into the base. As in a thrift store, the merchandise is irregular in its trash-to-treasures spectrum. But it shouldn't be missed, especially if you have never shopped in a jail before.

WATERVILLE

THE APOTHECARY MUSEUM

Waterville Historical Society, 64 Silver St., Waterville, Maine;
June–Sept Tues–Sat 2 PM–6 PM;
adults: $1, under 18: free

The Apothecary Museum is a small wooden-sided building attached to the Waterville Historical Society. It is the best re-creation of a turn-of-the-century drugstore we have seen. There is gleaming mahogany everywhere, richly burnished from years of polishing. There are stained-glass shelves, elaborate brass fixtures, and a mahogany counter with high stools. The counter is topped with marble, and a sign advertises nut sundaes for 15¢ (not available). Shelves in back are labeled "leeches" and "cocaine" (not available either). There are mortars and pestles, brilliantly colored brass bottles, and even an ancient capsule-making machine.

One fascinating thing we learned here was the origin of the word "heroin." Drugs, like ships, are considered to be of the female gender. When, after the Civil War, war injuries were treated with the new morphine substitute, it became known as the hero drug. In pharmacological circles, this became "heroine," and has since been shortened to "heroin."

WISCASSET

THE MUSICAL WONDER HOUSE

18 High St., Wiscasset, Maine;
June–Sept Mon–Sat 10 AM–5 PM, Sun 1 PM–5 PM,
special hours in Sept. & Oct; free, or $1.50 with guided tour

The Musical Wonder House is a sea captain's home, a classic white Georgian structure that now houses one of the world's most extensive collections of music boxes and mechanical music-makers. The house itself is wonderful, complete with classical moldings throughout and a great flying staircase just past the front door. If you just want to look around it's free, but we recommend paying for the tour, because only this way do you get to hear as well as look at the instruments.

In the Bird of Paradise Room you will see an eighteenth-century barrel organ, French mechanical singing birds, and the bed and nightstand that once belonged to the Archduke Ferdinand. In the Phonograph Room there are cylinder phonographs made by Edison, Columbia, and Pathé, and a rare player organ. The Music Room features European music boxes from 1810 to the present, including disc-player models and an Austrian "musical picture."

There are dozens of pieces on display—all in pristine condition, and all in tune—quite a rarity for music boxes, since there aren't many music-box tuners around.

There is a store in the Musical Wonder House where you can buy rare or common music boxes and at the touch of a button, make canaries sing, ballerinas twirl, and beer mugs issue forth "The Whiffenpoof Song."

MASSACHUSETTS

BABSON PARK

THE WORLD'S LARGEST GLOBE
and THE WORLD'S LARGEST RELIEF MAP
OF THE UNITED STATES

Babson College, Great Plain Ave., Babson Park, Mass.;
April–Oct daily 10 AM–5 PM, Nov–March daily 2 PM–5 PM; free

The world's largest globe is a twenty-five-ton, twenty-eight-foot diameter steel
ball that rotates daily, like the earth, and turns on its axis once a year. It is
outdoors, in a courtyard surrounded by shrubs, trees, and vines. In twenty
brilliant colors of vitreous enamel, it shows the topographical and political
features of the world and is the approximate size the earth would appear from
a distance of 5,000 miles. In addition to continents and countries, it shows
every city with a million-plus population, meridians for longitude and latitude,
the international date line, the tropics of Cancer and Capricorn, and the true
and magnetic poles. One of the expressed purposes of the Great Revolving
Globe is "to get students to be more world-minded and less provincial."

Inside the Coleman Map Building next to the Globe is the World's Largest
Relief Map of the United States. Standing up in the balcony of the building,
visitors get a stratospheric view of the landscape. It measures sixty-five feet
from Maine to California, and forty-five feet from Michigan to Texas. As on

all relief maps, the vertical scale is exaggerated. If it were the same as the horizontal scale—four miles to an inch—even Pike's Peak would look like a tiny pimple.

At the center of the Great Map, viewers will note a circle around the town of Eureka, Kansas. The circle has a four-hundred-mile radius, extending into Nebraska, Iowa, Illinois, Arkansas, Texas, and Colorado. It is called "The Magic Circle" because its material resources exceed those of any equal area in any other part of the world. "In fact," Babson College notes, "in the event of a national crisis, with the help of the ocean products, it could feed the entire western hemisphere, except Canada."

CARVER

SAVERY'S AVENUE

Parallel to Route 58 in Carver, Mass.;
always open; free

Parallel to Route 58 in Carver, Massachusetts, lies one of the most significant developments in the history of American civilization. It is the original two-lane highway, built in 1860–61 by William Savery as a public-works project to provide some employment to the men of Carver. It was macadamized in 1907, and is no longer a regular route, although anyone can drive along it, park, or enjoy a picnic in the surrounding pine trees. It is half a mile long, and shortly after it was built granite pillars were erected at each end, with a brass hand pointing and the words "keep to the right" written underneath. The hand is supposed to be that of Savery's daughter, Mrs. Mary Jowitt.

It is a lovely avenue, not in the least likely to induce the affliction of the modern superslab, "white-line fever." Savery made the stipulation when he built his boulevard that the pines between the lanes and on the outside were to be left standing "for shade and ornament for man and beast."

FALL RIVER

LIZZIE BORDEN'S ARTIFACTS

The Fall River Historical Society, 451 Rock St., Fall River, Mass.;
Tues–Fri 9 AM–4:30 PM, Sat 9 AM–noon, Sun 2 PM–4 PM; donation

Lizzie Borden took and ax
And gave her mother forty whacks.
When she saw what she had done
She gave her father forty-one.

. . . So goes the grisly rhyme about Fall River's most notorious citizen. Actually, Lizzie was acquitted of the crime and lived in Fall River until 1927, when she died at age 66, but the children's rhyme reflects the popular feeling that Lizzie was indeed guilty. Here in the Fall River Historical Society are displayed the pieces of evidence used at her trial: the hatchet, a bloody bedspread, and the pillow sham on which Lizzie's mother died. There are also pictures of the Borden family from "happier days."

Incidentally, Lizzie's mother was determined to have received nineteen hatchet blows, and her father a mere ten.

FRAMINGHAM

THE WILL C. CURTIS GARDEN IN THE WOODS

Hemenway Road, Framingham, Mass.;
April 15–Nov 1 Mon–Sat 8:30 AM–4:30 PM (best viewing time:
mid-April–mid-June); adults: $1, children: 50¢

The Garden in the Woods has over 4,000 species of native American plants growing across its forty-eight acres. The habitat varies from dry and acid woodland slopes for the early spring flowers to a sunny bog for pitcher plants, to shady brooksides for ginseng, to meadows, to pine groves, to rock gardens. Plants from every state in the union and several foreign countries are visible along the five miles of self-guiding trails. The garden was originated by Will C. Curtis in 1931.

Although its variety and beauty are delightful to the wild-flower lover, what is unique about the Will Curtis Garden is its several dozen strains of thriving albino flowers. Iris, rhododendrons, geraniums, and even some plants that produce albino fruits are represented, all white. They appear along the pathway like a page from a coloring book not yet filled in.

Many of the plants grown here—including the albinos—are propagated and offered for sale.

Nash-ional Dinoland, South Hadley, Mass.

The Original Diner, Worcester, Mass.

HADLEY

ROGER JOHNSON'S PRIVATE COLLECTION OF ANTIQUE AND ODD BICYCLES

120 Hockanum Rd., Hadley, Mass.;
April–Oct daylight hours; free

This collection of antique and odd bicycles is one of the most pleasant museums in the country. It is charmingly informal. When we visited, Mr. Johnson, Sr., was out on the great lawn raking grass clippings. We asked him if we could take a look inside the museum. "Sure, go ahead," he motioned, and we were on our own. The bicycles are kept in an old red barn. They are casually displayed, some with signs or indications of name and year, others lined up against the wall or upstairs in the loft. On the walls of the barn there are primitive paintings and old wood panels, plus bicycle prints, posters, and pictures. There is also a list of injuries—to the Johnson family, to friends, and to the cycles. It is these injuries that prompted posting of the sign "NO RIDING, except if trained by a Johnson." The museum is, in fact, so relaxed, that without the sign it would seem natural to hop onto one of these beauties and take it for a spin around the circular driveway in front.

Among the oddities on display are a bicycle built for four in 1895, an 1820 hobby-horse bike with a steering stick, a 1868 velocipede, a railroad track-inspector's bike, and a large selection of trikes, tandems, delivery bicycles, and racing bikes. There is even a one-cylinder, three-wheel Knox Runabout made in 1901 in nearby Springfield.

You'll be able to find the bicycle museum from the road if you look for Roger Johnson's mailbox. It is mounted on a turn-of-the-century high-wheel bicycle.

HAMPDEN

LAUGHING BROOK TOUCH-AND-SEE TRAIL

789 Main St., Hampden, Mass.;
Tues–Sat 10 AM–5 PM, Sun 1 PM–5 PM;
adults: $1, children: 50¢ (413) 566-3571

Laughing Brook is the former home of Thornton W. Burgess, the children's writer. It is now owned and operated by the Massachusetts Audubon Society as a wildlife refuge. Among its attractions is a "Touch-and-See Trail" for the blind and visually handicapped. The trail is 1,300 feet long, with several dozen labels written in both Braille and 1/4" type. It is called "the crooked little path" paralleling Laughing Brook and part of the Scantic River. One is guided along the path by nylon ropes, passing through woods and an open field along a wood-chip path.

A blind visitor is invited to feel the bark of trees and vines, to listen to the sounds of the forest and the river, and to breathe the scent of the woods. One post has a turtle shell mounted on the top to touch. Another offers a deer's antler, and if the visitor is lucky, Lightfoot, the resident deer, might decide to poke his nose through the fence to be touched, too. At one stop, a sign requests that the reader hoot like an owl. The horned owl who lives here usually hoots back.

In addition to the Touch-and-See Trail, Laughing Brook offers three miles of trails for sighted persons, live animal exhibits, and tours of Thornton W. Burgess's home.

PIGEON COVE

THE PAPER HOUSE

52 Pigeon Hill St., Pigeon Cove, Mass.;
July & Aug. daily 10 AM–5 PM, Spring and Fall hours erratic;
adults: 50¢, 6–12: 25¢

Have you ever felt guilty about throwing away that Sunday newspaper you never got around to reading? Why don't you save it and put it to some use? That's what Mr. Elis F. Stenman decided to do in 1922. Without using glue or varnish, Stenman and his wife rolled up over 100,000 newspapers and made them into a house. The walls and roof are newspaper, 215 pages thick. Funny papers were woven together to make curtains. A cot was made from papers Stenman had saved since World War I. Newspapers telling of Lindberg's flight were rolled up and made into a writing desk. The bookshelves are made from foreign newspapers. The front of a grandfather clock is made up of forty-eight tubes, reading *The Charleston Gazette, The Daily Oklahoman, The Des Moines Register,* etc.—one from each of the forty-eight state capitals. The fireplace mantel was made from the *Boston Sunday Herald* and *New York Herald Tribune* rotogravure sections. That's right, there is a fireplace in the paper house—a demonstration of newspaper's practicability.

Stenman and his family worked for twenty years creating an all-paper interior for their paper house. From a distance, the construction looks like bamboo. Up close, everything is covered with newsprint and occasional splashes of color. In theory, a guest sitting in the paper rocking chair who becomes intrigued by a line of type running across the seat could unfold the chair and read the paper. Since no glue was used, the entire house and all the furniture can be unrolled and read.

PLYMOUTH

CRANBERRY WORLD

Water St., Plymouth, Mass.;
April–Nov; daily 10 AM–5 PM; free

Cranberries are as American as a Thanksgiving turkey. To honor the native berry, a new museum has opened in the corporate headquarters of a growers' cooperative that markets almost all of the nation's cranberries. Walkways that lead to the museum's entrance serve as shelters for small "model bogs" in which real cranberries are grown. Inside the museum there are portraits of men and women who have contributed to the growth of the cranberry industry, a reproduction of the painting "Cranberry Harvest in Nantucket" from the 1880s, and a diorama depicting the topographical features of a modern cranberry plantation. There are assorted cranberry scoops and tools that have been used over the years to harvest the crop, and a slide demonstration showing modern processing methods.

Cranberry history is an important part of Cranberry World, and you can learn here how Indians introduced the first settlers to the wild berry's uses as food, dye, and medicine.

The building that houses Cranberry World overlooks Plymouth Harbor, a suitable place to honor the Thanksgiving turkey's long-time companion.

SOUTH HADLEY

NASH-IONAL DINOLAND

Aldrich Road, South Hadley, Mass.;
April–Nov, hours vary;
adults: 50¢, children: 25¢

Oh, how C. S. Nash loves dinosaurs! His Dinoland has been here since the 1930s, when he discovered some funny-looking footprints on the scrubby two-acre plot of land. Over the last forty years, dinosaurs have been his life. He has found so many footprints in the twenty layers of shale on his property that he has been selling them as stepping stones, doorstops, ashtrays, paperweights, and fireplace decorations. Customers for C. S. Nash dino-prints have included General Patton, Dale Carnegie, and Fritz Lang. A recent visit to Dinoland found a "bargain table" of 500-million-year-old trilobites piled up and selling for half price.

Nash-ional Dinoland is not the sort of dinosaur park that offers its wares in the name of science or paleontology. Nash's interest is clearly more aesthetic —a love of prehistorica based on its capacity to beguile and brighten the spirits. He is a man who has fun with dinosaurs, and his park is a reflection of his own amusement with the cold-blooded creatures. His house, for instance, is made of shale walls covered with footprints. His car is painted "Dino Delivery Wagon." He's got a Dino gasoline sign. And he has painted in naïve and wondrous style "billboards" depicting the types of dinosaurs that might have once wandered his land. There is only one sculpted dinosaur on the premises —a modest six-footer that is so emaciated, bug-eyed, and slack-jawed, he appears ready to become extinct any minute. The rest of the two acres are the quarry, or "farm" as Nash calls it, where visitors can see the bumper crop of footprints in their natural habitat.

Inside the museum shop, Nash sells everything dinosauric, from the bargain trilobites to Da-Glo red-and-yellow models. There are pictures of Nash's long career as a dinosaurophile, including his appearance on "To Tell the Truth" as a dinosaur footprint farmer, and his explorations out west, where he discovered "petrified dinosaur gizzards."

The photos and clippings are yellowing; the display tables in the store are in disarray; the skinny dinosaur outside and the billboards all look ancient. Somehow, the decrepit physical condition of Nash-ional Dinoland is fitting. It is fossillike itself, the imprint of a man who has been obsessed with dinosaurs all his life. While it may be found wanting in scientific rigor, C. S. Nash's

creation is among the most inspired and delightful environments we have seen
—a rare and precious personal landscape in which the dinosaur is still king.

A word of warning is in order: There is a new, slick dinosaur museum on
the main highway, to which we were sent when we asked directions to Nash's.
Do *not* accept this substitute. Go to Nash-ional, on Aldrich Road, just past
a gorgeous waterfall and working waterwheel. It's worth a detour. It is one
of a kind.

WEBSTER

LAKE CHARGOGGAGOGGMANCHAUGG-
AUGGAGOGGCHAUBUNAGUNGAMAU

Route 12 & 197 in Webster, Mass.

If you have only a small post card to send your friends while on vacation, steer
clear of Webster, Mass. The above-mentioned lake has an Indian name that
is supposed to mean "You fish on your side, I'll fish on my side, and nobody
fishes in the middle." And we always thought "antidisestablishmentarianism"
was a tough one!

WORCESTER

MISS WORCESTER DINER

300 Southbridge, Worcester, Mass.;
Mon–Fri 5 AM–2 AM, Sat 5 AM–2 PM;
always viewable from the outside; free

The Miss Worcester is the first diner. It is a working antique, a verifiable bit
of Americana right down to the blue-plate specials and 40-weight coffee, a
Roadfood shrine untouched by time or progress. The outside is still shiny blue
enamel with yellow trim. The interior pre-dates the stainless-steel era. It is
checkered tile and smooth-edged wood, trimmed with chrome. A visit here is
like seeing Neil Armstrong's space capsule or Johnny Carson's boyhood home:
an occasion fraught with history.

Not that there weren't dinerlike structures long before the Miss Worcester.

In fact, the diner descended not from the railroad dining car—as is the common misconception—but from the moveable lunch wagon, at least as old as the first wagon train west. Some time around the turn of the century, as cars started looking like the wave of the future, the Worcester Lunch Car Company was born. Their idea was to build elaborate lunch wagons. Borrowing principles of compactness and easy care from the railroad, they started building "dining cars." They were constructed and completely equipped at the factory. They were trucked to their location, hooked up to water, and they were ready to go. If business was slow, or if a new road was built somewhere else, you just disconnected the diner and moved it to where your mobile trade might be.

Since the Miss Worcester was built, the diner has taken on mythical proportions. It is part of the folklore of the road—celebrated for its honesty and damned for its greasy food; the location in a thousand movies of neon-nighttime encounters; the home of fallen angels and knights of the road; the only place in town that's open all night.

There are now luxury diners, "dineraunts," and neodiners with brick-faced façades and $9.95 sirloin steaks. But aficionados of dinerdom accept only those built by the Worcester Company, the simple enamel or chrome beauties of which the Miss Worcester is the original ancestor. We are not savage purists, nor are we one to bemoan progress—in fact some of the food in the new Hellenic diners is pretty good—but every time we see *They Drive by Night* or a 1949-vintage movie with Linda Darnell slinging the hash, we schedule a quick trip up to Worcester to soak up some of this rare and original diner air.

GORHAM

MT. WASHINGTON ALTERNATIVE VEHICLE REGATTA

Mt. Washington Auto Road, Gorham, N.H.;
last weekend in June; free;
to enter call Charles MacArthur (203) 289–6851

This is the only road race we know in which competitors are disqualified for going too fast. The point of the Regatta is to cover the sixteen-mile round-trip course using as little fuel as possible. Efficiency is determined in two categories: vehicles that use nonrenewable resources, and those that are powered by wind, solar energy, inertia, cooking fat, steam, chicken droppings, etc. Vehicles must ascend an eight-mile, 12 percent grade to prove their "strength," then descend to test braking and to allow vehicles with regenerative systems to recharge or reclaim energy lost during the ascent. Upon completion of the round trip, vehicle energy reservoirs are "topped off," and the costs of refueling are measured against overall performance.

Some vehicles look like ordinary cars or motorcycles, others are "stripped down" for efficiency, and some look like Martian mopeds. All are docile-looking, and nonagression is the rule. No contest vehicle may pass another contest vehicle without permission from the lead vehicle. Contestants are encouraged to use vehicles that operate with a minimum of pollution potential, in emissions of both gas and noise. Judges consider creative use of material and individual initiative along with mathematical efficiency. The Regatta symbol is a tortoise, and its slogan is Mahatma Gandhi's declaration that "There is more to life than increasing its speed."

HENNIKER

THE ONLY TOWN IN THE WORLD NAMED HENNIKER

Henniker, N.H. (Jct. of Rt. 114 & 202)

HILLSBORO

R. A. KEMP'S MACK TRUCK MUSEUM

River Street, Hillsboro, N.H.;
daylight hours; free

R. A. Kemp is an ex-truckdriver who thinks big. His hobby is collecting Mack Trucks, and a few other brands, too. They are displayed outdoors and in, divided up between the large garage on River Street and the yard next door. He estimates that he has seventy Macks altogether—a fine collection.

"The Museum" is a handle stuck on the place by townspeople. Kemp sees it more informally. He charges no admission, and viewing is strictly on the honor system. His biggest problem is theft—a dozen Mack bulldogs have been stolen from the hoods of his trucks. But he likes people to appreciate what he has, so he doesn't figure on changing the way he runs things.

What you can see here is a collection of just about every variety of Mack Truck made. His rarest might be a 1930 "Bulldog Mack," the original ugly piece of machinery with a growling engine and a snub nose. It is a green Texaco tanker now, and he got it years ago from a friend who was going to junk it.

If the new fancy Kenworths or duded-up Peterbilts leave you cold or remind you too much of California Van Culture, and if your idea of a nice truck stops with Bogey's rig in *They Drive by Night,* then R. A. Kemp's museum is the place to go for a double-dose of dieselmania.

KEENE

MAIN STREET

Keene, N.H.

Keene says that this is the widest Main Street in the world, 172 feet across and paved all the way.

KINGSTON

DARRELL'S THING (THE HORRIBLE ROOM)

Rt. 107 W. of E. Kingston, N.H.;
summer weekends; free

Darrell's Thing is Darrell O'Connor's backyard. It is populated with a menagerie of "junk sculpture" animals, made from scrap metal into vivid personalities. There is a pig made from a milk can, a colossal elephant made from a boiler with an auto axle for a trunk, an "astrobird," caterpillars, witches, and a variety of animals that Darrell has concocted from his own imagination, bearing no resemblance to anything in nature. "Very small kids and old people are the ones who love it," he told us.

More than the outdoor animals, we like The Horrible Room. It used to be Darrell's garage, and is now populated by snakes and bats, skeletons, gorillas, vampires, werewolves, and anything else that goes bump in the night. If you remember Zacherly or any of the other hosts of late-night "Shock Theater" TV shows, or if you are a reader of *Famous Monsters of Filmland,* you'll perfectly understand the logic of The Horrible Room. When you enter, a coffin creaks open and a gorilla face emerges. The spiders and snakes dangle and wiggle in the air. A snake pops out of a box and introduces himself. A talking hand appears from the wall waving a huge brassiere and asking your name. A tin-man robot taps his sneakers. It is a horror-fun house compressed into a single room.

Darrell's Thing and The Horrible Room are very informal, open when

Darrell or his wife are around to activate the monsters. There is no admission, but there is a box for donations "to the care and education of orphan vampire children."

LITTLETON

TRACKMASTER

Rt. 302, 6 mi. N. of Lisbon in Littleton, N.H.;
daily 10 AM–4 PM; adults: $2, under 8: free (603) 838–5533

Trackmaster is an outdoor museum of animal tracks that teaches visitors how to "read" the signs left behind by wild animals. There are several dozen exhibits laid out along a mountain stream. Most are sets of animal tracks. For instance, a straight line of moose prints leads toward a tree from one direction. From the other direction come bear paw prints, also toward the tree, at which point they disappear. What would the Mohawk Indian say about that natural "story"? If one consults the illustrated guide book that comes with admission to Trackmaster, one learns that the story is simple: A moose on the rampage scared the bear up a tree. Other sets of prints are more complicated, telling stories of porcupines or skunks encountering foes and scaring them off. Some show animals hunting, playing, or bedding down for the night. There is enough here to earn your wildlife merit badge, and for further study the museum shop sells tracks that you can take home and place around your backyard, creating "stories" of your own for your friends or your pet to analyze.

LONDONDERRY

THE LAWRENCE L. LEE SCOUTING MUSEUM

Bodwell Rd., Londonderry, N.H.;
last week of June–last week of Aug
Mon–Fri 9 AM–noon, 2 PM–5 PM, 6:30 PM–8:30 PM, Sat 9 AM–noon; free

We find it tough enough to start a fire in our backyard barbecue, so when we see evidence of one-match fires and similar wilderness survival skills, we must tip our hats. Here at the L. L. Lee Museum, all of those skills associated with scouting are represented in patches, badges, trophies and awards. It is the complete scouting museum, located at Camp Carpenter, which is run by the

The Paper House, Pigeon Cove, Mass.

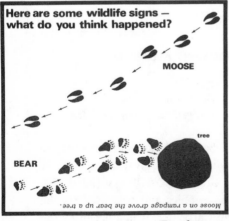

Here are some wildlife signs —
what do you think happened?

MOOSE

tree

BEAR

Moose on a rampage drove the bear up a tree.

Here are some wildlife signs —
what do you think happened?

PORCUPINE

LYNX

Porcupine drove a few quills into the lynx.

Trackmaster, Littleton, N.H.

Daniel Webster Chapter of the Boy Scouts of America.

The Museum is one large room, in which the entire story of scouting is told. It began in 1908, in England, as a movement founded by Baden-Powell and his wife. There are pictures of the Baden-Powells on display, as well as books they wrote and some of the original Boy Scout equipment. There are flags, belt buckles, neckerchiefs, mugs, uniforms, handcrafted items, and, of course, all the necessary tools to "Be Prepared" in the wilderness.

MERRIMACK

CLYDESDALE HAMLET

Rt. 3, Merrimack, N.H.;
daily 9:30 AM–3:30 PM; free

The Clydesdale horse is the "gentle giant" of the equine world, a relic of days when "horsepower" meant horse power. The work of the Clydesdale has been pretty much supplanted by the tractor, but there is at least one outfit around that still requires the services of that mighty workhorse. That is of course the Anheuser-Busch Company, who makes Budweiser Beer, and who uses the Clydesdales to pull the "Bud" wagon around in TV commercials and at special appearances. You can visit the Budweiser Clydesdales here at the Busch Brewery, where they also have oxen, a carriage house, a tack room, and exhibits about the history of the breed. When the team is not on tour, you can see the eight-horse hitch in action. If the big fellows are out of town, there are at least two left behind for visitors to see.

Clydesdales are unbelievably big horses. We were told that they consume four times the amount of feed eaten by an average riding horse, and that they eat only a special high-grade variety produced by the Merrimack Farmers' Exchange.

MERRIMACK FARMERS' EXCHANGE

Rt. 3, Merrimack, N.H.; Mon–Fri 8 AM–5 PM;
free; call ahead to insure a tour (603) 225–6661

A visit to the Merrimack Farmers' Exchange goes a long way to dispel any romantic notions one might have about the close-to-nature life of the New England farmer. The Exchange mills feed, packages seed, and supplies its own retail stores with items as diverse as nonburning lime for marking baseball diamonds and calcite that keeps cows from slipping on barn floors.

A tour of the feed mill takes you to the heart of the operation—two futuristic control panels that oversee ninety-nine separate motors in the plant, from grinders and corn crimpers to grain transfer systems and molasses mixers. The entire layout of the mill is visible on one control board, from which the operator automatically moves grains into proper sequence, selects which of the fifty-four ingredients ought to be used in a particular batch of feed, and dumps the finished product into individual bins. The tour also takes you to the top of the seventy-foot-high storage silos, and down into the basement where corn and oats are ground into meal. The machinery there includes a bagger that weighs seventeen bags a minute, a magnetized sieve to remove any nails or metal from the raw grain, and a device that coats pellets with molasses, like an M&M, so that cows will eat more.

NEWPORT

THE CLOCK MUSEUM

On the Common, Rt. ii, Newport, N.H.;
daily 9 AM–4 PM, Sun i PM–4 PM;
adults: 95¢, children: 50¢

The Clock Museum has one of the largest collections of horological art in the country. There are approximately four hundred timepieces, from sundials and hourglasses to digital clocks. Some are scarce collectors' items demonstrating the fine craftsmanship of men like Eli Terry and Seth Thomas. Others are one-of-a-kind anomalies, such as the clock run by a wagon spring and the eccentric "water clock" that includes a rocking sailboat, a small pond, a rotating waterwheel, and a railroad trestle with two trains. One of the strangest looking clocks is the Japanese Temple Clock that is designed with three miniature carved figures "holding up" its face. Two stand on either side, like pallbearers, and the third is in the center, underneath, squatting down as if the full weight of the clock is crushing his back. Another unique timepiece is the eighteenth-century French Night Clock with an alarm bell. It looks something like an automobile speedometer wrapped around a Lava Lite. The oldest mechanical timepiece here dates back to 1590.

Alongside the clocks, the museum also displays stamps, coins, canes, autographs, buttons, pistols, and piggy banks. Some of these items are for sale; none is cheap.

NORTH SALEM

MYSTERY HILL

Haverhill Rd, S. of Rt. III, North Salem, N.H.;
Spring & Fall 10 AM–4 PM, Summer 9 AM–5:30 PM;
adults: $2.50, Sr. citizens: $2, 6–12: $1

Mystery Hill calls itself "America's Stonehenge" because it is supposed to be a neolithic computer that once determined solar and lunar events for ancient peoples. In 1975, stone fragments were unearthed here that linked the mega-lithic complex to Celts who once lived on the Iberian peninsula. In fact, the signature of the stonemason is believed to be written in Iberian Punic on one stone. On another is a date which matches a known Celto-Iberian holiday. What this demonstrates is that North America was visited by European peoples approximately 4,000 years ago.

America's Stonehenge isn't as awesome-looking as England's, since many of the stone constructions have severely decomposed. You can see the Summer Solstice Monolith. In fact, if you happen to come here on June 21st, you will see the sun set directly over the pointy stone—providing you stand on the central viewing platform. You can also see the North Pole–Star Stone, lined up with the star "Thuban" in 2000 B.C., and used to compute the positioning of the other monuments. The central monument is a "sacrificial table," under which there is a "speaking tube" that runs back to a large "Oracle Chamber" as a sort of Bronze Age public-address system.

Doubting Thomases have attributed Mystery Hill's stonework to an eccentric early nineteenth-century farmer. If, in fact, he did build these rocks, caves, and altars single-handedly, then he is surely one of our country's most imaginative environmental artists. Whether 4000 years old or only 150, Mystery Hill is a singular ruin.

WARREN

THE MORSE MUSEUM

Rt. 25C, downtown Warren, N.H.;
Memorial Day–Labor Day, daily 10 AM–5 PM; free

The Morse Museum is a cavernous single hall containing skins, trophies, whole stuffed animals, and curios from around the world. It is one of the largest inventories of natural plunder we have seen anywhere, a monument to the hunting skills of Ira H. and Dr. Richard Morse, the two brothers who killed every animal on display. But aside from being a Great White Hunter, Ira H. Morse also ran a chain of shoe stores in New England, and during his world travels he collected shoes. Here amidst the beasts of the jungle is a vast collection of the world's shoes.

There are shoes made of hemp by prisoners of Zamboango, a Siamese princess's shoes made of pearl, solid rubber shoes worn on Island Miyajimi, Sunday shoes from the Isle of Amoy, wooden shoes, platform shoes, oval shoes, crescent shoes. There are three different types of Sunday shoes from Burma, shoes for wearing to a Chinese burial, and shoes worn by Mr. Morse on his visit to King Solomon's Temple in Jerusalem. There is a whole collection of shoes for bound feet, available in three sizes: 5, 6, or 7 inches. There are men's and women's shoes made from the skin of a zebra shot by Mrs. Morse. And there is even a tiny pair of child's sneakers, identified thusly: "Sneakers worn by Pamela Hollingsworth during her 8 days of wandering in the New Hampshire forest. Sept., 1941."

Ira Morse's fascination with feet and foot apparel extended to his trophies. Among the booty are elephants' feet made into trash cans and a rhino foot that serves as a humidor.

WOODSTOCK

ROCK OF AGES CHURCH

On the West side of Rt. 3 in N. Woodstock, N.H.;
always open; donation; (603) 745–8477

This is the most precarious-looking church in America. It is perched on top of a boulder on top of a hill. To get inside you mount a slim wooden stairway and enter the single door. It is one tiny room. A few nun dolls stand on shelves, a Mantovani album called "Songs of Praise" leans against the wall, and there are children's letters and sentiments posted near the door. There is one chair, one sofa, and a pulpit. Standing inside, the room *feels* more solid than it appeared to be from the road.

The church was built in the early 1960s when Charles Kimball thought he saw a bear by the side of the road one rain-soaked night. What he saw turned out to be a nun, kneeling by a boulder where she had seen a vision of the crucifixion. Kimball was so moved he built this church on top of the boulder. There is a small manger to the side of the boulder, and smaller rocks around the church stenciled "Mount of Olives," "Fountain Gate," and "Valley of Cedron." There used to be tiny white crosses leading from Route 3 up to the boulder, but they have disappeared in the last few years.

There are no regular services in the Rock of Ages Church, although one can be married here. To arrange the ceremony, call Mrs. Bartlett, who takes care of things and keeps the miniature church in tip-top shape. If you are married here, just remember to make plans for a symmetrical arrangement of your guests, by weight, so that the teetering church doesn't totter.

RHODE ISLAND

ADAMSVILLE

RED HEN MONUMENT

R.I. 179 in Adamsville, R.I., SE of Tiverton;
always viewable; free

To the long list of America's larger-than-life statuary we add the Red Hen Monument. It was built to commemorate the development of the Rhode Island Red Hen in 1854 by farmers at Little Compton. It is the bird that made the Rhode Island poultry industry famous. In fact, it is Rhode Island's state bird.

NEWPORT

INTERNATIONAL TENNIS HALL OF FAME

194 Bellevue Ave, Newport, R.I.;
May–Oct daily 10 AM–5 PM, Nov–April daily 11 AM–4 PM;
adults: $2, 6–18: $1

In 1874 Mary Outerbridge stepped off a steamship after vacationing in Bermuda. She brought with her a book of rules, a racket, balls, and a net for a new game she had learned about called "Lawn Tennis." In case you haven't heard, it is now America's favorite pastime. At first a game for the very wealthy, tennis has ballooned to fill the leisure time of everyone from suburban tykes to urban oldsters.

The Newport Casino was opened in 1880 as a deluxe resort facility. The lawn that was originally designed for bandstand waltzes and polite summer conversation was quickly turned into a "tennis court," and the Casino became host to the U. S. Lawn Tennis Association Championships from 1881 to 1914. It is now the site of the Virginia Slims Grass Courts Championships. It is also the home of the Tennis Hall of Fame and Museum, America's complete tennis shrine.

The best place to begin a tour is the Court Tennis Room—a kind of medieval shed in which the ancient history of the game is explained. The roots of tennis are traced back to the thirteenth century and games played in castle courtrooms and monasteries. Major Walter Clopton Wingfield is credited with adapting the game known as "court tennis" so that it could be played outdoors on his "hourglass" court. To do this, he borrowed rules from both badminton and rackets.

Along with a complete and detailed history of the game, the Hall of Fame traces the history and manufacture of tennis rackets, "one hundred years of women's tennis fashions," and the story of intercollegiate tennis. There are Davis Cup rooms, halls of trophies and miscellaneous memorabilia, a complete tennis library, a film room that regularly shows slides and movies, and a souvenir shop.

Outside, there are still a dozen grass courts open to the public. If you are the type of person who just can't get enough tennis, pay a visit to the Hall of Fame. You may never want to leave.

PORTSMOUTH

GREEN ANIMALS

Cory's Lane off Rt. 114, Portsmouth, R.I.;
May–Sept. daily 10 AM–5 PM, Oct weekends only 10 AM–5 PM;
adults: $1.50, 6–15: 75¢

This part of Rhode Island is the land of the "Newport Mansions," those baronial "cottages" built by people like the Wetmores and the Vanderbilts for those times they felt like "roughing it" away from the city. The grandeur of these homes far outdoes the White House or the Metropolitan Museum of Art.

They represent perhaps the most conspicuous of American consumption. And so this is a fitting environment for Green Animals, the most splendid topiary garden in the country.

Topiary art is the carving of living shrubbery into animals and abstract shapes. It began hundreds of years ago in England, where landed gentry did everything they could to eradicate the "natural look" from their gardens.

Green Animals was the garden of Thomas Brayton's Newport cottage, first sculpted in 1880. When Miss Alice Brayton died in 1972 at the age of ninety-four she willed Green Animals to the Preservation Society of Newport County, who today looks after her verdant menagerie. Altogether there are eighty sculptured trees and shrubs. Some are spirals, circles and symmetrical designs. The animals include a peacock, elephant, giraffe, cat, dog, lion, donkey, and wild boar. There is also a policeman. A pet cemetery on the premises is surrounded by a barberry hedge with urns sculpted of privet and filled with roses. In addition, there is a fruit and vegetable garden and formal flower beds. The whole is a spectacular example of nature conforming to human design.

WATCH HILL

THE OLDEST CAROUSEL IN THE COUNTRY

6. mi. S. of Westerly on Beach St. in Watch Hill, R.I.;
summers, till sundown 10¢

Watch Hill began as a summer resort in 1840, and since the early 1870s children have ridden the small carousel here called the Flying Horse. It is the oldest carousel in the United States in continuous operation (with brief interruptions to let the kiddies mount and dismount). The two white horses that originally propelled the ride have been replaced by a gasoline engine.

The central stem of the carousel is painted white and trimmed with elegant lines of black, gold, and red. The horses—the original wooden steeds—are small and red, with leather reins and black bridles. They do a fine if gentle job of going up and down on their poles. You'd never guess these nags are over one hundred years old.

WESTERLY

FLORENCE NIGHTINGALE'S CAP

The Westerly Hospital, Wells St., Westerly, R.I., in the main lobby;
visible during the day and early evening; free

Florence Nightingale's cap was put on display in 1965 on May 12, the anniversary of her birth. According to the display, the cap was worn by the famous nurse during the Crimean War, in 1854. She fought to overcome the unsanitary conditions in the British military hospitals, particularly in Scutari, and her efforts were reflected in the reduction of the hospitals' death rate from 42 percent in February, 1855, to 2 percent in June of the same year.

The cap is displayed in the Westerly Hospital to honor the originator and founder of modern nursing.

THE GLADYS ORMPHBY BENCH

Broad St. in Wilcox Park next to the Westerly Public Library, Westerly, R.I.;
always viewable; free

We can't guarantee that you will be accosted by a dirty old man if you sit on the Gladys Ormphby Bench, but don't be surprised if it happens. Westerly, Rhode Island is Ruth Buzzi's hometown. Ms. Buzzi, you will remember, made it big in the original "Laugh-In" with her characterization of the hairnet-headed frump Gladys, always ready to sock-it-to the park pervert. When the TV show "This Is Your Life" did Ruth Buzzi in 1970, they traced her roots back to Westerly and presented the town with this bench. A plaque in front of the bench is inscribed: "This bench presented to the town of Westerly, Rhode Island in honor of Ruth Buzzi–Gladys Ormphby by 'This Is Your Life,' November 25, 1970." Aside from the plaque, it looks like an ordinary park bench.

At the dedication ceremonies a Gladys Ormphby look-alike sat on the bench (the original Gladys refused to come because she wouldn't be allowed to wear her hot pants, Ruth Buzzi advised), and a local band calling itself The Sauerkraut German Band, dressed in overcoats, derby hats, and scraggy whiskers marched around the park fountain. Ruth Buzzi declared that she was probably the first celebrity to have her own park bench, and added that other stars like Sophia Loren or Raquel Welch might be better off with a Memorial Shelf.

WOONSOCKET

THE HEAD OF SAMUEL FOSS

The Woonsocket Call Building, 75 Main St., Woonsocket, R.I.;
always viewable; free

Poor Samuel Foss's head. It has been moved so much in recent years that it must be dizzy by now. The bas-relief carving of "the father of Woonsocket journalism" was originally embedded in glass and concrete next to the city parking lot, but Woonsocket vandals went to work on it, so it was removed. It finally wound up in its present spot in front of the Call building, high enough to escape the vandals' hands.

Foss was the editor of the *Weekly Patriot,* the city's first newspaper. He died in 1879. We hope his distinguished bearded visage has at last found a permanent resting spot, watching over Main Street. One can only hope that Mr. Foss did not suffer from vertigo.

VERMONT

BENNINGTON

THE WORLD'S TALLEST LADDERBACK CHAIR

Haynes and Kane Furniture Shop, Rt. 7, Bennington, Vt.;
always viewable; free

This jumbo ladderback sits in the parking lot of the Haynes and Kane Furniture Shop as a customer attraction in much the same way that fiberglass cows herald steakhouses. It weighs 2,200 pounds and is 19′ 1″ tall. It is listed in the *Guinness Book of World Records.* The chair was painted red, white, and blue for the Bicentennial, but it looks about due for another paint job soon.

BRADFORD

WILD GAME SUPPER

United Church of Christ, Bradford, Vt.;
2nd Sat of deer season (Nov. 18, 1978);
adults: $10, under 10: $5;
by reservation only at hourly sittings from 3 PM–9 PM—

call Mrs. Raymond Green (802) 222–4670 after Oct. 23,
or write Mrs. Eris M. Eastman, Box 182,
Bradford, Vt., 05033

Are you a meat-eater? If so, this is your meal—a cornucopia for carnivores. Last year over 1,500 people consumed over 3,000 pounds of moose, beaver, buffalo, venison, pheasant, rabbit, coon, wild boar, bear, elk, and caribou at Bradford's annual Wild Game Supper. The meal is served buffet-style, so you can try everything from coon pie to boar chops to bear sausage. Since most diners are not familiar with the difference in looks between creamed pheasant and glazed venison loaf, colored toothpicks are stuck into the various entrées to help you figure out what animal you are eating.

One of the most pleasant aspects of this event is the "church supper" atmosphere. If you arrive at the church before your sitting you wait upstairs in the church sanctuary where a local woman plays a medely of tunes on the piano. The vestry serves as the dining hall, where food is laid out by local residents who have volunteered to help. On the way out, every departing dinner guest gets a piece of fudge cooked by the church women.

The cooks have recently prepared a small cookbook with their favorite recipes for coon pie, buffalo burgers, and moose loaf. The recipes are simple and easy to follow, though you may have difficulty coming by some of the ingredients.

BRISTOL

THE LORD'S PRAYER ROCK

Rt. 17, 1 mi N. of Bristol, Vt.;
always viewable; free

Decades ago, a stern resident of Waitsfield became outraged at the language truckdrivers used negotiating a tight turn on Route 100. The Waitfieldian carved The Lord's Prayer into the surface of a strategically placed boulder, in full sight of the cussing gearjammers, reminding them that they might make it past this turn, but a certain well-known valley awaited them if they didn't slow down and live right.

CABOT

CABOT FARMERS' COOPERATIVE CREAMERY

(5 mi. S. of Walden off Rt. 15); Cabot, Vt.
Mon–Fri 8 AM–4:30 PM, May–Dec Sat 9 AM–3:30 PM; free

This is the largest butter-and-cheese plant in New England, a modern, scientific assembly-line operation that uses machinery to do all the primary dairy farm tasks that follow the milking of the cow. Tours begin in the Cheddar Cheese Room, where Cheddar from 31,000-pound vats is loaded into containers ranging in capacity from three pounds to 500 pounds. It is then pressed, dried, and waxed and sent to the Cheddar Cheese Aging Room, where it sits on wooden shelves for six to eighteen months. The Butter Room comes next. Here, 5,000-pound globs of butter are churned, then packaged into one-pound blocks and quarter-pound sticks. Then there is the Cottage Cheese Room, where the cottage cheese is cooked and where by-products like sour cream, yogurt, and dip are packaged. Last, you see the Milk Processing Room, where the sour cream and yogurt are manufactured, the milk is homogenized, pasteurized, and separated and the Milk Receiving Room, where 42,000 gallons are stored.

Despite the vast, mechanized nature of the operation, Cabot is quick to point out that at no stage in the process are preservatives added to anything they make.

At the end of the one-hour tour, visitors are taken to the Sales Room, where the Creamery's products, under the Rosedale Label, are offered for sale.

DANVILLE

THE DOWSERS' CONVENTION

U.S. 2, Danville, Vt.;
3rd weekend in Sept, Thurs–Sun;
free to watch, registration fee for seminars

Dowsers are the people who go out with a dowsing stick or divining rod to find water, gold, or whatever they need that is buried under the ground. We say "need" rather than "want," because selfishness is a vice certain to keep one from being a good dowser. Dowsers consider their ability a spiritual gift, not to be misused merely for personal gain.

Every September, about five hundred dowsers gather in Danville from all parts of the globe to talk dowsing and to go out on "field trips." Dowsing exhibits are given on the town green, and you will see sticks, rods, pendulums, and even bare hands used to locate hidden treasures.

One dowser we spoke to had never so much as struck water (the easiest substance to locate) until she was shown the way by an 87-year-old convention-eer who told her that dowsing can be learned by anyone. All it takes is the right kind of concentration and an altruistic frame of mind.

ESSEX JUNCTION

DISCOVERY MUSEUM

51 Park St., Essex Jct., Vt.;
July & Aug daily 10 AM–4:30 PM,
rest of year Sun–Fri 1 PM–4:30 PM, Sat 10 AM–4:30 PM; free

Visitors to the Discovery Museum are invited to touch the exhibits, play with the costumes on display, and even pick up and carry about an artifact they particularly like. It is a small museum, originally designed for children to counteract the hands-off, once-removed qualities of ordinary museum-going. Among the displays are a "Natural Science" corner, where visitors can pet a hamster, an iguana or a land crab, a hospital room where they can listen to their own heartbeat, put themselves in traction, and play with an electric bed, and a "Grandmother's Attic" upstairs, where children are invited to dress up in old clothes and snoop around.

The museum is one of the few institutions in Vermont licensed to keep native wild animals. They specialize in motherless or injured native birds. Visitors are allowed to take a racing pigeon outside the museum—even several miles away—release the bird, and watch it head directly back "home" to the museum.

Although it was designed for children, the Discovery Museum will delight anyone who ever stood on one side of a pane of glass under the watchful eye of a museum guard ready to pounce if you touched.

GRANITEVILLE

ROCK OF AGES QUARRIES

Rt. 14, Graniteville, Vt.;
May–Oct daily 8:30 AM–5 PM; free

The name of this place tells all about it. It is a granite quarry that has been providing stone for funeral monuments since the Civil War. Guided tours take you to see granite workers use jet-channeling flame torches and drills to carve out blocks of granite, which are then hoisted out of the quarry by great derricks that tower 115 feet above the edge. You are also taken to the Rock of Ages Tourist Center, which is made from granite, and told all about the quarrying industry. There is a Craftsmen's Center, where headstones are made, and a picnic area outside if this high-energy tour gives you an appetite.

For an extra dollar (on weekdays only) you can take a train ride through the site to conserve your own bodily resources.

HEALDVILLE

CROWLEY CHEESE FACTORY

Healdville Rd., S. of Rt. 103, Healdville, Vt.;
Mon–Sat 8 AM–4 PM (cheese-making usually completed by 2PM); free

A tour of the Crowley Cheese Factory is the most informal industrial tour you can imagine. The "factory" is two rooms of an old New England house. You enter one room and are given a piece of paper that guides you around the various steps of cheese-making. You are free to talk to any of the three or four employees, and when you get to the cheese drying shelves, there is a woman who will cut some cheese off a wheel for you to buy and take home.

The cheese is made here the same way it was when A. Winfield Crowley began the company in 1882—from curd sink to steam cabinet to press to waxing kettle to drying shelf. Every step of the process is visible, and the whole tour is hardly more complicated than going to a friend's kitchen to watch her bake a loaf of bread.

MIDDLEBURY

UNIVERSITY OF VERMONT MORGAN HORSE FARM

Weybridge St., Middlebury, Vt.;
May–Oct daily 8 AM–4 PM;
adults: $1.75, teens: 50¢, under 12: free

It all began with a small, rough-coated colt named Figure, owned by a school-teacher named Justin Morgan. Figure was barely fourteen hands, just over a thousand pounds, and yet he worked for twenty-eight years in Vermont, his strength earning him a good measure of fame. According to legend, he pulled logs that a draft horse couldn't budge. He once carried a U.S. president. He outran Vermont's winningest racehorse in the quarter-mile. He was also one of the greatest breeding horses of all time, his progeny including the best trotters of the 1850s, battle horses for the Vermont Cavalry during the Civil War, and the only survivor of the massacre at Little Big Horn. Figure was the first of the oldest and best of America's light horse breeds—now called the Morgan horse, after Figure's original owner.

The University of Vermont Morgan Horse Farm has been the primary source of Morgan horses throughout the twentieth century. Between 1907 and 1951 it was owned by the government. It is now run by the University, and the Morgan horse has become Vermont's state animal. A visit to the Morgan Horse Farm includes a guided tour through the stables and an opportunity to relax on the lush green grass, with mares and foals grazing all around. There is also a slide show about the history of the horse and the spacious farm on which they are bred. A bronze statue of Figure the horse is on display, and Morgan-related gifts can be purchased.

ROCKINGHAM

GRIST MILL MUSEUM

Rt. 103 (next to Vermont Country Store), Rockingham, Vt.;
always visible; free

This is more an exhibit than a museum; actually, more like a stage set than an exhibit. It is a postcard-perfect grist mill, complete with waterwheel, freshly painted trough, and New England covered bridge in the background. You can walk up to the side of the mill and look inside, through a glass window. Here are all the working parts of a grist mill—no longer used because of health laws. There are great grinding stones and huge gears in perfect condition, all forming an ideal backdrop to take that snapshot that epitomizes one's visit to Vermont.

ORTON EISENHOWER EXHIBIT

Rt. 103, Rockingham, Vt.;
Mon–Sat 9 AM–5 PM; free

We walked into the Vermont Country Store Wholegrain Bakery to buy some cookies to eat along the road. We bought our cookies—beautiful six-inch-round oatmeal and chocolate chips—and turned to walk out the door. There before us stood a glass case. In the glass case was the most complete collection of Dwight D. Eisenhower bibliographica in the world. Every book ever written by or about Ike is here, including *Invincible Ike, Eisenhower and the Jews, The Man from Abilene, Eisenhower's Six Great Decisions,* and *Eisenhower the Liberator.* There are scores of pamphlets representing every phase of his career, proclamations in French announcing his arrival on the continent, letters, buttons and telegrams relating to political campaigns, and even a 45-rpm record called "I Like Ike," with words and music by Irving Berlin.

Aside from the record, and a few pictures on dustjackets and posters, all the material is in print form. There are no souvenir plates or ashtrays, and scarcely a single portrait of Mamie. Of course, Nixon's face crops up here and there, especially in campaign memorabilia. Everything is contained in one great glass case along one wall of the bakery.

Why? Vrest Orton, who owns the bakery, was a Vermont delegate to the Republican Conventions during the 1950s. Ike asked him to compile the material, much of which was donated by the president and Sherman Adams. It is here in the bakery, a salesgirl explained, "because the display case is too big to fit anywhere else."

ST. JOHNSBURY

THE MAPLE MUSEUM and MAPLE GROVE TOURS

U.S. 2 E. of St. Johnsbury, Vt.;
museum: May–Oct Mon–Fri 8 AM–5 PM, Sat & Sun 9 AM–5 PM; free,

Maple Grove Tours: Mon–Fri 8:30 AM–noon, 1:15 PM–4:30 PM,
every 10 minutes; 50¢

The Maple Museum is a sweet-smelling replica of a sugar house in St. Johnsbury, the "Maple Center of the World." In the middle of the museum there is an Evaporator, with a recorded voice explaining "This is an Evaporator, hear how it works . . ." Around it in the small wood cabin are displays of sap spouts, tap screws, maple leaves, old buckets, and yokes once used on oxen. There is also an exhibit of elaborate, charming old molds used to make maple-sugar candy. As you peruse the exhibits, the voice from the Evaporator tells you how sap from trees is boiled down from its three percent sugar content into maple sugar. It takes forty gallons of sap to make a single gallon of pure maple syrup.

Next to the Maple Museum is the Maple Grove Factory, where you can see the kitchens and packing departments in which candies and fudge are prepared. The tour is unbelievably appetizing. You watch great ladles of fudge poured out over molds, amber vats of syrup poured into buckets, and an endless stream of maple candy emerging into the packing room. An invigorating, woodsy smell wafts everywhere.

In the gift shop next door, free samples are available as you shop.

WINDSOR

THE AMERICAN PRECISION MUSEUM

196 Main St., Windsor, Vt.;
June–Mid–Oct daily 1 PM–5 PM;
adults: $1.50, children: 50¢ (families $4 maximum)

This place calls itself "The national museum of tools and the 'American system' of manufacturing." The American system was first displayed at the Crystal Palace Industrial Exhibition of 1851 in London by a firm named Robbins & Lawrence. Its principle is interchangeability of parts. The American Precision Museum is now housed in a beautiful three-story brick building that was once Robbins & Lawrence's machine shop. The collection touches on every imaginable aspect of modern life, including hand and machine tools and their products. There are scales, typewriters, computers, engines, generators and an automobile. And there are more esoteric devices, like the linear dividing engine of 1850, which is described as having made vernier calipers a practical reality, and the "double-acting high pressure V-type reversible, two-cylinder marine steam engine" made by Herbert I. Boynton as a graduation piece at the completion of his apprenticeship as a machinist.

The breadth of the museum's collection is suggested by one of their reference sets—an 800-volume *Patent Digest* describing American and foreign inventions. Among the significant tools and esoteric devices the museum places mundane objects which incorporate significant instrumentation, like the sewing machine or a simple steel ruler. Some of the machines reflect an era when workpieces were made to be as beautiful as possible, embellished with carved sea shells, paneling, polished brass, or painted designs. Others are beautiful in a more abstract way—for the clarity or invention of their design.

Even if you have no interest in mechanical things, this is a fascinating museum. If you are mechanically-inclined plan to spend a long day here. You'll be mesmerized.

DELAWARE

DOVER

DELMARVA CHICKEN FESTIVAL

Early June–Friday and Saturday
Dover, Delaware (location changes from year to year);
For specific information contact Delmarva Poultry Industry,
Box 47, Georgetown, Del.: (302) 856–2971

Every June Delmarva (that's Delaware, Maryland, Virginia) goes chicken-crazy. Delmarva calls itself the "birthplace of America's broiler industry." It is also the home of the world's largest chicken frying pan—a ten-footer that's hauled out Friday afternoon to start the bird celebration. By late Friday, chicken fans have gobbled down a few thousand pounds of fried chicken, and a few more thousand of barbecued chicken. Friday night the poultry princess is crowned, the last of the barbecue sauce is licked from the fingers, and serious competitors in the chicken contests are warming up.

The fire under the fry pan is stoked again Saturday morning, and the real festivities begin. The main event is always the chicken cooking contest, with expert poultry preparers lined up at a few dozen stoves creating everything from plain and perfect fried chicken to elaborate renditions of creole, French, and Italian original recipes.

Cooking is only one way the Delmarvans enjoy their chickens. "Chicken Capers" follow the cook-off, with such attractions as a chicken-plucking contest (record time: one minute, 48 seconds), a chicken-scratching contest (in which participants imitate chickens and scratch for coins buried under corn meal), a rooster-crowing contest, and, of course, the best-dressed chicken award. Previous winners of this last contest have included Alphonsa, a white-crested black Polish bird dressed as General George Washington, and Hanna Hooper, another white-crested Polish who wore a yellow polka-dot muumuu and sun bonnet.

MARYLAND

BALTIMORE

BABE RUTH BIRTHPLACE SHRINE AND MUSEUM

216 Emory St., Baltimore, Md.;
Weds–Sun 10:30 AM–4 PM; Adults: $1.00, Children 12–18: 50¢

The Babe was born in the front room of the second floor apartment at 216 Emory, and while we are not particularily interested in birth sites (since there is usually little to see except for the space in which the grand event occurred), this shrine to the Sultan of Swat is something special. The Bambino's artifacts are on display in other baseball museums around the country, but there is something poignant about viewing them in this natal setting. There is Mother Ruth's old sewing machine, and the toys once played with by Baby Babe. There is a stick . . . could it be the first one hefted and swung by the toddler Babe?

Other than childhood mementos, the shrine does display some of the Babe's uniforms and bats, an original home plate from Yankee Stadium, and even his traveling kit, open and on display for posterity.

EDITH'S SHOPPING BAG

726 Broadway, Fells Point, Baltimore, Md.;
daily, hours erratic, late Fri & Sat nights

This is the only thrift store we know run by a movie star. Edith Massey—
known to her fans as "Edie the Egg Lady"—appears in the not-so-firm flesh
almost every day to oversee the goings-on in her very casual store in Fells
Point. In case Edie the Egg Lady isn't a household word in your household,
let us remind you that Edie's big break was in John Waters' *Pink Flamingoes,*
and she has had featured roles in the motion pictures *Female Trouble, Multiple
Maniacs,* and *Desperate Living.*

Edie loves her fans. If you ask her she'll give you one of her autographed
postcards—a poignant study of the star herself, looking rather down in the
mouth, seated in front of a cash register and a roll of paper towels. But Edie
is sweet and saucy, a real charmer whom success has not spoiled a whit. She
is still the same chubby lady who won America's heart sitting in a crib in her
trailer eating a dozen eggs at a time. "I wove my wittle eggies," she says,
practically swooning over her favorite food.

In Edie's words, the Shopping Bag's offerings include "new and old clothes,
knickknacks, hats, dishes, purses, and et cetera." We wouldn't go to Edith's
Shopping Bag to purchase a gift for a fussy aunt. But if your taste runs more
to 1950s funk or 1960s vinyl—displayed in *haute* thrift-store fashion (that is,
piled up on shelves at random)—then this is the spot for you. It is rumored
to be a major supplier of artifacts to the National Sleaze Convention.

BARNESVILLE

ARABIAN HORSE MUSEUM

Cloppers Rd, Barnesville, Md.;
Tues–Fri 9 AM–5 PM, Sat 10 AM–5 PM, Sun 1 PM–5 PM; free

The Arabian horse has always been the most romantic of steeds, carrying
sheiks and Shebas across the sands under a magical moon. From Ali Baba to
Lawrence of Arabia, desert heroes have relied on this strong and steadfast
breed of horse, and today the Arabian Horse Owners' Foundation watches
over its rich heritage. They offer courses in horse management, a training film
called *You Owe It to Your Horse,* and an "Endowment for the Future," which

consists of eighteen purebred Arabian mares which they lease to breeders across the country, to keep the strain going strong. The last we heard, they were preparing a film on Arabian horses that was reputedly shot by that old sheik of the Hollywood backlot himself, Rudolph Valentino.

Of interest to nonbreeders is the Arabian Horse Museum, Art Gallery and Hall of Fame. On display here are portraits of Mesaoud, Bobha and Skowronek—Hall of Famers all, as well as exhibits showing their natural habitat, the desert. There are some saddles, Syrian riding clothes, and a new acquisition—the rearticulated skeleton of Indraff, the first son of the great stud Raffles. Also on exhibit are works by contemporary artists, selected for their ability to paint a good Arabian horse portrait.

BELTSVILLE

THE POULTRY HALL OF FAME

In the U.S.D.A. National Agricultural Library, Beltsville, Md.

This is big-time poultry. That doesn't mean high-profile media chicken men like Frank Perdue or the Colonel, either. It means prominent poultry personnel like the Bird Brothers (Charles and Cyrus) who are world famous "for their Bronze Turkeys and Partridge Plymouth Rocks." It means Arthur O. Schilling, the "World's most famous poultry artist," creator of the Standards of Perfection illustrations. It means Mrs. Kathryn Niles, a Hall-of-Famer for her twenty-eight-year project, which involved creating over ten thousand recipes featuring new ways to use eggs, chicken, and turkey.

The American Poultry Historical Society is ever-vigilant in its evaluation of the bird and egg industries. Hall-of-famers and chicken-loving dilettantes alike will be interested to know that the sixteenth-century Italian treatise *Aldrovandi on Chickens* is now available in English, as is their own *American Poultry History 1823–1973.*

The latest brochure of the American Poultry Historical Society suggests we "pause a moment to reflect . . . to take pride in the Poultry Industry's heritage." We can't think of a better place to reflect on chickens, turkeys, and Rock Cornish hens than here in front of the grand portraiture in the Poultry Hall of Fame.

CAMBRIDGE

NATIONAL MUSKRAT-SKINNING CONTEST

Dorchester High School, Cambridge, Md.;
2nd weekend in Feb.; for info call Roger Webster (301) 228–1454

If you are a tender-hearted animal lover, skip this event. The point of the contest is to skin as many muskrats as neatly as possible in a minimum amount of time. This celebration of frontier skill has been going on in Cambridge every winter for years, as soon as the fur-trapping season draws to a close. And despite the annual protests of humane societies, it seems that the muskrat is such an ugly beast that the majority of Cantabrigians are happy to see them get turned en masse into piles of small fur pieces.

Contestants come from all over the United States and Canada—wherever muskrat-trapping and skinning is still an active sport or business. Finalists are judged by quality of pelt as well as quantity, since a hastily removed and nicked-up piece of fur is less pleasing than one removed neatly and without a scratch.

The annual event also involves selection of a Muskrat Queen (a human being) who reigns over things, and who is sent to Louisiana each year on an exchange program with the Mississippi River Muskrat Queen.

CORDOVA

OLD ST. JOSEPH'S JOUSTING TOURNAMENT

Church Lane, Cordova, Md. First Weds. in August; Entrance Fee: $2.50

If you think jousting went out with King Arthur, take a look around Cordova, Maryland the first week in August. Here are modern Southern gentlemen knights and their ladies fair competing in the oldest ring-riding tournament in the United States. The contests began in 1868, and now include such events as a horse show, a pony jump, a pole-bending race, an egg race, and a musical-chair race for children.

But it is jousting that makes the Old St. Joseph Tournament special. The idea of this sport is for riders to spear a tiny ring on the end of a lance while riding on a charging horse. It appears about as easy as trying to thread a needle as you ride a roller coaster.

Tradition is the keynote at Old St. Joseph's (which is the oldest Catholic Church on the Eastern shore). In 1917 an attempt was made to modernize the proceedings by substituting automobiles for horses. Jousters perched on running boards with their lances poised; but this version of jousting proved so unpopular that the discouraged Cordovans didn't even bother to hold a contest in 1918 (when most of the riders were in the Armed Forces anyway). The tournament was soon revived—using horses instead of Model T's as mounts. Today it's not at all unusual for several of the contestants to be female knights.

The jousting tournament always includes a public dinner of fried chicken, country ham, and beaten biscuits, with a mint julep or two for refreshment.

CRISFIELD

THE NATIONAL HARD CRAB DERBY

The Somers Cove Marina, Crisfield, Md. Sept 1–3, 1978

> It is soft crab time in Crisfield,
> you can hear the hammers ring;
> They are fitting up the skipjacks
> it's the first sure sign of spring.

These verses by Stephen Ward, poet of Maryland crab country, give some idea of just how crab-crazy the residents of Crisfield can get when Derby time rolls around. One would think that the crabbing industry in this town is just year-around practice for the big three-day event.

Some of the more peripheral events are the Miss Junior Crustacean contest (held, of course, in the Crab Bowl), a crab-cooking contest, a dance in the Crab Bowl, and a crab-picking contest in which entrants demeat a maximum amount of crabmeat in fifteen minutes. The record so far is 79.5 ounces, set by Betty Lou Middleton in 1975.

As exciting as these goings-on are, they are secondary to the main event, the Hard Crab Derby itself, the *grand prix* of crabdom. While not as fleet as greyhounds, the blue-shelled beasts do have enough torque to propel themselves admirably—if somewhat aimlessly—along the track.

If, after three days in Crisfield, you find yourself a bit crabby and crabbed-out, longing for a change of pace, take a look at their Bicentennial project—a scale model of the Great Pyramid of Cheops. Inside is a time capsule containing what Crisfieldians think will be of interest to Americans in 2076.

We wouldn't be a bit surprised if one of the artifacts turned out to be a racing crab—cryogenically preserved and raring to go in the 2076 Crab Derby.

KENT ISLAND

THE CHESAPEAKE BAY HYDRAULIC MODEL

Kent Island, Md.; Mon–Fri, tours at 10 AM, 1 PM, 3 PM,
drop in 9 AM–3 PM.
For tour reservations call (301) 962–4616; Free

As children we spent many a thrilling Saturday afternoon in our local movie theater watching Godzilla, Mothra, Gamerra or some other Japanese monster smash its scaly way through miniature villages and small-scale Tokyos. Whatever made that microcosmic technology so fascinating to us then is still magic today in the form of the Chesapeake Bay Hydraulic Model.

This perfect re-creation of the Chesapeake Bay is housed in a fourteen-acre shelter. It is the largest model of its kind in the world. The purpose of this detailed facsimile, built by the U. S. Army Corps of Engineers, is to allow scientists to observe the effects of erosion, tides, natural and unnatural disasters, and changing weather conditions in miniature.

There are controls to produce storm conditions here and enough jellyfish and noxious weeds and parasites to simulate the Bay at its boggy worst. Every watery condition imaginable can be simulated by the people at the control board . . . except the appearance of Godzilla.

The Chesapeake Bay Hydraulic Model is a must for lovers of planetariums, aquariums and dioramas as well as for those who believe that nature is best enjoyed behind glass.

LILYPONS

THE GOLDFISH FARM

Three Springs Fisheries, Lilypons Rd., Lilypons, Md.;
Open daily 9 AM–3:30 PM, Sun. 12:30 PM–3:30 PM; free

There is something nostalgic about the Three Springs Fisheries. Even their catalogue reminds one of a vintage Esther Williams movie, with 1940s glamour

The Late Jiggs and Friends, The Aspen Hill Pet Cemetery, Wheaton, Md.

The Gingerbread Castle, Hamburg, N.J.

girls wading thigh-deep amongst the lily pads. This is the largest goldfish "farm" in the country. Along with America's Number-One House Pet, they also raise and sell bullfrogs, ready-made plastic lily ponds, and an assortment of aquatic plants.

The business was started in 1917 by a farmer named G. L. Thomas, who was then only interested in aquatic aesthetics as a hobby. Pretty soon friends and curious visitors started dropping in and wanting goldfish of their own. In those days goldfish were a rarity. Almost single-handedly, Mr. Thomas started the national craze by selling his beauties to five-and-ten-cent stores around the country. There is no evidence that he encouraged the 1920s fad of swallowing the little golden fellows, but without his pioneering efforts, to be sure, the goldfish might never have become the collegian's favorite back then or the home companion it is today. The business is still run by one of Mr. Thomas's sons, who probably knows more about goldfish and their habits than anyone else in the country.

Whether your goldfish memories are happy ones of Mom and Dad helping you net that beauty in the corner tank at Woolworth's, or heart-wrenching visions of flushing old goldie down the john, the Three Springs Fisheries is a good place to renew your interest.

TOWSON

LADEW TOPIARY GARDENS

Jarrettsville Pike (Route 146); 14 Mi. N. of Towson, Md.;
April through Oct., Sat & Sun 10 AM–5 PM;
Adults: $2.00, Children: 50¢

To anyone who has tried to plant a straight row of flowers or hold their arm steady enough to trim a neat hedge, the Ladew Gardens are nothing short of a miracle. It is a showcase for the nearly lost art of topiary gardening—sculpting figures and intricate shapes out of living bushes, hedges, and trees.

The gardens are the work of Mr. Harvey Smith Ladew, winner of the Distinguished Service Medal of the Garden Club of America "for his great interest in developing and maintaining the most outstanding Topiary Garden in America without professional help." There are more than fourteen acres of his spectacular living art. It is a garden of sculpted swans, pyramids, birds of paradise, spirals, squares, urns, and even a lifesize fox hunt—horses, dogs, and fox all frozen in midflight.

These gardens conjure up visions of English royalty, or Hollywood movies depicting the leisure class. A day spent here is one of quiet grace. The only liability is returning home to one's own shaggy "natural look" vegetation.

WHEATON

ASPEN HILL PET CEMETERY

13630 Georgia Ave. (at corner of Aspen Hill Rd.), 3 mi. N. of Wheaton, Md.; daily 7 AM–dusk; free

We asked Mrs. Nash, the owner of the Aspen Hill Pet Cemetery, if there were any famous animals buried here. "If a person loves their pet enough to bury it, then it's a famous pet. Across the street there at the Gate of Heaven Cemetery, everyone *had* to be buried. That's the law. There's no law that says you have to bury your pet. You only do it because you love them. Let me tell you, there's more love here than across the street."

Nonetheless, we pressed on, looking for more conventionally famous animals that might be interred here in the eight-acre cemetery. Sure enough, here is the J. Edgar Hoover plot, with a memorial stone marking Mr. G-Man's passed-away pooches. And here too is the grave of Jiggs, Spanky and Alfalfa's pal, the "Our Gang" dog with the ring around his eye. He is pictured on the tombstone with the sentiment "RKO–Peace." Finally, at Aspen Hill you can see the graves of all the Washington D. C. K-9 corps—gone, but Mrs. Nash will assure you, not forgotten.

NEW JERSEY

ATLANTIC CITY

PLANTERS' PEANUT STORE

1011 Boardwalk, Atlantic City, N.J.;
Open daily Summer 9 AM–midnight, Winter 10 AM–4 PM.

It is hard to miss the Planters' Peanut Store. It is next to a looming giant statue of that suave old goober himself, Mr. Peanut. Dressed to the nines in top hat, monocle, and cane, Mr. P. has spent the last fifty years watching Atlantic City change from elegance to dilapidation, and now, to a nascent Las Vegas of the East.

Whatever the future of Atlantic City, we are convinced that the Planters Store will remain the same. Aside from the peanuts you buy here, which taste fresh and delicious, there is a gold mine of original kitsch at original prices. Mr. Peanut banks, swizzle sticks, salt and pepper shakers, pencils, and endless other nut icons can be had at prices seldom over a dollar.

For us, this Atlantic City shrine recalls nostalgic days when a smiling peanut was something you ate by the bag- and fistful with your beer, long before the days of presidential peanut jokes.

CAMDEN

THE CAMPBELL MUSEUM

1 Campbell Place, Camden, N.J.;
Mon–Fri 9:30 AM–5 PM; free

Soup can be as plebian as Salvation Army gruel served to derelicts, or as swanky as the perfect, clear consommé that is the mark of an accomplished chef. Or it can be the stuff you buy in cans at the supermarket, the "umm-mm-good" brand, the soup so utterly ordinary that Andy Warhol chose it for his most famous pop art emblem. Campbell, the makers of this most popular brand of soups, has set up a museum of soup bowls.

Contrary to the democratic image of Campbell's Soup, the Campbell museum displays only the most aristocratic of tureens. They are exhibited like jewels at Tiffany's, in glass cases under indirect lighting, each item identified as to country of origin and date of manufacture. Three centuries worth of soup bowls and tureens seem to float within the rarified display area, which is decorated in the classic shade of tomato-soup red.

Museum literature informs us that soup tureens have customarily been the most decorative food service containers on European and Chinese tables, a contention borne out by the several hundred silver, porcelain, and faïence beauties on display here. There are Spode china, Wedgewood, and laquered serving sets from the Orient. There are gold-embellished bowls and bowls of pure white porcelain. There are soup containers made to look like chickens, cabbages, rabbits, cows' heads, frogs and fish. There are broth bowls, ladles, soup plates and *pot-à-oilles*. There are even soup bowls here that date back to the sixth century B.C.

The Campbell Museum is fascinating, scholarly, and beautiful. After it, a cup of soup can never look the same.

CAPE MAY

INTERNATIONAL CLAMSHELL PITCHING TOURNAMENT

Steger's Beach, Cape May, N.J.;
Sat & Sun before Labor Day Weekend; Contest begins at 10 AM each day;
entry fee: $1; free to watch

"If you can't eat what came out of it, I don't want any part of it," says Bill

Ward, the defending clamshell pitching champion. His statement of principle is in response to recent developments in artificial quahogs that have rocked the sports world—or at least that part of it concerned with the sport of clamshell pitching. You see, a few years ago Leo Curren of the Cape May Clamshell Pitching Club invented a resin-based plastic substitute for the real thing. He's been trying to get the annual contest to adopt these bogus shells, but so far they've stuck with the natural quahogs.

The reason anybody would go to the trouble of perfecting an artificial shell is that the real ones become brittle, and they occasionally break. Since the purpose of the sport is to pitch the shells over twenty-five feet into a tiny three-inch hole dug in the hard-packed sand, breakability can cost a contestant points. Judges measure that part of the broken shell that is furthest from the hole, and since points are scored for being closest, nobody wants a broken shell.

But would the sport of clamshell pitching really be the same if competitors didn't have to worry about broken shells? We predict that the natural bivalve will never be replaced. After all, it is the unpredictable shell that has made this sport the game of skill and fortune it is today.

FREEHOLD

THE NATIONAL BROADCASTERS' HALL OF FAME

19 West Main St., Freehold, N. J.;
Tues–Sun 10 AM–5 PM;
Adults: $2.00, Children 6–12: $1.00

If you have ever basked wearily in the glow of a TV set as it spewed forth reruns of bionic bores and Gilligan's islanders, we prescribe for you a time-capsule tour back through history to the mellower days when radio was king.

The National Broadcasters' Hall of Fame recalls when families huddled together in front of giant, ornate cabinets bearing the names of Stromberg-Carlson or Atwater Kent, from which emanated the strains of the Lone Ranger's theme and the antics of Fibber McGee and Molly.

On display here are those very radios, along with recordings of America's favorite shows, from *Amos 'n' Andy* and *Ozzie and Harriet* to *The Shadow* and *Your Hit Parade*. There are old fan magazines, radio schedules, and shrines dedicated to Kate Smith, Red Barber, George Burns, H. V. Kaltenborn, and Walter Winchell.

If the names Kay Kayser, The Green Hornet or Harry Von Zell mean nothing to you, head down to Freehold for an earful of what was once a revolutionary medium.

HACKETTSTOWN

THE NEW JERSEY PHEASANT FARM

Grand Ave. 3 mi. W. of Hackettstown, N.J.;
daily 7:30 AM–4:30 PM
free; for tour call (201) 852–3461

Forty thousand pheasants born and raised on this farm are released into the New Jersey woods each year. The public is welcome at these facilities, and if you come in a large enough group you will be shown around the premises and told about the techniques involved in hatching, incubating, and raising birds until they are big enough to make it on their own in the woods.

The pheasants are visible year round in their huge wire cages, but if you come during the months of May and June it is likely you will be able to see some of the baby birds hatching. There is also an outdoor display of "sports birds," including exotic Chinese pheasants, gold and silver pheasants, and the standard pheasants, which are brown and multicolored if male, and a drab brown if female. You can also pet a tame deer.

The Pheasant Farm is only a few miles away from the Hackettstown Fish Hatchery, so you can round out your day of nature by going from fowl to fish.

HAMBURG

THE GINGERBREAD CASTLE

Rt. 23, Hamburg, N.J.;
April 1–Oct 31, open daily from 10 AM, Nov–March, Sat & Sun only

As you approach the winding stairs to the Gingerbread House, you find yourself flanked by pink elephants. This fairyland is a charmingly personal monument to childhood. It was built in 1930 by F. H. Bennett after he saw a production of the opera *Hansel and Gretel.* Bennett approached the stage designer and told him how much he loved Grimm's fairy tales. $250,000 later, the Gingerbread Castle was completed.

According to Grimm, a gingerbread castle has walls made of spicy brown cake, a roof of frosted sugar, candy-cane towers, and plum-pudding pools. This castle is only stone and plaster, but its ornate construction reflects that style of architecture called "gingerbread."

The tour of the castle is not for the cynical. There is a pre-Disneyland charm about the characters who appear around this storybook land, from the pink elephants to Humpty Dumpty sitting on a wall with his skinny legs dangling over the side to a Snow White who looks a bit like Annette Funicello.

After your tour you can purchase a few gingerbread cookies in the adjoining shop.

MARGATE

LUCY THE ELEPHANT

9200 Atlantic Avenue, Margate, N.J.;
May 29–Sept 15 10 AM–5 PM daily,
other times group tours by appointment (609) 823–6473; donation

Lucy the Margate Elephant is an architectural folly left over from an era of ornate Victorianism. She is a building shaped like a pachyderm, six stories tall, sculpted from a million pieces of wood, and weighing ninety tons—perhaps the original "white elephant." Lucy was built by James V. Lafferty in 1881 as an attraction to draw prospective buyers to what was then called "South Atlantic City" (now Margate). He sold it to people who operated it as a tourist attraction, and in this century it has served as a real-estate office and a summer home for eccentrics. After World War II Lucy hit the skids and began to deteriorate into an abandoned elephant carcass, the salty sea winds blowing through her rattling frame.

The citizens of Margate decided they couldn't let Lucy turn into a ninety-ton derelict, and so the elephant was moved in 1970, and restored in 1973. Her "howdah" (the box on top), which had been blown to sea by a storm during the 1920s, was reconstructed in 1977. Lucy today is a bit sleeker than before, due to her new, modern skin. Her interior is still being restored to its original sumptuousness, but you can see what there is of Lucy's innards for a dollar donation.

MT. HOLLY

THE FABULOUS FIFTY ACRES

5 1/2 mi. S. of Exit 7 of N.J. Tpk. on Rt. 206 in Mt. Holly, N.J.;
hours vary;
admission free if Mahalchik likes you; otherwise, keep out!

There are a lot of things Mahalchik doesn't like. He sure doesn't like Nixon or Kissinger. As you drive past his place on Route 206 you will see his billboard-painting of Nixon and Kissinger, declaring both to be traitors, "America's two biggest rats." Their heads are painted onto large, red rodent bodies.

Another thing Mahalchik doesn't like is the guy from the Smithsonian Institution who came down to ask him to donate one of his seven dirigibles. "I paid for all this. Let somebody else buy it and get the tax dodge and a gold plaque." They wanted one of his two gliders as well. "There are only four known WACO gliders in the world, and I've got two of them. They were used in the Normandy invasion."

Mahalchik doesn't much like the American two-party system, either. "We've got free elections here, Russian style. There is only one party in America, and that is the Judicial Party." He says he ran for president in 1972, and came in just ahead of Dr. Spock.

One thing Mahalchik *really* doesn't like is people who call his "Fabulous Fifty Acres" a junkyard. "Anybody says that to me, I punch their teeth down their throat. I've got 128 antique cars here. I used to be the largest army surplus dealer east of the Mississippi. You gonna call that junk??"

You'll know Mahalchik's place by the Nixon-Kissinger sign looking out over the road, and a great white locomotive nearby. From the road, you can see a vast array of signs, poems, and paintings indicating the many, many things Mahalchik doesn't like, as well as what political offices he is running for. We suggest casual passers-by limit themselves to this roadside vantage point.

OCEAN CITY

THE HERMIT TREE CRAB RACE AND BEAUTY PAGEANT

The 12th St. Beach, Ocean City, N.J.
(Mid–Late August) for specific date contact: P.O. Box 174, Ocean City, N.J. 08226

Two events of great magnitude—if you are a hermit crab—take place every August at Ocean City. For athletic specimens, there is the Hermit Tree Crab Race; and for those crabs vain enough to crawl out of their mollusk shells, there is a beauty contest. In order to create the most aesthetically appealing tree crabs, owners groom their crustaceous hopefuls by affixing and glueing as many baubles and beads as possible to the soft shells of their entries. Since it is practically impossible to figure out the sex of a hermit tree crab, he or she always wins the Miss Crustacean U.S.A. crown, and parades about Ocean City to the strains of the Mermaid Singers and their rendition of *Here It Comes, Miss Crustacean.*

But the frills of the beauty contest don't compare to the fevered excitement surrounding the hermit tree crab race. Contestants are confined beneath pie tins until a bugle sounds, at which point they break from the starting plates, scuttling for the finish line. Past winners include Awful Kanawful, a sprinter known for brutal tactics and a particular bigotry toward oysters, and Ugly Sam, trained on a high-protein diet of fried beetles and seaweed. The champ each year wins the Cucumber Rind Cup.

Ocean City's most celebrated crab is Martin Z. Mollusk, a local weather prognosticator who performs a seaside version of Groundhog Day by searching for his shadow on the sand each spring.

SEASIDE HEIGHTS

GRANDMOTHERS' BEAUTY CONTEST

The Boardwalk at Franklin Ave; Seaside Heights, N.J.;
weekend after Labor Day; free

We don't know how the Gray Panthers feel about this event—whether it exploits or celebrates the oldsters who enter. The fact is, though, that a lot of the grannies who enter this contest are not at all the steely-haired octogenarian variety. Some are much younger. There was one last year who reported her age to be thirty-eight. But don't bother to do any quick arithmetic; just enjoy the parade.

WILDWOOD

NATIONAL MARBLES TOURNAMENT

At the "Ringer Bowl," Wildwood, N.J.
Late June; free

Do the expressions "clodnockers," "moonaggies," or "solid pee-wees" send your blood racing? To the marble shooter knuckling down to shoot for keeps, these terms are what the game is all about. Marbles may not be the national sport, but there is something about the sight of these twelve- and thirteen-year-olds bending over to concentrate on a game of Black Snake or Potsies that is all-American. Every year they get together in Wildwood to hold the grand play-offs.

This championship tournament is played just like every other sidewalk marbles game. It is open to any girl or boy under fourteen. Of course, the top competitors are several-year veterans, here to represent their home state. For others, it may be the first time they've seen the ocean or stayed in a motel.

The City of Wildwood seems to have lost interest in the tournament, perhaps because marble shooters don't add a lot to the local economy. Over the years the prize money has decreased, and one report quoted the mayor as saying he wished all the marbles "would just roll into the ocean."

But as long as there are kids and marbles, it looks as if Wildwood will stage the tournament, which is just fine with us. In their elemental simplicity, marbles recall happy childhood times before the creation of the bubble-headed Barbie Doll and banana-seat souped-up kiddie trike; times when boys and girls sat around a circle wearing sailor hats, arguing the fine points of a game of Chasies.

NEW YORK

ALEXANDER

THE WORLD'S TALLEST BARBER POLE

2725 Walker Rd., Alexander, N.Y.;
always viewable; free

James Boatfield once ran an ordinary barbershop in an ordinary home in Alexander. One night his neighbors played a practical joke on him by erecting a fifty foot, three-inch barber pole where his mailbox post used to be. Boatfield tacked his mailbox onto the red, white, and blue pole, and continued with his tonsorial work, now in the shadow of the world's tallest barber pole.

BROOKLYN

TRANSIT EXHIBIT

Boerum Place and Schermerhorn St., Brooklyn, N.Y.;
Open daily 10 AM–4 PM;
Admission: one token

What do the words "New York Subway" bring to mind? A dank, dark network of holes in the ground? Flashers, weirdos and pickpockets? Power failures and blackouts? If that is your image of the subways, you might visit the Transit Exhibit for a look at the grandeur that was once the MTAS.

Here is subway art (not graffiti) in the form of inlaid mosaics that once graced each individual station's walls. Here are perfectly preserved cars with preplastic wicker chairs for seats. Here are mementos of the days when each subway stop had its own insignia—Astor Place was a beaver, we presume representing the top-hatted gentlemen who once walked above; South Ferry was, of course, symbolized by a ship. IRT, BMT, IND . . . you name it, and there is a car from it here. After walking through the old subway cars, you can take a look at films of the old transit system, then proceed to some vintage New York City buses on display. One of our favorite exhibits is the three-dimensional map of the entire subway system—looking more like a work of modern sculpture than an engineering layout. There are also tiny scale models of subway stations, lovingly hand-built by a local doctor who donated them to the exhibit.

BUFFALO

Q.R.S. MUSIC ROLL FACTORY

1026 Niagara Street, Buffalo, N.Y.;
tours daily Mon–Fri 10 AM & 2 PM;
free; (716) 885–4600

Who hasn't seen the movie where the suave-looking type is seated at the piano playing away passionately—and then the doorbell rings, he gets up and the keyboard is left playing itself? That is the way a player piano operates—

mechanically—and we were surprised to learn that there is a company still manufacturing piano rolls like those used generations ago.

Q.R.S. offers tours of their plant (although they discourage young children and warn senior citizens that the steep stairways may be too much to contend with). Every piano roll requires six hand operations: stamping title and tempo, cutting leader to a point, attaching the eyeletted end tab, printing of sing-along lyrics, and packaging. You see all these operations, as well as the special recording piano where master rolls are created.

If you thought these things went out with "Sweet Adeline," you will be surprised to find piano rolls as modern as the "Theme from Batman" and "Aquarius." Of course, it is hard to pass by available standards like "Lindbergh, the Eagle of the U.S.A.," "My Little Bimbo Down on the Bamboo Isle," and "Yacka Hula Hickey Dula."

CARROLLTON

STUDEBAKER PARK

Rt. 17, 7/10 of a mile W of junction Rt. 219, Carrollton, N.Y.;
daily usually 6 PM–10 PM;
free (716) 945-3994

"My buddy next door was a Ford man," Lance Oaks told us. "But I converted him. Now he's got my '62 Studebaker Champion truck and two Hawks." Here in New York State is a small but highly selective collection of prime Studebaker cars, from the last, dying years of the breed in the 1950s and '60s. Lance Oaks's three gems are a 1960 all-black Lark convertible, a 1957 Studebaker President 4-door sedan, and the original 1953 Lowey hardtop coupe. The Lowey—a streamlined blue-and-white job—was the model that Studebaker had intended to introduce in 1952 as their anniversary car. But they didn't get it out until 1953, which is when Mr. Oaks fell in love with the ill-fated Stude'.

The Lowey Coupe was the last attempt to modernize the Studebaker image. It was re-dressed in 1956 and came out as the Studebaker Hawk, but by the late '50s the line was swamped by the heavy sales of the "big three" automakers. Studebaker's last gasp was the futuristic Avanti, which can still be custom-ordered today. Mr. Oaks is working on getting one of these.

If you visit Studebaker Park—and Mr. Oaks is happy to show any interested people around—take a look as well at the collection of his neighbor (the converted ex-Ford man). He's not only got the Champ truck and two Hawks, but an original Lowey Starlite Coupe as well.

COOPERSTOWN

THE BASEBALL HALL OF FAME

Main St. Cooperstown, N.Y.
Nov–April open daily 9 AM–5 PM, May–Oct 9 AM–9 PM.
Admission $2.25 adults, $1.00 children, or $6.00
for all three Cooperstown museums

The Baseball Hall of Fame wins our vote as the best sports Hall of Fame in the country. This is the compleat baseball shrine, a national treasure as much as baseball is the national sport. Everything you ever dreamed about as a little boy (or girl) is here: lockers once used by Joe DiMaggio, Stan the Man and others, Ted Williams's bat, balls signed by every world championship team, gloves, uniforms, bats, and masks from baseball's past, the original baseball, one century old, baseball paintings, uniforms and trophies, a huge replica of the United States Capitol Building made out of baseball bats and crowned with a huge baseball, and the solemn Hall of Fame itself—a hushed sanctum made of polished marble in which baseball's greats are immortalized on bas-relief plaques. There is practically a whole floor devoted to Babe Ruth, with everything from his locker to a wall telephone that you can pick up and hear him tell you how he's doing.

Everything here is all-baseball. The waiting benches outside the washrooms are benches from famous dugouts. There are baseball movies shown every day; exhibits of Little League history; displays of every baseball card that ever came in a pack of gum; even an exhibit of "beep baseball"—a form of the sport played by the blind. The men who work here, ushers and guards, all wear red uniform jackets. They look and act exactly like umpires—cool, unruffled, with little escaping their attention. Except that they all seem to have good eyesight, and we've never once heard one yell at a visitor to the Hall of Fame.

THE CARDIFF GIANT

The Farmers' Museum, Rt. 80, 1 mi. N. of Cooperstown, N.Y.
9 AM–5 PM daily, closed Sun & Mon mornings during winter months.
adults; $2.25, children $1.00, or special $6.00 ticket
for all three Cooperstown museums

The Cardiff Giant was the all-time great American hoax. When he was "discovered" near Cardiff, New York in 1869, he was supposed to represent an ancient specimen of man, ten feet tall, who had apparently fallen asleep sometime in the distant past, only to petrify in his position of repose. The hoax was engineered by a fellow named George Hull, a cigar maker, in whose likeness the giant was supposedly made. It was manufactured in Chicago from a block of gypsum, shipped to Cardiff, buried, and unearthed, shortly after which Hull started charging 50¢ for a peek. (Now it costs $2.25.)

The giant caused such a sensation that P. T. Barnum, not to be outdone, quickly manufactured his own giant and put it on display in New York City. The real Cardiff giant, whom Hull sent on tour, showed up in New York only a few blocks away from Barnum's—but, needless to say, could not compete with the master showman's attention-grabbing imitation fake. Eventually, both the real giant and Barnum's faded into oblivion. The once-famous Cardiff Giant hit the skids, was bought and sold several times, winding up in the rumpus room of a citizen of Des Moines, Iowa. In the late 1940s the giant was rediscovered—this time as a valuable artifact of American folklore—and was finally moved to its present, pleasant enclosure at the Farmers' Museum, where it resides as part of the museum's extensive collection of Americana. Beyond its folkloric value, the Cardiff Giant still provides juicy material for occasional tabloid exposés.

DOUBLEDAY BATTING RANGE

Next to Doubleday Field, Cooperstown, N.Y.
Open in good weather. Helmet and eyeglasses required; no cleats.
10 pitches: 75¢, 30 pitches: $2.00

Since our visit to the Doubleday Batting Range we have not once booed a ball player for striking out. This place allows you to pit your batting skill against major league pitching machines, set alternately for right-hand overhand curve, left-hand sliders, and fast balls. There are no screwballs, knuckle balls, change ups, or spit balls, and the machines are mostly set at medium speed. Still, you've got to be pretty good to get a piece of wood onto one of these pitches; damn good to get what would be a solid base hit. But despite our consistently terrible performances the machines are hypnotic; and we can't help but feel that with enough practice we could soon give up our humdrum existence and join next year's free agent draft.

The batting range is open only in good dry weather, we were told, because if the balls get wet the machines start tossing wild pitches.

ELMIRA

NATIONAL SOARING MUSEUM

Harris Hill, Elmira, N.Y.;
Mid-May–Mid-June weekends only 11 AM–5 PM, Mid-June–Sept daily 11 AM–5 PM,
Sept–Mid-Nov weekends only 11 AM–5 PM;
adults: $1, students and children: 50¢

Glider pilots consider Harris Hill the Soaring Capital of America, the best place to glide silently into the blue and float with the hawks and gulls, high above it all, surrounded by the blue sky and warmth of the sun. On weekends throughout the year, and on a daily basis throughout the summer, the Harris Hill Soaring Corporation offers rides to the public (with experienced pilots) for a small fee, giving nonpilots an opportunity to experience the unique pleasure of motorless flight.

For those who will never climb into a glider, the National Soaring Museum serves as a nice substitute. Here on terra firma, near the glider field, are displays and exhibits that explain the principles and history of gliders through pictures and models. There is a "soaring map" that shows where the wind currents are best, and explanations of how pilots search for lift. You can even sit in the cockpit of a sailplane, close your eyes, and pretend you're up there.

One of the joys of coming to Harris Hill is simply sitting near the field and watching the graceful moves of the silent aircraft up in the blue, or landing gently and precisely back on the earth.

FLANDERS

THE BIG DUCK

Rt. 24, Flanders, Long Island, N.Y.;
daily 8 AM–7 PM

Ten years ago in a controversial article called "On Ducks and Decoration" Robert Venturi used The Big Duck as a paradigm of architecture as sculptural symbolism. He saw duck-type buildings proliferating along the highways as a means of announcing to motorists what the building "stood for." It's pretty easy to know what this big bird symbolizes. "Duck" goes with Long Island as sure as steak with Kansas City or lobster with Maine. And what better way to pay homage to the bird that made the island famous than building a two-story plaster duck and carving out of its belly a store that sells—what else? —ducks. You enter a door just under the beak, carved into the plaster pinfeathers and once inside, there's nary a quack to remind you that you are inside the largest specimen of poultry sculpture in the East—and an architectural landmark besides.

FRESH KILLS

THE WORLD'S LARGEST GARBAGE DUMP

Fresh Kills, Staten Island, N.Y.;
free; by appointment, call (212) 556–5527 or write Dept. of Sanitation,
125 Worth St., NYC

This is known as Reclamation Plant #1, chosen by the *Guinness Book of Records* as the world's largest. It can be seen by appointment only, the resident "san men" told us, because it is too smelly, too dangerous, and too huge to have members of the general public tramping around without a chaperone. They also told us that the dump is a favorite spot for diplomats and foreign dignitaries visiting New York.

GOSHEN

HALL OF FAME OF THE TROTTER

240 Main St. Goshen, N.Y.
Mon–Sat 10 AM–5 PM, Sundays & Holidays 1:30 PM–5 PM closed Dec. & Jan.;
located at the Gate of the track; free

The harness-racing track at Goshen is the oldest operating track in America, the only one registered as a national historical landmark. Goshen, in fact, likes to think of itself as the "birthplace of trotting." A plaque at the gate of the track notes that in 1801 "Imported Messenger, progenitor of trotters, grazed under this tree." The tree is called "Messenger's Tree," and is a huge old oak under which the granddaddy of almost every trotter alive today once gnawed on Goshen grass.

Inside the museum is everything the trotter tout could hope for: exhibitions of Currier and Ives lithographs, wood carvings, bronzes, dioramas, statuary, harness-racing films, and lifelike full-color statuettes of the great personalities of the harness-racing world. Here you will see the world's first mobile starting gate, sulkies once hitched to the trotting and pacing greats, and mementos of Dan Patch, Hambletonian, Nevele Pride, and Steady Star. There are free art classes for children, instructing them and encouraging them to draw horses. And finally, there's the Weathervane shop, which sells souvenirs, jewelry, and, of course, horseshoes.

HAMMONDSPORT

THE GREYTON H. TAYLOR WINE MUSEUM

Bully Hill Rd., Hammondsport, N.Y.
May 1–Oct 1, Mon–Sat 9 AM–4:30 PM, Sun 1 PM–4:30 PM;
Adults: $1.00, Children and students: 50¢

We were intrigued by the Greyton H. Taylor Wine Museum when we heard that they had a "living grape library." Indeed they do have over two hundred varieties of grapes from all over the world, cultivated here on the vine for visitors to see but not touch or eat. Aside from the living exhibit, there are displays, objects, paintings, and diagrams all related to the subject of winemaking. The most intriguing exhibit is a tool used in the nineteenth century to secure the tops of champagne bottles by means of a knotted wax string. There is a *Scientific American* picture of one in use, but the museum staff and local vintners still cannot figure out how it was supposed to work.

HORSEHEADS

ANN PAGE FOOD-PROCESSING PLANT TOURS

Rt. 17, Just West of Horseheads, N.Y.
Mon–Fri, Memorial Day through Labor Day, 9 AM–2 PM (607) 796-4411

This is the world's largest kitchen, or, more precisely, the world's largest food-processing facility. One is informed that "something yummy is always cooking" somewhere in the thirty-five-acre cookhouse, where an "efficient straight line flow of raw materials and packaging supplies" ensures the 2,000 cooks and helpers that they won't be wasting any time as they prepare the 550 separate items on the menu. Tours of the Horseheads plant begin with a 17-minute film then proceed along efficiently designed corridors with observation windows looking out onto the gargantuan enterprise. The whole tour takes just over an hour. Some of the highlights are the preserves and syrups area, where jams and jellies prepared on the second floor flow, like The Blob, downstairs into the glass packing area; the "candy-enrobing" department, where nuts and fruits are coated with chocolate; the sugar silos containing 1,750,000 pounds of sugar; the semolina silos with 740,000 pounds of semolina on call for use as needed by the macaroni department; and the giant kettles cooking up beans and soups.

If your appetite is whetted by seas of chocolate, mountains of sugar, and carloads of colossal olives, there is a small A & P market in the plant where you can buy everything that is made on the premises.

HUNTER MOUNTAIN

NATIONAL POLKA FESTIVAL

Late August; Ski Bowl Rd., Hunter Mountain, N.Y.
Adults: $5, Children 6–12: $2, under 6: free.
For further info call (518) 263–4278 June–August

This is the premier blow-out for polka fans. The National Polka Festival features the largest tent in the United States, a dance floor big enough for a thousand dancers, and top name bands like Casimir Wulkowicz and his Mischief Makers, Stanky and His Pennsylvania Coal Miners and Ed Guca and the Polish Canadians. There's plenty of kielbasa, pirogen, and wursts, and enough beer to keep the polka party going for a full three days. Authentic ethnic dances are performed by the Polka Dolls; championship demonstrations are given by the Imperial Polka Dancers; and if you don't want to polka, you can just make yourself comfortable in the flower-decorated beer garden on the side of Hunter Mountain.

HYDE PARK

TOUR OF THE CULINARY INSTITUTE OF AMERICA

Rt. 9, 3 mi. S of Hyde Park, N.Y.
Tuesday only, by appointment (914) 452–9600; free

It is difficult to get a place on one of the booked-up Tuesday tours of the CIA, but well worth whatever hassles or wait is involved. This is the mecca for students, aficionados, and lovers of food. It is the only institution in the country that trains students to become expert chefs. The program here is so successful that each graduate can expect approximately three job offers. A tour of the place explains why. There are two demonstration amphitheater kitchens, rather like operating theaters, where students can watch expert chefs at work. There are twelve production kitchens, four bakeshops, four instructional dining rooms, two classrooms designed especially for the wines and spirits classes, a butcher shop, a working diner, and a working restaurant specializing in *haute cuisine.*

On the CIA tour you are likely to see everything from instructions in chicken boning to Chinese cooking to cold buffet layout. One hallway is devoted to the baking of bread and pastries. In the classical bakeshop, students learn to sculpt nougat and pulled sugar. In the wines and spirits class, one can watch earnest students—always dressed in their spanking clean "whites"—learning the five S's of wine tasting—see, swirl, sniff, savor, and swallow. There are classes in bartending, breakfast cookery, and restaurant bookkeeping; everything from coffee shop to *garde manger.* Tour guides try to show you all of this, but tourists must tread these halls and classrooms ever so lightly. Instructors here are chefs and most are famous; some are from the U.S. Olympic cooking team. *All* are reported to be very temperamental.

A tour of the CIA is likely to tease your appetite toward a state of frenzied hunger; this is fine, because at the end of the day there is the Escoffier Room, named for Auguste Escoffier, "the king of chefs and the chef of kings." A jacket is required to dine here, and the prices are not low ($14.50 prix fixe dinner). But the CIA serves an elegant five-course feast that is, by New York *haute cuisine* standards, a bargain. Of course, you are served by students from the advanced table service class; and the food is prepared by students in the final à la carte kitchen class. We'd give them an "A." If the Escoffier Room is too rich for your blood, try the diner planted in the middle of the campus. It is a traditional chrome dining car; but it is cleaner than any diner we have ever seen, and the food is all prepared right here, including the dinner rolls! Come as you are. No reservations are necessary.

LEWISTON

ARTPARK

Lewiston, N.Y. along the Niagara River Gorge;
June through September Activities are staged from Noon Wednesday through Sunday when there is a parking fee of $1.50 per car. No parking fee before noon or all day Mon & Tues.

Artpark is a Disneyworld for aesthetes. It is a government-supported open-air gallery of two hundred acres along the Niagara River. There are nature trails, picnic grounds, and fishing docks for outdoor enjoyment, but what is special here are the facilities available to artists: a theater with multilevel terraces and a computerized lighting board; an earthwork amphitheater overlooking the river; and the ArtEl, a boardwalk construction on which artists are free to realize their most grandiose conceptions.

The last time we looked, Artpark's astonishing landscape included Phil Simkin's human maze, Ree Morton's paintings draped on rocks, Abe Rothblat's network of aluminum tubing along the upper gorge trail, and Margaret Wharton's rows of luminous chairs. Mary Miss has created some of Artpark's most monumental works, including a piece called "Four Horizons," which required bulldozers and a full crew of construction workers to reach its aesthetic perfection. Jim Roche, who describes himself as "an artist of bad taste," used an $8,000 grant to buy a vintage Cadillac and drape it with just about every conceivable automotive gizmo and gimcrack he could find. This work of art was called "The Bicentennial Welfare Cadillac."

There are works of art, and there is art that happens, and Artpark is a prime location for the latter. Last year Helene Valentin decorated the park's air ever so briefly with smoke sculptures. One conceptual piece, staged by Douglas Davis, was guaranteed by the artist to occur at exactly the same time two artists in Russia were creating similar pieces. Many events involve the use of film and videotape. One of our favorites was a work of art for which the artist flew in a genuine chili chef from Texas to watch over his brew as part of the piece.

The agenda for planned creations is as enigmatic and intriguing as some of the art itself: "An art work that deals with star patterns and the migration of birds;" or "A 'logical concept' is inscribed into the earth;" or "Miracles with tree trunks and chain saws;" or, simply "Strange Protuberances."

Artpark is wide open, informal, and always surprising. If stuffy galleries and suffocatingly quiet museums have turned your feelings about art into weary surrender, go to Artpark for fresh air and a recharging of your aesthetic battery.

LILY DALE

LILY DALE

Exit 59 off I–90, N.Y.;
daily: $1.25, monthly: $20,
season (June–Sept): $30

Lily Dale is the world center of the Universal Religion of Modern Spiritualism. Each summer session at Lily Dale consists of almost three straight months of lectures, religious services, seminars, talent shows, bake sales, and seances— all dedicated to an expression of the Living Spirit, to affirmation of life after death.

If you are a medium, Lily Dale requires that you register at the Assembly office before doing any professional work. Bulletin boards around the community list all registered mediums, their locations, and their respective phases of mediumship.

If you are not a medium, but merely curious, there is much to do here. Of course, you can make an appointment to speak with dead friends or relatives. Or, if you are ill, there is daily healing in the Healing Temple between noon and 1:00 P.M., and between 7:00 P.M. and 8:00 P.M. Lectures and services are given in the auditorium and the assembly hall. Since these are of a religious nature, no shorts, swimsuits, or bare feet are allowed. The Forest Temple is one of the most popular meeting places. Here, voluntary demonstrations of mediumship are encouraged by nonprofessionals. You may want only to seek rest and quiet. If that is the case, proceed to the Inspiration Stump in the Leolyn Woods, a virgin forest. There are also a library, a picnic area, a gift store, a cafeteria, and a hotel. Guests and visitors are welcome: "We ask not what thou art If Friend, we greet thee hand and heart. If Stranger, such no longer be; If Foe, our love will conquer thee!"

NEW YORK CITY

THE BOXING HALL OF FAME

120 W. 31st St., 6th floor, NYC
Mon–Fri 10 AM–3:30 PM; free

If you think you're tough, match your fists against those of Muhammed Ali, Ken Norton, or "Smokin' Joe" Frazier. Once you do, you will be very happy that these fists—on display in the Boxing Hall of Fame—are only plaster casts, and not the real thing. It is astounding that real people have mitts this size; and quite reassuring to find them mounted inanimately in the showcases that line the walls of *Ring* Magazine waiting room, which houses the Boxing Hall of Fame.

Besides casts of famous fists, there are Joe Lewis's gloves, the bell used in James "Boilermaker" Jeffry's fights, and an assortment of plaques and souvenirs honoring the immortals of the ring from Georges Carpentier and Jack Johnson to Ali and Norton. The Hall of Fame is just one block away from Madison Square Garden, where many of these champs earned their laurels.

CHINATOWN CHICKENS

The Arcade below the Chinese Museum; 8 Mott Street; NYC;
Open 10 AM–11 PM weekdays, Fri & Sat until 2 AM; Admission: Free

We've lost several games of tick-tack-toe to a chicken. It's a fact, and we're big enough to admit it. Of course, the champion chicken of Mott Street is *always* allowed to make the first move; and as long as we're beefing, we want the world to know that this so-called champ happens to be aided in his play by a computer. So much for sour grapes. If you're a good loser, it costs 25¢ to pit your skill against chickie. You can be sure you'll never win—unless (and here's the secret tip) you wait until very late in the day, or until the early-morning hours. By that time, it is rumored, the champ is so chock-full of chicken feed (he gets a grain every time he makes a move), that he just might make a mistake. But don't count on it. The champ plays only every other day. He alternates with the dancing chicken, who prances about every time someone pays him a quarter. The dancing chicken appeals to those of a more artistic bent, rather than to avid sportspersons. There's no competition on dancing-chicken days, just as there's no dancing when the tick-tack-toe champ is holding court. They alternate days, we were told, so they don't overeat and develop the heart conditions to which overweight chickens are prone.

THE FIRE MUSEUM

104 Duane St., NYC;
Mon–Fri 9 AM–4 PM, Sat 9 AM–1 PM; free

The Fire Museum is housed in what was once Ladder Company #1, a large three-story building now crowded with mementos that tell about three hundred years of firefighting in New York City. You enter past an antique watch-desk equipped with telegraph instruments and an electronic "trip" that released horses from their stalls at the sound of the alarm. The first major exhibit is the 1898 LaFrance engine, formerly of the Brooklyn Fire Department, equipped with a harness for three horses abreast, which dropped onto the horses from the ceiling at the call for action. Nearby are two other gleaming "steamers."

On the second and third stories of the firehouse are pieces of hand-operated equipment, certificates and memorials, and hundreds of pictures depicting fires, firefighters, and firehouses of the past. There is even a firefighting sleigh, for use in heavy snow, and a section of the fireboat "Zophar Mills," which saw duty between 1882 and 1934. One case contains a display of scale-model firehouses.

One small part of the old firehouse is now used as a theater, where guided tours and special groups are shown films that depict the story of New York firefighting. The theater seats were taken from the old Polo Grounds just before it was torn down.

HARLEM "AS IT IS"

The Penny Sightseeing Co. 303 W. 42nd St., NYC
(212) 247-2860, reservations required, $5.00 per person.
Tours given Mon & Thurs 10 AM, Sat 11 AM, March through Nov. Additional tours given July 1–Sept., 1 10 AM Tues.

The Penny Sightseeing Company is operated by black Americans whose goal is to give "a true and honest picture of the Black Capital of the World." And so a Penny tour of Harlem shows you the poverty, the wealth, and places of

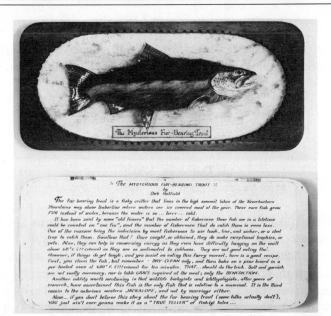

Gladding International Sport Fishing Museum, South Otselic, N.Y.

Movie Star News, New York, N.Y.

cultural interest from the Schomburg Library to the Apollo Theater. "Harlem has two faces," the guide says. "One is a stereotype, the other is a Harlem of hard work and hope."

The tour begins with a drive into Harlem, past the City University, Strivers Row, Sugar Hill, the former home of Alexander Hamilton, and Harlem's shopping and business areas. On foot you see a church, the Freedom Bank, and Harlem Hospital. Religion has been an important part of Harlem history, and so the tour takes you to several churches, as well as to the unfinished Cathedral of St. John the Divine.

Harlem is known throughout the world; and yet many who *think* they know, have never really seen it. If you have ever wanted to visit this fascinating part of New York but didn't know exactly what to look at, Penny Sightseeing provides a fine way in which to get a feel for the real Harlem.

MOVIE STAR NEWS

212 E. 14th St., NYC;
Mon–Fri 11 AM–5 PM; free

Movie Star News inhabits the second floor of a rather seedy building on East 14th Street, a neighborhood overrun with peep shows and hangers-on at the local methadone clinic. A dingy window looks out onto the street. Painted black and silver, it promises "Pin-up photos of your favorite movie stars, latest movie scenes, bathing beauties, popular cowboy stars and vocalists, bandleaders." At the top of a narrow staircase you enter a vast stockroom that is quite literally filled with 8" × 10" glossy photos. There are aisles between the shelves, but one senses that the aisles are always lessening, crowded out by the ever-expanding collection of stills. It is estimated that there are over two million pictures, piled up floor to ceiling, and stacked on groaning shelves.

In this room you will find Paula Klaw—the owner—and her helpmate, Howard Mandelbaum. Howard knows more about movies and movie stars than anyone; and miraculously, his mind contains an organized inventory of Movie Star News's holdings. And so it is possible to come here with only the name of an obscure film or bit player, or perhaps merely an estimated film title or approximate description of a star or starlet, and it is likely that Howard will be able to locate a whole range of stills, pin-ups, studio shots, or whatever is called for. Prices range from a dollar or two for common pictures of big-name stars to substantial double-digit prices for the rarest pictures treasured by collectors.

Paula Klaw is the sister of the late Irving Klaw, the man who was known as America's Pin-Up King from World War II to his death in 1966. Paula has taken over the kingdom, and has maintained Irving's supply of rather unusual and risqué photos, items which come under the heading of "special collections." Happy hunting!

THE MUSEUM OF BROADCASTING

1 E. 53rd St., NYC;
Tues–Sat noon–5 PM, suggested contribution: $1

We confess to being television addicts. Gone are the days when we tried to conceal this mania by hiding the tube in a hall closet, or quickly switching to educational TV when a knock was heard at the door. We now brazenly answer the phone with "The New Treasure Hunt" blaring in the background, and unashamedly quote Johnny Carson or Gene Shallit as readily as others might invoke Spinoza or Thomas Jefferson.

Even those who are not tube-hounds ought to know about The Museum of Broadcasting. It is one of the very few places in the country where the medium's great moments are preserved for pleasure or serious study. It is a sleek little place, classy and well-architected enough to assuage any guilt pangs one might have about watching *Amos 'n' Andy* tapes, rare *I Love Lucy* episodes, or the culturally more reputable Ernie Kovacs. For the serious-minded viewers, there are tapes of the Kennedy-Nixon debates, Edward R. Murrow in his trenchcoated glory, and the very best examples of the pioneering days of *Playhouse 90* and *Studio One*.

Enjoying these samples of what Eric Barnouw has called "The Tube of Plenty" is as simple as looking through the card catalogue and finding the TV (or radio) show you want, filling out a card, and going into the next room to watch your show. Visitors are invited to watch a videotape of Alistair Cooke introducing the Museum. After that, it's just you and your favorite program, just like home only better—since here there are thousands of shows from which to choose.

THE MUSEUM OF HOLOGRAPHY

11 Mercer St., NYC;
Weds–Sun noon–6 PM;
Adults: $1.50, Children: 75¢

If you see a woman blowing a kiss at you as you visit the Museum of Holography, don't be flattered. "It's only a hologram," you must say to yourself— words that people in the future might find themselves saying quite a bit. The fact is that holograms are amazingly real-looking; at least, at the present state of the art, amazingly *tangible.* They are everything that 3-D movies claimed to be with their silly headache-producing glasses. You need no glasses to look at a hologram. As you peer at it, you know it is three-dimensional. Move your head to the side, and you see the object depicted from a slightly different point of view. Holograms truly appear to occupy three-dimensional space.

The Museum of Holography is as shiny new as the medium itself. It occupies a five-thousand-square-foot loft in Lower Manhattan, and as far as we can tell is the only holography museum in the world. There is a permanent collection of works, as well as exhibits by working hologramists. Some are static pictures, like *Iguana,* which is set in an aquariumlike tank in the museum wall. Others are closer to moving pictures—actually hologram filmstrips, like the above-mentioned *Kiss II.*

It's all done with laser beams, and one can't help but feel that the holograms on display at this museum are like the first primitive moving pictures. A few decades from now, when people matter-of-factly create holographic scenes in their living pods (that's a futuristic living room), they will look back and chuckle at us and our primitive amazement at these truly dimensional pictures.

NEW YORK POLICE MUSEUM

The Police Academy; 235 E. 20th, NYC;
Mon–Fri 9 AM–4 PM

This is the world's largest collection of police memorabilia. Detective Al Young, museum curator and official NYPD historian, has created a remarkable display of some of the more colorful aspects of police history, from handguns and handcuffs to billy clubs and rattles. Rattles? Yes, in New York's colonial days, policemen carried wooden rattles—the precursor of whistles— to sound an alarm. In those days, cops were called "the rattle watch."

Some of our other favorites here include "the flute"—a glass bottle shaped like a billy club, the purpose of which was to carry the "little nip" that kept many a bluecoat walking his beat through the cold winter nights; the 33-inch billy club that looks like Babe Ruth's bat; a display of confiscated homemade weapons; and fancily-carved personalized nightsticks. In a less menacing vein, the museum displays a collection of every shield issued by the NYPD since

1845, the oldest known medal of honor, uniforms, hats, and a collection of sheet music with titles like "Oh Girls, Never Trust a Policeman."

ROSELAND'S WALL OF FAME

Roseland Ballroom, 239 W. 52nd St., NYC;
viewable during daylight hours; free

Roseland. The name conjures up visions of Vaseline-haired tango dancers, shimmying flappers, broad-shouldered zoot-suited lindy hoppers, and just about any popular dance fad of the twentieth century, right up to disco madness. The Wall of Fame is in Roseland's lobby, just before you get to the ticket booth to buy your passage into the terpsicary. The Wall consists of two glass cases, in which are displayed approximately thirty pairs of shoes.

These are the shoes of the Great Dancers: Ann Miller, Ray Bolger, Hal Leroy. Here are the shoes of Kathleen Murray (Arthur's wife), of Bill "Bojangles" Robinson, of George Raft; shoes worn by the winner of the Harvest Moon Ball and sometimes emcee at Roseland, Don DeNatale. The most popular pair is Ruby Keeler's—outrageously flashy, and symbolic of the magic spell that fleet feet can have over an audience. Each pair of shoes in the Wall of Fame is marked with a plaque and a picture of the star.

SONGWRITERS' HALL OF FAME

1 Times Square (8th Floor), NYC;
Mon–Sat 11 AM–3 PM; free

If you stroll down Broadway in the Times Square area, music emanates from almost every storefront, movie theater, souvenir store, massage parlor, and dance studio. Even the street people who linger around the clock carry transistor radios to keep themselves plugged in to the music. The beat of New York City is everywhere here at its crossroads. The Songwriters' Hall of Fame—honoring those men and women who created that musical pulse—is nestled in the midst of it all.

The Hall of Fame is one large room, filled with instruments, photos, and sheet music of the Greats. There is a revolving exhibit, changed every six months, devoted to a particular theme: women songwriters, vaudeville, record production, etc. Among the permanent exhibits are Victor Herbert's desk—high enough so that he could stand and work at the same time, the drum box used by Jerome Kern to tap out tunes, a piano marked with cigarette burns where Hoagy Carmichel forgot his light, and an upright piano at which Fats Waller sat, and at which visitors to the Hall of Fame are invited to tickle the eighty-eights themselves.

Once popular music enters the national repertoire, it is easy to forget that these "most hummable" tunes were once the brainchildren of some very talented songwriters, here given an appropriate fanfare by the Songwriters' Hall of Fame.

THE TREE OF HOPE

Seventh Avenue (Adam Clayton Powell Jr., Dr.) at 131st St., NYC, NY

Nobody knows how the legend began, but there was a time in the 1920s when show business performers would walk blocks out of their way just to rub the trunk of the Tree of Hope. Touching it meant good luck, perhaps because the Lafayette Theater, in front of which it grew, had been a "good-luck place" for New York's black entertainers. Unlike the Cotton Club, which by the 1930s was run by downtown whites for the amusement of slummers, the Lafayette represented black show business for the people of Harlem, along with Connie's Inn, Small's Paradise, and the Entertainer's Club. It was here that James P. Johnson and Leonard Harper first put on all-black stage shows in the early '20s, where Fats Waller performed in "Jr. Blackbirds," where Florence Mills debuted in "Keep Shufflin'." The Tree of Hope stood in front of the place that advertised itself as "The Most Widely Known Negro Theater in America."

But by the 1930s the tree was crowded by new layers of pavement, and was choking to death. Bill "Bojangles" Robinson, who had himself rubbed the lucky trunk, had the tree moved to the center of Seventh Avenue and replanted behind a plaque that reads: "The Original Tree of Hope—Beloved by the People of Harlem. 'You asked for a Tree of Hope, so here 'tis.'—Bill Robinson." The plaque is still there, worn almost flat, but the tree has been replaced by a modern sculpture, presumably symbolizing the same hope for which the original tree stood forty years ago.

PENN YAN

THE FINGER LAKES GRAPE FESTIVAL

Yates County Fairgrounds at E. Main St. & Old Rt. 14A, Penn Yan, N.Y.;
last weekend in Sept.;
free (charge for barbecue)

This festival celebrates the grape in all its incarnations from jelly to champagne. Starting at 9:00 A.M. on Saturday, buses leave the fairgrounds taking visitors on tours of the nearby vineyards, where you see the grape crop in its fullest glory. September is harvest month, and at the time of this festival the vines form a dense cover over the trellises. If a bus tour isn't good enough for you, planes take off from the Penn Yan airport starting at 10:00 A.M. to provide aerial views of of the grapes.

Saturday afternoon at 2:00 P.M., the "wine refreshment area" opens up, where you can have a few glasses to put you in the mood for the most enjoyable event of the weekend—the grape stomp, where all are invited to jump in and feel the cool, squishy grapes 'twixt the toes. Meanwhile, homemade wines are judged nearby the stomp, and there is a pork-chop barbecue beginning at 4:30. Your chops are eaten on the grass, picnic-style, and if after all this you can't move, that's fine, because there is an outdoor concert that runs from 7:00 P.M. to midnight.

Sunday begins with a pancake breakfast, plane rides and a twelve-mile marathon run—all just to get the blood circulating again for the afternoon cooking competitions (using grapes).

It all adds up to a heady weekend, and although specific events and times change from year to year, you can be sure if you come here that there will be plenty of grape-oriented activities to keep your spirits high.

PORT CHESTER

GIANT LIFE SAVERS

Horton St. & N. Main St., Port Chester, N.Y.;
always viewable; free

Ever since Andy Warhol painted soup cans, the border between industrial advertising and Art (capital "A") has been uncertain. As you round the bend on Route 1 heading from Connecticut into New York State you are struck by what appears to be a pop art sculpture garden. Giant packs of Life Savers, ten feet high, line the road: peppermint, wintergreen, orange, cherry, and a variety pack.

These giant candies were around long before such visual overstatement became aesthetically fashionable. In fact several years back there was a movement afoot among Life-Saver executives to tear down the colossal candies and replace the Life-Saver factory's old-fashioned stone front with a classier façade. Life-Saver workers—a Mr. Ray Sammarco in particular—rebelled, and finally convinced the powers-that-were that the great candy rolls were a Port Chester landmark.

"I look out my window and see families drive by," Mr. Sammarco says. "They stop and take pictures, sometimes a gag shot of the kids licking the candy."

RHINEBECK

MONTFORT REPTILE INSTITUTE

Schultz Hill Rd., 1/4 mi. off 9G, Rhinebeck, N.Y.;
Summer Hours, Daily 10 AM–5 PM, rest of year Sat & Sun 10 AM–5 PM or by appointment (914) 876–3769
Adults: $2, children 5–11: $1, under 5: free

"Each and every individual during his lifetime will encounter a snake in its wild state, and knowing what to do and how to do it may save your life or the life of a companion." So proclaim Charles and Peter Montfort, who have made it their personal business to tell the world about reptiles. Their institute is a strange cross between educational exhibits and circuslike manipulation of ophidians designed to thrill and scare you. Nobody just walks around Montfort at their leisure. You are taken through the collection of copperheads, rattlers, cobras, boas, alligators, and tropical lizards, with stops along the way to explain where you are likely to encounter each, and exactly what you ought to say or do at the time. Charles will pick up a cobra and "play" with it, and let lizards crawl around on his shirt, and demonstrate venom extraction from poisonous American snakes. One leaves the Montfort Reptile Institute a little weak-kneed but better-educated about snakes and lizards.

RYE

THE MUSEUM OF CARTOON ART

Comley Ave., Rye, N.Y.;
Tues–Fri 10 AM–4 PM, Sun 1 PM–5 PM;
adults: $1, students, sr. citizens, & under 12: 50¢

The Museum of Cartoon Art has just recently moved from its once-cramped Greenwich, Connecticut residence to a grandiose castle in Westchester County. Looking a bit like something out of a fairy tale or cartoon itself, the building is in fact the first prestressed concrete structure in America. But it is not for architectural splendor that we direct you here.

In the castle you will find the quintessential collection of cartoon art. Virtually every facet of cartooning is represented—strips, cartoons, books, newspaper drawings, panel cartoons, sports cartoons. Just about anything drawn that can elicit a chuckle is displayed or available here. From "The Yellow Kid," which was the first comic strip ever (1896) to modern film animation, the Museum of Cartoon Art takes its laff-a-minute subject seriously enough to be a valuable resource for collectors and historians of the subject. Slide shows are offered regularly, and there is a small theater in which some of the best vintage cartoons (Remember "Out of the Inkwell" . . . ?) can be seen. There are ongoing programs, or specific works can be requested.

The museum also runs a gift shop where you can buy rare comics at rarified prices, books on the art, and prints of famous cartoons. The only thing you can't buy is the latest "Archie" or "Sgt. Rock." For that you go to the local candy store.

SARATOGA SPRINGS

NATIONAL MUSEUM OF RACING

Union Ave. & Ludlow St., Saratoga Springs, N.Y.;
Mon–Fri 9:30 AM–5 PM, Sat & Sun noon–5 PM, August racing season 9:30 AM–
7 PM; free

The National Museum of Racing exists to encourage the idea of racing as a *"gentleman's sport"* (italics theirs). It is located across from the Saratoga Racecourse, the oldest working track in the country. It is an impressive Georgian colonial building, its walls lined with portraits of famous horsemen and horses, from George Washington to Seabiscuit. The East Gallery is all racing silks, endless combinations of color and design, each of which represents an individual horse owner registered with the Jockey Club. Aside from equine art, silks, statuary, and portraits of "Patrons of the Turf," the Museum displays historical artifacts. You can see the boots worn by Johnny Loftus on Man o'War, War Admiral's triple crown, and the jockey scales used at Saratoga between 1906 and 1946. There is an entire exhibit devoted to James E. Fitzsimmons, the "Grand Old Man" of racing, and dean of American thoroughbred trainers. A Hall of Fame in the rear of the main building immortalizes trainers, jockeys, and horses who have done the sport proud.

Each weekday during racing season, movies are shown of the great horses and their historic races.

SOUTH OTSELIC

GLADDING INTERNATIONAL SPORT FISHING MUSEUM

Octagon House, South Otselic, N.Y.;
Memorial Day–Labor Day, Tues–Sun 10 AM–5 PM; free

South Otselic is the Fishing Line Capital of the World, so named because for over a hundred and fifty years they have been making fishing line–as much as two hundred million yards per year. For avid fishing fans, and for others who, like us, have never caught anything outside of a restaurant lobster tank, the Sport Fishing Museum is an enchanting place. It is in an octagonal house in the rolling wooded countryside—so simple and pleasant to look at that the exhibits are practically a bonus.

On display here are some of the beautifully intricate rods, reels, lures, landing nets, and flyrods that have been used over the centuries. Some were used by famous fishermen for their macho encounters with half-ton swordfish. Other exhibits are as simple as the polished stone trolling rig used by Greenland Eskimos centuries ago. Of course there are mounted fish, pictures of fish, and books about fish, too. Incidentally, the first book ever published on sport fishing, *Fysshe and Fysshynge* (1496), is here. It was written by a sporting nun named Sister Juliana Berners.

The Sport Fishing Museum sponsors an annual Tall Tales Contest, with categories for amateur BS artists (mere fishermen) and professional liars (writers).

STANFORDVILLE

COUNTRY FARE ANTIQUE DOLLHOUSE AND TOY MUSEUM

Route 82, Stanfordville, N.Y.;
Mar–Jan, Sat & Sun 1 PM–5 PM;
Adults $1.25, children 75¢

It is a pity that the Incredible Shrinking Man, of 1950s horror-movie fame, did not know Anne and Arnold Schack. He might have happily lived out his minuscule life in style in any number of the Schack's antique dollhouses. He could have gone riding in one of their miniature stables (saddling up a mouse, perhaps?), climbed into the hayloft of a miniature barn, gone shopping in a miniature store, served himself tea from a miniature porcelain tea service, and played a tiny grand piano by the light of a minicandelabra.

These are among the dozens of miniature artifacts that make up the Schacks' collection, all housed on the second floor of their farmhouse barn. Among the unusual houses, there is one made entirely of tin (too hot for summer residence), a beautiful example of "tramp art" design whittled into a rococo Victorian mansion—all from cigar boxes—and one home with a genuine miniature Persian rug on which stands an eighteenth-century gateleg table.

Downstairs, the Schacks often have coffee brewing for guests, and a dish of free peanuts. There is a checkerboard set out if you want to while away the afternoon in this most informal miniature museum, the best collection of dollhouses we have seen.

TROY

UNCLE SAM'S GRAVE

The Oakwood Cemetery, Oakwood Ave., Troy, N.Y.

Uncle Sam Wilson died in 1854 and is now buried under a bronze plaque that declares him to be the inspiration for the same bearded Uncle Sam who walks around in a top hat and striped suit, lives in Washington, D. C., and used to point menacingly from army posters. This fellow Sam Wilson was a meat packer in Troy who supplied pork to the Army of the North during the war of 1812. The meat came to the army camp in Greenbush, N. Y., where the soldiers from Troy (who knew Sam Wilson) started calling it "Uncle Sam's meat." The other soldiers (not from Troy) thought that they were referring to the "U. S." stamped on the barrels in which the army meat was shipped. And so "U. S." came to be associated with "Uncle Sam" because of a few hundred barrels of Sam Wilson's meat.

The fact is that the original Uncle Sam did not have chin whiskers, and was never known to parade around in a red-white-and-blue striped tuxedo. Nor did he ever try and recruit people for the army. But he did quite well in the meat business.

WANTAGH

CHECKERS' GRAVE

Bide-A-Wee Pet Cemetery, 3300 Beltagh Ave., Wantagh, L.I., N.Y.;
daily 9 AM–5 PM; free

Before the Nixons moved to Washington they buried their cocker spaniel Checkers on the grounds of the Bide-A-Wee Pet Cemetery under a pink marble headstone bearing the inscription:

Checkers
1952–1964
NIXON

The people at Bide-A-Wee don't recall the Nixons coming back to Checkers' final resting place, but we are sure than anyone who remembers the famous "Checkers speech," or who is interested in Nixon family history will find this marker worth a special trip to Section 5 of the well-manicured cemetery.

Any man who buries his pooch under a pink marble headstone can't be all bad, can he?

WARREN

PETRIFIED CREATURES MUSEUM

Route 20, Warren, N.Y. (Cooperstown North);
Open Memorial Day to Labor Day 9 AM–7 PM,
Labor Day through Oct. 9 AM–6 PM.
Admission: $1.25

Petrified Creatures, Warren, N.Y.

What is it about dinosaurs that makes them so celebrated by roadside entre-
preneurs? Is it the fact that in the last few million years the mighty beasts have
become the oil and gas that speed us on our way? Whatever the explanation,
dinosaurs abound along America's highways, and upon us falls the difficult
task of recommending those dinosaur parks that are the best. Should we select
the most elaborate? The most scientific? The most educational? The most
beautiful? Petrified Creatures wouldn't win on any of these counts. But Petrified Creatures has personality.

It's run by John Mlecz and his son Richard, who bought it five years ago
and are fighting an uphill battle to turn it into the finest dinosaur shrine in the
country. Their first problem was the dinosaurs themselves. When they bought
Petrified Creatures, it had already been around for a quarter of a century, and
some of the dinosaurs were in terrible disrepair. So they took several thousand
pounds of plaster and tried to reconstruct them. All went well, except that they
got a little carried away in their sculpting. The neck of the brontosaur grew
longer and longer as they rebuilt it, and it now extends so far from the
trapezoidal body that it touches the ground in one place and is held up by steel
posts in another. It looks now like an ancestor of the giraffe, crossbred with
a full-leg cast. Lacking museum materials, the rebuilders used red rubber balls
for eyes. They enlarged the dinosaurs' teeth, and tried to paint a bit of expression onto the faces of the gawky plaster forms. There are five huge creatures
in all—some more free-form than others; all propped up in the woods behind
the indoor museum.

There is a diorama in back, too, depicting some sort of duckbilled creature
having a bloody fight with a *Triceratops* as a flying pterodactyl gazes down
from its all-too-visible wires overhead. The *Triceratops* looks as if it is suffering
from the heartbreak of psoriasis. Its horns are eaten away, and part of its back
is gone. "A mouse got into the diorama," Richard Mlecz explained.

There are other exhibits outside, complete with push-button recordings that
explain prehistoric life. There's a pit where kids can dig for fossils. And inside
the museum there is a large selection of rocks, fossils, dinosaur literature, toys,
and ashtrays.

John Mlecz is himself a dinosaur buff, and once he gets started on the
subject, be prepared for a lecture. "Those babies were hot-blooded!" he began
to us. "Don't let anybody tell you different." Young Richard takes a lighter
approach. He wants to install foot-activated recordings of "dinosaur voices"
so that as a tourist approaches, the animals roar and start to talk. Both John
and Richard are constantly at work—repainting, refinishing the monsters'
skin, cutting the grass on which they graze, fighting the inevitable natural
erosion of the Petrified Creatures. We wish them well. What their park lacks
in class, they make up for in their determined, eccentric efforts to keep the
dinosaurs from disintegrating.

WOODSTOCK

CLARENCE SCHMIDT'S ENVIRONMENT

Spencer Road, off Ohayo Mountain Drive, Woodstock, N. Y.

Schmidt's Environment is a legend in the Woodstock area. We had heard it talked about for years as a fantastic, kaleidoscopic place, an eccentric artistic creation. Unfortunately, most such recommendations ended with the lament that Schmidt's environment had burnt down; that there was nothing left; that we had missed our chance to see evidence of the environmental genius of Woodstock. We asked around the town, and sure enough, everyone knew of this place. In fact, everyone seemed perfectly able to direct us to the site. And just as surely, each person ended the directions by warning us that there was nothing left to see.

All you can see from Spencer Road is a mailbox, encrusted with bits of mirror and colored glass, decorated with a Datsun 1600 emblem. The terrain drops sharply to the side of the road, and as we inched our way back we saw the burnt remains of what was once Clarence Schmidt's home. We climbed down the side of the hill—an eerie terrain dotted with rubber life masks, burnt mannequin forms, bottles, boxes, TV tubes, and all the junk throw-away stuff of which folk art environments are made. As we descended, the scene of destruction took on apocalyptic resonance. Here were the remains of civilization as gathered together by Clarence Schmidt, now burnt and scattered, overgrown with vegetation, in the process of being swallowed up by the earth. We had climbed past the area that had been his house and roof garden, past what was once the House of Mirrors, and now found ourselves in the remains of The Silver Forest—acres of trees and bushes all still wrapped carefully in aluminum foil. Lurking behind bushes and trees there are faces everywhere. Some are the faces of burnt dolls; some are life masks, still painted bright red or blue. It was morning, and the faces dripped with dew that looked like tears. Some faces were surrounded by hands—open hands, hands like fists, hands clutching the silver-wrapped trees.

We finally arrived at what must have been the bottom-level entrance to Schmidt's environment—an ancient Studebaker station wagon, half planted in the earth. Perched atop it were three mannequin heads acting as sentries. Near it a sign: "Children at Play." Now deep in the forest, we heard a rustling above us. A young man swung out of the trees and cried "hello!" He had evidently been watching us all the while. He introduced himself as Michael Schmidt, Clarence's son. He wore only a pair of cut-off jeans. His body was daubed with tar, which he explained by telling us he was continuing his father's work. He was friendly and accommodating, but he seemed uncomfortable conversing with us, as if he were more at home up in the trees, swinging through the man-and-nature-made environment like some Woodstock Tarzan. He receded into the forest, promising that the next time we returned the environment would be in A-1 shape. As we continued to look around, we sensed Michael somewhere above us. We heard sawing, the dragging of branches—the sounds of someone altering the environment. What Michael Schmidt has in store for this bizarre place we do not know.

Schmidt's environment is an explorer's delight. If you plan to visit here, wear your climbing gear. Be prepared for shocking, amusing, morbid, playful, visionary, schlocky and always surprising vistas along every pathway, behind every bush, and half-buried in the earth. And if you see somebody swinging overhead in the foil-wrapped trees, you'll know that Michael Schmidt is at work, creating art out of the Ohayo mountainside.

PENNSYLVANIA

CENTRAL CITY

THE SHIP HOTEL

Rt. 30, 17 mi. W. of Bedford in Central City, Pa.;
open all year; rooms from $12; (814) 733–9918

The view from the Allegheny Mountains is spectacular. The valley below is a wavy blue-green stretching out toward the horizon. It looks like the ocean. That's what Mr. Paulsen thought when he decided to build The Ship Hotel. So he built the hotel in the shape of a ship. The medium-sized concrete structure is nestled on the heights overlooking Pennsylvania, Maryland, and West Virginia. The hull is white, painted sea-green below the "waterline." On the "bridge" you'll find what they claim to be the world's largest outdoor telescope (twenty feet long) and five sets of high-powered binoculars with which you can take bearings. The cabins are fitted with wall-to-wall carpeting, and there is a promenade deck reserved for hotel guests. Even if you can't come aboard for the night, you can visit the dining room with plate-glass windows overlooking the panoramic view.

This is a unique, eccentric, and inexpensive hotel—shipshape as well as shipshaped.

CENTRALIA

CENTRALIA, PA.

Rt. 61 between Ashland and Mt. Carmel, Pa.

Centralia is a hellish place. It is a town perched upon an unquenchable chasm of fire, in the Appalachian Mountains of Pennsylvania. The trouble started in 1962 when the Centralia town dump, situated in an abandoned coal-mining area, caught fire. A vein of coal ignited; the fire crept underground; and the populace of Centralia began to experience a communal hot-foot. Experts have tried pumping water, sand, and fly ash into the ground, but this is one inferno that will not be put out.

Of course, living on top of a fire isn't all bad. The winter heating bills here are practically reasonable. Ice is never a problem on the roads and sidewalks near the fiery pit. But Centralians are not entirely happy living on top of a private hell. They tell the story of one woman who left Centralia nine years ago when her canary died. She knew that canaries were once used by miners to test the breathability of mineshaft air. And so when "Tweetie Pie" croaked, his owner moved out fast. They say that occasional sulphur clouds waft through the streets. And the temperature has been going up.

It is estimated that there are eight million tons of coal under Centralia, so there is little hope that the fire will burn itself out. That's enough fuel to keep the town's muffins toasted well into the next century.

DELAWARE WATER GAP

THE WORLD'S LARGEST URINAL

In the Deer Head Inn (Main St.), Rt. 611, Delaware Water Gap, Pa.

The Deer Head Inn is a locally popular tavern—beloved for its long, cool draughts and for the jazz piano playing of John Coats. It is easy to imagine spending a whole evening inside this slightly faded inn, especially if you want to tell your drinking buddies out of town that you have come face to face with the world's largest urinal.

The diploma to the side of the urinal modestly proclaims it to be "one of the world's largest," and also discreetly rumors that Teddy Roosevelt personally consecrated it.

It is indeed on the large size, but not excessively so. Certainly fame has not turned the heads of the Deer Head's owners, who have casually crowned it with a half-empty can of Ajax and a sponge—just like any ignoble urinal. The enamel bears a thin veil of cracks, and it is flanked by another run-of-the-mill *pissoir;* but, given the choice, who'd settle for second best?

During off-hours, groups of daring and curious women have been seen sneaking into the men's room for a peek. The management seems to treat these men's room raids with the patience of those who are accustomed to living with greatness.

DURYEA

WORLD SHRINE

631 Ann St., Duryea, Pa.;
free, any time

The World Shrine is an inconspicuous monument built by John B. Salek to honor his parents, who came to America in the early 1900s. It is a small, grotto-style structure in his backyard, presided over by a statue of the Virgin Mary. The base is a concrete rectangle to which John Salek affixed stones from each of the fifty states, thirty-two foreign countries, and eighteen other "points of interest"—one hundred locations altogether. Among the stones are Hawaiian lava, catahoula sandstone twenty-five million years old, Indiana limestone two-hundred-and-ninety-five million years old, a piece of marble from Israel sent by the Bethlehem Lions Club, and a rock from Pennsylvania that still shows the bloodstains of men killed during the Revolutionary War.

Mr. Salek welcomes visitors to his very personal monument any time they wish to drop in. He never meant it as a tourist attraction, but travelers have been stopping by since 1958 when it was dedicated.

KENNETT SQUARE

PHILLIPS MUSHROOM MUSEUM

Route 1; Kennett Square, Pa.
(215) 388–6082; Museum open 10 AM–6 PM Daily;
Admission Adults: $1.00, Children 7–16: 50¢, under 7: free

If you've got any phobias about a poisonous toadstool fungus lurking at the bottom of your bag of supermarket mushrooms, or if you've ever thought of picking some wild ones for your picnic salad, then hesitated, fearing the mushroom might turn your picnic into a psychedelic freak-out circa 1967, go to Phillips Mushroom Museum and get wise to the *agaricus bisporus,* the edible, no-trip mushroom. More mushrooms are grown in the ten-mile area around Kennett Square than anywhere else in the world. The Phillipses, who lord over this empire of fungus, have named it "the mushroom capital of the world."

In the Mushroom Museum you'll find mushroom history going back to the Egyptians who thought the eating of it ensured immortality, to the Greeks and Romans who considered it fit for royalty alone, and to the United States (in the 1890s), where it was first imported to fill empty space in greenhouses. In the 1930s William Phillips first experimented with year-around mushroom farming in Kennett Square; and once he got that perfected, business mushroomed to a million pounds a year. The Phillips Museum also answers the question "What is a mushroom?" and explains how they are grown and harvested.

After a tour of the museum, you can visit the Cap and Stem Shop, which sells every conceivable mushroom-shaped, mushroom-decorated and mushroom-inspired gift, as well as fresh mushroom bread and, of course, fresh mushrooms.

LANCASTER

ANDERSON PRETZEL BAKERY

Route 340, Lancaster, Pa.
Mon–Fri 8:30 AM–5 PM, tours free

Did you ever get to wondering, after a few too many beers, how those pretzels you're munching on got their twist? Wonder no more. At the Anderson Bakeries you'll see the Bavarian twisting machine in action, taking a single strand of pretzel dough into its pincers and turning out a perfect pretzel every time. They then proceed along the "extruder loading proofing belt," into the pretzel oven, out to cool, then into boxes, bags, and vendor packs, ready for a TV snack or beer party. There are no free samples at Anderson, but at the retail store on the premises you can buy everything they make, including gift tins to send to your friends.

LEBANON

WEAVER'S FAMOUS LEBANON BOLOGNA TOURS

15th & Weavertown Rd., Lebanon, Pa.;
Mon–Fri 9 AM–4 PM; free

Pennsylvania is bologna country, and Lebanon—home of Weaver's Famous —is the bologna heartland. It is only in this town that you will see menus with items like bologna tetrazinni or Lebanon cutlets. The people of Lebanon, in fact, are known for their robust and pink bologna-cheeked good looks.

If you have ever pondered the mystery of what goes into that pale-red circle of meat that fits so neatly between the bread slices, here is your chance to find out. Despite rumors that the Lebanon bologna production is a deeply guarded town secret, Weaver's is happy to take visitors on a tour of the whole process, from steer meat to stockinette stuffing.

It begins in large tubs, where the meat is cured. Here, bacteria goes to work —friendly microbes, to be sure, "aging" the meat the way bacteria ages cheese. Eventually, the meat is shoveled into a "stockinette"—a large canvas sock— in which it is hung for several days in just the right atmospheric conditions. The finished bologna is cleaned of excess cellulose and shrink-wrapped into its polypropylene skin. It is now ready to eat.

This product is treated with the same respect a gourmet cook has for a juicy little quail or a tin of truffles. When you tell someone in Lebanon that they're full of bologna, they're likely to agree.

LITITZ

CANDY AMERICANA MUSEUM

46 N. Broad St., Lititz, Pa.;
Mon–Sat 10 AM–5 PM; free

A visit to this museum is a delight for anyone who longs for the sweet old days when ornate, chocolate-molded valentines, bunnies, and squirrels were as commonplace as the flat, slablike chocolate bar is today. Wilbur Chocolate Company is a venerable old candy manufacturer, still producing Vanilla Buds, Ideal Cocoa, and Mint Buds. Because of their long involvement with America's favorite sweet (since 1884), they have put together this museum as an ode to the way sweets used to be. Here you will see the original chocolate molds and other kitchen equipment, ancient packaging tins, and best of all, a factory outlet where you can buy every sort of Wilbur Bud they make.

OXFORD

LEMONGROVE (EDSEL PARK)

Rt. 472, 4 mi. W. of Oxford, Pa.;
weekends are best, call (717) 529–2126; free

Lemongrove has every Edsel model but one. Station wagons, hardtops, coupes, and convertibles cover the landscape like strange vehicles from another civilization. Even when it was first made, the Edsel was a nonconformist car—from its push-button transmission in the middle of the steering column to the notorious design of its front grille. It was speculated at the time of Edsel's demise that its failure was due to its "feminine looks"—an anomaly amongst the finned and phallic cars that streamed from Detroit in the late 1950s. Jack Parr called The Edsel "an Oldsmobile sucking a lemon," and its name has come to symbolize any gross marketing miscalculation.

Today the car is a fascinating anachronism. Hugh Lesley's collection is the world's largest, consisting of some showroom-shiny restorations and a great number of originals in varying states of driveability, some in disrepair. The pride of the fleet is a "cherry" 1958 red-and-white convertible with a Continental kit "out back." The best models are kept in a garage. The others are lined up outside in rows, or nestled in a grove of trees. "It's a grove of lemons," Mr. Lesley says. "Get it?"

The one model not displayed at Lemongrove is the 1960 four-door hardtop. That was the year Edsel tried to get away from the horse-collar grille, and came up with a car that looked like a customized Ford with a Pontiac grille. If you see such a thing driving down the street, parked in a junkyard, or abandoned in an empty lot, call Hugh Lesley. That car could make him an Edsel man who has everything.

PHILADELPHIA

THE MÜTTER MUSEUM

College of Physicians of Philadelphia, 19 South 22nd St, Philadelphia, Pa.; Tues–Fri, 10 AM–4 PM; Free

The Mütter Museum is the country's most extensive collection of pathological specimens and medical instruments. If you have a morbid medical curiosity, the Mütter is hypnotic. If you are a hypochondriac, here you will find a lifetime supply of diseases, aberrations and anamolies to worry about. If you are a student of medical oddities or medical history, this is *the* place for you.

The anatomical collections include the Hyrtl collection of skulls and ear ossicula; the Chevalier Jackson collection of foreign bodies removed from the lungs and bronchii; the Matther Cryer collection of internal facial anatomy; the Sappey collection of mercury-filled lymphatics, and various wax models depicting diseases of the eye.

In the pathology collection you'll find every known type of bone fracture, tissue injuries from the Spanish-American and Civil Wars, benign tumors, malignant tumors, assorted skeletons demonstrating bone diseases, the B. C. Hirst pelvis collection, syphilitic bones, syphilitic tissues and a collection of human and animal anomalies. This includes examples of hydroencephalism (waterheads), anencephalism (pinheads), gigantism, and a full case history of the Siamese twins Chang and Eng including their torso death cast and actual jointed liver(s).

There is an instrument collection, too, showing the development of the microscope, stethoscope, syringe, and obstetrical forceps. Here are instruments and medical tools from Pompeii, as well as ones used by Curie, Lister, and Pasteur, even illustrations of the old "purge and bleed" school of medicine.

THE WISTAR MUSEUM

The Wistar Institute of Anatomy and Biology, 36th & Spruce St.,
Philadelphia, Pa.;
Mon–Fri 10 AM–4 PM; free; (215) 387–6700

A visit to the Wistar makes us think of those hundreds of cop movies in which bad guys of various height and girth are lined up for identification under the glaring lights of the precinct house. At the Wistar, there are line-ups everywhere. Only here the suspects are all skeletons, and the light isn't glaring. The room is quiet and suitable for study and contemplation. The Wistar is a bone museum.

Osteology exhibits are organized to demonstrate contrast and continuity from one skeleton to the next. Some line-ups are chronological, from youthful skeletons to ones whose owners were octogenarians. Some display cases contrast racial morphology. Some show male and female. There is a collection of skulls of all ages. A favorite exhibit is the one that shows hybridization in dog bones (the ones inside their body, not what they eat). In addition, there are specimens of the fetus from the tenth to the eighteenth week of intrauterine life, and exhibits of cell structure, division, and mutation.

The Wistar Museum is a spacious, comfortable hall in the Wistar Institute of Anatomy and Biology. A taped, thirty-minute tour is available to explain its exhibits—highly recommended unless, like us, your interest in bones is purely aesthetic.

SHARTLESVILLE

ROADSIDE AMERICA

Rt. 22, Shartlesville, Pa.;
July–Labor Day 9 AM–8 PM, Sept–June Mon–Fri 10 AM–5 PM,
Sat & Sun 10 AM–7 PM;
adults: $2, children 6–11: 50¢

In 1903 five-year-old Laurence Gierenger looked out his bedroom window onto the Pennsylvania countryside. The legend of Roadside America is that little Laurence was inspired by what he saw. To him the landscape looked like a sparkling miniature scene out of a fairy tale. He never forgot this vision, and when at sixteen he became a carpenter he began to make miniature buildings —houses, farms, stables, churches—eventually a whole miniature world.

Roadside America, Shartlesville, Pa.

13 Month SOLUNAR and 12 Month GREGORIAN CALENDAR side by side

SOLAR YEARS 0 to 100,000			**SOLARIUS** *Universal International*			7TH LUNAR MONTH (28 Days each)	
MONDAY	**TUESDAY**	**WEDNESDAY**	**THURSDAY**	**FRIDAY**	**SATURDAY**	**SUNDAY**
18 ☼ 169th DAY JUNE ☼☼ **1** 25TH WEEK	19 170th DAY **2**	20 171st DAY **3**	21 172nd DAY **4**	22 173rd DAY **5**	23 174th DAY **6**	24 175th DAY **7**
25 176th DAY JUNE ☆ **8** 26TH WEEK	26 177th DAY **9**	27 178th DAY **10**	28 179th DAY **11**	29 180th DAY **12**	30 181st DAY JUNE **13**	1 182nd DAY JULY *second quarter* ☆ **14**
2 183rd DAY JULY **15** 27TH WEEK	3 184th DAY **16**	4 185th DAY **17**	5 186th DAY **18**	6 187th DAY **19**	7 188th DAY **20**	8 189th DAY **21**
9 190th DAY JULY **22** 28TH WEEK	10 191st DAY **23**	11 192nd DAY **24**	12 193rd DAY **25**	13 194th DAY **26**	14 195th DAY **27**	15 196th DAY **28**

The Calendarium, Washington, D.C.

Roadside America might be described as the world's most elaborate train set, or, more accurately, as a condensed American cosmos, in scale at 3/8″ to the foot, depicting the history, variety, and topography of rural America. Here are idealized small towns, miniature zoos, mountains, streams and lakes (stocked with live fish), country clubs, historic Indian battles from the past, coal mines, waterfalls. Miniature airplanes fly overhead; the seasons change; day dissolves into night. Laurence Gierenger created the American countryside as it might be seen by a giant if he could look from coast to coast and back into a mythical past. Gierenger pursued his microcosmic work with a single-minded intensity until his death in 1963. It was a labor of love.

Roadside America is now run by his descendants, who keep it in good order as a tourist attraction. The sign on the faded pink building warns "Be prepared to see more than you expect." The admission concept is like that of a freak show: the attraction is hidden from view until you pay your money. Only then are you allowed behind the curtain to gaze upon Laurence Gierenger's creation. This is one case where the quality of the attraction far surpasses the sales pitch out front.

The lobby is stocked with made-in-Hong Kong souvenirs, post cards, and gag gifts. But for all the hard sell and junky gimcracks up here, the miniature world behind the partition is a delicate place, an elaborately imagined vision of a Roadside America that could only exist in fairy tales.

DISTRICT OF COLUMBIA

WASHINGTON, D.C.

THE GARDEN OF ALMANALOGY AND ASTROMETRY
(CALENDARIUM)

Visible by appointment:
call Mrs. Walter Rothe (202) 244-4511, or write to 4767 Indian Ln. N.W.,
Washington, D.C. 20016; donations

Quick—what day is it? On what day of the week does your anniversary fall? What date is payday? If you can't immediately answer all of the above, don't blame yourself. Blame your outmoded calendar. Throw that Gregorian laby-rinth of leap years out the window and forget "Thirty days hath September, April, June, and November." Get yourself a Solunar Calendar and you'll never be confused again. "Isn't it high time we stop kidding ourselves and start printing calendars which conform to present-day activities?" That is the ques-tion Dr. Walter Rothe asked himself. And the answer to our present calendari-ous confusion will be found in what was once his backyard in Washington, D.C.—the Garden of Almanalogy and Astrometry. Here is the Birthplace of the Universal Calendar, as invented and celebrated by Dr. Rothe.

The yard is a series of monuments cut from stone, each illustrating vital aspects of the New Astrometric Order. Each is made up of giant numbers, like three-dimensional Jasper Johns paintings. But each conveys a specific message. One sets forth the numbers 7, 14, 21, and 28. It is entitled "Sundays Forever," because in the Solunar Calendar those dates are always Sundays. Another series of digits forms a concrete equation: "$13 \times 28 = 364$." This demonstrates how the solunar year is made from thirteen identical months (a new one, Solarius, falls between June and July). The 365th Day is called Orbit Day, honored here in the yard with a great arch and the inscription: "Climax Day after orbiting 687,803,131 miles in 365 days at 66,000 m.p.h." There is one quadrennial "catch-up" day. There is never a Friday the 13th.

Dr. Rothe died in 1976, but his wife carries on the work of the Calendarium Foundation. She is pleased to show interested parties around the Birthplace of the Universal Calendar, and gives a convincing argument for Dr. Rothe's work. His calendar only leaves twenty-six seconds per year unaccounted for. These will be adjusted for every 3,323 years when they have accumulated to a full twenty-four-hour day. But other than that, it is as precise as the movements of the planets. Dr. Rothe saw it as a "perpetual calendar impartial to all nations, races, and religions." A sign in the Calendar Yard expresses his credo: "The calendar is the most important item in our entire lifetime. It is a guide from the cradle to the grave. Is it not obvious we should be adhering to the best calendar available?"

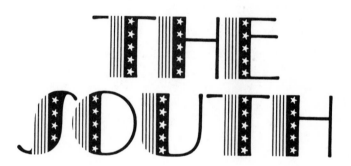

ALABAMA

ATHENS

TENNESSEE VALLEY OLD TIME FIDDLERS' CONVENTION AND ANVIL SHOOT

Athens State College, Beaty & Pryor Sts., Athens, Ala.;
Oct. 6, 7, 1978;
Admission Fri: $2.00, Sat.: $3.00

The fiddle was at one time known as the devil's box for its ability to cause people to dance, whoop it up, and generally raise hell. Limestone County, Alabama in the 1920s was a thriving center for such hell-raising. In the early 1960s a local resident named Bill Harrison, fed up with the plastic Nashville sound that passed for "country," created the Tennessee Valley Old Time Fiddlers' Association "to preserve, but not embalm" traditional Southeast country fiddle playing. Now, every year in early October, these people really raise some hell.

The convention begins with a traditional anvil shoot, an old folk custom that involves putting one anvil on top of another with a generous supply of black gunpowder in between. The powder is ignited and the top anvil blasts off into the air like an overweight cannonball, and crashes back near its "launching pad." In fact, the custom was originated by settlers too poor to afford a cannon but in need of convincing hostile Indians that they had some artillery. Bill Harrison claims to be one of two men in the country who still know how to shoot an anvil properly.

But all that is only a fanfare to the business at hand, which is choosing the annual grand champions of the fiddling world. Winners in both the junior category (under sixty years old) and senior are selected for rhythm, creativity, authenticity, expression, and execution. Trick fiddling is frowned upon by judges, so you won't see any contestants pulling the old tricks of playing with their heads between their legs, or their bow in the mouth, or imitating roosters and hens as part of their repertoire.

The contest is carefully organized into categories, including guitar, old-time banjo, mandolin, dulcimer, harmonica, and a specialty, buckdancing. And in case you have any doubts about the seriousness of this contest, these are the buckdancing rules: "Dancers will be judged according to the authenticity of the dance, rhythm and timing. The following steps will *NOT* be allowed: clogging steps, Charleston steps, backward steps, and sidewise steps. Arms should not be flayed up and down, but should be held loosely at the side of the body. Feet should be kept close to the floor and should cover as small an area as possible. Knees should be held to a low level to accomodate the true flat-foot style. *NO* taps will be allowed. Dancers should keep the head as level as possible."

If, however, you feel inclined to flay your arms about, kick your feet up and bob your head around like crazy, all in a very unprofessional way, don't worry. For all the seriousness with which fiddle playing, anvil shooting, and buck-dancing are treated here, there's still plenty of room for raising hell in the tradition of the devil's box. There is a big country-style supper on Saturday night, and there are jam sessions everywhere on the Athens campus during the two-day contest.

BIRMINGHAM

VULCAN—THE WORLD'S LARGEST IRON MAN

Vulcan Park, Birmingham, Ala.;
daily 9 AM–10 PM

"How many places can you speed right up 179 feet to an iron man's head?"

This question is posed by the Alabama Department of Tourism, but only rhetorically. They know the answer is "one," and that is Birmingham, Alabama, where you can ride an elevator up to the six-ton iron head of the world's largest iron man.

If you remember your Greek mythology or the iron-suited Vulcan character from *Flash Gordon,* you know that Vulcan is the god of metalworking. According to the Greeks, he was thrown out of heaven by Zeus, injured his foot in the fall, but earned back the respect of the gods by making them flashy brass houses and sleek golden shoes in his shop near Mount Etna in Sicily.

Birmingham's Vulcan was erected in 1904 to symbolize the city's mining, iron, and steel industries. He looks not unlike a male version of the Statue of Liberty, holding up in his right hand what at night is clearly a torch, but by day appears to be an ice-cream bar. The torch glows green, unless an automobile fatality has occurred that day in town, in which case it is switched to red. Vulcan thereby becomes (the tourism people say) "the world's largest safety reminder."

CHEROKEE

COON DOG MEMORIAL PARK

(12 mi. S. of Rt. 72 on Colbert County Rd. 21)
Cherokee, Ala. Always open

If the idea of a "dog cemetery" conjures up images in your mind of little old ladies with shaky Chihuahuas or decadent Hollywood types who come to bury pink poodles under pink marble headstones, go out of your way to visit Coon Dog Memorial Park. If you like dogs, this place will make you cry. It is a simple clearing in the middle of pristine Alabama woodland, miles from anywhere, quiet except for the chirping of birds. There is one well-crafted monument here, that tells you the park was begun in 1937 by Key Underwood, when his favorite "Old Troope" died in his sleep after a hunt. Old Troope is buried beneath the monument, which depicts two hounds cornering a racoon at the top of a tree.

The rest of the hounds are interred in the simplest of plots, marked with some of the most touching headstones we have ever seen. They are crudely hewn pieces of marble, or simply large stones. Some are draped with old and weatherbeaten collars, while on others there are faded photographs of the dogs. On many, the teary-eyed good old boys who have come to bury their hounds have scratched messages, or simply a name: "Bo—the best blue tick to ever hunt the Tennessee Valley;" "Old Queenie, killed by car 4–28–59;" or, plainly, "My Boy—age 13."

Clearly, this moving place is anything but decadent. These are the dogs of "jes' folks," who traditionally make a pilgrimage each Labor Day to Cherokee to decorate the stones of their once favorite pets with wreaths, racoon skins, and old bones.

MUSEUM OF THE FREEDOM HILLS

County Rt. 21 (White Pike Rd.) Cherokee, Ala.;
hours flexible, admission free

Admission to the Museum of the Freedom Hills is attained by knocking on the door of the house nearby, or hunting up Mr. or Mrs. J. H. Durham. Mrs. Durham was taking an afternoon nap when we arrived, but she was happy to get up and show us around the museum. The exhibit consists of a large, newly built log cabin, stocked with artifacts of old-time Alabama life. All things are arranged as if the place were lived in. There is a kitchen with a wood-burning stove and a beautifully crafted tin-front pie safe. In the living area there is a spinning wheel and a caned rocker and a single bed with a simple quilt.

All the items on display are either originals found in local farmhouses, or hand-crafted reproductions made by Mr. Durham. We are not ones who go out of our way just to see some nice antiques and craftwork, but the informality of this museum won our hearts. There is no admission charge, and no proselytizing purpose. "We had all these things around the house, and my husband likes to work with wood, so we put together this museum," is Mrs. Durham's statement of principles. It is a lovely stop in the Alabama woods, surrounded by the Durhams' dozing dogs and cats, open and friendly to all who pass.

The Coon Dog Cemetery, Cherokee, Ala.

The I.Q. Zoo, Hot Springs, Ark.

CULLMAN

AVE MARIA GROTTO

1 mi. E. of Cullman, Ala., on U.S. 278 & 69;
Daily 7 AM–sunset;
Adults: $1.50, children: 50¢

Ave Maria Grotto began early in the century as a hobby of Brother Joseph, O.S.B. He was boss of the St. Bernard Abbey power plant, when he decided to take up a hobby—the building of miniature shrines. As he built, he became inspired, and pretty soon Brother Joseph found he had constructed practically the entire city of Jerusalem in miniature. People around the world heard of this miniature city, and began sending Brother Joseph stones, shells, rocks, chandelier prisms, beads, and local icons. He continued to build, including all these gifts in his intricate constructions.

There are now four acres of miniature life in Cullman. The original Jerusalem is flanked by Rome, which includes St. Peter's, the Pantheon, the Coliseum, and the viaducts. Elsewhere there is Noah's Ark, the Basilica of Lourdes, shrines and churches from around the world. There is even a small Hanging Gardens of Babylon. There are tiny waterfalls, fountains, a whole miniature landscape etched into the side of the mountain along with the buildings.

Little Jerusalem and the Grotto are today one of the South's most elaborate and popular tourist attractions. But for all their renown, they are still a very personal work of art—one man's miniature world made from scraps.

ENTERPRISE

BOLL WEEVIL MONUMENT

Town Square, Enterprise, Ala.;
Always visible

If ever a contest is held to crown the country's ugliest monument, the judges need look no further than here. The bug-faced Boll Weevil monument was erected in the town square by the citizens of Enterprise "in appreciation of what it has done to herald prosperity." How, you ask, does that destructive insect, the boll weevil, herald anything but headaches for a farming community? Well, when the boll weevil struck, destroying the local cotton crop, farmers turned to peanuts as an alternative. They found peanut farming far more profitable than cotton. And for their newfound source of income, they had not only George Washington Carver but that ugly pest, the boll weevil, to thank.

FLORENCE

W. C. HANDY HOME AND MUSEUM

620 W. College; Florence, Ala.;
Tues–Sat 9 AM–noon, 1 PM–4 PM,
Adults; $1, students: 25¢

W. C. Handy is the father of the blues. Of course, he didn't invent them. They evolved, and they were the expression of a whole world of experience. Handy was dedicated to this music. He "lived" the blues, knocking around the country until he wound up in St. Louis, a center of ragtime music. It was there he found the inspiration for what became—according to Guinness—the most recorded song in history, "St. Louis Blues." His method of working was to take "hand-me-down" tunes that he heard in his travels and give them his own interpretation, mood, and rhythm. He "fathered" the blues because he was the first to put them down in musical notation, and to dedicate his life to that unique sound of black America.

Many of Handy's original compositions are on display here in the Handy Museum, the cabin (restored) in which he was born in 1873. Also on display are his piano, on which he first worked out "St. Louis Blues," his famous "Golden Trumpet," and other bluesy memorabilia. There is Braille music here too, and Handy's Braille watch (he was blind in his later years). W. C. Handy commemorative record albums are sold for $3 each.

MONTGOMERY

THE LURLEEN B. WALLACE MEMORIAL MUSEUM

725 Monroe St., Montgomery, Ala.;
Mon–Sat 8:30 AM–4:30 PM, Sun 1:30 PM–4:30 PM; free

There are some who believe that Lurleen Wallace was merely an extension of George B., his puppet in the Alabama governor's mansion. This museum is a good place to learn about Lurleen Wallace—as Alabama's first woman governor, and as a woman with a distinct and unique personality.

There is official memorabilia here in this ante-bellum home in the Montgomery capitol complex. The governor's desk and her specially made petite chair are shown, placed for comparison alongside her girlhood desk. What is especially nice here is that the Lurleen B. Wallace Museum tries to give one an understanding of and a feeling for her personality. She was a pretty good fisherwoman and hunter, and some of the beauties she bagged are on display, right beside her favorite tablecloth and napkins. Some of her distinctive ensembles are also on display, including the "Pink Lady" dress she wore for hospital work, and the modest black suit and pillbox hat she wore at her inauguration.

ARKANSAS

EUREKA SPRINGS

CHRIST ONLY ART GALLERY, THE BIBLE MUSEUM, AND CHRIST OF THE OZARKS

Art Gallery: Mt. Oberammergau, Eureka Springs, Ark.;
June–Oct daily 8 AM–8 PM, Nov–May daily 9 AM–4 PM;
adults: $1, 6–14: 50¢
Bible Museum: 3 mi. E. of Eureka Springs, Ark. on US 62;
Daily 9 AM–5 PM;
adults: $1, 12–16: 50¢
Christ of the Ozarks: Mt. Oberammergau, Eureka Springs, Ark.; always visible;
free

These three attractions are each part of one man's master plan to turn Eureka Springs into a town of sacred projects. The Art Gallery contains approximately five hundred portraits of Christ—in wood, metal, paint, embroidery, ivory, marble, ceramics, gold, and silver. The Bible Museum contains seven thousand books in six hundred and twenty-five languages, and display cases of Bible-oriented artifacts. Christ of the Ozarks is the largest Christ figure in North

America. It weighs two million pounds and is strong enough, its builders say, to support the weight of two full-sized American cars if one were suspended from each of His arms.

These are all the legacy of Gerald L. K. Smith, the man whom H. L. Mencken described as a "first-rate rabble-rouser," and who was widely known as "the old hatesmith" for his rabid publication, *The Cross and the Flag*. They are now managed by the Elna M. Smith Foundation, which is currently planning a twenty-million-dollar life-size reconstruction of the Holy Land. This was Smith's dream project—vital, he felt, because the original Holy Land was so in danger of being destroyed by war.

MRS. QUIGLEY'S CASTLE

Highway 23, S. of Eureka Springs, Ark.;
Mon–Sat 8:30 AM–5 PM, Sun 1 PM–5 PM;
Admission: $1.00, under 15: free

Mrs. Quigley's Castle is a home and a rock collection all in one. Her story is that one day in 1943 when her husband left for work she decided to tear down their house. "When Bud got home that night, he was living in a chicken house, where I'd moved all of our stuff." The idea behind Mrs. Quigley's one-woman demolition Derby was that she wanted a house with more room; and a house "where you felt like you were living in the world instead of in a box." Mrs. Quigley is not a professional architect, and her blueprint was a small model made from cardboard and matchsticks. The house was made of earth, with fossils, petrified wood, marbles and pretty rocks all pressed into the surface. The first story was ringed with bare earth, into which Mrs. Quigley planted shrubs, trees, flowering plants and cacti—all now growing into the house and up toward the second-story ceiling. Huge windows provide the plants with light and the occupant with a true feeling of living out in the world.

The sparkling, colorful house is ringed with more flora, and with birdbaths, dove cages, small archways and a fish pond—also made from rocks and fossils and colored glass from bottles.

Mrs. Quigley estimates that she spent altogether only $2,000 making her castle. "I live off what God put in the world," she says.

HOT SPRINGS

I. Q. ZOO

Highway 270, W. of Hot Springs, Ark.;
Memorial Day–Labor Day 9 AM–5 PM, rest of year 10 AM–4 PM;
adults: $1.50, children: 75¢

The I. Q. Zoo is the home of the most well-behaved animals in the world. Take Bert Backquack and his band, or Chickey Mantle the slugger, or Red, the roller-skating parrot. These guys keep their beaks clean, never get into trouble, and do exactly as they are told. Why? Because they are treated right, the I. Q. Zoo informs its visitors. They never hear a harsh word and never get hit.

The I. Q. Zoo is a project run by Animal Behavior Enterprises as a tourist attraction and a demonstration of the techniques of positive reinforcement. They have trained animals for movies and TV, and here in Hot Springs put on shows for visitors of what their menagerie can do when they put their not-so-limited minds to work.

If you have ever had problems disciplining a pet, this place will seem like one of the wonders of the world. There are dogs here who can play chess. They're not masters yet, and they'd probably lose to Bobby Fisher (unless they were trained to undermine his concentration as well as play the game). But what the I. Q. Zoo animals lack in refined skills, they make up for with charming personalities. They love their work, and it shows. Look at the fireman rabbit extinguishing the blaze. He's showing off! And Ruby the twisting chicken looks like she's auditioning for "Soul Train." This place is an animal-lover's delight, and an inspiration to pet owners. Remember—your dog or cat is smart. All it needs is a little education.

ROGERS

DAISY B B GUN PLANT AND AIR GUN MUSEUM

U.S. Highway 71 S., Rogers, Ark.;
Museum open 9 AM–5 PM daily Mon–Fri; Factory tours daily at 1:30 PM; free

Were the names "Buzz Barton" and "Red Ryder" part of your childhood? If so, then the Daisy air gun company can chalk up another victory in their campaign to "put an air rifle within reach of every boy." Daisy is the world's largest and oldest manufacturer of nonpowder guns and ammo. A tour through the plant shows you how those Red Ryders, Buzz Bartons and vintage Number 25 Pumps were made. You also see several thousand of the plant's daily output of sixty-five million BBs being made (where, oh, where do they all go?). And at the end of your tour—or before it—you can look through the Air Gun Museum. Here is air-gun history beginning with the reservoir guns of the seventeenth century—so feared by Napoleon that he ordered the death sentence for anyone caught with these silent bullet dispensers. The modern air gun is so accurate that there is a special category for it in the Olympic competitions, and it is championed by the National Rifle Association as a weapon the use of which is not only within reach of every boy, but of every girl, too. But air rifles are not all fun and Olympic games. Astronaut Edward White blasted himself through space in 1965 by shooting a specially made air pistol—thereby making the air gun the granddaddy of any space weapons of the future.

SPRINGDALE

ALBERT E. BRUMLEY SUNDOWN TO SUNUP GOSPEL FESTIVAL

Parsons Rodeo Arena, Rt. 62–71, Springdale, Ark.;
1st week in August, Thurs, Fri & Sat, 7:30 PM–1 AM Thurs & Fri, 7:30 PM–Sunup Sat;
Adults: $4.50 per night, or $10 for three nights; further info, call: (501) 751–4694

This is the big blow-out for fans of Ozark-style gospel music. Each of the festival's three nights features six of the country's top-rated gospel groups— performers like Willie Wynn and the Tennesseans, the Cathedrals, and the Thrasher Brothers. It is three nights of mountain music at its best, and on Saturday afternoon the doors are open for the amateur talent contest.

The *Gospel-Singing Journal* reports that conventions such as this began in 1869 at a "Peace Jubilee" in Boston at which there was a chorus of ten thousand people, an orchestra of eight hundred pieces, and fifty anvils used to beat the rhythm. Most performers in Springdale are quartets or families, and the instrumentation is simple. The human voice is the gospel's instrument.

STUTTGART

WORLD CHAMPIONSHIP DUCK-CALLING CONTEST

Registration at 507 Main St., Stuttgart, Ark.;
Late Nov (the 1st Sat. of duck-hunting season)
call (501) 673–2687

When ducks fly south, most of them pass over Arkansas. Their flyway takes them right over the rice fields around Stuttgart, and it seems fitting that every November there are dozens of humans on the ground, quacking right back at them. This contest began in the 1930s and it has become an elaborate ritual. The main street of Stuttgart is blocked off and contestants appear one by one and start to quack. There are four types of call: 1) the open water call, 2) the woods call, 3) the mating call, and 4) the scare call. The excellence of each contestant's performance is not based on whether they attract a curious (calls 1 and 2), sexually aroused (call 3), or alarmed (call 4) mallard. They are rated instead by a panel of expert human judges.

Most contestants use artificial duck calls, but some old-timers (and two recent world champs) need nothing but their lips and virtuoso vocal chords to produce prize-winning quacks.

In addition to the World Championship, there is a Junior Championship Duck Call, a Women's Duck Call (for women who call ducks, not people who call woman ducks), and an annual crowning of Queen Mallard (also a person).

Every five years Stuttgart holds a Champion of Champions Contest, to which all previous world champions are invited. Until 1980, the superchamp is Harry Richenback, a local boy.

FLORIDA

CARYVILLE

INTERNATIONAL WORM-FIDDLING CONTEST

Caryville, Fla. off U.S. 90;
1st weekend in Sept.

Worm fiddling has nothing to do with Isaac Stern or Jack Benny. It is a way of luring the wrigglers up above the ground by placing a wooden spike in the earth and dragging a heavy metal bar across it. This creates a vibration that, to worms, is a siren call. Whether they find the noise irresistibly alluring, or whether it drives them to madness, nobody seems to know. In any case, the worms surface and are bagged by Worm-Fiddling contestants. The one who has played the sweetest (or most hideous) tune—and has therefore captured the most worms—wins.

The captured worms are then used as bait—a logical fate, since the fiddling is soon followed by a grand-scale fish fry.

CASSADAGA

CASSADAGA, FLORIDA

Near Orange City on Highway 17–92

Although the population of Cassadaga, Florida is listed at 350, there are several hundred million souls who exist just within reach of every Cassadaga resident. Cassadaga's people are all mediums, and each is in the business of bridging the boundaries between life and death. They are not fortunetellers, and there are no crystal balls in town. Do not ask any of them if you should invest in AT&T, or when you will meet your dream lover. Talking with the dead is an entirely different proposition from looking into the future.

Cassadaga was founded in 1895 when spiritualist George Colby, who had been led here on a psychic journey by three spirits, willed thirty-five acres to the Spiritualist Church, so that there might be a permanent haven for its followers. Cassadaga was built on that land, and today practically every doorway in town is marked with a sign indicating that a medium is inside. The village is a quiet, Gothic-looking sort of place, with narrow streets and moss-draped gnarled oaks.

If you do plan to visit Cassadaga, either to look around or to contact a spirit, don't come between January and March. That is when the town hosts the Southern Cassadaga Spiritualist Camp Meeting, at which spiritualists from all over congregate for religious services, lectures, and medium sessions with an assortment of friends, living and dead. It's hard to get a reading at this time because most of the population is busy talking shop or off in another world, so to speak.

FT. LAUDERDALE

INTERNATIONAL SWIMMING HALL OF FAME

501 Seabreeze Blvd., Ft. Lauderdale, Fla.;
Mon–Sat 10 AM–5 PM, Sun noon–4 PM;
adults: $1.25, students: 75¢, under 6: 50¢, families: $3.00

Swimming is a sport of heroes and heroines from Johnny Weissmuller and Esther Williams to the gold-medal-draped Mark Spitz. According to the International Swimming Hall of Fame, swimming's heroes and fans go back 3,000 years; and they do their best here to memorialize the sport and its famous gods and goddesses through the ages.

What we love about this Hall of Fame are its inventively designed displays. At the entrance there is an artificial Hawaiian waterfall where Arthur Godfrey's voice eulogizes a wax statue of swimmer Duke Kahanamoku. There is a 3,600-tile mural of King Neptune's courts. There are stuffed swimmers too, including stingrays, porpoises and turtles. There is a mounted marlin to honor Hemingway's *Old Man and the Sea,* and a spitz dog (alive) named Mark Spitz.

Here you will find the world's largest collection of sports stamps, the world's smallest trophy (a gold thimble mounted on a gold collar button), and a collection of dummies modeling swimming gear through the ages. The exhibits are vast, extending far beyond the Hall of Fame itself, which is designed to honor Buster Crabbe, Weissmuller, Esther Williams, Mark Spitz, and swimming's other sleek heroes.

If your visit has inspired you, it costs only 80¢ (40¢ for kids) to jump into the Hall of Fame's Olympic-sized pool and paddle around just like the champs.

HOMESTEAD

CORAL CASTLE

28655 S. Federal Highway, Homestead, Fla.;
open daily 9 AM–5 PM,
adults: $2.00, children: $1, under 7: free

Edward Leedskalnin died of starvation in 1951. He left behind several thousand dollars in cash, hidden in a drainpipe at Coral Castle. The Castle was his home —a fairy-tale place built over a period of twenty-five years, now a monument to Leedskalnin's eccentric life and one of the wonders of roadside America. The castle is made from coral rock—an estimated thousand tons of it altogether—excavated and carved by Mr. Leedskalnin with nothing more than hand tools.

What could drive a man to devote superhuman energies to so complex and awesome a task? Edward Leedskalnin was lovesick. He had been jilted on his wedding night. He spent the rest of his life waiting for his sweetheart to come back to him; waiting and building. The Coral Castle was to be their dream home. And so he built a Feast of Love Room in which they might dine at a heartshaped table around a heartshaped coral centerpiece weighing six tons.

And after dinner they could retire to the Throne Room where Edward could sink back into his carved contour chair, and his sweetheart could rock in the perfectly balanced three-ton rocking chair. Their children would play in the Grotto of the Three Bears with its coral porridge bowl. Late in the evening, for Mrs. Leedskalnin's ablutions, there is a coral bathtub. And when they retired, it would be to the carved coral-rock bedroom.

But not all of Leedskalnin's creations here at Coral Castle are merely practical home furnishings. There is whimsy too—a thirty-ton telescope, carved crescents and planets, and a table shaped exactly like the state of Florida, surrounded by coral chairs.

The mystery of how he did it has yet to be explained. Coral Castle has been used as proof by the book *Flying Saucers Are Watching Us* that superintelligent beings have lent their skills and/or construction crews to selected humans through history. Leedskalnin was always secretive about his work, saying only that he knew the secrets of the Great Pyramids, as well as electromagnetic engineering.

"Sweet Sixteen," as Edward Leedskalnin called his once-wife-to-be, never returned. He died broken-hearted, leaving behind Coral Castle as a monument to unrequited love.

JENSEN BEACH

SEA-TURTLE WATCH

Jensen Beach, Jensen Beach, Fla.;
June; free (call 305–334–3444 for details and up-to-date turtle reports)

It is a strange sight for sure: as night falls, kids and adults with flashlights and Instamatics squat on the sand at Jensen Beach and look for signs of turtles flipping out nests in the sand. Every year for the last twenty years giant sea turtles weighing as much as 500 pounds crawl onto the beach to lay their eggs. There are no hordes of turtles, and sometimes nights can go by when none is spotted. But during the height of the season, in late June, organized turtle watches prowl the beaches looking for signs of the great beasts digging nests in the moist sand with their tough flippers.

The event has been sanctioned by the Jensen Beach chamber of commerce as a fine way to "gain an unusual understanding of the mysteries of Mother Nature."

KEY LARGO

CHRIST OF THE DEEP

John Pennekamp Coral Reef State Park;
U.S. 1, Key Largo, Fla.

We have seen icons and statues in some pretty strange places, including a shrine placed in the belly of a brontosaur model, but this is the first underwater one we have come across.

When the weather permits, glass-bottom boats cruise the waters off the mainland for impressive views of the marine life underneath. There are nearly a hundred square miles of coral formations, and right in the middle of the reef is Christ of the Deep. This is a nine-foot tall statue of Christ, arms outstretched, reaching from underwater toward the surface. The folks in charge here regard this statue as "unique in the western hemisphere, a symbol of peace," although we find it a bit distressing to see a statue with its arms raised looking up at you from underwater.

KISSIMMEE

MONUMENT OF THE STATES

Monument St., Kissimmee, Fla.;
always viewable; free

Being only a stone's throw from Walt Disney World, Kissimmee gets its share of tourists. At the Tourist Courts just two blocks from the downtown area there is an imposing step pyramid made of concrete and rock, rising over a hundred feet in the air. It is the Monument of the States, built in the early 1940s. Tourists from forty-eight states and several foreign countries each added a trinket, bauble, stone, rock or shell to represent their home. In addition to the matter affixed to the sides of the pyramid, there are inscriptions—signatures, names of the states' governors at the time, and sentiments now somewhat eroded by time. The monument is a bit like an inside-out time capsule —a message from tourists at Kissimmee thirty-five years ago to Disney World-goers of today.

The monument sits in front of a recreation area where one can play shuffle-board or tennis.

LABELLE

SWAMP CABBAGE FESTIVAL

Barron Park, LaBelle, Fla.;
last full weekend in Feb.

We doubt if New York or Kansas City steakhouses will take notice, but "Steak 'n' Swamp Cabbage" makes for a pretty decent duo. This is but one of the many ways the swamp rat's favorite vegetable is served during this uniquely Floridian festival. Swamp cabbage grows freely in this hot, humid part of the country, and late in February the LaBellites put their heads together and try to devise some new ways of cooking it. The old standards are boiled, raw, or fried, but we have heard exotic recipes that involve drying out swamp cabbage leaves, rolling them in cigarette paper, and smoking the resulting stogie. Swamp cabbage is devoid of tar and nicotine.

At the festival LaBelle crowns a swamp cabbage queen, and holds an exhibition of the most aesthetically pleasing swamp cabbages, the hugest swamp cabbages, and other cabbage-oriented creations. The festival is rounded out by a score of other countryish events, from gospel singing to beard-growing contests.

ORLANDO

TUPPERWARE MUSEUM GALLERY OF HISTORIC FOOD CONTAINERS

Tupperware International Headquarters; U.S. 441 & 17–92 Junction, 15 mi. S. of Orlando, Fla.;
Mon–Fri 9 AM–4 PM;
free; groups call in advance (305) 847–3111

If the magnitude of Earl Tupper's contribution to modern civilization can be measured by the enthusiasm of his Tupperware salespeople, then he must be considered a giant among men. The Tupperware spirit is as indestructible as the Tupperware container. And a tour of the Tupperware International Headquarters is as precise as the patented Tupper seal.

First you see the gardens, lakes, and friendship fountain. You see the spot on which a bicentennial flag made entirely of Tupperware containers was once constructed. Past the manicured grounds, you are greeted by a hostess in the reception area. She narrates a photographic essay that tells the tale of Tupperware and how it is made. You are then led through a lovely home setting where you see the many uses of Tupperware products, from kitchen and dining area to baby's room. The highlight of the tour comes when you are escorted through the Museum Gallery of Historic Food Containers. Here you may browse on your own amongst containers as old as 4000 B.C., some made of stone, leather, horn, or shells. All are displayed in glass cases—all except the Tupperware, which is the high point of the gallery and the apotheosis of the food container. This is out in the open: Over a hundred pieces of Tupperware, demonstrated by your hostess to reveal the product's unique qualities.

It is all too lovely to miss.

SAN ANTONIO

RATTLESNAKE ROUNDUP AND INTERNATIONAL GOPHER RACE

San Antonio, Fla., N. of Rt. 52;
3rd Sat in Oct.; free

By the third Saturday of October, most residents of San Antonio, Florida have collected bags full of rattlesnakes. This is the day they bring their catch into town and collect a bounty on all rattlers, living and dead. The roundup originated in the necessity of keeping the rattlesnake population low, but it has evolved into a festive pageant. There are venom-milking shows, first-aid exhibitions (treatment of snakebite is the first topic examined), and a chicken dinner.

The concurrent gopher races are not run by the furry things that most people think of as gophers, but by a particular sort of burrowing land tortoise native to Florida and known here as a gopher. Individual heats lead up to the International Gopher Race Championship Run at the town's fairgrounds. This determines from among all the molasses-paced beasts which is the fleetest-flippered in all turtledom.

For information on where to bring your rattlesnakes, call (904) 588–2611.

SANFORD

GOLDEN AGE OLYMPICS

Sanford, Fla. (all over town); 2nd week in Nov.;
Spectators free, entrance fee for each event: 50¢

Somewhere in Sanford, Florida at this moment, there is an over-fifty-fiver jogging, gardening, perfecting pinochle moves, or greasing the wheels on a wheelchair in preparation for the Golden Age Olympics. These games are open to anyone over fifty-five. For those out-of-shape oldsters, there are horticulture events, bridge and canasta, dominoes and ceramics competitions. But just as in the youngsters' Olympics, it is athletic prowess that makes these games exciting. The dance contest, bicycle race, bowling competition, and unisex pancake race are the major events, and you'll see sportspeople in Adidas and sunbonnets earnestly warming up before their heats.

Somewhere toward the end of the contests there is a two-dollar-a-plate spaghetti dinner. The competitors' ability to run around all day in the hot Florida sun, then wolf down a plateful of spaghetti is a dramatic demonstration of what good shape these elderly athletes are in.

SARASOTA

ANNUAL SANDCASTLE-BUILDING CONTEST

Lido Beach in front of the Sheraton Sandcastle Hotel, Sarasota, Fla.;
1st Sat. in May;
free (for info. call 813–388–2181)

Sandcastles, like flowers, are charmingly impermanent. But this does not deter the ardent builders at work each May on Lido Beach in Sarasota. The finished sandcastles are elaborate structures, some complete with drawbridges and turrets, others eccentrically designed to express their architects' sandy imagination.

Some builders compete just for fun. Others are aiming for the free dinners or T-shirts given by the Sheraton Sandcastle for the winning castles. Any design is acceptable, the management says. Winners are selected for artistry, originality, and structural integrity.

The same hotel holds a kite-flying contest on the beach in February.

CIRCUS HALL OF FAME

6255 N. Tamiami Trail, Sarasota, Fla.;
daily 9 AM–5 PM;
$3.50 when there are circus acts; $1.75 other times, children $2.50 & $1.25

Sarasota is a mecca for circus buffs. It has been since 1929, when John Ringling brought his circus here for the winter. Now, what with Ringling theaters, Ringling museums (of art as well as of the circus), and Ringling residences all over town, Sarasota is not a place for the timid sightseer. The circus is by nature a frenetic business, one of stampeding elephants and maudlin or mischievous clowns. The Circus Hall of Fame enshrines all of the biggest and best things that have made the circus the most colorful of entertainments.

It was founded in 1954 by Colonel B. J. Palmer, "the father of chiropractic medicine" and creator of Iowa's "Little Bit o' Heaven" (see Davenport, Ia.). It is, appropriately, the largest hall of fame in America. What is enshrined here are not only the great performers and ringmasters of circus history, but actual bandwagons and tents and "all performers and all circuses whether living, dead, or out of business" (the museum's stated aim). Here is the largest bandwagon ever built—ten tons—and the smallest—Tom Thumb's. There is a vast museum of puppetry, a side-show museum (with only the tamest stuff —this *is* a family hall of fame), and a collection of lithographs and posters.

Between Christmas and Easter and during the summer, the circus comes to the Hall of Fame, under the blue-and-white striped tent around which the regular exhibits are organized. It is an old-fashioned one-ringed circus, with enough noise and clamor for any circus lover.

RINGLING MUSEUM OF THE CIRCUS

U.S. 41, 3 mi N. of Sarasota, Fla.;
Mon–Fri 9 AM–10 PM, Sat 9 AM–5 PM, Sun 11 AM–6 PM;
Adults: $3.00, under 12: free

Do not go to the Ringling Museum of the Circus if you suffer from bozophobia. Too many clown artifacts, calliopes, and circus wagons might set off an attack. But for those who feel nothing but pleasure at the carnival colors and sights of circusdom, this is a spot not to be missed. The museum was opened in 1948, and is now a treasure house of circus history from ancient times to the present.

The centerpiece here is the museum's collection of encrusted, jewel-bright circus wagons, some with lion motifs, some draped with figurines of half-clothed ladies. There are circus posters, miniature parades, and a large collection of gaudy circus costumes worn by the stars of the highwire and clown alley.

In one building there is a re-created circus yard as it might have looked in the 1930s, including lions' dens and a blacksmith's wagon.

The Museum of the Circus shares space with two other Ringling Museums devoted to high art. For anyone with guilt pangs about choosing circus art over the serious stuff, we suggest you carry a notepad, prominently marked "Notes for Dissertation on Popular Culture." This museum is, in fact, a great source.

SPRING HILL

ANNUAL WORLD CHICKEN-PLUCKIN' CONTEST

Spring Hill Recreation Center, Spring Hill, Fla.;
1st week in Oct.

How does one begin to explain this event? Perhaps with the Miss Drumstick Contest: In this competition girls parade around on stage covered with flour sacks from their thighs up to the top of their heads. How about the Chicken Concerto: contestants each perform "The *William Tell* Overture" or "Gaieté Parisienne" using only chicken-clucking sounds. Perhaps one should begin at the heart of the matter, and explain that at the sound of a bell teams of women with names like The Featherweights or The Mud Hens start tearing feathers out of chickens so fast you'd swear a fox got into the henhouse.

Wherever you start, the Chicken-Pluckin' Contest is a day of madness. It is held in Spring Hill, which is known as the egg basket of Florida. Some come here with only a large appetite to contribute to the festivities. They are shuttled to the hard-boiled-egg-eating contest. Some bring their bellow-lunged roosters for the crow-off. Here, the birds are accompanied and encouraged in their crowing by a human choral group called the Hernando Harmonizers. Some people come here just to sit back and enjoy the C&W music, the skydiver who attempts to land in a large nest, or the annual hatching of "Mr. Chicken" and lighting of the Chicken Torch.

Here indeed may be the answer to the riddle of why the chicken crossed the road—to get away from this organized lunacy, which we recommend only to nonfeathered fairgoers.

TAMPA

VILLAZON CIGAR COMPANY

3104 N. Armenia Ave., Tampa, Fla.;
Mon–Fri 8:30 AM–10:30 AM, 1 PM–2:30 PM (except the last week in June, 1st 2
weeks in July, and Dec. 20–Jan 10);
free (813) 879–2291

Truck drivers on the C.B. radio call Tampa "Cigar City" because it is believed that the stogies made here are almost the equal of real Havanas. The best cigars made in Tampa are the Bances, Punch and Hoyo de Monterrey brands. They are manufactured by Villazon, where, during a twenty-minute tour, you can see the whole process. Some cigars are made by machines, but the best ones are made by hand, just like in *Carmen*. Here you will see people wrapping, binding, and rolling tobacco with skill that anybody who has tried to "roll their own"—cigar or cigarette—will envy. The hand-rolled beauties are given names like Corona Inmensa, Gran Ducs, or Demi-Tasse. This is the only factory we know that still makes the once-popular "torpedo" style cigar, now called "The Aristocrat."

GEORGIA

ATHENS

THE TREE THAT OWNS ITSELF

Dearing and Findley Streets; Athens, Ga.;
always visible

It is hard enough to say you are your own man. But there is a tree in Athens, Georgia, that is entitled to say it is its own tree. In fact, it owns the property on which it grows. This tree became a landholder when William H. Jackson, a professor at the University of Georgia, grew so fond of the oak on his property that in his old age, he recorded a deed: "W. H. Jackson . . . for and in consideration of the great affection which he bears this tree, and his desire to see it protected, has conveyed, and by these present, does convey unto said oak tree, entire possession of itself and of the land within eight feet of it on all sides."

The deed kept the ancient oak safe from all squatters, land developers, highway construction, and shopping-center sprawl. But nothing could protect it from the windstorm that uprooted it and scattered it through the Athens streets.

Shortly after the storm, though, the Junior Ladies' Garden Club of Athens planted a sapling in the great oak's place. It was grown from one of the acorns of the original tree, and is therefore deserving of its name, "Jackson Oak, Jr.," duly recorded heir to its father's land.

ATLANTA

BAILEY'S SCULPTURE GARDEN

396 Rockwell, S.W.; Atlanta, Ga.
(Always visible)

Folk art is mostly a country thing—from Grandma Moses to some of the environmental artists in this book, most of the primitives draw their inspiration from the countryside and the simple ways of life. But there are a few rare and wonderful exceptions that appear on the city landscape, and are inspired by urban life. Watts Towers and E. M. Bailey's sculpture garden are the most notable examples. Bailey's is in the middle of Atlanta's black section, not far from the baseball stadium and the airport. In a minuscule front yard next to a prim and well-kept home Bailey has built a collection of monuments and shrines that reflect the sensibilities of the urban black artist.

Bailey's best-known piece is the Henry Aaron statue—a dramatic plaster figure swinging a mighty bat through the air. Below the body is the plaster-cast number "715," commemorating Aaron's surpassing of Babe Ruth. Nearby is the Kennedy Monument, which Bailey designed as a model for what he hoped would become *the* Kennedy Memorial in Washington. It shows a jet plane— a symbol of modernity—flying over a bust of JFK. Not all the plaster statues crowded together in this garden are commemorative. Some are more whimsical, like the sinuous dancing muses that skip by the front fence, or the goddesses of Bailey's imagination.

E. M. Bailey is relaxed about his work. He knows he is good. "These new fellows, these artists," he said. "I've got it all over them. I was plastering for thirty years before I made this garden. I know how it's done."

THE FOX THEATER

660 Peachtree St. N.E.; Atlanta, Ga.
Public tours three times a year: call 892–5685 for reservation;
adults: $2, children: $1

Here is the splendor of Egypt's Pharaohs, set inside the courtyard of an ethereal Moorish city. Here clouds waft through the air, stars twinkle in the ceiling, and the sun and moon rise and set several times a night. This is the Fox Theater in Atlanta, the last of the great movie palaces. It is an ode to the movie megalomania of the late 1920s, a fantasy land that appropriates all the splendors of all the ages, as if no project, no building, could possibly be too grand for Hollywood.

It has had a rocky career since opening in 1929. It is now used for ballet, concerts, theater, and Liberace when he comes to town. But three times a year, the Fox is opened for tours—grand tours, tours fit for a king or Pharaoh. Everything about this place is deliriously gaudy. There are three "retiring rooms" for patrons—one Egyptian, one Turkish, one Moorish—each designed personally by Mrs. Fox. The orchestra pit seems big enough for the London Philharmonic. It was here that on Christmas Eve, as the Fox orchestra played "Jingle Bells," white cornflakes fell from the ceiling. There is a cloud machine that puffs vapors into the "atmosphere" above the audience. And there is the Fox organ—the most powerful in the world. This at one time was equipped with a "grand crash box," a steel cage filled with nuts, bolts, and tin cans that shook mightily to create a crash effect at the whim of the organist.

The wonders here are endless; and if they do not transport you to exotic visions of the Middle East, they are sure to conjure up that madly conspicuous era of American movie-going.

BUENA VISTA

EDDIE MARTIN'S HOME

Buena Vista, Ga. (Take Rt. 37 West, turn right on the second paved road)
Always visible.

"I have built my house as a monument to all the primitive peoples of

Mrs. Pope's Museum, Meigs, Ga.

Eddie Martin's Home, Buena Vista, Ga.

the world," Eddie Martin told us. "And I don't mean folks that live in closets, either." If this last remark strikes you as a bit enigmatic, that is appropriate, because Eddie Martin is himself an enigma. He is by profession a seer and spiritual reader who, having spent thirty years in New York City, decided to return to his mother's Georgia home and here continue his work and build his own home. His house defies categorization. It is huge and sprawling, immaculately clean and fastidiously maintained, half-hidden in the brush by the side of the road.

The house, in fact, seems literally to peer onto the road, because it is designed as a series of faces. There is one dominant set of eyes toward the back, overlooking the entrance drive. You get the distinct feeling as you approach Eddie Martin's property that you are being watched.

The designs that cover and create the form of the house are colorful and eclectic. Some look Polynesian; some Indian; some African. Between the faces there are red, green, yellow, and blue zigzags, shiny designs cut from tin, and always there are eyes.

Because he and his house are different, Eddie has been bothered by some local citizens annoyed at his visible, colorful individuality. So there are signs on the property that warn "bad dog—beep your horn and I will come out." We suggest you not bother Eddie unless you come here for a reading, or really want to know about this remarkable house. You can see the place quite well from the drive, where the house has a good view of you, too.

CALVARY

MULE DAY

Calvary, Ga. (15 mi. S. of Cairo);
1st Sat in Nov.; free

Why would 25,000 people congregate in a tiny Georgia town to celebrate the happy animal that has been judged "the Ugliest Mule in Town"? We do not have the answer to this question, but you will find us here the first weekend in November, voicing our choice of the Ugliest Mule, the Prettiest Mule, and the Most Stubborn Mule. This is mule country, and we can think of few more enjoyable weekend vacations than coming to Cairo and celebrating that rather ridiculous-looking animal.

The day begins with a Mule Parade at about 11:00 A.M. The mule-judging is interspersed with contests that give local farmers a chance to show off, too: plowing (with a mule, of course), cane-grinding, syrup-making, and greased-pig-chasing. There is a mule race in the afternoon, which mostly consists of trying to point the animals in the right direction and getting them to move. At midnight the day ends with a square dance. Heehaw!

DECATUR

THE MUSEUM OF SUNDAY SCHOOL HERITAGE

Baptist University of America, 2009 White's Mill Rd.; Decatur, Ga.

Elmer Towns—the man known 'round the world as "Mr. Sunday School"—put this museum together in anticipation of the two hundredth birthday of the first Sunday School in 1980. It is a quiet, low-key museum with display cases showing Sunday School-related artifacts such as the ring donated by Rebecca Thomas in 1836, which inspired hundreds of contributions that established Sunday Schools across America, music hand-written by Francis Scott Key (an early Sunday School supporter), and a Bible pierced by a marauder's bullet. There is a Christian Hall of Fame, with pictures of men and women instrumental in the movement, and a room devoted to the facts and figures of the largest and fastest growing Sunday Schools in the country.

Considering the quiet tone of this place and the gentle dignity displayed by the elderly gentleman who acts as a guide, it is hard for us to understand their brochure, given out at the door, which reads like an ad for a 1950s epic movie: "See! Original Pictures and Woodcuts . . . See! Full Color Film . . . See! Records and Music." Sunday School history has in fact had a cast of thousands and has been years in the making, and this little museum is sure to tell you all the things you ever wanted to know about Sunday School.

THOMAS JEFFERSON FLANAGAN'S MURAL

Antioch A.M.E. Church, 912 Atlantic Ave., Decatur, Ga.;
Viewable when church is open; free

Reverend Thomas Jefferson Flanagan has been discovered recently by folk-art cognescenti, who declare him to be an authentic American primitive. His paintings depict old Georgia life, and there is a well-known memorial portrait of John F. Kennedy. But it is inside the Antioch A. M. E. Church in Decatur that he has created perhaps his greatest work. It is a wall mural expressing Reverend Flanagan's concern over all the portraits of Christ in which He is shown on His knees surrounded by thorns. In the Reverend's picture, lilies take the place of thorns, and Christ, depicted in Reverend Flanagan's energetic style, is surrounded by lush foliage. He calls the mural "Christ in the Garden."

Reverend Flanagan is also a poet, a teacher, and a retired minister. He is apt to give you a personal account of the mural if you are fortunate enough to arrive at the church on a Sunday morning, when he is usually there.

EATONTON

UNCLE REMUS MUSEUM

In Turner Park, Highway 441 in Eatonton, Ga.
Closed Tues., Open daily 10 AM–noon, 1 PM–5 PM, Sun 2 PM–5 PM;
Adults: 50¢, students: 25¢

As history is written and rewritten, the significance of Joel Chandler Harris's Uncle Remus stories has been re-examined. His work was once considered folklore, but folklorists today see it as "once-removed"—a whitewashed version of the authentic folk tales told Harris by local slaves. Whatever his fate in the official history books, Joel Chandler Harris was a man whose stories affected millions of American children. And for those with fond memories of Uncle Remus's land of humanoid rabbits and foxes, we recommend this museum.

It is a log cabin similar to the one in which Harris sat and listened to "Uncle" George Terrell and "Uncle" Bob Capers tell him stories. One end of the cabin is a reconstruction of Uncle Remus's fireplace, where he sat and told stories to "the Little Boy." At the other end of the museum is a collection of first editions and other Harris- and Remus-related artifacts.

Further into the town of Eatonton there is a giant statue of Br'er Rabbit, corncob pipe in hand, wearing a sports jacket and tie, and looking very dapper.

MADISON

SPACE VIEW

U.S. 441 & 1–20, 1 mi. S. of Madison, Ga.;
Daily 1 PM–5 PM, or ring the bell; free

We frankly have some doubts about recommending Space View, "the park that promises you a future." Space View consists of a large open space through which you can drive or walk, in which you see religiously inspired plaques telling of what will happen to those who are wicked. That was fine, but what gave us the heebie-jeebies was "the world's most unusual art exhibit" inside the Space View building.

The sign on the door says "Ring bell." Since nobody seemed to be around, we hunted for a buzzer or doorbell and found nothing. But in back we saw a huge Liberty Bell-sized gonger, hung in the air with a rope dangling. We sounded it and almost instantly Brother Morris appeared. He is a gaunt and friendly fellow, who ushered us immediately into the Space View auditorium. He began speaking of the expulsion from the Garden of Eden, and as he spoke the lights dimmed, and he moved to close the doors. We were alone with him in the darkened, cavernous space. At the precise moment he stopped speaking a voice sounded from somewhere in front. A curtain drew back, and there before us was an eight-by-ten-foot painting of "The Expulsion," made from glittering gold, glass, and mother-of-pearl. The recorded voice stopped speaking and Brother Morris took up the story, continuing to "Nativity." Again, as his words ended, the recorded voice issued forth and a new eight-by-ten-footer appeared onstage.

So it went, alone in the auditorium with Brother Morris, the Voice, and "the world's most unusual art." We do not recommend Space View for those with claustrophobic tendencies. While you are in the auditorium, there is no means of escape from the Voice and the Story. But then, that seems to be the point of Space View.

MEIGS

MRS. POPE'S MUSEUM

Meigs, Ga. (Follow Rt. 111 South of Meigs 8 mi. to blue silo on the right. Take the second paved road after the silo to the left. Proceed approx. one mile); always visible

Mrs. Pope's is more of an outdoor catacomb than a museum. It is an isolated home in the Georgia farmland that has been turned into a personal memorial, sculpture garden, and environment. Mrs. Pope is now deceased, but it was during her lifetime that the townspeople of Meigs started calling her place a museum, partly because of rumors of what she had inside. The Meigs policeman told us that many believed her to be a witch. "She buried three husbands," he said. "Upstairs she had a coffin that she made, and a skeleton to go in it. Some said she was crazy. Now people come around to look and say she was a genius."

When we came around the house was empty, but well–kept and obviously lived-in. Most of Mrs. Pope's creation is visible from the road. Her sculptures create a lacy environment that grows up out of the ground into sculpted latticework, hanging gardens, and endless rows of faces. There is a great concrete edifice out front, a wall on top of which perch the heads of General Eisenhower and other heroes of D-Day. Elsewhere in Mrs. Pope's yard are galleries of famous women of both history and fiction—Scarlett O'Hara, Cleopatra, and the first woman seated in the United States Senate, Rebecca Ann Latimer Felton of Georgia. Some are mythological, like the Goddess of the Deep—festooned with shells, beads, and strings of pearl-like baubles.

These mute presences were all cast in the 1940s and '50s from Mrs. Pope's friends' faces, from her own face, and perhaps from the faces of her three husbands. Each group of sculptures seems to have a very specific meaning. But if the exact subject of the commemorations become hazy with time, the strength of Mrs. Pope's vision is not a bit diminished. It is a haunting place, whimsical and solemn—a monument, more than anything else, to one woman's ability to render her vision in concrete and stone.

PLAINS

THE PEANUT MUSEUM

Main St.; Plains, Ga.;
Daily 8 AM–6:30 PM (til 9 PM summer); free

John and George Williams opened the Peanut Museum to cash in on the fame of their once-unknown hometown and its two most famous products—Jimmie Carter and peanuts. Like most of the other places on Main Street, it is laden with every imaginable Jimmy, Rosalynn, Amy, and Billy gewgaw—enough junk to keep a crazed family of souvenir hounds happy all day.

The Peanut Museum proper is in the back of this store and by contrast is an uncommercial, low-key place. Artifacts are displayed over hand-lettered signs, and only a few of the busy souvenir hunters up front ever wander this far away from their quarry. In addition to implements such as shellers, pickers, and combines, the museum has a continuously running videotape that tells the story of peanuts. The Williams brothers are always here, and seem quite happy to talk peanuts with anyone interested. They are most amused by visitors who are obviously shocked to learn that peanuts don't grow on trees, hatch from eggs, or sprout out of the ground presalted. Until the ascension of Jimmy Carter, goobers were the lifeblood of Plains, and the subject that the Williams brothers enjoy the most. But if the boys like you, they might dish up a little local gossip about the first family.

QUITMAN

SOUTH GEORGIA HORSE AUCTIONS

Rt. 84 E. of Quitman, Ga.;
horse sales Tues at 1 PM, tack sales Tues at 11 AM; free

There is nothing that says "country" as sure as the bullet-fast cry of the auctioneer, and few places that give as good a feel for South Georgia life as the horse auctions held in Quitman. These people who buy and sell horseflesh are true red-dirt Georgians, and an afternoon here will give you a chance to peruse equine specimens from nags to thoroughbreds, as well as soak up the flavor of the clay-eatin' life, as it is known in these parts.

SAVANNAH

THE COCA-COLA COLLECTION

Tic Toc Museum, 125 W. Congress St., Savannah, Ga.;
Mon–Sat 10 AM–5 PM;
Adults: $1.00, children under 15: 50¢

It is not for the elegant timepieces, or the early music boxes and musical instruments, or the antique furniture all on display here that we like the Tic Toc Museum. It is for their display of an item that seems truly at home in Georgia; a part of the Southern landscape . . . Coca-Cola. The Tic Toc has

Plant Farm Museum, Summerville, Ga.

Space View, Madison, Ga.

probably the best collection in the country of artifacts relating to that sticky, sweet and wonderful soda.

Here at the Tic Toc, the drink that is synonymous all over the world with the U.S.A. is celebrated in all its shapes, labels, logos and incarnations, from the days it contained cocaine and was drunk by Gibson Girls, through leggy Coke-drinking pin-ups of the 1950s, to the present-day image of Coke equaling Life Itself, being "the real thing."

Can somebody explain why there is a Pepsi machine on the ground floor?

JULIETTE GORDON LOW GIRL SCOUT NATIONAL CENTER

Oglethorpe Ave. and Bull St., Savannah, Ga.;
Daily except Weds 10 AM–4 PM, Sun (except in Jan) 2 PM–4:30;
Girl Scout Adults: 75¢, Girl Scouts under 18: 50¢,
Non-Girl Scout Adults: $1.50, under 18: 75¢

This place is a good antidote for the automatic association of Girl Scouts with those intensely caloric chocolate-mint cookies they purvey. There is more to Girl Scouting than the encouragement of obesity, and much of interest will be found here. This is the girlhood home of Juliette Gordon Low, the founder of Girl Scouting. Girl Scouts emeriti act as hostesses and show you around the antique uniforms, old badges, and letters and diaries written by early scouts. When we were here the place was packed with Brownies and Scouts learning of their foremothers' exploits, and poring over archives and records inscribed with the names of the earliest Girl Scouts.

THE KAHLIL GIBRAN COLLECTION

Telfair Academy of Arts and Sciences, 121 Barnard St., Savannah, Ga.;
Tues–Sat 10 AM–4:30 PM, Sun 2 PM–5 PM;
adults: $1, students: 50¢, under 12: 25¢

Anyone who attended a wedding of flower children in the late 1960s or early '70s has probably heard the oft-recited words of "The Prophet" himself, Kahlil Gibran. For years his books have sold like Lebanese hot cakes, inspiring generation after generation of devotees to his mystical philosophizing. As any

Gibranophile can tell you, the Master was an artist as well as a profound thinker, and many of those cloudy sketches and watercolors that adorn *The Prophet* and *The Garden of the Prophet* are on display in the Telfair Academy of Arts and Sciences.

The Academy is the oldest art museum in the Southeast (founded 1886), with a collection that includes silver, porcelain, miniatures, nineteenth- and twentieth-century American paintings, and America's only collection of art works by Gibran. Even those paintings that are not illustrations from his books bear the unmistakably swarmy mystery that characterizes his vision. Mere mention of some of the titles makes the point: *The Medusa, The Head of Orpheus Floating Down the River Hebrus to the Sea,* and *The Blessed Mountain.* There are also portraits of the artist's mother, self-portraits, and portraits of Mary Haskell Minis, who donated the collection to the Museum.

MAMMY'S KITCHEN'S PIT

Highway 17, South of Savannah, Ga.;
6 AM–6 PM, 7 days a week (restaurant open until midnight); free

It is a source of deep frustration to us, living as we do in the Northeast, that it is impossible to get good barbecue within a several-hundred-mile radius of New York City. Apparently Northerners don't have the patience to sit at a hickory pit for hours on end, watching ribs or brisket or pork shoulder ever-so-slowly turn the deep reddish-brown color that marks the genuine article. While the restaurant at Mammy's Kitchen is a little too corny for our taste (Mammy dolls on display everywhere; "ye olde-timey-cooked-in-de-pit" Southernoid menu), the actual barbecue pit here is one of the best working exhibits of barbecue technique we know. And as far as we're concerned, the ritual of the pit is an essential element of American culture.

Even before you see this pit by the side of the road, you will smell the hickory smoldering. Inside the cookhouse is Pappy, half-asleep but with one slitty eye watching the meats. At appropriate times that no clock or schedule can determine, Pappy rises, turns the meats, and slathers them with sauce. Around the room are all the important implements—the brushes, the sauce vats, the hand-labeled jars of secret ingredients, the piles of different kinds of wood—all layered just so for the perfect smoke. This is a working museum, and at $4.25 a pound for ribs and $3.75 for shoulder, you can take home the most valuable exhibits.

SUMMERVILLE

PLANT FARM MUSEUM

Off Rt. 27; 4 mi. N. of Summerville, in Pennville, Ga.;
always visible; visiting hours approx. 6 AM–3 PM daily

> I took the pieces you threw away
> Put them together by night and day
> Washed by rain, dried by sun—
> A million pieces all in one.

. . . So says one of the several dozen signs on the front of Reverend Howard
Finster's Plant Farm Museum, a backyard environment that wins our vote as
America's best. Also known as Finster's Paradise Garden, the Plant Farm
Museum is a cornucopic maze of inspired creation—a million pieces of found
or constructed art; specimens from nature and manufactured gimcracks;
scenes from the Bible and shrines to Henry Ford next to pictures of Sal Mineo;
water wheels and rooms made entirely of mirrors; plots of vegetation and
sidewalks made of poured concrete into which Finster has pressed bits of
mirror, ball-point pens, souvenirs, wrist watches, castor-oil bottles and colored
buttons. There is a collection of tumors given to Finster by a local doctor.
There are miniature alligators preserved in brine. There is the first model of
the Snapper lawn mower, complete with its turtle masthead. There are piles
of discarded TV sets, because Finster's son runs a TV repair shop and Finster
uses the backs of old TVs as boards on which to create his paintings. Finster's
self-portraits are everywhere. Some are miniature cut-outs, only six inches tall,
that he nails to posts or free space on a wall. Some depict him delivering
sermons, or verbally battling with the infidels whom he sees on local television.
Some merely include Finster among hundreds of faces—Washington, Lincoln,
Billy Graham, Jimmy Carter, Dakota Dick, "Alvis" Presley, Lassie the Dog,
and dozens of children and adults who visit the plant farm. Other portraits are
painted onto the sidewalks that wind through the environment. There are nests
of turtle doves and a corpse from a nearby Civil War battlefield . . . This is
a created garden which could have been the inspiration for the expression
"mind-boggling."

If you plan to visit the Plant Farm Museum, give yourself a full day—half
a day to walk through, and half a day to absorb what you have seen and to
recover from Finster's high-energy omnipresence. For the most complex and

fascinating aspect of this man-made universe is the man himself, Reverend Howard Finster. He is always here, either chatting with neighbors, extending his garden, painting new pictures, or explaining to visitors what each and every exhibit, sign, shrine, or object means. He is a charismatic fellow, driven by an inner force to create and to offer his creations to the world. He is over sixty years old, but he left us breathless. Whether you call his spirit "artistic genius" (as we would) or "divine inspiration" (as he does), there is no doubt when you are at the Plant Farm Museum that you are in the presence of a gifted human being of Promethean energies. Unschooled in art and primitive in his craft ("just a grease monkey who got the calling," he says), Howard Finster is nonetheless a national treasure. And what is best is that you can meet him and stroll with him through his greatest creation. That's the way Howard Finster likes it. He and his museum are there for people to enjoy. "You know," he confided, "if I only had the time I could create the whole world here." We believe him.

BARDSTOWN

THE BARTON MUSEUM OF WHISKEY HISTORY

Barton Rd.; Bardstown, Ky.;
Daily 8 AM–5 PM; free

Did you know that George Washington once ran a whiskey distillery? We didn't until we went to the Barton Museum of Whiskey History, and learned of the Father of our Country's fondness for the amber stuff. Neither did we know that the word "booze" originated in the mid-1800s when whiskey-maker E. C. Booz had his bottles in nearly every tavern in America. At one point even honest Abe ran a grocery store that sold liquor. They've got his liquor permit on display here.

This is a complete museum of whiskey history, with everything from silly things like pilfer-proof bottle stoppers to illustrations of the Whiskey Rebellion and photographs of Prohibition-era gangsterism. And, of course, for an up-to-the-moment look at whiskey production, you can take a tour of the Barton distillery with which this museum shares space.

CORBIN

THE MOONBOW

Cumberland Falls State Park, U.S. 90 SW of Corbin, Ky.

There are only two places on earth where you can see a moonbow. One is on the Zambezi River in South Africa. The other is over Cumberland Falls in Kentucky. It occurs about four or five days each month, when the moon is full and atmospheric conditions are right. The light from the moon is refracted in the mist produced by the falls, which results in an arch of white light occurring at the base of the Falls and continuing downstream. The moonbow is a perfect place for wishing, marriage proposals, and midnight picnics.

DEST

WILLIE OWSLEY'S HOUSE

Off Rt. 80, Dest, Ky. (near Hindman);
always viewable

Eighty-year-old Willie Owsley has been a farmer and a creator all his life. If you visit him he will show you the dozens of houses he has designed, all on the backs of other pieces of paper, because he doesn't like to waste things. But the house he lives in now he never designed. He just went ahead and built it. From a distance it looks like a normal wood-frame house. But up close you see the walls just above ground level are made from stone and concrete. Into these walls Willie Owsley has imbedded mementos of his life. There are marbles, bottles, dolls, toy guns, combs, shoe soles, horseshoes, saucers, half-clothed figurines, and geometric shapes, arranged in neat rows or patterns. The overall effect is quite orderly, like a *tableau vivant* of a man's life—three dimensional hieroglyphics that form Willie Owsley's autobiography.

But Willie doesn't see himself as any kind of great artist, just a man who has made the most out of what he's had. His vivid home is a testimonial to his ingenuity.

FORT KNOX

PATTON MUSEUM OF CAVALRY AND ARMOR

Off Rt. 31 W near Chaffee Ave Exit in Keyes Park, Fort Knox, Ky.;
Mon–Fri 9 AM–4:30 PM, weekends and holidays 10 AM–6 PM; free

It was George C. Scott who reintroduced Patton to the postwar generation, but lest that overblown character study take the place of the real man, we suggest a visit to the Patton Museum. There are no actorly histrionics here. There is a Patton Gallery, containing personal artifacts, ranging from his boyhood toys to the famous Patton pistols, a magnum and a Colt .45 he wore throughout "the big show." There are displays of cavalry and armor, weapons from the Revolutionary War to the present, and a "Red" Davis Memorial Library of military literature.

The outdoor exhibit is the one Patton would have loved. It is a park full of tanks. You can wander around and look at the gargantuan machines close up, and on the Fourth of July you can see them in action. Every Independence Day the Patton Museum presents what they call a "Living History Program," in which the tanks, jeeps, and half-tracks are activated, and roll around the park firing blanks instead of bullets.

FORT MITCHELL

THE VENT HAVEN MUSEUM

33 W. Maple St., Fort Mitchell, Ky.;
Open by appointment May 1–Sept. 30,
call Susan Defalaise at (606) 341–0461; free

This is the only ventrological museum in the United States. It is three buildings filled with nearly five hundred "retired" dummies, sitting up, propped up, lying down, boxed everywhere. It is an eerie and fascinating place. Vent Haven has the body (corpse? wooden shell? lifeless form? . . .) of Frank Barnes, Jr., who was the dummy belonging to Frank Barnes, the father of ventriloquism. There are elaborate dummies here who do everything including spit and stick their tongues out—that is, when they are in the company of their "master." What you will not find here are modern dummies like Charlie McCarthy because they have not yet retired. You won't find Howdy Doody here either, because he was a marionette—dummy!

Tours are conducted by Susan Defalaise, who will tell you a little about ventriloquism history since before the Civil War, then conduct you around the dummies, the pictures, books, and memorabilia of this intriguing profession. If you are a little paranoid or if, like us, you saw the seemingly several dozen *Twilight Zones* in which the ventriloquist's dummy takes on a life of his own, you will find this a most disconcerting tour. The little people are everywhere; and there is something undeniably scary about dummies, living-working or dead-retired. They are usually nasty things, saying what their human companion is too decent or too sane to say. And there is nothing reassuring about seeing them all here, apparently lifeless. After all, they are immortal. Made of wood, all they need is a fresh human companion to snap back to life.

Every year, on the weekend after the Fourth of July, there is a ventriloquist's convention in Fort Mitchell. The official entertainment—open free to everyone—is a show staged on the last day of the convention. But for the most bizarre experience of your life, come before the show and watch the ventriloquists talking shop. There are voices everywhere, and after only a short while you may find yourself having an intimate conversation with a dummy and ignoring the man whose lap he's sitting on.

HARLAN

HARLAN POKE SALLET FESTIVAL

Stone Mountain Park, Harlan, Ky.;
last weekend in June

We had long been admirers of Tony Joe White's catchy country-western tune "Poke Sallet Annie," and had even taken to humming the song and singing it in the shower when—in a moment of embarrassment—we learned that he was not singing about "Pork Salad Annie," but rather about *Poke Sallet* Annie; a woman who made salad not of pig meat, but soul sallet, from greens. Sallet is an Elizabethan word that means greens or weeds, and pokeweed or poke sallet is similar to collards or swamp cabbage. That is, it's available to people who don't mind tramping about in some pretty funky terrain to get it. Pokeweed is cooked until it takes on the flavorings of whatever it's cooked with (like hambone), and gets soft enough to eat. Eaten with a plate of ribs or equally soulful food, poke sallet is "good vittles."

As you may have guessed, the Poke Sallet Festival serves up a mess of this stuff, along with some great mountain entertainment in the form of pickin' and flat-foot dancing.

MAYFIELD

HENRY C. WOODRIDGE MONUMENTS

Maplewood Cemetery (U. S. 45, North end of town), Mayfield, Ky.
Daily 7 AM–6 PM; free

Some of us are content to shuck our mortal coils in a pine box. Others choose to be immortalized in stone. Henry C. Woodridge was one of the latter. But he didn't want his stone memorial to be lonely. So not only did he have a sculpture made of himself to perch over his grave, but he had some made of his girl friends, his parents, his brothers, his hunting dogs, a deer and a fox. And then for good measure, he had another statue made of himself. One shows him on a horse. The other is more contemplative, showing him with his head resting on a Bible.

To be sure, these monuments resemble a party more than a solemn remembrance. Everybody, including the animals, looks pretty happy. There's only one unexplained thing—all the statues are facing east. Did Henry know something we don't?

LOUISIANA

BREAUX BRIDGE

CRAWFISH FESTIVAL

Breaux Bridge, La.;
held even-numbered years in the spring;
for specific information call Mulate's Crawfish Plant (318) 332–1420

Breaux Bridge calls itself the Crawfish Capital of the World, and to honor the rare and delicious crawdaddy, they hold a festival every even-numbered year. The date of the festival depends on how the crawfish are running. The annual season is short, and they are biggest in the spring (tapering off to shrimp-size by summer). The best thing about coming here is the chance to eat at Thelma's, a roadside restaurant that is world-famous for its crawfish recipes, and so discriminating that it closes when the supplies are not up to standards of size and taste. While at the festival, you may find your own crawfish and enter the critter in the crawfish races, in which the pokey crustaceans crawl to the outside of a circle from the bull's-eye in which they are dropped. If this sport is too far removed from gustatory gratification, you can try your hand at the crawfish-peeling or crawfish-eating contests.

While here, visit Mulate's Crawfish Plant, and see them boiled, peeled, and packed *en masse* (tours are free). You can buy them here raw or cooked.

BRIDGE CITY

GUMBO FESTIVAL

1701 Bridge City Ave., Bridge City, La.;
2nd weekend in Oct.

Gumbo is the name for okra in Bantu. In Louisiana it has come to mean a dark, stewlike soup that has been thickened with filé powder, and contains shrimp, oysters, frog meat, or duck. It has been immortalized in songs as the one dish above all others that says "Louisiana." Bridge City is Louisiana's Gumbo Capital, and each year they hold a mammoth eating festival centering around several great vats of gumbo. There are cooking and baking contests, and a Mr. Gumbo Pageant, in which the most impressively constructed body builder is crowned to represent Gumbo City.

GALLIANO

LOUISIANA OYSTER FESTIVAL

South LaFourche High School (Highway 308), Galliano, La.;
2nd weekend in July

Almost anywhere outside Louisiana, oysters are a rich man's food—unless one is satisfied with a mere dozen or two. Down here, workmen's lunch pails are filled with oyster sandwiches, and ordinary people think nothing of spending the sultry afternoon sipping Jax beer and downing several dozen oysters between lunch and dinner. The Louisiana Oyster Festival is one place where everybody gets their fill. There are eating contests, and shucking contests, and the election of an oyster king. There are even crab patties and shrimp for variety between the dozens, and a Cajun-spiced seafood dinner Sunday afternoon.

KAPLAN

BASTILLE DAY

Kaplan, La.;
entire weekend prior to or including July 14

Kaplan is the only town in America that officially celebrates the French Independence Day as well as our own. In France they dance in the street. Here in Kaplan, as a reflection of the cultural richness of Louisiana, they have a *fais-do-do*. This is an old Louisiana custom that began when mothers sang their children to sleep with those Cajun words. It has now come to mean the wild, noisy street fairs that Louisianans love so much. Bastille Day here is celebrated to the music of Blackie Forestier and the Cajun Aces, not *La Marseillaise*.

KROTZ SPRINGS

THE CYPRESS NEE SHOP

Rt. 190 W. of Krotz Springs, La.

The Cypress Nee Shop looks like a huge roadside bush with a door in its side. We had no idea what a cypress nee was, so, intrigued by the sign on the top of the bush, we entered. Nobody was in. The bush turned out to be a small square shack, overgrown with foliage. Inside there are shelves along the walls and a table in the center of the room. There are cypress nees everywhere. They are the knobby projections that grow up out of the water around cypress trees. They have been cut and polished to a high gloss, some turned into weirdly shaped lamps and ashtrays, others just "standing" on the shelves. These are not the kind of household decorations one sees in the pages of *House Beautiful*. Even cut and polished, they look as if they should have a little moss draped around them, or at least be set into a small mud puddle.

Aside from the eccentric knobby nees, what is fascinating about this shop is the way it is—or is not—run. At the back of the room there is a cigar box. On the box is a handwritten note from Reverend James Carter, proprietor, explaining that he had to go out for a while, but that if any of the nees catch a customer's fancy, he ought to leave the money (prices are marked on each

FROG FESTIVAL
RAYNE, LOUISIANA
SEPT. 16, 17 & 18. 1977

The Frog Festival, Rayne, La.

Jimmie Rodgers Memorial and Museum, Meridian, Miss.

nee) in the cigar box and take the nee with him. There are bags under the table. We don't know how often Reverend Carter entrusts his business to the good will of passers-by, but we waited a full hour, admiring the nees and the fanciful plaid linoleum floor of the nee shop before we left—four dollars poorer, and one cypress nee ashtray richer.

LAFAYETTE

THE MINI-SWAMP

On Campus at the University of Southern Louisiana
(off Hebard St.) Lafayette, La.;
free

A complete miniature swamp has been built into the center of the campus of the University of Southern Louisiana. In it live alligators, swans, frogs, and God-knows-what-else. It is a gloomy, moss-shrouded place, incongruously surrounded by modern collegiate buildings. Near the college cafeteria there is a walkway that goes over the swamp; here you see students tossing remnants of their junk-food lunch into the muddy water, where it quickly disappears. We have always felt rather apprehensive about venturing into the likes of the Everglades or the Great Dismal, but this little swamp is just right. One can get near enough to the alligators to take a close-up picture, and still rest assured that the gators are so filled up with popcorn, potato chips, and cafeteria frankfurters that they have no interest whatsoever in your thigh.

NEW IBERIA

McILHENNY TABASCO CO.

Avery Island, 8 mi. S. of New Iberia (Hwy 14 to Hwy 329), La.;
Mon–Fri 9 AM–11:45 AM, 1 PM–4:15 PM, Sat 9 AM–11:45 AM;
25¢ vehicle charge to get on island;
tour free; (318) 365–8173

It is *hot* on Avery Island, so hot that snowy egrets, alligators, nutria, and other jungle exotica breed like crazy throughout its 5,000-acres. But of course the McIlhenny Company didn't get its reputation by breeding jungle wildlife. The animals they keep on their paradisiacal tropic island share space with the tabasco pepper plants. A tour shows you both.

In the factory you see peppers mashed and put into barrels, then covered with a thick layer of salt from nearby mines. During the aging process air escapes, but the natural gases are retained to ferment the mash. After three years the substance is diluted with salt and vinegar, then siphoned off into the tiny glass bottles that spell trouble to taste buds all over the world. If you've always felt there was something savage about Tabasco sauce, a visit to its jungle homeland will confirm your feelings.

NEW ORLEANS

BRUCE BRICE'S TREME WALL MURAL

1127 St. Phillips St., New Orleans, La.;
always viewable; free

Treme was a black neighborhood in New Orleans that was torn down to make room for a park. Bruce Brice was moved to paint a protest mural on one of Treme's remaining walls, expressing his anger at the people's displacement. His work has since been discovered by folk-art cognoscenti, and his energetic, untutored style has been celebrated as among the best of the urban street artists.

There are actually two murals here, side by side. One depicts the jazz heritage of the Treme area. There are portraits of the great musicians, colorfully portrayed against the crumbling red-clay bricks. The other mural shows crowds of black New Orleans citizens playing and working. Some ride in horse-drawn carts, others pile into cars. Animals romp at their feet as a jazz band plays. In the background, an octopus-armed policeman points to the people, and directs a wrecking crew to smash the pink-and-red houses. Rats and roaches stream from the buildings. It is a scene that is both frightening and exuberant.

Bruce Brice continues to work in New Orleans, and he hopes to get enough money to keep restoring the mural as time takes its toll on the paint.

MARIE LAVEAU'S GRAVE

St. Louis Cemetery #1, 400 Basin St., New Orleans, La.;
Mon–Sat 8 AM–4:30 PM, Sun 8 AM–4 PM; free

Inside the gates of St. Louis Cemetery #1, twenty-five feet to the left, there is a grave covered with chalked X-marks. It is the grave of the voodoo high priestess Marie Laveau—one of the most superstition-ridden spots in all of America. Marie Laveau lived in New Orleans in the 1800s. She performed black magic rituals in Congo Square and became the most powerful voodoo queen of all time. She has been in her grave for a hundred years; but her voodoo powers have not been forgotten.

Believers come here to mark an X on her tombstone for luck. Even better is to snatch a handful of dirt from her plot and sprinkle this "gris-gris" about the home to ward off evil spells. Some say that to bury a coin in the earth around her grave ensures good fortune.

Like most Southern Louisiana cemeteries, the crypts and tombs at St. Louis #1 are above ground so they're not washed away by the high water table. The vista of elaborate raised monuments around Marie Laveau's grave is appropriately spooky in this spirit-haunted part of the country.

THE PHARMACY MUSEUM

514 Chartres St., New Orleans, La.;
10 AM–5 PM, Tues–Sat.;
Adults: $1, children: 25¢

Upon entering a strange town in a new locale, there is no better place to take the pulse and temperature of the populace than the local drugstore. A quick look at the shelves lets you know whether you are in a Pluto Water Town, a Snake Oil Village, an Ex-Lax Development, or an Extra-Strength Aspirin Berg. The Pharmacy Museum isn't a working pharmacy, but it's still a mirror of modern New Orleans. A few souvenirs are sold, and a few post cards, too, but the emphasis here is on authentic pharmacological history—seen in the antique building and fixtures, and in the museum's collection of medical instruments, potions, placebos, and voodoo powders. It is called *La Pharmacie Française,* and is surprisingly untouristy considering its location in the Vieux Carré. It is to the soul of New Orleans what Caswell-Massey is to New York, or Schwab's to Hollywood.

NEW ROADS

POINTE COUPE DRIVE-IN FUNERAL HOME

Morganza Highway, New Roads, La.;
free; (504) 638–4981

There is a ferry boat that takes you to New Roads, and the trip is like one across the River Styx. In fact, on the other side you will find the Pointe Coupe Funeral Home, the only one in the country that offers drive-in service. The deceased is displayed in a seven-by-five-foot plate-glass window at the side of the building; just like at a drive-in bank or a Jack-in-the-Box hamburger stand, drivers need never get out of their car to do what they came to do. In this case, people come to pay last respects. A register is set up outside the window, requiring you to roll down your car window and reach out if you want to sign, but other than that it's as easy as a drive through a Robo-Wash.

Many who come by, funeral director Alvin Verrette told us, are merely curious, and don't even know the identity of the deceased. We asked him if this disturbed the family of the corpse. "Not at all," he said. "Some ask me to extend the hours he's out there. If you get the window when you die, that's a real honor."

OPELOUSAS

THE YAMBILEE

Yambilee Grounds, Highway 190 W. of Opelousas, La.;
Last weekend in Oct. (318) 948–8848

Towns all over the country hold festivals to celebrate whatever it is they produce the most of, but we haven't seen any that go to it the way Opelousas honors the yam. Notices printed on yam-colored paper are handed out by yambassadors and yamettes, telling you to get to the yamitorium for yaminal judging and selection of the Yam Queen. (Yaminals are animals made from yams, Mr. Potato Head-style; Yam Queens are local girls who walk around carrying armfuls of yams.) There is, of course, a sweet-potato show, with prizes for the largest, sweetest, cutest, longest, widest, heaviest, and oddest. There is a yam slogan contest, a yam dance (only so-named—people dance with people), a yam product display, and a yam invention contest, at which we sampled yam pizza (back to the drawing boards, please) and yam chips (like sweet-potato chips). If you come to the Yambilee, wear orange.

RAYNE

FROG FESTIVAL

Rayne, La.;
3rd week in Sept.; (318) 334–2332

Rayne is the Frog Capital of the World. Pictures, icons, statues, and assorted frog faces are everywhere. Local frogophilia is a natural result of the abundance of these creatures in the swampy countryside. Three companies in this moist community survive on frogs alone. Two export frogs' legs; one supplies scientific specimens. On almost any fair-weathered day, all you have to do is to step off the main road and you can pick up bullfrogs as big as plates from their natural hopping grounds.

But the best time to come to Rayne is the third week in September, when they stage the most spectacular frog festival in the country. Other towns hold frog jumps or frog fries, but nobody revels in reptilian glory quite like Rayne. Each year they publish a book called *Potpourri de Ouaouarons* (an *Ouaouaron* is a bullfrog), a cornucopia of frog facts, frog fun, and frog festivities. Frogs often come here from Croaker College in Sacramento, and last year's *Potpourri* had photos of some of these West Coast stars dressed as rhinestone cowboys, doctors, and graduate students (the latter to symbolize their completion of degree requirements at Croaker College).

During the festival, there are fireworks that light up the sky in frog shapes, frog-eating and -cooking contests, and the selection of the frog with the best body. You will see girls walking through the frog fairgrounds carrying whips and buckets. They are frog jockeys, an elite corps of beauties selected each year to spur on frogs during the jumping contests. Frog jockeys can be seen everywhere, grooming their entries for the three-jump event. Jumping champions from all over the country compete here. Winning frogs return home to glory. Losers never plunk their magic twangers again.

MISSISSIPPI

BOONEVILLE

SORGHUM MUSEUM

Rt. 45, Booneville, Miss.
Mon–Sat 8:30 AM–5:30 PM;
Adults: $1.50, children 8–12: 75¢

We can't quite figure out James Frank, the collector, host, and curator of the Sorghum Museum. If you called up Central Casting and said, "Send me a hick," they might send James Frank. He seems at times like a professional bumpkin, playing the part to perfection. When we arrived at the Sorghum Museum it was just after 8:00 AM and there he was, setting on the porch, whittling. Dressed in old overalls, sporting a scraggy white beard that it must have taken years to grow, he "howdy-doo'd" and "dad-gummed" us through a tour of his museum. It was the collection inside the museum that made us suspect James Frank's "act." You see, if you called up the prop department and said "Send me prime, pristine, vintage antiques," they might send you the contents of the Sorghum Museum.

On the ancient Victrola is an original 78-rpm recording of Jimmie Rodgers singing "T.B. Blues." All the farm implements, household goods, clothes, caskets, cars, and musical instruments in his collection are in mint condition

—perhaps used once, if that, then preserved seemingly immune from the ravages of time. The Sorghum Museum is an extremely informal place, nonetheless. Things are scattered about, piled in corners, stacked up; and visitors are free to wander about or listen to James Frank tell them about the way things were "way back when."

We gave up trying to figure him out. The fact is that this is one of the best and most accesible collections of vintage Americana; and James Frank is a perfectly friendly host. In fact, he is the Sorghum Museum's most intriguing exhibit.

GAUTIER

THE SINGING RIVER

The Pascagoula River off Rt. 90,; Gautier, Miss.
Generally audible in the evenings during August, Sept, & Oct.

At first it's like the sound track of *The Deadly Bees*—a low buzz that you can hear from what seems like downstream on the Pascagoula River. Some call it a singing sound; some hear a melody working its way up the river. We don't want to throw a wet blanket over such romantic fantasies, but to us the Singing River sounds either like the aforementioned swarm of bees or the hum of an electrical generator. Any way you listen to it, however, it is certain that the more you concentrate on the mysterious and unexplained sound, the more you hear it—sort of like a Rorschach test for the ears.

There is a legend that the buzzing is the echo of a death chant sung by a tribe of Pascagoula Indians when the Biloxi tribe pushed them back into the river.

You can hear the sound either from the shore, or from the river on the *Magnolia Blossom,* a sternwheeler out of Gautier.

GUNNISON

WARFIELD QUAIL FARM

Rt. 1, Gunnison, Miss.;
Mon–Fri 7 AM–5 PM, July through April; free

This is not a place we would recommend to bird lovers or to the faint of heart. On Thursday and Friday it's a lovely place; and if you visit on those days it's likely you'll be shown all the cute little quails, some just born, some grown up, some breeder birds, all hopping about in their comfortable little cages. Mike McCaleb, the manager, who calls himself "just an old Southern boy," and who looks not a little like a large quail himself, is as hospitable and as friendly as can be. Even the quails seem to like him. They are timid birds, and run from strangers. But old Mike is their friend, and they seem to hop and chirp when he walks near their cage.

But come Monday, it's a different Mike those quails see. Between Monday morning and early Thursday, the Warfield Quail Farm—the nation's largest processor of Bobwhite Quail—kills three to four thousand birds. It's the kill room that is likely to set your hair on end. For it is here that two ladies sit and kill the quails by cutting off their heads with scissors. The rest of the assembly line blurs in our minds into disconnected images of the egg room, the automatic pluckers, and the freezing chambers.

Frozen birds can be bought here for $20 a dozen.

LORMAN

OLD COUNTRY STORE

Rt. 61, Lorman, Miss.;
Mon–Sat 8:30 AM–6:30 PM, Sun & Holidays noon–6 PM; free

This is a genuinely ancient business establishment, still selling groceries, dry goods and hardware to the local populace. Most of its customers seem over sixty-five years old—black men in overalls coming for their week's supply of tobacco chaws, ladies in bonnets buying sacks of flour and sugar, oldsters just lounging on the porch out front. But the Old Country Store knows that antiquity can be a business asset, too, and so some of its old-time charm has been purposely preserved for the sake of tourists.

The nicest thing here is the floor, made of ancient long-leaf pine and worn smooth by a century of customers. Antique fixtures are still in use, including a tobacco cutter, cheese cutter, ladders on the walls for reaching high places, and a wind-up display case for shoes that enables the merchandise to be rotated. There is also a good selection of locally carved canes and Shankstowne sunbonnets.

To the side of the store is a funky museum annex, once used for the storage of flour barrels. It is now filled with farm implements, and its walls are covered with the calling cards of thousands of visitors who have come here to soak up a bit of the store's authentic old-fashioned atmosphere.

LUCEDALE

PALESTINIAN GARDENS

Lucedale, Miss., Highway 98;
Daily Feb–Oct 8 AM–5 PM, Nov–Jan 8 AM–4 PM;
Adults: $1.00, children: 25¢

Palestinian Gardens is a scale model of the Holy Land at the time of Christ, a three-dimensional map constructed at the scale of one yard to the mile. Mrs. W. H. Jackson who, with her husband, takes care of the gardens calls it a "place book" where, instead of reading the Bible, you walk through it. "When one sees the Jordan, the Dead Sea, Jerusalem and the other places, it makes the Bible come alive," she told us.

A full tour of the Gardens takes about one hour, and involves about a quarter-mile walk up and down the mini-Middle Eastern terrain. You enter at the place where Joshua led the Children of Israel across the Jordan; and after seeing Jericho, Bethlehem, and Jerusalem, you follow in Christ's miniature footsteps toward Golgotha and the Holy Sepulchre.

Some of the cities have a few small carved people in them in order to create that "lived in" look. We felt, however, that the botanical environment tended to detract from the desired authenticity. Lush Mississippi foliage and chirping finches hardly suggest an arid Middle Eastern terrain. But they do make a visit here into an enjoyable stroll through nature, as well as an unusual "reading" of the Bible.

MERIDIAN

JIMMIE RODGERS MEMORIAL AND MUSEUM

39th Ave. in Highland Park, Meridian, Miss.

"Oh, come hear my story of heartaches and sighs . . ." That is the way Jimmie

Rodgers introduced one of his best-known songs. It is a line that perfectly expresses the simple and pure spirit of the music sung by "America's Blue Yodeler," the father of country music. Jimmie sang the wandering blues until he died in 1933 at age thirty-five of tuberculosis—a condition he grieved over in his song, "T.B. Blues."

Jimmie was laid to rest in Bonita Cemetery in his hometown of Meridian, Mississippi. Every year on the anniversary of his death Meridianites hold a country music jamboree around the memorial they have built to their favorite son in Highland Park. (The festival is held during the week of May 26th—the date of his death.)

The memorial consists of a museum, a shiny red locomotive outside, and a monument. The museum building is a reconstruction of an old railroad depot —the kind that Jimmie, "The Singing Brakeman," might have wandered through during the 1920s. Inside there are mementos of his life alongside a wealth of train memorabilia—souvenirs of the kind of traveling life he sang about. Outside in front of the red locomotive is the monument. It shows Jimmie in his famous "thumbs-up" pose, guitar in lap, trainman's cap on his head. Below him are inscribed these words:

> "His is the music of America
> He sang the songs of the people he loved,
> Of a young nation growing strong.
> His was an America of glistening rails
> Thundering boxcars and rain-swept nights
> Of lonesome prairies, great mountains,
> And a high blue sky.
> He sang of the bayous and the cotton fields,
> The wheated plains, of the little towns, the
> Cities, and of the winding rivers of America.
>
> We listened, We understood."

NATCHEZ

MAMMY'S CUPBOARD RESTAURANT

Rt. 61 S. of Natchez, Miss.;
Always visible; restaurant open Mon–Sat 8 AM–7 PM

Built in 1940, Mammy's Cupboard is a roadside attraction that has etched itself into the American traveler's psyche. Almost every road-person we know has seen it, or seen pictures of it. What it is is a restaurant in the shape of a Mammy. She is twenty-eight feet tall and wears a five-foot chain necklace. Her earrings are horseshoes. You eat inside of this Mammy, in the domed area under her skirt.

The restaurant was originally opened to serve food to those few tourists who came to Natchez to see its ante-bellum houses. Now, Natchez and the mansions are big tourist business, with their own more predictably designed eateries. But Mammy remains, an eyesore to those Natchezites who want only the whitest and most graceful mansions of the past to mark the city's history. To the connoisseur of roadside Americana, Mammy is a prime exhibit—far more interesting than the carefully packaged Natchez mansion tours.

A bonus on your visit to Mammy's is the surprisingly good fried chicken served here. "It's terrific 99 percent of the time," a regular customer told us. We were lucky—we found it to be a crisply fried, tender dish served with home-cut French fries and presweetened tea. Another fringe benefit of a visit here is that Mrs. Vedrenne, the owner and cook, will, if not too busy, bring out your meal and sit down with you, family style, and talk as if you were old friends.

OXFORD

ROWAN OAK

Old Taylor Rd., 1 mi. S. of Oxford, Miss.;
10 AM–noon, 2 PM–4 PM Mon–Fri; 10 AM–noon Sat. (Old Taylor Rd.)

William Faulkner named his home Rowan Oak because legend has it that the presence of a rowan tree (also called a mountain ash) discourages unwanted intruders. Today Rowan Oak is maintained as a home, not a museum, and is as relatively inaccessible as Faulkner would have wanted. There are no signs pointing the way, no parking lot for visitors and tour buses; no souvenir stands or snack machines. To get here you've got to ask around Oxford until you find someone who knows where the Faulkner home is. And when you come upon it, it is as if he still lives there. You have to walk up the long, straight road lined with oak trees and knock on the front door. Having made it this far, you have proven you are deeply interested in Faulkner, not just a gawking tourist, and are treated with full honors by the chivalrous graduate students who stay here and—as personally as possible—act as guides. Howard Bahr showed us around, much as somebody might show a person around their private home. There is no prepared speech, no lecture, no pretentious awe at Faulkner's greatness. Bahr knew his Faulkner, but spoke of him less as a grand eminence than as a fellow Southern gentleman. As a matter of fact, Bahr's courtly manners, worthy of a Colonel Bayard Sartoris (or a Colonel William C. Falkner, William's great-grandfather, a Civil War gallant) were among the most memorable—and appropriate—aspects of our visit to Rowan Oak.

The house is preserved exactly as it was in Faulkner's lifetime. In his study, on the wall, is written his outline for *A Fable*. Across the room is his old Underwood typewriter; next to it a bottle of horse liniment and an ashtray he had made from an artillery shell casing. Outside is the stable he built, and the old kitchen he used as a smokehouse.

But the memorabilia is less interesting than the carefully preserved tone of the place. It remains private, intimate, and gracious. It is these intangible qualities, so often missing from the "home-shrines" of famous people, that make a visit to Rowan Oak a very special experience for the Faulkner enthusiast.

RALEIGH

TOBACCO-SPITTING CONTEST

Rt. 18, Billy John Crumpton's Pond, Raleigh, Miss.;
Last Sat in July

The Tobacco-Spitting Contest is actually two different contests—one for distance, one for accuracy. Nobody has ever won both. Qualifying spit-offs are held during the morning of the contest and in the afternoon the championship matches are staged. Each contestant in the accuracy spit gets three shots at a target. The combined total score determines the winner. To determine the distance champ, each spitter gets three tries. The longest shot wins. The 1977 distance champion was Mark Wilks, who sent his clam flying twenty-eight feet, ten inches. Mark is eighteen years old, and has been entering the contest for the last five years. He practises one hour every day, and intends to come back in '78 to defend his crown and to try and top Don Snyder's all-time record of thirty-two feet, six inches.

There have been several woman entrants in recent years, although none has yet made it into the finals. One contestant speculated that her lack of success was due to inadequate opportunity to practise, as well as her personal affinity for snuff, which is not allowed in the contest.

TUPELO

ELVIS PRESLEY BIRTHPLACE

Elvis Presley Park, Saltillo Rd., Tupelo, Miss.;
Tues–Sun 2 PM–5 PM,
Admission: 25¢, or by appointment, call 842–6640

"Who would have ever thought that Elvis Presley would amount to anything?" asked Mrs. Billie Boyd, the woman who almost single-handedly has made a shrine out of the two-room shack in which Elvis was born. It's a tiny house —what's called the "shotgun style"; that is, two rooms lined up, double-barrel fashion. Elvis was born in the Depression. His parents were too poor to have a place of their own, so they were staying here with the grandparents. At the time, Saltillo Road was far outside the city limits of Tupelo. It was the sticks, the bad side of town. Times were so bad that the Presleys couldn't keep up payments even on this place. It was repossessed and rented out for several years. For a long time it remained vacant, and in disrepair.

That's when Mrs. Billie Boyd instituted the East Heights Garden Club and made it her business to turn the dilapidated shack into a national shrine. She has made everything as authentic as possible—although the area is no longer a soulful swamp, and the house does look a bit cleaner than it might have looked when Saltillo Road was only a muddy path running through the woods. There are lace curtains on the windows and the white siding and green roof and porch swing are painted like new.

Mrs. Boyd says that there are rumors Elvis once returned to his home—but only under cover of darkness.

VICKSBURG

U.S. ARMY ENGINEER WATERWAYS EXPERIMENT STATION

Halls Ferry Rd., Vicksburg, Miss.;
Guided Tours 10 AM & 2 PM Mon–Fri, or self-guided tours 8 AM–5 PM Mon–Fri;
Free

This is one of the best tours in the country for those with a microcosmic sensibility. Unlike the Chesapeake Bay Hydraulic Model, which exactly duplicates that body of water in miniature, this W.E.S. (to use their acronym) is a miniature generalized world. There are some specific topographies that are duplicated, such as the Niagara River and Falls, New York Harbor, and a simulation of DeGray Lake, Arkansas (in fact, one of the ego-inflating thrills of a visit here is the opportunity to turn the flow of Niagara Falls on and off), but for the most part W.E.S. tries to come up with universally applicable findings.

To this end, there are weapons-effects study areas, where you see miniature rivers, dams, and locks being blown up; an environmental laboratory that throws miniature waste into miniature rivers and lakes and then studies the ecological effects; a soils and pavements department that develops portable landing mats for military aircraft; and a hydraulics laboratory that not only studies navigation, flood control, etc., but studies *how to study* these phenomena by experimenting with different ways of constructing miniature worlds.

If you have the time, take the guided tour. They're likely to set off atomic blasts and cause a few floods just for you.

NORTH CAROLINA

COLLARD FESTIVAL

Downtown Ayden, N.C.;
2nd weekend in September

Last year's collard-eating champion consumed five pounds of boiled greens in thirty minutes. Collards—if you are a Yankee—are like spinach only tougher and stronger-tasting. They are served in an iron brew of a broth usually flavored with bits of pork or hambone. They are the most invigorating tonic we can imagine. They provide instant comprehension of the nutritional mythology at work in Popeye cartoons.

The Ayden Collard Festival is the most healthy food festival we can imagine. A Collard Queen is crowned, there is dancing in the streets, and everybody spends the day eating lots and lots of collard greens—as an entrant in the eating contest, or simply as a festival-goer who is here to celebrate one of the foods that makes eating a favorite Southern pastime.

BAILEY

COUNTRY DOCTOR MUSEUM

Rt. 264, Bailey, N.C.;
Weds & Sun 2 PM–5 PM; free

Some may find this hard to believe, but there was a time when doctors came around to visit sick people in their homes. This practice was known as "a house call."

Country doctors did little else than make house calls. Often traveling late at night, any time of the year, they covered the back roads of America delivering babies, setting limbs, doling out pills, or maybe just offering spiritual support to those in need.

The Country Doctor Museum is a tribute to this old-fashioned kind of "sawbones." It was put together by two country doctors themselves, one the daughter of a long line of other country doctors. Some of the displays here are quaint, some mysterious, and some—by modern standards—barbaric. There are leech jars and scarificators for emptying the patient of "bad blood," pocket spittoons for victims of "galloping consumption," apothecary jars, bivalve speculums, bone-handled delivery forceps, and a huge, horrible-looking gunshot forceps from the time of the Civil War.

The museum tells of the kind of improvisation that made the country doctor a hero in his time. When they first started doing their rounds in automobiles, they were able to shine the car's headlights into the windows of small farmhouses to provide light for operations. When they had to recruit help, they always chose women—because they fainted less than men. And the best surgeon was always the fastest. Before anesthesia, a forty-second amputation technique was what made one doctor more popular than the one-minute man. But our favorite story here about a country doctor making do with very little is this, told by a Dr. Macartney: "A three-year-old girl had inserted a small bean in her ear. The bean had pushed up against the eardrum, had softened and swelled to some extent, and we failed to dislodge it by any of the usual means. We procured some bicycle spokes and, by bending and sharpening these, improvised some satisfactory hoes and spuds."

Also at the Country Doctor Museum there is a Medicinal Garden, where "healing plants" and herbs are grown. The garden is an exact replica of the Medicinal Garden in Padua, Italy—the oldest botanical garden in the world.

BARNARDSVILLE

BIG IVY RAMP FESTIVAL

Dillingham Rd (The Big Ivy Community Center), Barnardsville, N.C.;
1st Sat. in May

We have often mused about what might happen if somebody decided to market ramps on a nationwide scale. Somehow this pungent, scallion-like vegetable doesn't fit into that mass of food products, refrigerator deodorizers, and breath aids that promise us an odorless life. Perhaps it is as a reaction to this anti-odor media blitz that small towns in North Carolina, Tennessee, and West Virginia reserve one day a year to celebrate the foul-smelling ramp.

In Barnardsville, you can by ramp T-shirts ("Ramp eaters make Stinkin' Lovers"), ramp bumper stickers, and raw ramps. A Ramp Queen is crowned with a tiara made from woven ramps. Teary-eyed contestants try to eat more ramps than anyone else (the record is forty-six at one sitting), and average folks enjoy all the ramps they can eat at a public dinner.

Actually, the ramp *tastes* quite sweet. It is only its odor that has made it a pariah among vegetables, allowed into town only once a year, "and cooked downwind!" a local ramp-eater volunteered.

BENSON

MULE DAYS CELEBRATION

Singing Grove Park, Benson, N.C.;
third week in Sept.; call (919) 894–3825

This is one time of the year that the hardworking mule gets a break. The citizens of Benson gather in celebration of all things mulish, and elect from their town's stubborn ranks the Ugliest Mule, The Oldest Mule, The Youngest Mule and other specimens of mule pulchritude. Winners are draped with blankets and crowns and paraded around the town park, or just left alone to be stubborn and ornery.

Meanwhile the residents of Benson elect a human beauty queen, put on a rodeo and a barbecue, dance in the streets, and generally make jackasses of themselves. The most interesting contest at this celebration is the "scoop race," in which cowboys sit on large shovels attached to mules' behinds. The object is to get the mule to drag the cowboy and shovel across a finish line.

CHARLOTTE

BILLY GRAHAM'S BIRTHPLACE

The IBM Building, 4601 Park Rd, Charlotte, N.C.;
outside; no admission

Billy Graham sure has a nice mom. We had circled Charlotte unsuccessfully trying to find Billy Graham's birthplace, and so sent out tracer letters. Months later a soft, sun-colored piece of stationery came to us with a little sticker in the corner: "Mrs. W. F. Graham."

Billy's mother said that Billy's birthplace was torn down years ago because the Grahams couldn't meet the taxes on it. A giant IBM building was eventually built in its place, but IBM wasn't totally heartless, and put a nice plaque outside and a marker showing people exactly where he came into this world. According to Mrs. Graham, "IBM keeps the plot well-manicured, also some lovely landscaping around it, and that's about it." The rest of her letter explained that "a good snap" could be had outside the building, near the plaque, if we venture there again. We pass on this advice to you, straight from Billy's mother's pen.

IRMO

THE OKRA STRUT

Recreation Center, Irmo, N.C.;
1st week in Oct. (803) 772–2802

We once endured an embarrassing communications breakdown in a North Carolina restaurant. The waitress seemed to be asking if we wanted a side dish of "bald okra." Such a question seemed to make sense, since the one thing many people find objectionable about okra is its hairy texture. She was, of course, saying "boiled okra," and the combination of her accent and our ambivalent feelings about the odd-textured vegetable made us wish that this restaurant had somehow invented a new strain of hairless pods.

No such produce has been developed, but that doesn't bother the people of Irmo, North Carolina, who hold a "strut" each year to celebrate okra. Events begin with an okra parade. (They have not developed walking okra, either. It is called the okra parade because the grand marshal wears a necklace made of pods.) The festival winds up at the recreation center, where there are, of course, okra-eating contests, okra-cooking contests, and plenty of "bald" food for those who don't like Irmo's favorite vegetable.

LINVILLE

HIGHLAND GAMES AND GATHERING OF SCOTTISH CLANS

Grandfather Mountain, MacRae Meadows, Linville, N.C.;
2nd full weekend in July
$5 per adult per day; under 12 free; No Pets

Tartans, kilts, sheepdogs, and bagpipes do not fit into stereotyped pictures of Dixie, but you'll find all of them at this traditional gathering of Scotsmen in North Carolina. The point they want to make here is that there are deep Scottish roots in the Carolinas; in fact a lot of what we think of as "mountain talk" can be traced back to the Britannic tongues of the people who first settled here.

There are two days of piping, dancing, and athletic events such as the hammer toss, cabar toss, the hop-step-and-jump, and fifty-six-pound weight throw. Kilts and bonnets are the favored attire, and the sponsoring clans invite participants to display their own tartans.

SINGING ON THE MOUNTAIN GOSPEL FESTIVAL

The MacRea Meadows on Grandfather Mtn (U.S. 221), Linville, N.C.;
4th Sun in June; free

This is the gospel-singing extravaganza of the year, held in the open air on the side of Grandfather Mountain. People attend wearing everything from shark-skin and leisure suits to baggy overalls and sunbonnets.. There are preachers from the old school regaling all who will listen about the damnation that awaits as payment for drink and sin; and there are farmers selling homemade apple jack and cherry cider by the side of the road. Over the years, performers as famous as Johnny Cash have come to join in the singing along with local stars like Johnny Dee Loudermilk and Happy John Coffey. This festival is nonprofit, non-denominational, and disorganized. But every year it works, as it has been doing for over half a century. Their motto is 'Who so ever will may come.'

MOREHEAD

OLD QUAWK'S DAY

City Park, Morehead, N.C.;
2nd week in March (919) 26–6831

We don't know of another hideous human who has served so happy an end. Old Quawks, the legend says, was the meanest man in Carteret County—and Carteret is a county known for fighting, cussing, and just plain ornery folks. But Quawks was the worst. One day he went to sea, after being warned that bad storms were brewing. But he cursed the person who warned him, and disappeared, followed by a lone night heron screeching its harsh call.

The town couldn't have been happier to see Old Quawk go to the bottom of the deep, so they have celebrated every year since with Old Quawk's Day. The day's main event is "Quawk-calling," in which contestants are judged according to who makes the ugliest-sounding screech. There is a flounder-flinging contest too, usually accompanied by the best of the Quawk calls.

We can't think of a better way to let off steam than a full day of screeching and flounder-flinging. Try it next time your friends come for dinner—or go to Morehead City the second week in March, where the mayhem is organized.

MORGANTOWN

BROWN MOUNTAIN LIGHTS

Off N.C. 181 between Morgantown and Lenoir, N.C.
(At night only in Fall)

Some say they are the lights of UFOs, peering down through the night air to get a glimpse of North Carolinians necking in their parked cars on the side of Brown Mountain. Others say they are the glow of a spirit belonging to a man whose corpse was found at the foot of the mountain. Scientists say they are an electrical discharge, like slow lightning, that turns the air over Brown

Mountain from a pale red glow to something that occasionally resembles skyrockets.

The more spectacular sightings of the lights are indeed perfect to neck by; they have, in fact, given rise to the belief that if a courting couple parks here and sees the lights, their love is true. If the lights fail to show . . . forget the affair.

They are best seen on a clear, moonless night.

MURPHY

THE LARGEST TEN COMMANDMENTS IN THE WORLD

Field of the Wood, Highway 294, W. of Murphy, N.C., E. of Turtletown and Ducktown, Tenn.,
sunup to sundown daily; free

If it is true that anything gets better as it gets bigger, then here in the "Biblical park" called Field of the Wood are the best Ten Commandments anywhere. They are the familiar ten admonitions, carved in stone letters five feet high and four feet wide. They are enclosed in a border that measures three hundred feet across and three hundred and fifty steps from bottom to top.

At the top of those three hundred and fifty steps is a colossal likeness of the New Testament, thirty-four feet wide and twenty-four feet high, open to Matthew.

Visible one mile away is the "All-Nations Cross," the largest of its kind in the world, three times larger than the "World's Largest Wood and Bronze Crucifix" in Indian River, Michigan. The All-Nations Cross is 150 feet high, 115 feet wide, and is perched on top of 2,210-foot All-Nations Mountain; and can accommodate flagpoles of all the nations of the world.

NEW BERN

FRED THE HORSE

The New Bern Firemen's Museum, 1420 Broad St., New Bern, N.C.;
Tues–Sun 9:30 AM–noon, 1 PM–5 PM; free

New Bern is an exceptional town, a town chock-full of "firsts:" the first death sentence issued by a U. S. Federal Court; the first torpedo put to practical test; the first four-faced clock on a public building in the state, "if not the world." It is a town also well-stocked with "oldest" things: oldest theater in America; oldest "self-kicking machine;" "oldest instance of paternity on medical record." (We could not verify these last two claims, having no idea what a self-kicking machine is, and not understanding how any one place could be the "father of paternity." Both facts are given as a matter of record at the New Bern Firemen's Museum.)

Fred is not the oldest stuffed horse we have seen, nor is he any kind of "first" we can think of, but for our money he's New Bern's nicest attraction. There wasn't room for all of him in the Firemen's Museum, so only his head and neck are displayed in a glass case as a memorial to his heroic life. The official literature describes him as a horse driven just after the turn of the century "by John Taylor, colored." Fred had put in seventeen years of service with the fire department when in 1925, while answering a false alarm, he succumbed to a heart attack. New Bern didn't want to forget him. They say he knew the numbers and locations of all the most frequently used fireboxes in town.

PINEHURST

WORLD GOLF HALL OF FAME

Gerald R. Ford Blvd., Pinehurst, N.C.;
Daily 9 AM–5 PM; Adults: $2, children 8–17: 50¢

North Carolina is the Golf State. Pinehurst is the Golf Capital of the state. And so the World Golf Hall of Fame is here. It was inaugurated by the nation's ex-first golfer, Gerald R. Ford, who follows in the spiked footsteps of Dwight Eisenhower, Lawrence Welk, and Bob Hope. Surprisingly, golf is not an all-American game. In fact, as the Hall of Fame demonstrates, it was being played in Scotland centuries ago. One sees here the evolution of the tee and club, and a mock-up of what a club-maker's shop was like years ago. And of course there are the greats of the game, enshrined here at Pinehurst's Second Hole.

As we browsed, we pondered the nature of golf, which is called "the most human of games"—presumably because it does not involve tackling, pushing, gouging, or even running and yelling—and we wondered, why is it that people spend years trying to knock a tiny dimpled ball across endless grass into an unseen hole? "Because it is like life," the Hall of Fame told us.

SALUDA

COON-DOG BARKING CONTEST

Main St., Saluda, N.C. (Rt. 176 E. of Hendersonville);
1st Sat after July 4; free

Each year Saludians honor that faithful Southern pet, the coon dog. Festivities begin with a coon-dog parade through town, for which homemade floats are constructed around actual trees with raccoons on top. Around the tree, of course, is a pack of coon hounds going nuts. There is a public dinner, after which the entire town (population 600) turns out to watch the coon-dog judging. Hounds are awarded prizes for beauty and barking. Barking is judged by the number of barks, bays, and howls a dog lets loose during one minute at the base of a coon-topped tree.

We are told that the population of this town has been honoring the hound this way for over twenty years, and that while the coon-dog population has stayed the same, the coon population has increased dramatically. Could it be that the Saludian hounds are all bark and no bite?

SHEPARDS

KILROY BAUMGARDNER'S HAUNTED HOUSE, JUNK STORE, AND HUBCAP COLLECTION

Rt. 115–21 in Shepards, N.C., just N. of Mooresville;
Daily 6 AM–9 PM

"That is an *outstanding* store," the black farmer told us as he saw us gawking at the exterior. He laughed as he got into his battered pick-up, because he knew that we were in for a treat. Kilroy's store *is* outstanding. It is to junk what the Smithsonian is to museums: he's got the market cornered.

Kilroy himself is a quiet man. His name is sewn in script onto his gas-jockey shirt. He told us his wife doesn't like a lot of miscellanea in her house, so she makes him take it all down here. He has been doing so for several decades. Looking through his merchandise is like going on an archaeological field trip. On top there is junk from the 1970s; below that, from the '60s and '50s and '40s. It all seems randomly arranged. TV ornaments in the shape of flamingos share space with artificial limbs. There are jars of fishing worms and dough to catch catfish; pickled pigs' feet; time-worn comic books; a penny-candy machine from World War II (you shoot a coin at Hitler's face to win your candy). Kilroy's supplies are endless—you get the feeling that if you looked hard enough you could find anything you'd need . . . and plenty no one could ever imagine needing.

The haunted house is next door to the store. It is an old white house, covered from foundation to roof with hubcaps Kilroy has been collecting since 1946. We asked him why he called it haunted. "Because," he drawled, "when the wind blows, the hubcaps sing; and besides, a man who built coffins used to live inside." Now the house is a silvery monument to automania, surrounded by Kilroy's store, a few rusting vintage cars and hearses, steam cabinets, paperback book racks, silk stocking displays, dry goods, wet goods, hard goods—an amazingly eclectic collection that is a tribute to one man's curatorial magnetism.

SNEAD'S FERRY

SNEAD'S FERRY SHRIMP FESTIVAL

Snead's Ferry Bridge over New River, off Highway 172, Snead's Ferry, N.C.;
2nd Sat. in Aug.

Shrimp is a food that no restaurant ever serves enough of. Like truffles or Beluga caviar, they are doled out stingily, in shrimp cocktails or geometric arrangements designed to make three or four little fellows look like more. Sneads Ferry has the answer to such miserliness, beginning with the "Shrimp-a-roo," at which a huge outdoor kitchen dishes up endless plates of shrimp, flounder, and "Dot's Special Fish Stew." Shrimps are eaten and celebrated throughout the day, and we can practically guarantee that a visit to Snead's Ferry is sure to satisfy the most deep-seated prawn cravings.

SPIVEY'S CORNER

NATIONAL HOLLERING CONTEST

Spivey's Corner (Highways 13 & 421), N.C.;
3rd Sat. in June

Hollering, Carolina style, began long before there were telephones. When one wanted to get in touch with a neighbor, one hollered. Simple enough, but it became necessary to distinguish one farmer's holler from another, and so each man and woman developed an individual call. Some yelp; some send forth long, uninterrupted cries; some vary their holler with rhythmic grunts or abrupt changes of pitch. It is said that farmers could communicate for distances of several miles this way, aided by the natural acoustics of the Carolina hills.

Now that most folks around Spivey's Corner have telephones, they don't do much hollering, but every third Saturday in June, local bellow power is aired at the National Hollering Contest. Prizes for loudness and originality are awarded to both male and female contestants. Last year a man did a hollering duet with his dog, and the woman hollering champ was a 300-pound redhead whose warbles and shrieks were said to have seriously affected the local water table.

Hollering is a fine country tradition, and this is one of the most exciting and unusual contests we know. But after a day of it, we give thanks to Alexander Graham Bell for having invented the telephone. Life in most places is noisy enough without hollering from building to building.

CHARLESTON

MIDDLETON LANCING TOURNAMENT

Middleton Place, 14 mi. NW of Charleston on Highway 61, Charleston, S.C.;
3rd week in Oct.;
adults: $4, children: $2

Middleton Place was one of the great rice plantations of the eighteenth century. Every October it stages a lancing tournament as part of its Plantation Days Celebration, during which it aims to capture the spirit of genteel eighteenth-century fun. While most of us associate knights, jousting, and the like with a much earlier period, the fact is that these aristocratic activities were a characteristic of leisure life on Colonial American plantations. The game played at Middleton is called lancing, also known as "tilting the rings," the point of which is to ride full speed ahead on a horse and try to collect a series of small, dangling rings on the end of a lance. The men who ride, and the "ladies fair" who watch, all dress in Colonial costumes. The knight who collects the greatest number of rings has the honor of choosing his "Queen of Beauty," with whom he enjoys the rest of the day's activities.

Other events at Middleton include a jumping exhibition, a "Parade of Ladies Faire," and a game of musical chairs on horseback. Throughout the afternoon, spectators can enjoy plates of barbecued chicken, although somehow the sloppy process of eating chicken seems out of place amid these elegant activities.

Middleton Place, which can be visited any day of the year, is surrounded by America's oldest landscaped gardens—terraces, ornamental lakes, and allées. There is a stableyard with horses, mules, goats, peacocks, and rabbits, and working exhibits of tanning, corn-grinding and candle-making—all part of Middleton's well-tended "Colonialism."

COLUMBIA

TUNNELVISION

The Farm Credit Bank Building (North Wall), 1401 Hampton St.,
Columbia, S.C.; free

It would not surprise us if Columbia, South Carolina reported an extraordinarily high incidence of people and cars running into brick walls—one brick wall in particular. It is the north wall of the Farm Credit Bank Building, upon which has been painted a spectacularly realistic tunnel. It is four stories high, and appears to be surrounded by craggy rocks. "Through" the tunnel you can see a low-hanging sun and a single twinkling star. It is uncannily accurate in color and perspective, the best modern example of *tromp l'oeil* we have seen.

It was painted by a local artist named Blue Sky who wanted it to be a "refuge for contemplation both day and night." At night it is illuminated to look like the evening version of the same tunnel that appears to be there during the day. A source of contemplation it most definitely is. A refuge, Mr. Sky, it is not. It is one of the most disconcerting urban vistas anywhere.

DARLINGTON

JOE WEATHERLY STOCK CAR MUSEUM

3 mi. W. of Darlington at the Speedway, S.C.;
June–Sept Daily 9AM–5PM,
Oct–May Mon–Fri 9AM–noon, 2PM–5PM, Sun 2PM–5PM; free

Here is the car that belonged to the man whom Tom Wolfe called The Last American Hero. The man who, to locals, was just a "good ol' boy"—but a *real* good one, and fast: Junior Johnson. Here's Junior's '63 Chevy, the one he took to first place at Atlanta and Charlotte without the backing of General Motors. He did it like a hero, on his own; and his car now sits in this hall of honor among the great stock cars of the South.

The legendary names are everywhere in this museum: Cannonball Baker, Fireball Roberts, Lee Petty, Cotton Owens, and Joe Weatherly himself, after whom the museum is named. Joe had seen the museum they have in Indianapolis to honor the tube-shaped "cucumber cars" that race there, and he felt it was about time that the all-American sport of stock-car racing got its due, too. The museum was begun shortly after he died at Riverside.

Junior Johnson's Chevy may have the most charisma, but it wasn't the winningest car of all time. That would be Curtis Turner's 1965 ragtop, on display here with pictures of its "reincarnation" as a hardtop, which is the way it won the Southern 500. Our vote for most beautiful car would go to Fireball Roberts's lavender Ford; and for most futuristic car to Herb Thomas's Hudson Hornet; and for most dignified car to Buck Baker's smooth honey of a 1950 Olds . . . There are dozens here to choose from.

The most touching exhibit is little Joe Weatherly's black-and-white saddle oxfords, the shoes that were his trademark.

There is also a room full of illegal parts used during the short history of stock-car racing, displays of engines, trophies, tires, and personalized driving helmets. There is one car you can sit in and pretend to drive around the two-mile Darlington oval. We suggest you give this a try, and thereby let off enough steam to avoid getting a speeding ticket on the way home.

HARTSVILLE

THE WORLD BEHIND YOUR WALL SOCKET

H. F. Robinson Nuclear Plant, Old Camden Hwy, Hartsville, S.C.;
Mon–Fri 9AM–5PM; free

The name of this place made us think of H. P. Lovecraft's ghoulish fables, in which whole civilizations of grotesque beings live on the other side of one's wallboard. Actually, it is just a tiny museum set up to explain how electricity is made from nuclear power. The exhibits are the kind of thing one finds in science and technology museums, but on a small and intimate scale. There are bicycles to pedal and thereby generate enough power to light up a bulb, and colorful "talking" exhibits of what goes on inside a reactor.

And while you're in the neighborhood, the road to The World Behind Your

Marine Corps Recruit Depot, Parris Island, S.C.

National Hollering Contest, Spivey's Corner, N.C.

Wall Socket takes you past one of our favorite-named eateries, the Nucleus Pit Bar B Que.

MOUNTAIN REST

HILLBILLY DAY

Mountain Rest, S.C.; (8 mi. above Walhalla on S.C. 28)
July 4, 1978

The Fourth of July 1978 will be the eighteenth annual Hillbilly Day held in Mountain Rest, and we can hardly imagine a more down-home way to spend this national holiday. The day is filled with corny fun activities such as egg-throwing, the greased pole, the greased pig, tugs o' war—and shoe kicks and rolling-pin throws "for the gals." Or you can just relax on the grass with a plate of Brunswick stew, barbecue and a jug of 'shine and listen to the fiddle contests. Although most of the townsfolk here in overalls and straw hats are a put-on, the clog-dancing, guitar-playing, and hillbilly music are the real McCoy.

OYOTUNJI

THE KINGDOM OF OYOTUNJI

Oyotunji, S.C. (near Rt. 21); $1.50

Oyotunji is a kingdom of one hundred black Americans who have seceded from the United States. "The black man is not a European," King Efuntola explains, "and we refuse to be Europeanized." As you enter the twelve-acre kingdom, a sign announces "You are now leaving the United States of America." In fact, the village does look like Africa—or at least like the Hollywood Africa we have seen in *Mogambo* and *Hatari.* Tribal drums are used for communication; goats wander the dirt streets; and tourists are welcome to take pictures, purchase "native" crafts, and take home some authentic voodoo spells. There is a village altar, on which goats, frogs, whiskey, and cigars are offered as sacrifices.

Oyotunji's economy relies on tourism and revenue from its voodoo-based religion. Payments are made for the performance of rituals and the production of appropriate curses. The citizens of Oyotunji are perfectly serious about their venture, and believe that it will eventually lead to an African empire on the East Coast. Efuntola, their king, is an ex-dancer from New York who has seven wives.

PARRIS ISLAND

MARINE CORPS RECRUIT DEPOT

Rt. 21, Parris Island, S.C.;
always open; free

We don't train recruits . . . We make Marines.
—U.S.M.C. Brochure
Behold a Marine . . . A mere shadow and reminiscene of humanity.
—Henry David Thoreau

We had assumed that Marine training was some sort of top-security operation; that the turning of men into Marines was a secret process known only to members of that elite corps. But Parris Island is open to any citizen, and once on the island you're free to roam around almost as if you owned it. There are some sensible restrictions—no trespassing downrange at the rifle range, and no snooping in the men's barracks. Gunnery Sergeant Matthews also cautioned us about picnicking near the shore, where combat maneuvers are held. But other than that, visitors are free to see everything, from close order drill to bayonet and pugil training. You can even try your hand at the ups and downs and ropes and abutments of the "confidence course."

Since a recruit's day starts before 7:00 A.M. and proceeds vigorously until after dinner, we were advised that visitors coming at night would find little to observe except bone-weary sacked-out leathernecks.

Rather than the bleak isle of physical torture we had imagined, Parris Island turned out to be a nicely gardened community with every modern convenience, from a movie theater to a bowling alley. Only the "hup-two!" of marching troops and battle cries of charging soldiers distinguish it from any Small Town, U.S.A.

Tunnelvision, Columbia, S.C.

Greetings from the

ANNUAL "CHITLIN STRUT"

The WORLD CHITLIN CAPITAL
SALLEY, SOUTH CAROLINA

The Chitlin Strut, Salley, S.C.

PARRIS ISLAND MUSEUM

Marine Corps Recruit Depot, Parris Island, S.C.;
Mon–Fri 8AM–4:30PM, weekends and holidays: 10AM–4:30PM; free

The Parris Island Museum tells all about the Marine Corps. It is a large, two-story building that contains everything from Marine art (some by, some about Marines) to examples of what Marine rations have looked like in various wars. In the rotunda of the Museum there are displays of uniforms placed against appropriate period backgrounds. A spotlight in the ceiling illuminates a bronze model of the raising of the flag on Iwo Jima. To the right is the Contemporary Room, which tells the whole grueling story of how men are turned into Marines during the eleven weeks of recruit training. There are pictures of heads being shaved, drill instruction, marksmanship, and pugil training. A talking mannequin tells you all about it.

Elsewhere in the museum are photographs of Marine history, displays of weaponry, a library of historical books, and a room dedicated to the Woman Marine Corps. There is even something called a "Wet Bulb Globe Temperature Index Station" (WBGT) that is placed in strategic locations all over camp to indicate when the South Carolina sun has made it too beastly hot to train. And of course there is the famous Marine's ode to his rifle, depicting it in terms an ordinary civilian might use to describe a sweetheart or a favorite pal.

ST. MATTHEWS

PURPLE MARTIN FESTIVAL

St. Matthews, S.C.;
last full weekend in April

When we first saw the sign for this event, we read it as "Purple Martian Day" and imagined a festival of small three-legged purple people with antennae roaming the streets of St. Matthews. This festival does celebrate creatures who soar in the air—but by wing power, not in flying saucers.

The purple martin is a bird that eats several times its weight in mosquitoes every few days. This makes it a beloved addition to any humid, swampy place. Until local Rotarians decided to erect birdhouses all over town, St. Matthews was infested with mosquitoes. Now the purple martins flock to town each summer to feast on the local mosquito population—making it a much more pleasant place for people.

The birds' arrival is celebrated in April by a festival that includes everything from tobacco-spitting contests and tractor pulls to exhibits of microwave cookery.

SALLEY

THE CHITLIN STRUT

Salley, S.C., Rt. 394;
1st Saturday after Thanksgiving;
$3 a plate.

Chitlins—formally known as chitterlings—have always been considered poor man's food, the last part of the pig to be eaten before the squeal. They are intestines, cleaned and boiled, then deep-fried. Some folks never acquire a taste for them. Others come to Salley every year and eat them by the pound. This tiny South Carolina community (pop. 450) sets aside one day each fall to celebrate chitlins in all their ignominy. The day's events begin with a parade and proceed rapidly to the Crescent Cities Vocational Cafeteria, where chitlins are served throughout the day. In recent years, five tons of chitlins have been just about enough to feed the 25,000 people who annually attend the Chitlin Strut.

But you don't have to love chitlins to come to Salley every year for their celebration. The day has become one of the great festivals of the rural South, filled with dancing, country music, gospel singing, and general whooping it up. The saying around town is "It takes guts to make a Chitlin Strut," but you don't have to eat them to have a marvelous time.

SPRINGFIELD

THE GOVERNOR'S ANNUAL FROG-JUMPING CONTEST

Main St., Springfield, S.C.;
2nd week in April

They grow some gargantuan frogs in the slime-green swamps of the Carolinas, and no self-respecting kid can get through childhood without netting one or two. But what fun is a frog, other than to cure a wart or catch a fly, if he isn't a good jumper? The strongest-legged local froggies are pitted against one another each April in Springfield, and the winning frog gets a free trip to California and the grand national jump in Calavaras County.

Judging at this contest is done by state dignitaries, and although the population of Springfield is a mere 700, over 7,000 people annually attend the festivities. Events other than amphibian antics include horseshoe-pitching, square-dancing, a barbecue, and lots of country music.

TENNESSEE

CHATTANOOGA

THE CHOO CHOO HILTON

Terminal Station, Chattanooga, Tenn.;
rooms from $20, rail car: $40,
reservations: (615) 266–6484

Trains are known for their ability to lull passengers into a deep, hypnotic sleep.
We always thought this had something to do with the cradlelike rocking of the
moving train along the tracks, but this theory was disproved by a night at the
Choo Choo Hilton, where one sleeps in a firmly anchored railroad car that
happens to be one of the most soporific places to bed down we know.

We recommend the Choo Choo Hilton to insomniacs, to lovers or honeymooners who prefer the romantic Victorian style of this redone railroad car
to the anonymity of an ordinary hotel, and to families with kids (or grown-ups)
who think that trains are terrific. At the Choo Choo, the cars are set out on
tracks, and they are boarded just like a regular train, by climbing up the
outside metal steps. Each car has been cut into two halves, allowing for two
very generously proportioned rooms. The furnishings are old-fashioned, including velvet swags, tassels and brass headboards. But unlike old-fashioned
Pullmans, there are conveniences such as bathtubs and drink-and-snack dispensers in each room.

The old station around which the hotel has been built contains a restaurant, several fancy shops, and a huge model railroad. You can take a trolley ride around the whole operation for a nickel. For all its commerce and convenience, this hotel is dominated by a feeling of nostalgia for the days when travel by trains was the classy way to go.

COOKVILLE

HIDDEN HOLLOW

Poplar Grove Rd., Cookville, Tenn. (Exit 290 off I–40);
daily 8:30 AM–10:30 PM; 50¢

Hidden Hollow is one man's idea of paradise, a man-made wonderland of waterfalls, lakes, and covered bridges. Arda Lee, who built it, calls it "The Never Ever Land." It costs 50¢ to get in, a dollar to swim, and a dollar to go cane pole fishing in one of Arda's well-stocked mini-lakes. It is a kind of naïve Disneyland, where a small menagerie of peacocks, silky Japanese chickens, ducks, and geese wander about the landscape. Guests are free to wander too, or to play volleyball on Arda's court. Among the things you can see here are a reassembled antique water wheel, a colored fountain Arda built in memory of his mother, a barbecue pit made from a 150-year-old fireplace, and hundreds of signs and slogans that people have given Arda Lee from all over the world. There are bamboo and plum trees, and a rock garden in which natural stones are arranged to look like alligators, penguins, hands, and other familiar shapes.

Standing over this fairy-tale land is Arda Lee's 52-foot tall aluminum cross. It is decked out with light bulbs to be visible at night, and serves as the gathering spot for an annual sunrise Easter service in Hidden Hollow.

COSBY

COSBY RAMP FESTIVAL

Kineauvista Hill, Rt. 32, Cosby, Tenn.;
last Sun in April

Like many towns in Appalachia, Cosby, Tennessee celebrates the rites of spring with a mass eating of the unpleasant-smelling ramp. They explain the purpose of this festival in medicinal terms: "For generations people in the mountains have considered raw ramps, ramps parboiled and fried in grease, scrambled with eggs, or served up in various other ways, to possess wondrous medicinal properties; to be, in fact, a necessary spring tonic and the best way to overcome winter's sluggishness."

If partaking of this vile wild leek is not your idea of fun, you still might enjoy the spring festivities in Cosby. There is always lots of barbecued chicken to go with the ramps, and gospel singing and mountain music are performed throughout the day. Lester Flatt and the Nashville Grass were the stars of last year's show.

The Cosby Ramp Festival is now approaching its twenty-fifth year, the oldest such celebration in the country. In 1976, Governor Ray Blanton declared the last Sunday in April to be Ramp Day in honor of "the lowly ramp [that] grew unheralded in the rich, moist coves in the Appalachian Mountains for ages beyond the memory of man."

GATLINBURG

GATLINBURG, TENN.

Rt. 73

The town of Gatlinburg is the Main Street of Southern Tourism. Even Florida's Orlando-land can't compete with the effusion of unadulterated hucksterism one finds here. This place is P. T. Barnum's vision of heaven. Let us dip into the attractions, and select a few of Gatlinburg's quintessential come-ons for your consideration:

In the Believe It or Not Museum there is a ship made entirely from chicken bones, and an Eiffel Tower made of toothpicks. Abe Lincoln's log cabin is made from pennies, and there is a circus made out of tiny sugar cubes.

At the World of the Unexplained you can see a statue of a man that changes into a werewolf before your eyes.

At the National Bible Museum there is a Bible that weighs thirty-two pounds, and one that weighs one ounce.

Christus Gardens has a six-ton block of Carrara marble into which has been carved Christ's face. Wherever you walk, His eyes seem to follow you. They used to have a wax re-creation of hell and roadsigns inviting travelers to "Go to Hell." But hell no longer exists here, having disappeared or burnt down.

LOOKOUT MOUNTAIN

THE BIRTHPLACE OF MINIATURE GOLF

Fleetwood Drive (The Fairyland Club), Lookout Mtn., Tenn.

On the way to Rock City—Tennessee's most publicized tourist attraction—
you have the opportunity to view a unique, unmarked historical spot. It is on
the property of a country club, but is visible from the road.

Miniature Golf was invented here. In the 1920s a man named Garnet Carter
devised what he called "Tom Thumb Golf," played on a course constructed
around the unusual rock formations in this area. The idea caught on quickly,
and soon Carter laid down plans for other courses all over the country for
golfers who couldn't avail themselves of eighteen full-sized holes.

Who knows what Mr. Carter would think if he were to come back and see
the sprawling acres of dinosaurs, Fred Flintstones, and Fairyland Terrains that
now identify the game. His pure and simple original rock formations are a bit
overgrown, but still a vital landmark in the evolution of leisure-time activities.

LYNCHBURG

JACK DANIEL'S DISTILLERY

Rt. 55 (Jack Daniel's Hollow), Lynchburg, Tenn.;
Daily 8 AM–4 PM; free

You can't get a drink in the town where Jack Daniel's is made, because
Lynchburg is in a dry country. That's the only disappointment about touring
the Jack Daniel's Distillery, which is likely to leave you with quite a thirst.
The nicest thing about a tour is Lynchburg itself. Although Jack Daniel's is
a major distillery, the town has not been turned into "Whiskeyland," or any
such commercial nightmare. You'll see a place little-changed by success. Men
in bibbed overalls sit on their benches in front of the hardware store, and the
perfume of hard sugar maple and corn squeezin's wafts through the trees
around the distillery.

Jack Daniel's has whiskey license #1, the oldest in the United States. A tour
takes you to see the limestone caves from which they extract pure water, Jack
Daniel's cluttered office, and all the steps involved in brewing, filtering, and

aging the whiskey that has been sipped by Faulkner, Hemingway, and generations of Southern gentlemen.

If you are lucky, you will be picked from among the morning tour groups for a free lunch at Mary Bobo's boardinghouse. We don't know how they select the twenty people who get to go. Perhaps one should look extremely hungry, or convivial, because the lucky ones are led to a "family-style" table piled high with fried chicken, biscuits, salads, roasts, and vegetables. You can trade drinking and travel stories, or spend the time trying to sample from among the mountainous quantity of food that is passed along. Mary Bobo, who runs this very old-fashioned place, is over a hundred years old, and stands by the door to say "howdy" as Jack Daniel's well-fed guests file out into Lynchburg's lovely town square.

NASHVILLE

ELVIS PRESLEY'S GOLD CADILLAC

Country Music Hall of Fame Museum, 4 Music Square East, Nashville, Tenn.;
June, July & Aug Daily 8 AM–8 PM, Sept–May 9 AM–5 PM;
adults: $2, children 6–11: $1.50

This finned, sparkling beauty is the most popular attraction in the museum. It is a 1960 Model 75 limousine, made from what looks like a thousand layers of gold dust, looking like a great fish hoisted from the waters of a mythical kingdom, beached here in the Country Music Hall of Fame. People crowd around it; polyester double knits scrape against rough denim as the late king's fans strain to get close to his royal coach. "Oh, my God, it is more beautiful than I thought!" "Can you *imagine* what they'd say in Eudora if I drove home in that?"

This particular car is referred to by the cognoscenti of Presleydom as "the less gaudy" one from among his fleet. It shares space here with a mock-up of a "star's touring bus," cut open for all to gaze upon the air-conditioned plushness and brass-bedded comfort in which the likes of Loretta Lynn travel. The museum also houses famous musicians' guitars, boots, overalls, glitter-shirts, and lots of plaques to honor people like Hank Williams and Ernest Tubb. But there is no exhibit that can set the adrenalin pumping like the Cadillac that once belonged to the Rockabilly King.

PATSY CLINE'S BOOTS

Ryman Auditorium, 116 5th Ave. N., Nashville, Tenn.;
Daily 8:30 AM–4:30 PM; $1

Patsy Cline was perhaps the original Queen of Country Music. She met her death in 1963 in the same plane crash that killed Hawkshaw Hawkins and Cowboy Copas. She is now a cult figure, a Blue Ridge version of James Dean. The faithful still trek to Nashville to pay homage before the glass case in Ryman Auditorium that contain her cowgirl boots and other personal artifacts. These boots were Patsy's trademark, and although they are not as gaudy or as fancily designed as those that stomp across the stage of Opryland today, they look as if they could have just stepped out of her hit, "Walkin' After Midnight." They are hand-tooled leather beauties, calf-high and polished so brightly they could well have reflected the moon that shone over her midnight walk.

TOOTSIE'S ORCHID LOUNGE

412 Broadway, Nashville, Tenn.; (615) 251–9725

Do you feel that there is something missing in Opryland and *nouveau* Nashville? Have you looked for that white soul of country-and-western music and found only pop polyester imitations? If so, come to Tootsie's Orchid Lounge for a beer and a sandwich. It is the ultimate Music City bar. It is an after-hours landmark in this town. You'll know it by its orchid skin ringed with neon. Inside, the walls are plastered with star photos and graffiti inscribed by the royalty themselves. On some nights Tootsie's back room looks like a parade of album covers as the stars themselves stop in for a quick brew or an earful of the live music. Tootsie's has enough character to make up for all the rest of glossy Nashville. It is a tattered shrine to the humble origins of country-western music.

VANDERBILT TELEVISION NEWS ARCHIVE

6th Stack, Main Building, Joint University Libraries, Vanderbilt U.,
419 21st Ave. S., Nashville, Tenn.;
Mon–Fri 9 AM–6 PM (615) 322–2927

The cliché about yesterday's news being uninteresting has always seemed to us all wrong. Yesterday's news—whether it be about hula hoops sweeping the country or Nixon and Agnew making their pleas—sometimes seems much more interesting than tonight's 11:00 P.M. report. The Vanderbilt Archive contains over five thousand hours of videotaped television news. They have recorded all three networks' evening news programs from 1968 on, as well as presidential speeches, political conventions, Watergate hearings, and other top TV stories. No other archive in the country has this material—not even the networks themselves.

The Vanderbilt Archive is open to the public, and you can sift through material for $2 per hour of machine use. There are monitors set up in a viewing room, where you will sit elbow to elbow with other students of the tube, poring over the proclamations of newsmen, presidents, sports heroes, and foreign correspondents. If you don't have the time to look at the raw news as it was aired (which can provide the most fascinating perspective of day-by-day shifts in attitude and tone), the Archive provides a compiling service—at a substantially higher fee. You give them the subject and they provide you with tapes so that you can compare how ABC, NBC, and/or CBS covered it on any particular day or over a given period of time. Whatever your field of study—the New York blackouts, Billy Carter, or the changing face of Barbara Walters, they've got the goods on it here.

WEBB PIERCE'S GUITAR-SHAPED SWIMMING POOL

801 N. Curtiswood, Oak Hill, Tenn.; (greater Nashville)
Thurs, Fri & Sat. (or whenever the gate is open); free

In the old days of hillbilly jazz, stars' cars were decorated with silver pistols and silver dollars, and their mansions were fenced with giant half-notes made of gold (paint). The Great Ones wore a sequin for every fan. In this glittery tradition of stardom, Webb Pierce has constructed a guitar-shaped swimming pool in his backyard. And he has invited all his fans to come and see it.

Cars and buses began crowding the streets of Oak Hill after Webb's invita-

American Museum of Atomic Energy, Oak Ridge, Tenn.

Webb Pierce's Swimming Pool, Nashville, Tenn.

tion went out, and the mayor got so fed up with tourists asking "Which way to Webb's pool?" that he tried to get a court order to stop the pilgrims from coming. Whether or not Webb Pierce has a right to invite fans to see his pool is now a court case which could drag on till the cows come home. In the meanwhile, it is still possible to catch a glimpse. Webb has plans to build a ramp overhead big enough to hold a Greyhound bus. His fans deserve the very best.

OAK RIDGE

AMERICAN MUSEUM OF ATOMIC ENERGY

Tulane & Illinois Aves., Highway 61, Oak Ridge, Tenn.;
Sept–May Mon–Sat 9 AM–5 PM, Sun 12:30 PM–5 PM,
June–Aug Mon–Sat 9 AM–6 PM, Sun 12:30 PM–6 PM; free

The town that was a top secret during World War II, "the birthplace of the A-bomb," is now the site of the American Museum of Atomic Energy. Oak Ridge is still a center for the development of atomic power.

The museum is filled with models, gadgets, and machines, all designed to show how atomic energy works. You can stroll through the core of a breeder reactor (inactive), and use atom power to detect an art forgery or test the wear and tear on a car engine. There are demonstrations throughout the day (check for times at the desk) at which you can see Felix the Ferret (an energy research animal), the actual harnessing of an atom, and a high-energy globe that makes your hair stand on end when you touch it—a sort of nuclear fright wig.

There is a "science boutique" here that sells books and toys designed to make you think of the atom as your friend.

PALMYRA

ENOCH WICKHAM'S SCULPTURE GARDEN

Head out of Clarksville towards Palmyra on highway 149,
turn left on Oak Plains Rd., right at stop sign, go 3/4 mile to Garden;
always viewable; free (Palmyra, Tenn.)

Enoch Wickham died about five years ago, and his sculpture garden is slowly receding into the earth, a process accelerated by vandals. But there is enough remaining to make an exploratory mission through the foliage an exciting trip. Some of the sculptures are visible from the road.

Wickham's art was basically rough-hewn: monuments to American folk heroes and local war dead formed from cement, trees, and wire. Still emerging out of the greenery are Babe the Blue Ox, a Virgin Mary, and a monument to Estes Kefauver, Patrick Henry, John Kennedy, and Robert Kennedy. A plaque is etched with the names of Montgomery County Tennesseeans who were "engaged in the medical art."

Many of the sculptures are now decapitated, and some have fallen onto the weed-covered ground. The paint is chipping, and the wires connected to an electric halo around the Virgin Mary are partially pulled down. It is difficult to tell what Enoch Wickham's Sculpture Garden was like when he was around to tend it, but one guesses that it was never neat and tidy. His sensibility, like that of so many folk artists, is made up more of strength and audacity than refinement. To see this work decompose, essentially unappreciated, is pitiful. On the other hand there is some poetic justice in the fact that Wickham's art, in itself so independent of the world of galleries and museums, is returning to the natural world from which its creator drew his inspiration.

PIGEON FORGE

HANK WILLIAMS, JR.'s CAR

Smoky Mountain Car Museum, U.S. 441, Pigeon Forge, Tenn.;
July–Labor Day 11 AM–5 PM Daily;
Adults: $2, children: 50¢

"See! Hank Williams, Jr.'s $22,000 car!!" Big deal. On today's car market that could mean a Dodge with an FM radio or air conditioning. But this car was constructed in the days when a dollar still bought you lots of chrome and leather, and Hank's car is no disappointment. It is a country-western dream.

The car is a Pontiac Bonneville convertible ornamented with 547 silver dollars inlaid into the dashboard, the steering wheel, and the gearshift. Fifteen silver horseshoes are affixed in appropriate spots on the exterior. There are ten pistols for decoration and two serving practical duty as door handles. There are three rifles, seven silver horses, and seventeen silver horseheads. Hank, Jr.'s name is emblazoned across the continental kit (a rear bumper-mounted spare tire).

This car makes Stringbean Akerman's '56 Cadillac (also on display here) look like a utility vehicle.

THE MAZE

The Parkway (across from the Coliseum), Pigeon Forge, Tenn.;
June 1–Labor Day daily 10 AM–11 PM,
weather permitting; weekends year around;
Summer admission: $1.50; rest of year: $1

Mazes have fascinated human beings for thousands of years. They have been used as amusements, prisons, or as symbols of the earth itself by everyone from the Greeks to American Indians. The maze here in Pigeon Forge is like the ones used in Old England. It is a lawn game, a 160 foot by 110 foot labyrinth into which players are sent and out of which they try to find a way. There are over forty dead ends, and endless confusing roundabouts. Entrants are given a flag so that if one person does manage to complete the maze, he can climb a platform and direct his friends. The shortest time through the maze is five minutes. Average time is half an hour. For the chronically confused, we recommend you pack lunch. For the chronically anxious, there are two emergency exits.

VIRGINIA

FREDERICKSBURG

THE DOG MART

Downtown Fredericksburg, Va.;
1st Sat in Oct.; free

1978 will be the Dog Mart's 280th year. Yes, fourscore years before the United States was born, proto-Fredericksburgians were busy trading, buying and selling dogs with the Pamunkey Indians. It began as part of a peace plan, with perhaps one useful dog offered in exchange for a sack of corn flour. The Dog Mart has evolved from such primitive détente to a celebration that fills the streets of Fredericksburg with marching Shriners, old-time fiddlers, Pamunkey Indian dances, high school marching bands, floats, turkey-calling contests, hog-calling contests, and a demonstration of foxhorn blowing.

The dog is still paramount here, but now more as a celebrated guest than an item used for barter. There is in fact a dog auction; but our favorite events are the contest for the ugliest dog, the selection of best-dressed dog, and the judges' choice of the funniest dog. Canine ugliness is generally equated with a pushed-in face, and so this contest has long been the province of breeds such as the bulldog, boxer, Pomeranian, and pug. We feel that these flat-faces have been getting a raw deal, and that there is much beauty to be seen in their accordionlike muzzles; it therefore gives us some satisfaction to see that dog ugliness at recent Dog Marts has been defined more in terms of the contestant's asymmetry, mismatching ears and eyes, and general dishevelment. As for the best-dressed dogs, well, frankly, Fredericksburg is *not* New York, and the fashions on display here are—by Park Avenue standards—a teeny bit *outré*. The people of Fredericksburg do have enough good sense to consider handsomeness a vital attribute of canine beauty; and so the most beautiful dog might just as easily be a sturdy retriever or golden Labrador as a poufed and powdered poodle.

All the contestants—ugly, pretty, or dressed-to-kill—are paraded up and down the main street of Fredericksburg by their masters before the judging at the town fairground.

GALAX

OLD FIDDLERS' CONVENTION

Felt's Park Rt. 58–221; Galax, Va.;
Aug 10, 11, 12, 1978 (always 2nd weekend in Aug.)
$3 each day, or $8 for all three days

Traveling through the small mountain towns of the Southeast one could easily get the impression that there are as many people down here who play the fiddle as drive a car. Fiddler conventions and play-offs are everywhere. The fact is that only a small number of musicians can qualify for this soul-stirring musical event, but people love to hear them, and the fiddlers love to play, so America's fiddlers travel all over the country to pit their skills against one another.

The convention in Galax is "big time" for fiddlers, beginning Thursday night with individual competition, Friday night with band play-offs, and Saturday night with band championships and a big sheebang of a dance. You'll see virtually every stringed instrument from a Jew's harp to one bull fiddle so big, it is permanently displayed on the top of of a station wagon. There are old, old timers fiddling out "Fly around My Pretty Miss" and "Bile Them Cabbage Down," and new fiddlers with their own compositions. Individual competitions are held for each instrument, as well as for the mountaineer's favorite toe-tapper, the Flat-Foot Dance.

LEBANON

"CREEK" CHARLIE FIELDS' POLKA-DOT HOUSE

Lebanon, Va.;
always viewable; free

"Creek" Charlie's house is just outside the town of Lebanon, but the directions, across unmarked rural roads and paths, are so convoluted that we suggest you do as we did—ask a local cop or gas station attendant. Although Charlie died about ten years ago, almost everyone in town knows his house well. Once you see it, it's hard to forget.

The house is made of wood. "Creek" Charlie painted it with polka dots and intermingled squiggly lines. These dots and lines thread through every piece of wood, every window sill, door jamb, porch slat and step, and even spread out over the tin roof. The dots and lines are many-colored, once vivid but now slightly bleached to pastel tones. There are one or two designs—a flag, a square, a circle—but these scarcely affect the overall pattern that vibrates out of the surrounding green foliage.

It is said that "Creek" Charlie's clothes and furniture were painted with dots, too, and that the entire inside of his home was as brightly patterned as the exterior. But it has been vacant for a decade, and the elements and vandals have taken their toll. There is nothing left to see inside, but the exterior remains a striking sight, a unique, eccentric, and inspired creation.

LEESBURG

THE AMERICAN WORKHORSE MUSEUM

Rt. 622, Paeonian Springs, Va., 4 mi. NW of Leesburg;
by appointment only (703) 338–6290

"The workhorse served his master for hundreds of years in thousands of useful ways, until replaced by the tractor and machine-age craze that swamped our every way of life, almost relegating the workhorse to extinction." Readers may note wistful—if not downright frustrated—sentiments in these words from the American Work Horse Museum's brochure. To commemorate that faithful steed, to remind people just how important the workhorse has been in our nation's development, there are three acres worth of exhibits.

Among the implements on display are plows, reapers, binders, cultivators, and planters. There is a small dump cart—forerunner of the dump truck, and Army gun carts as well. But not all of the horse's drudgery was intertwined with human toil. The museum has what is called a "Roving Carousel." Dr. Henry Buckhardt, the museum's president, explained that these carousels used to travel the city streets, playing music until they attracted a crowd of children. The carousel would stop, the kids would get on, and the horse would pull them around in a circle.

Among the other unusual items here are a bobsled, a one-horse sleigh, and a surrey with a fringe on top. There is a harness shop with collars, bridles, breast chains, and all the full-dress gear needed by a working horse. There is a treadmill on which a horse produced one horsepower worth of power, and there is even an anomalous dog treadmill, apparently for smaller tasks.

The museum is dedicated not only to the horse, but to those times in which it seems that people worked like horses. There is an entire building filled with tools and gadgets, from common saws and axes to a Conestoga wagon jack. There is also a "country kitchen," containing such handy devices as a sauerkraut cutter, a venison spit, and a sausage stuffer.

It seems like a woman's, a man's or a horse's work was never done. Although this charmingly antique collection is meant as an ode to the good old days, we get vicariously tuckered out just thinking about all the chores the tools and implements here represent.

LEXINGTON

STONEWALL JACKSON'S STUFFED HORSE

The Virginia Military Institute Museum, Jackson Memorial Hall on the
Campus Lexington, Va.;
Mon–Fri 9 AM–4:30 PM, Sat 9 AM–noon, 2 PM–5 PM, Sun 2 PM–5 PM,
closed school holidays; free

If the Virginia Military Institute ever runs into hard times and wants to break up their collection of military memorabilia, they can count on us to put in a bid for Little Sorrel. For those not brushed up on their equestrian history, Little Sorrel was Stonewall Jackson's horse. He has survived the sands of time far better than his compatriot horse, Robert E. Lee's Traveller. The latter has wound up a handful of ashes under a stone near a power plant at nearby Washington and Lee University. Little Sorrel is in one proud piece—stuffed, and a little tatty around the edges, but still a handsome steed. What is especially appealing about him is his face—a cross between Julie Andrews and Eleanor Roosevelt—and his expression, which is kind, perky, and good-willed. He still wears a full saddle and bridle, and stands in a small diorama surrounded by a wooden fence so visitors don't touch and wear him out. "Kids love him," the lady at the desk told us. So do we.

TRAVELLER'S GRAVE

Outside Robert E. Lee Chapel at Washington and Lee University, near
Jefferson and Washington Streets, Lexington, Va.
Always viewable (in back)

Leave it to the United Daughters of the Confederacy to see to it that a good Southern-born and -bred horse is laid to rest with honor and dignity. This horse is Traveller [*sic*], who spent his youthful days carrying Robert E. Lee around. Traveller was originally preserved in skeleton form in the nearby chapel, where Lee's life and posessions are enshrined. But time took its toll on the old bones, and eventually he got too dilapidated to have around. So the U.D.C. cremated what was left of the skeleton and buried it with fitting ceremony under a plaque near the back of the chapel. You can find it if you look hard—a tasteful, understated monument at the crest of the hill leading up to the chapel's power plant.

LURAY

PETRIFIED FRIED EGGS

Luray Caverns, Rt. 211, Luray, Va.;
March 16–May 15 9 AM–6 PM, May 16–Labor Day 9 AM–7 PM, after Labor
Day–Nov 15 9 AM–6 PM, Nov. 16–March 15 9 AM–4 PM;
Adults: $5.00, Children 7–13: $2.00, Under 13: free, uniformed servicemen: $3.00;
tours every twenty minutes

If it weren't for the Petrified Fried Eggs, we would never recommend a trip to the Luray Caverns. They are too large, too expensive, and too crowded for our liking. But the eggs won our hearts.

We were first smitten when a friend traveling with a movie crew went post-card shopping in Luray. There appeared in our mailbox a color post card of two fried eggs in shades of bilious green, yellow and off-white. We took a casual look and tacked the card up on a bulletin board. It was at least a week later that we made the awesome realization that these "eggs" were actually "carbonaceous lime building a new stalagmite." Since that discovery, our lives haven't been quite the same. We have switched to scrambled eggs and omelets, because "sunny side up" now immediately makes us think of those petrified lime deposits. And whenever the word "egg" pops into a conversation, we feel compelled to tell the world about these carbonaceous friers down in Luray.

The eggs are affixed to the cave wall. We have seen old photos of the caverns in which a slightly pudgy "Betty Homemaker" type in a gingham apron is holding a frying pan with two holes cut in its bottom to accommodate the "egg formation" as if she is cooking them for John Doe's breakfast. It's a real subterranean *tromp l'oeil,* the highlight of a trip through the caverns, surpassing even Luray's underground wildlife—the eyeless red beetles and the blind albino shrimp.

PETERSBURG

OLD BLANFORD CHURCH'S TIFFANY WINDOWS

319 S. Crater Rd., Petersburg, Va.;
Mon–Sat 9 AM–5 PM, Sun 12:30 PM–5 PM; free

This would be just another modest chapel if it weren't for the fact that the ladies of the area—in an effort to restore the church in the late 1800's—hired Louis C. Tiffany to create fifteen windows for them. Now the Blanford Church is the only building in America to have had its every window designed by the master of Art Nouveau. Even then they were expensive—$400 each. Today, with single Tiffany lamps and vases selling for five-figure prices, the value of these windows is inestimable.

The Old Blanford Church is a Confederate shrine and holds only one service a year, on June 9th, Petersburg's Memorial Day. But it is open daily for visitors.

QUARTERMASTER MUSEUM

Fort Lee, Rt. 36, Petersburg, Va.;
Mon–Fri 8 AM–5 PM, Sat & Sun 1 PM–5 PM; free

The Quartermaster Corps is that part of the army that concerns itself with uniforms, symbols, equipment, and military hardware. They provided the black drum used symbolically in JFK's funeral cortège. They furnished Patton with his jeep, and Patton's dog with a collar. They supplied balloon baskets for artillery observers during World War I, and the bell that called in the camels when—briefly—the animals were used by the cavalry in the Southwest.

A vast array of this paraphernalia is on display here at the Quartermaster Museum, just inside Fort Lee's main gate. You get a map of the exhibits so you may propel yourself around on what they call a "self tour." The tour leads from uniforms and footwear, past musical instruments and into the dog equipment area, where you see all the accouterments worn by the well-heeled dogfaced dog. You can also see the country's only collection of presidential colors. There are endless insignias, chevrons, medals, decorations, and crests. The tour ends with a display of weapons, and then "subsistence"—facsimiles of what the army has eaten over the years.

POWHATAN

THE SPIDER MUSEUM

8 mi. E. of Powhatan on County Rd. 614, Powhatan, Va.;
April–Oct, Mon–Sat 10 AM–5 PM, Sun 1 PM–5 PM;
adults: $2, children: $1, under 6: free

"I've got spider egg sacs all over the ceiling. I've got two golden silk spiders from Florida. And there are over twenty tarantulas from around the world in here too." Anne Moreton is surrounded by arachnids, and she loves it. She is the founder and curator of the world's only live–spider museum. The museum is housed in an 1850–vintage building called the Woodward Mill, a grist mill built of stone. The tarantulas are inside, along with scorpions from Thailand and South Africa, displays of real spider webs "captured" on paper, and whatever else Ms. Moreton happens to have discovered on her daily walk through the woods. She gives an informal lecture to anyone who enters the mill, explaining, for instance, that a spider's silk is stronger than steel, tarantulas live to be twenty-five or thirty years old, and that spiders eat more insects than all other animals put together. She also tries to convince visitors that spiders make swell pets. "An orb-spinning spider—that's as nice a pet as you could want." Only two spiders are poisonous to humans, she points out. The rarest spider here is the *Listiphus desultar* tarantula, a species thought extinct until 1972, when this specimen—called "Desi"—was discovered.

But the real museum is outside. After meeting Ms. Moreton, she sends you out on the two miles of trail to see spiders for yourself in their natural surroundings. She regularly puts signs along the trail, pointing out spider colonies, or an area in which spiders happen to be transacting some special business. Last August, signs pointed to a group of Fishing Spiders guarding their young along the creek. Outdoor tours are self-guided, the only rules being no fishing, no collecting, and no picnicking.

Anne Moreton publishes a newsletter in which fellow-members of the National Arachnid Society exchange views and discuss any problems they may have about their pets. In Newsletter #15, she queried, "When I press gently on the left fang of my orange-kneed tarantula, I find it is stiff. Could it be out of joint? There is no doctor of spiders in the world. Does one consult a dentist?" The same issue contained a "human" interest story: "Judy Rush of Biloxi placed a small Christmas tree in the cage with her tarantula and to her surprise and delight, the spider spun a web all over the tree!"

RICHMOND

THE VALENTINE MUSEUM

1015 E. Clay St., Richmond, Va.;
Mon–Fri 10 AM–5 PM; Free

Do not come to this museum expecting hearts and flowers or a lover's missive decorated with arrows and Cupids. It was named after its founder, Mr. Valentine, about whose amatory inclinations the museum provides no clues. What you will find here is the country's largest collection of tobacco broadsides. These are paste-on tobacco ads once used to identify the thousands of individual varieties of tobacco grown and sold in America. They range in size from one-inch squares to wall posters, although most are the 10″ × 14″ labels that were affixed to the sides of tobacco boxes. They are comparable in lithographic beauty to the kind of artwork one can still find on the sides of wooden fruit boxes. The subjects of this tobacco art range from a blissfully nostalgic scene of two lovers in a rowboat to more sensuous portrayals such as a half-nude beauty stroking her tabbycat.

SHAWSVILLE

THE GINGERBREAD HOUSE

Rt. 11 on Christiansburg Mtn., S. of Shawsville, Va.;
always visible

The late William Preston, Sr., of Shawsville built the Gingerbread House; the last time we looked it was vacant and up for sale. It is a local landmark, and there is hardly a citizen of this town that can't be tapped for directions to it if you get lost.

One glance explains its popularity. It is a rambling white house merrily decorated with red, white, and blue hearts, stars, crescents and other festive shapes, all carved out of wood. These are attached everywhere, to the roof, windows and sides. There are carved steeples and turrets arising out of the roof. Each window is shuttered with its own unique woodwork.

If this description reads like a real estate ad, it is no wonder. Any copy-writer's fantasy about that "adorable country doll's house" or the "little snow-white cottage in the brush" pales before the reality of Preston's creation. It is startling in its naïve frivolity—a busy eccentricity that is essence of "gingerbread."

Since the fate of this house is in the hands of whoever buys it, we recommend a quick trip to see it as it is. It's truly one of a kind.

VIRGINIA BEACH

ASSOCIATION FOR RESEARCH AND ENLIGHTENMENT

67 Atlantic St., Virginia Beach, Va.;
Mon–Sat 9 AM–10 PM, Sun 1 PM–10 PM (804) 428–3588

Edgar Cayce was not only a psychic, but a devout believer in the Divine Plan. The Association for Research and Enlightenment was founded on the spot where he died in order to propagate his teachings and provide a place for meditation, study, and psychic research. There is a large library of psychic literature, a rooftop meditation area, and a Braille library for use by sightless seers.

Visitors are welcome to A.R.E. Each day at 3:00 P.M. there is a lecture on Edgar Cayce's life, and at 4:00 a movie is shown. These presentations explain Cayce's gifts, and tell of his ability to diagnose illness in Latinate terms otherwise unknown to him. They also remind visitors that Cayce always refused payment for the use of his psychic powers, since he felt they were God-given, and therefore not to be sold. A casual visit here gives one a hint of the activities of A.R.E. A longer stay, or enrollment in one of the study groups or lecture series, might help one penetrate the mysteries of Cayce's life.

YORKTOWN

WALTER FLAX'S ARMADA

Yorktown, Va.

You will know you have arrived at Walter Flax's place when you come upon a one-room shack in the middle of the woods, surrounded by a miniature version of the Sixth Fleet. His front yard looks like the special-effects department from the movie *Midway*.

For years, this black man (now in his seventies) has been building ships. His construction materials consist of metal scraps and cast-off appliances. All have been recycled into a wonderful flotilla surrounding his little white cabin. The ships' prows all point away from his house, toward the woods. There are at least fifty ships altogether, many rusting out from the damp salt air that blows in from the bay, others still maintaining a bung-up and bilge-free appearance. Although none of these tin battleships looks as if it could float, each has elaborately crafted decks, gun turrets, and smokestacks.

Walter Flax's nautical vision is well worth a half-day's wandering through the Yorktown woods—which, in fact, may be necessary to find it. Rather than try and reproduce the mind-bending directions that lead to his woodsy clearing, we suggest you visit the local sheriff's office, where they will draw you a map that will take you to the landlocked regatta.

WEST VIRGINIA

CHARLESTON

LONGEST BLOCK IN THE WORLD

The 1500 block of Virginia St., Charleston, W.Va.

West Virginia tourist literature proclaims this block to be the world's longest. They make the claim without equivocation, but we found several Charleston residents who modestly allowed that there might indeed be longer city blocks in the world—perhaps even in the United States—but decidedly not in West Virginia.

We have seen no city blocks longer than this. It runs about a mile, and the only cross-traffic for that whole distance comes from a couple of pedestrian alleyways. It is, to be sure, not a spectacular sight; although it is a pleasant enough walk, lined as it is with nice old-fashioned homes from the late 1800s.

NATIONAL TRACK AND FIELD HALL OF FAME

1524 Kanawha Blvd. (Exit 8 on I–64), Charleston, W.Va.;
Mon–Fri 9 AM–4:30 PM, Sat 9 AM–5 PM, Some Sundays noon–5 PM; free

Here is "the world's fastest uniform." Of course, had it not been affixed to the body of Charles Paddock, "the world's fastest human," it might never have won a race. Paddock dominated the sport of sprinting during the 1920s. His sons donated the uniform to the Hall of Fame in 1976, and it now forms the core of a growing collection in a shrine dedicated to a sport that is rapidly gaining in popularity. Also on display are the late Steve Prefontaine's shoes, the ones "Pre" wore during his undergraduate days at the University of Oregon.

Plans for the future here include museum expansion, an indoor–outdoor track facility, and an auditorium. Every year the Hall of Fame stages the fifteen-mile Charleston Distance Run. In light of recent less-than-successful attempts to "professionalize" the sport of track and field and the concurrent fascination with amateur jogging and running, it will be interesting to see how this relatively new Hall of Fame develops.

GRAFTON

MOTHER'S DAY SHRINE

Andrews Church, Main St., Grafton, W.Va.;
Daily 9:30–noon, 1 PM–4 PM;
free (donation box) 304-265-1589

The woman who initiated the observance of Mother's Day died blind, penniless, and childless. Her name was Anna Jarvis, and she spent all her life and all her money trying to spark the world with her idea.

Anna's own mother worshiped and taught at the church that is now the Mother's Day Shrine, and it was three years after her death that her daughter became obsessed with the deification of motherhood. Now, years after Anna Jarvis's death, America has taken her idea to heart. From pillows with "Mother" emblazoned across the shiny silk to greeting cards and tattoos, Mother is big business.

Inside the Andrews Church parlor are two stained-glass windows—one depicting Anna Jarvis and one her mother. In the summer of 1978 the church hopes to have a small museum set up to house some of the founder's personal belongings. They do sell Mother's Day cards here—year 'round.

LEWISBURG

ROBERT ADDIS'S STALAGMITE SITTING BENCH

Lost World Cave, Court St., Lewisburg, W.Va.;
April–Oct, 9 AM–dusk, closed Nov–March;
adults: $2.25, children 6–12: 90¢, under 6: free

Frankly, caves give us the creeps. As in an airplane, the air is too dead, the space claustrophobia-inducing. And the darkness seems just barely pushed aside by the artificial lights. And so we are amazed that one man—Robert Addis—sat on top of a stalagmite in the Lost World Cave for over two weeks. This established the world record, although we are unaware of any serious competition for the honors of "World Champion Stalagmite Sitter." Addis perched on the "War-club" stalagmite. You can still see it here, and still see the tiny platform upon which he perched deep inside the Lost World. We wonder what he thought of all those days. If he was like us, he thought about daylight.

WILLIAMSON

THE COAL HOUSE

Corner of 2nd Ave. & Court Sts., Williamson, W.Va.;
Mon–Fri 9 AM–5 PM; free

If energy ever becomes a serious problem in West Virginia, the Tug Valley Chamber of Commerce has little to worry about. All they have to do to keep warm is to tear down their building with a pickax and burn it. The Chamber of Commerce is made of coal.

Its outside walls were made from sixty-five tons of coal cut into smooth blocks. It looks like stone, although pitch black, and the finish is preserved by several layers of varnish. It's really quite sleek-looking. It was built in 1933 by several local coal companies as a tribute to the industry that made West Virginia the most important source of bituminous coal in the nation.

The interior of this strange building is incongruously modern, furnished with wall-to-wall carpeting, fluorescent lights, and air conditioning. There's not even a pet canary inside to test the air.

THE
MIDWEST

ILLINOIS

CHICAGO

LAVA LITES

Lava Simplex Internationale, 1650 W. Irving Park, Chicago, Ill.;
Mon–Fri 9 AM–5 PM; free

Who managed to make it through the 1960s without getting caught in a room
with a Lava Lite? What were those strange, undulating blobs that symbolized
the head trip (remember?) of the psychedelic sixties? What were they, and who
put them there? Having mused on this deep question a few times, we were
happy to stumble upon the Lava Lite factory in Chicago. "Oh, wow," we
exclaimed, and went in to see whatever happened to the Lava Lite.

It's more popular than ever, Mr. William Rubenstein, the Lava Lite Internationale executive director told us. "It's a poor man's fireplace," he said. "Most
of them wind up on top of the TV, as ornaments. They're a tranquilizer." He
told us that the Lava Lite was perfected in the 1960s by an English chartered
accountant. He also told us that, contrary to popular opinion, the blob is *not*
made from oil in water. It is a secret mixture of eleven chemicals—known only
to two employees of the company. The chemicals react to heat when the lamp
is turned on, and it is the warmth that starts the globule undulating. But
because of the top-secrecy of the mixture, no visitors are allowed to observe
the manufacture of Lava Lites.

However, there is a showroom here that is open to the public. It is a Lava

Lite museum, with every model displayed in its own niche cut into the "wood"-paneled wall. Overlooking the scene is an oil painting of a sad-eyed little boy gazing up at an illuminated Lava Lite. Some of the Lava Lite models are available here as factory seconds for a 50 percent discount. Among the choices are:

The Lava Coach Lantern 6000 Series . . . "captures the elegance and mood of Old World England and modern Americana."

The Enchantress Planter 8200 Series . . . "Stylish, elegant, and complete with blooming artificial flowers that brim the planter bowl."

The Capri "Can-o-Lite" 9000 . . . "New contemporary version Lava Lite with a mod approach in a brushed brass finish beverage can base and matching cap."

THE MIDGET'S CLUB

4016 W. 63rd St., Chicago, Ill.;
Mon–Fri 4 PM–2 AM, Sat 4 PM–3 AM

We know a Chicago photographer who went into Midget's to recruit elves and munchkins to pose for an ad he was shooting. He got the bum's rush. "Normals" are tolerated in this tavern, as long as they respect the feelings of the little people who come to lean against the three-foot high bar and sit in the seats with the sawed-off legs. Everything is scaled to accommodate the dwarves and midgets who are the regular patrons.

If you are over four feet tall, you are a giant here. The phone is at waist level. When you sit in a chair you find your knees up to your chin. Using the toilet is like squatting on a toadstool. Everything but the drinks is scaled down.

There are plenty of full-sized customers here, so normals needn't feel they are entering a land of hostile Liliputians. Just don't call anyone "Shorty," and don't go looking for elves—unless you want a swift kick in the shins.

QUAKER TEST KITCHENS AND "WORLD'S LARGEST COOKIE JAR"

Rm. 234 Merchandise Mart, Wells St., Chicago, Ill.;
Mon–Fri 10 AM–12 noon, 1:30 PM–3:30 PM, closed Fri afternoons in June & Aug;
free; (312) 222–6809

The guided tours of Quaker's Test Kitchens are designed to answer questions like "How are recipes created?" "How can I bake an upside-down cake in five minutes?" and "How is Cap'n Crunch made?" These questions and others are answered by showing visitors through six "dream kitchens" in which home economists test, taste, and experiment. The kitchens are not scientific-looking or industrial. They are made to look just like the one you have (or should want to have) at home. Two are paneled in "rare South American wood." Others are furnished in soft tones of mustard and olive, warm browns and beiges. Each is filled with ultramodern appliances; and in each the home economists are stirring, baking, and smiling. Four kitchens are separated from viewers by glass partitions, so that if confidential testing is being conducted, shades can be pulled down to ensure secrecy.

Also on view is the "attractive dining room" where taste panels are conducted by experts with trained taste buds. On the 30-minute tour one sees historical kitchen utensils, *objets d'art,* food photos, and a gigantic wrap-around photograph of a cookie jar—the world's largest, as the Quaker people humorously advise us. A real jar that size would hold three thousand dozen oatmeal cookies, but in the photo it is filled with larger-than-life pictures of cookies and cereal confections, "so realistic viewers are almost tempted to sample them."

DEERFIELD

THE KITCHENS OF SARA LEE

500 Waukegan Rd., Deerfield, Ill.;
Mon–Fri tours at 9:30 AM, 10:15 AM, 1 PM by appointment (312) 945–2525;
free; no cameras, no crutches due to slippery floors

The tour begins in a hospitality room where the hostess tells the history of Sara Lee. Tour members introduce themselves (Floridians on vacation, birthday partying preteens, cheesecake-loving college students), and everybody gets a big laugh at the sanitary garb that is given out and must be worn—hair nets, beard nets, and caps.

The tour then begins. About the only thing not seen is the breaking of eggs (a special factory does that). But you do proceed along a mammoth production line, through the cheesecake room, the Danish pastry room, the oven room and the freezing chamber. You see sixty-pound bricks of butter blended with egg whites and yolks, then creamed into thin, uniform layers. You see machines that deposit precise numbers of cherries onto cheesecakes, dough-spreaders that create 108 identical layers for pastries; frosting spritzers for the Danish. The huge rooms are deafening. The heat in the oven room is almost overwhelming. The freezing area is freezing. It is a cataclysmic tour—not a bit like your hometown bakery.

At the end, there is coffee and an assortment of cakes, cut into small pieces.

DEKALB

THE LITTLE HOUSE AT ELLWOOD PARK

509 N. 1st St., DeKalb, Ill.;
May–Nov Wed & Fri–Mon 2 PM–4 PM;
adults: $1.25, 12–17: $1, under 12: 35¢

It used to be that there were two sizes of automobile—compact and full-size. Now, with the "intermediates," "precision sized" models, "subcompacts" and "downsized" designs, it's hard to know what is, in fact, a normal-sized car and what is a mini. Similar confusion prevails at the Little House in Ellwood Park. We have seen mansions and miniature dolls' houses, but nothing this size. It is ten feet high and appears from the outside to contain two stories. When you enter the front door (you have to stoop if you are over four feet) you see that the interior is in fact only one story, tall enough to stand in comfortably, although all of the furniture is too small for adult bodies. There is a sitting room, a dining room, and a bedroom—about as much space as a small mobile home. The house rests on a solid concrete foundation, has a miniature sidewalk leading up to its front porch, and is surrounded by beautifully landscaped grounds.

The Little House at Ellwood Park was built in 1892 to commemorate the opening of a DeKalb shoe company, and was later used by wealthy DeKalb families as a child's playhouse. It was finally moved to the grounds of the Ellwood House mansion, a French-English-Victorian mélange of conspicuous consumption built by a nineteenth-century barbed-wire manufacturer. The Little House can be seen as part of the tours of the large mansion.

It is truly something to behold. Anyone building a house today would be very happy to get construction quality of this caliber. The porch railings are delicately turned, the festive gingerbread scalloping along the shingled roof is hand-cut, and the moldings, windows, and door jambs all fit perfectly. The wood siding was designed to show off the carpenter's skills. Each panel is different, with some wood parallel to the ground, some vertical, and some at a 45° angle. Children may love to play inside, but adults will marvel at its workmanship.

On a plaque near the door, the Little House says "For every child who looks through my windows or walks through my rooms, and especially for those who do not have to stoop to enter."

DES PLAINES

THE ORIGINAL McDONALD'S

400 Lee St.; Des Plaines, Ill.;
Mon–Thurs 7 AM–11 PM, Fri&Sat 7 AM–midnight, Sun 8AM–11 PM

On April 15th, 1955, Ray Kroc opened the original McDonald's hamburger restaurant on this spot in Des Plaines. He had bought the name from a prosperous burger stand in Southern California and brought it here to the Midwest, where he created the "McDonald's Speedee Service System" under the sign of the golden arch. But all that is already the stuff of legend. Twenty-two billion burgers later, for better or worse, McDonald's is a way of life.

A bronze plaque at 400 Lee Street marks the spot's historic importance. The original sign is still standing—a single arch, more pointy than the current double models. As at every other McDonald's, the old red-and-white tile has here given way to the modern "towne house" design; and once you step up to the counter, you won't be able to tell this original "Mac" from any other.

EVANSTON

BIRTHPLACE OF THE WOMEN'S CHRISTIAN TEMPERANCE UNION

The Rest Cottage, 1730 Chicago Ave., Evanston, Ill.;
Mon–Fri 9 AM–noon, 1 PM–4 PM,
or by app't: (312) 864-1397

Miss Frances Willard was the founder of the W.C.T.U., and it was in this home —now called the "Rest Cottage"—that she spent much of her very active life. She combined her leadership abilities (she was first dean of women at North-

Petrified Fried Eggs, Luray, Va.

The Original McDonald's, Des Plaines, Ill.

Doggie Place Mat, The American Pet Motel, Prairie View, Ill.

western University) with a fervid feminism and an abhorrence for any intoxicants, and began The Women's Crusade in 1873. Members of the group wore a white ribbon to symbolize purity as they fought for the preservation of the American family against the threats of alcohol and drugs.

"Just look at the character in that face!" our guide remarked as she pointed to a portrait of the strong and sober Miss Willard. Her organization lives on today, operating from the Rest Cottage to advocate a life style that seems to be a peculiar mixture of modern feminism and bedrock abstinence. They carry on her work from here—now the national W.C.T.U. headquarters—and maintain the home as a shrine to her life and work and character.

It is a peaceful home, but not at all stuffy. It reflects the family life that is at the core of W.C.T.U. teachings, and it shows a commitment to action that encouraged individuality and outspokenness. Near the front door is a bell cast from one thousand opium and tobacco pipes; Mrs. Stanley, our guide, smacks it with a gavel to grab the attention of visitors to the home. There are thousands of other artifacts relating to temperance over the last century. Perhaps the most telling is Miss Willard's family Bible, in which she inscribed a pledge, signed by all who lived here:

> A pledge to make
> No wine to take
> No brandy red
> To turn the head
> No whiskey hot
> That makes the sot
> Nor fiery rum
> That ruins home
> Nor will we sin
> By drinking gin
> Hard cider too
> Will never do
> Nor brewer's beer
> Our hearts to cheer
>
> To quench our thirst
> We always bring cold water
> From the well or spring
> So here we pledge
> Perpetual hate
> To all that can intoxicate.

MUSEUM OF FUNERAL SERVICE ARTIFACTS

1600–1628 Central St., Evanston, Ill.;
Mon–Fri 9 AM–4:45 PM; free

About ten years ago a cast-iron coffin containing the body of an unidentified woman found its way into the sewer system of Belleville, Illinois. The body was reburied, but the coffin—a mummy-shaped structure believed to be over two hundred years old—went to the Funeral Museum that is part of the National Foundation of Funeral Services in the Chicago suburb of Evanston.

The Foundation explains the origins of the museum this way: "Through the past ten or a dozen years, individual funeral directors would decide that they had something of no immediate or practical value to them, but which was too old, too historic, too interesting or too unusual simply to discard. Then the thought would strike them—why not send it to the Foundation for display and safekeeping, where others could enjoy these artifacts of funeral service? And so they did."

The museum consists of a single, sedate room watched over by a miniature stone statue of Anubis, the Egyptian funerary god. On display are a selection of old and new caskets, burial garments, and urns selected from the Foundation's collection (too large to be displayed in its entirety.) A recent acquisition, contributed by the Frank E. Campbell "Funeral Church," Inc. of Manhattan, is a Civil War embalming kit, contained in a 6″ × 12″ mahogany box lined with navy blue velvet. The museum considers itself "a modest place," and disdains the exhibition of anything that might be considered bizarre or potentially offensive.

HIGHLAND PARK

THE WORLD'S LARGEST LIQUOR STORE

Gold Standard Internationale, 153 Skokie Valley Highway, Highland Park, Ill.;
Mon–Sat 9 AM–9 PM, Sun 11 AM–6 PM

There are liquor stores with more snob appeal, and ones with lower prices, but Gold Standard Internationale is the world's largest. Customers work their way through the aisles pushing supermarket shopping carts. Rows are marked with "street signs" separating vodka from vermouth and wines from cordials. There are booths set up for wine tasting, a kitchen in back for cooking demonstrations, and an area in the center of the store for bands and small orchestras that are brought in to highlight German, Italian, or French wines.

The variety here sets one's head spinning. We found seven different types of aquavit, all nine Hennessy cognacs, five Remy Martin cognacs (top of the line was $300 for a bottle), and all varieties of the best champagne in sizes from splits to jeroboams.

The store occupies fifty thousand square feet, five thousand of which devoted to wine alone. "Did you know," an overhead sign inquires, "that wine is mentioned 165 times in the Bible?"

METROPOLIS

METROPOLIS, ILL.

Rt. 45, NW of Paducah, Ky.

The people of Metropolis have been waiting a long time for their rocket to stardom. They have tried once before to exploit their town's name by making it into a Superman-Land. The attempt was unsuccessful. The day the press came to town, the minister was dressed in a Superman suit, but came down with a flu virus that made him so weak he was unable to burst through the door of the dry-cleaning store from which he was supposed to emerge. A Superman Center was constructed as a museum dedicated to the Man of Might, but it closed after only one summer.

Metropolis still has much to offer dedicated fans of "Supe." There is a giant mural of him on display at Fort Massac, a local park. The local paper is called the *Daily Planet,* but there don't seem to be any clothing hooks in the town's phone booths. Bob Westerfield, former Green Bay Packer halfback and now owner of the aforementioned dry cleaners, displays a life-sized rendering of the man from Krypton in his store window. The Chamber of Commerce distributes free samples of kryptonite, the rock from Superman's birthplace that holds sway over his powers. This Southern Illinois version of kryptonite looks very much like mussel shells painted red and green and sprinkled with glitter.

PRAIRIE VIEW

AMERICAN PET MOTEL

1 Pet Lane, Prairie View, Ill.;
tours Mon–Fri 1:30 PM & 3:30 PM;
free; for pet reservations call (312) 634–9444

In the aviary of the American Pet Motel sits a parrot under a heat lamp. "He's sixty years old," his attendant says. "It's for his arthritis." The parrot spends his days here soothed by stereo "easy listenin' " music. The halls of this motel are awash with the sound of the FM radio, although if your pet prefers hard rock or Sousa marches or Delta blues, the management will accommodate the animal's taste. Sleeping quarters here are individually prepared and stocked with favorite bones or blankets. Deluxe suites are, of course, carpeted and furnished with brass beds. There is a maternity ward, a day-care center, a summer camp, and a senior citizens' home.

Well-heeled pets are sometimes fussy eaters. During our visit we met a resident terrier who liked soft-cooked eggs and crisp bacon in the morning. The chef's offerings had been rejected twice—once because the eggs had gotten cold, another time because a yolk had broken and run over the bacon, causing it to lose its crispness. Standard fare from the kitchen includes beef-bone parfait and milkbone roulades.

Tours of these sumptuous accommodations are offered twice daily. One sees the dogs in their imperial suites, the pampered snakes in the serpentarium, the simian salon, and the pet boutique. There is a large mailboard behind the front desk, with a letter slot for each "guest," just as in a regular hotel. The management swears that they read any post cards or correspondence sent to the residents, and then report back to the pet owners in detail as to how the animal responded to his master's missive.

SCHAUMBURG

THE WORLD'S LARGEST SHOPPING MALL

The Woodfield Mall, Rt. 90 in Schaumburg, Ill.

The Woodfield Mall is almost twice the size of Vatican City. On a good day, its population exceeds two hundred thousand, and there is more money exchanged here than in the entire state of Utah. It is a police precinct by itself.

Shopping centers are everywhere, but Chicago (or Chicagoland as it is called locally) has seen a phenomenal boom in the last ten years. Shoppers trek from one mall to another, to shop, eat, or loiter in the environments, where "the weather is always perfect" and the Muzak never stops. We were wandering through one mall last summer and were passed by a children's parade, led by a clown, winding its way past the indoor fountains and into the Astroturf park to play. Malls are the closest thing yet to the "enclosed cities of the future" promised to us by popular science in the 1950s.

If you have but one mall to visit, go to Woodfield. It is an X-shaped shopping plan on three levels, containing two hundred stores. Some walkways are marble, some are carpeted. In some areas the "room tone" is intimate, hushed; in others sounds are magnified, as in an underground cave. The music is the same everywhere, and the temperature is always 72 degrees. Whether you see it as a shopper's paradise or a claustrophobic nightmare, there is no denying that Woodfield is the definitive mall.

UNION

ILLINOIS RAILWAY MUSEUM

Olson Rd., Union, Ill.;
June, July & Aug daily 11 AM–5 PM; Sept–Nov Sat & Sun 11 AM–5 PM;
March, April, May Sun only 11 AM–5 PM;
adults: $1, children: 50¢; train fares adults: $1.25, children: 75¢

Illinois means trains. Railroad buffs know it. So do trainmen, hobos, and everyone who ever switched connections at Rock Island or Moline or Peoria. Here in the Illinois flatlands is the sprawling Illinois Railway Museum—a perfect place for the connoisseur of railroadology or the passer-by who wants to learn about the mystical lure of the locomotive.

The museum is run by a nonprofit group of people who love trains. There are over one hundred and forty steam locomotives, gas electric cars, steam road cars, inter-urban cars, elevated cars, and streetcars. There is a complete Silver Zephyr Streamliner that looks as if it's flying even when standing still. Much of this equipment is in working order, and can be boarded for a brief ride along the museum's 1 1/2-mile track.

The museum bookshop is located in an 1851 railroad depot. It sells everything having to do with trains, including records with famous train whistles and chugs, train schedules from across the country, destination flags, and hundreds of other varieties of railroadiana.

AUBURN

AUBURN-CORD-DUESENBERG MUSEUM

1600 S. Wayne St.; Auburn, Ind.;
daily 10 AM–9 PM;
Adults: $2, students and senior citizens: $1

Who could argue that the three types of cars displayed here are not the most beautiful ever produced? They are the products of an Olympian era, when the gods of luxury and power ruled the road. Restraint and economy were unheard-of here in Auburn. The mighty and beautiful Duesenberg is the epitome of the great machine, its heavy metal body propelled at speeds up to one hundred and thirty miles per hour by an eight-cylinder, supercharged seven-liter engine. The classic Cords are more modest in dimension, but unique in design. They are Art Deco cars—buffed chrome inside, ultrasleek fenders and grille outside. The Cord may be the most futuristic car ever made, looking like a cross between a space-age refrigerator and a guided missile. The museum that houses these rare beauties is itself a spectacular example of art deco design—

the restored factory showroom of the Auburn Automobile Company.

In these days of "down-sizing," "personal luxury," and "sensible styling"—all euphemisms for cramped and bland look-alike transportation—the world celebrated by the Auburn–Cord–Duesenberg Museum seems like a golden age, when cars were king and the people who could afford them didn't have to worry about the price of gas or finding a place to park.

FAIRMOUNT

JAMES DEAN'S GRAVE

Park Cemetery, County Rd. 150E, Fairmount, Ind.;
daily dawn to dusk

The gravekeeper told us "People have written to me from Germany asking to buy a plot here, just so they can be buried near Jimmy. We tried to keep place mats with his picture on them in the café, but they were snatched up—just like the sign I put here saying 'This Way to James Dean's Grave.' That lasted only one afternoon."

Some do not believe that the blue-jeaned hood with the face of an angel ever died. In the early 1960s, Joan Collins, a dimestore salesgirl, was possessed by an inner voice that dictated to her "I am not dead. Those who believe I am not dead are right. I, James Dean, have rejoined my mother." Collins made a record of her revelation that sold over half a million copies. Some believe that it was a hitchhiker who was killed in the famous car crash, and that James Dean escaped, or was disfigured and lives to this very day in an insane asylum or hospital. When the film *Giant* was released, girls in the audience cried out "Come back, Jimmy, I love you! We are waiting for you!" The crash had occurred four days before *Giant* opened. Thousands of bolts and scraps of metal alleged to have been taken from James Dean's death car have been sold as magic amulets, or charms, or relics of the divine star. Handfuls of dirt are regularly carried away from the Park Cemetery.

"We get people here who weren't even born when he died. I can't understand it myself, but any time, any weather, all year, I just look around and there over my shoulder is somebody asking, "Which way to James Dean's grave?' "

MARTINSVILLE

THE MIDWEST PHONOGRAPH MUSEUM

State Rd. 252 at Hwy 37, Martinsville, Ind.;
May–Oct Sat, Sun & Holidays 2 PM–7 PM

Poor Dr. Drake. As a little boy his great-uncle wouldn't let him play with the phonograph. That was decades ago, and as Dr. Drake grew up, attended medical school, served in the army, married, and went into practice, phonographs receded to the distant corners of his mind. Then in 1964 a patient mentioned to him that her father-in-law had an antique Victrola for sale. Years of phonograph deprivation flooded back. He bought the antique phonograph, and has been buying them ever since. He now runs the Midwest Phonograph Museum—on weekends when he isn't at the office—and has a spectacular collection open to the public.

Dr. Drake has every type of talking machine one could imagine, including a facsimile of the original phonograph (1877) and a Bell and Tainter Graphophone from 1886 that uses cardboard recordings. There are machines covered with gold leaf and hand-painted scenes, coin-operated machines, hand crankers, automatics, and 3,500 records of every shape and material. In the main display room of the museum is a six-foot model of Nipper, RCA Victor's trademark pooch. His head is cocked as always, waiting for "His Master's Voice."

NASHVILLE

THE JOHN DILLINGER HISTORICAL MUSEUM

State Rt. 46, Nashville, Ind.;
March–Nov daily 10 AM–6 PM, Dec–Feb call (317) 342-3120;
adults: $1.50, children: 50¢, under 10 not admitted without adult; free to police

As a boy Joe Pinkston wanted to be just like John Dillinger. Fortunately for the banks, he grew up to be a criminal investigator instead of a criminal, and authored several books about his boyhood hero. He now runs the only museum we know devoted to the study of a single criminal. Along with Bonnie and Clyde, Dillinger was one of the "popular" bank robbers of the 1930s. Like them, he became a folk hero by knocking down banks, evading the G-men, making a spectacular prison escape, and creating around himself the legendary aura of a Depression-era Robin Hood. Stories about this larger-than-life man persist today. Joe Pinkston has put together his collection of Dillinger memorabilia in order "to preserve and display an authentic if regrettable part of American history." In fact, the museum is as much a shrine as it is a study of Dillinger's extraordinary criminal personality.

Upstairs in the museum Pinkston has the "funeral parlor"—an exact re-creation of the one Dillinger reposed in—complete with a wax likeness of the man in his coffin. As you enter, a funeral dirge plays on a Victrola, and the whole scene is so life (or is it death-) like that Joe has remarked "No one leaves here laughing." He's also got Dillinger's tombstone on display, complete with vandals' marks, a "lucky" rabbit's foot Dillinger once carried, and bank robbery plans written in Dillinger's own hand.

The only aspect of the Dillinger legend not covered here is the speculation that it was not Dillinger who was killed outside Chicago's Biograph theater; that the cops killed another man just to say they had gotten the "#1 Most Wanted"; that they trumped up stories about Dillinger having changed his fingerprints in order to explain how dead "Dillinger's" didn't match those of the famous criminal; that perhaps Dillinger made a deal . . . Like fellow-Hoosier James Dean, Dillinger was too much a legend to die and not leave some part of himself here on earth . . . if only in the minds of his followers.

PERU

CIRCUS CITY FESTIVAL

Peru, Ind.;
3rd Weds. in July

Peru was once the winter home of a dozen circuses. Everyone from Buffalo Bill to Baron Julius von Uhl brought their troupes here, and the town contained more lion-tamers, clowns, and acrobats than it did butchers, bakers or bartenders. Since the circuses stopped coming (they discovered Florida) the citizens of Peru have banded together every year since 1960 to put on their own show. Every third Wednesday in July the circus "comes to town"—which is not precisely true, since it never left. There is a mammoth street parade, a midway, and plenty of human pyramids, clowns, and tightrope walking. All performers are local "Peruvians." It is a volunteer circus good enough to warrant Peru's title: Circus City, U.S.A.

THE PUTERBAUGH MUSEUM

11 N. Huntington St., Peru, Ind.;
daily except Weds & Sun 1 PM–5 PM; free

The Puterbaugh is a local historical museum and contains much of interest, but since Peru is Circus City, we especially recommend their collection of sides and carvings from circus wagons. They are ornate and colorful, primitive in sentiment but elaborate in execution. One from the Floto Circus depicts "Motherhood" and "Innocence." Another shows a carved ape's head in a medallion. A John Robinson Hippopotamus Wagon has Egyptian figures across its sides. A tableau of elk and buffalo decorates a specially constructed wagon used in a wild-animal show.

Among Puterbaugh's other exhibits, we recommend their display of seven different coffins, Mark Twain's goggles, and the inkwell "probably used by Harriet Beecher Stowe."

TWELVE MILE

THE ANNUAL RUNNING OF THE TWELVE-MILE RIDING LAWN MOWER RACE

Plank-Hill Park, Twelve Mile, Ind.;
1st Mon in July

If you are cruising around Twelve Mile, Indiana, on a Sunday and hear the drone of lawn mowers, don't automatically assume that the sound is made by your average lawn-tending suburbanites, hard at work keeping up property values. It might be the sound of Twelve Mile's racing drivers, practising or tuning up for the town's big event—the annual lawn-mower race.

Come July the mowers line up Grand Prix-style along the town's lawn-ish Le Mans track. At the call "Gentlemen, start your engines," the machines rev up, and the Twelve Mile "500" is underway. In the 1960s the winning speeds had edged up into the 30-mile per hour range, but in 1970 a new track (grassless) was put into use, and the top speeds dropped into the mid-20s. The rules for entry are that the mowers must be factory models with the "original factory look" intact. The engine and drive train may be rebuilt or replaced, so the racing vehicles really are the "funny cars" of the mower world—looking like the one you have sitting in your garage, but with a volcano under its blades.

We don't see Paul Newman trading in his Porsche and Coors for a Snapper and Pepsi, since there's not a whole lot of macho aura surrounding the sport of mower racing. But you can bet that Twelve Mile, Indiana, has some of the nicest lawns in the state.

AMES

FRANCE BETTEN BEER TRUCK SUPERMARKET

Rt. 30 E. of Ames, Iowa;
Mon–Fri 8 AM–5 PM; free

About the only company that doesn't drive a France Betten Beer truck is Coors. "Coors is too fussy," says owner Mr. France Betten. He runs the country's only beer truck supermarket. Why it is called a supermarket we don't know, since there are no carts to wheel around and only one thing is sold here. What Betten does is to take beer trucks and paint or repaint them to suit almost all the beer companies in America.

Visitors are welcome to look into the showroom, where Mr. Betten always keeps a beautiful newly painted truck on display. Or you can take a tour behind the scenes and watch the workmen stripping down old Bud trucks and making them into Schlitz trucks, or vice versa.

Outside you will find the reason why this place is called a supermarket—a giant inventory of painted trucks, ready to drive home. Each costs about $20,000, but we wonder—what with all the interest in beer-can collecting—how long it will be before a rich beer-lover gets himself a collection of his favorite brands—on wheels.

AUDUBON

ALBERT THE BULL

Rt. 71, Audubon, Iowa.

Albert is a lot of bull. He is the world's largest—not flesh and blood, but concrete and steel. He weighs forty-five tons and stands thirty feet tall. He is painted bovine brown and cream, and has big blue eyes and dark eyelashes. He projects a personality that is more like Ferdinand the flower-sniffer than a fierce El Toro. He is, however, complete anatomically—and gigantically so.

BRITT

THE HOBO CONVENTION

Britt, Iowa. U.S. 18, W. of Mason City;
August; write "Hobo Convention," Britt, Iowa 50423 for specific date.

Hobos belong to a vanishing America. Like the trains they once traveled, these raggedy free spirits are now symbols of older and slower times. Housewives no longer offer to trade a meal for an afternoon's labor. Trainmen don't make it their business to roust the 'bos when the freights leave the yard. It is rare to see an open boxcar with a drifter sitting in the wind, riding "ol' dirty face" from ocean to ocean.

There are still enough of these professional vagrants around to hold a convention in Britt, Iowa, every year, as they have been doing since 1896. In Britt you can hear them spin out the legends of hobo glory—stories about King Scoopshovel Scotty, Hairbreadth Harry, Polly Ellen Pep, and the all-time hobo hero who scrawled his moniker on watertowers all over the country—"A #1." There are modern mendicants, too: Box Car Myrtle, Slow Motion Shorty, Roadrunner Brown (a hitchhiking double amputee), and the current king, Hardrock Kid.

There is an art show in honor of hobo artist Ben Benson, a hobo parade, and free mulligan stew all around. King and Queen of the hobos are crowned. Don't be surprised if last year's king doesn't attend—he may be cooling his heels in jail.

CLARINDA

GLENN MILLER FESTIVAL AND BOYHOOD HOME

Clarinda, Iowa;
May 26–July 1978—call (712) 542-2166

It is a dark redwood house with brown shutters on a shady street in a small Midwestern village. Where else could one expect Glenn Miller to have been born? The man whose name is synonymous with the big-band sound is the pride of Clarinda. They have a Glenn Miller Museum planned, for which the Miller Archives at the University of Colorado has already pledged the original hand-written copy of "Moonlight Seranade," his trombone, and a copy of his birth certificate. In 1977 they staged the first annual Glenn Miller Festival in his honor. The Eddie Haddad band of Omaha played the tunes. Clarindans from generations that should have loved Elvis, the Beatles, or even Kiss, swirled around the floor, extolling their native son: "Now *that* is music you can dance to."

CORNING

JOHNNY CARSON'S BIRTHPLACE

13th and Davis Sts., Corning, Iowa.

In the Jane and Michael Stern Hall of Fame, Johnny Carson reigns over all. Having always liked "the prince of blends," we grew to worship him while researching this book. We spent the days looking into every sort of eccentric and unusual place or happening we could find, from the Hollering Contest to the Hobo Convention to the country's two largest balls of twine. By evening, our minds were spinning, and there was only one thing that kept us sane— the regular, dependable, unruffled and unshakable personality of Johnny. We went to sleep with him all across the country, and each morning we were ready for any surprises America had to offer.

One may pay homage to the king at 13th and Davis Street, in Corning, where he was born.

Albert the Bull, Audubon, Iowa

Mrs. Olson's Hometown & World's Largest Coffee Pot, Stanton, Iowa

DAVENPORT

A LITTLE BIT O' HEAVEN

Palmer College, on Brady between 8th & 11th Sts, Davenport, Iowa;
Memorial Day–Labor Day daily 10 AM–5 PM;
adults: $1; children & Sr. cits: 50¢

A Little Bit o' Heaven is a lot like a little bit o' San Simeon. It is a garden of exotic foliage and *objets d'art* from around the world. It is filled with worshipful and worshiping religious figures of pre-Christian, Christian, and Oriental beliefs. It contains what they claim to be the smallest Christian church in the world—eight feet deep, eight feet wide, and ten feet long, with a crucifix made from fourteenth-century Spanish ivory. There is a waterfall made from five hundred tons of glacial rock. It falls into a pool filled with tropical fish and water lilies. In one statue Venus is born, in another Buddha laughs, in a third a man sits in a rubber tree reading a book. All this is preserved as a perpetual reminder of Dr. B. J. Palmer, the founder of chiropractic medicine.

Palmer opened A Little Bit o' Heaven in 1924 to display some of the curios and plants he had collected in his travels around the world. As he travelled, he collected more, and the garden grew. Intricate stonework surrounds the religious statues and flora—tables, planters, columns, and gazebos all constructed like three-dimensional mosiacs. The design is completely eclectic, with no aesthetic logic other than the desire to create a lush and wondrous garden full of treasures.

One has the advantage of knowing that if one gets a crick in the back while gawking at the many bits o' heaven, there is a college full of chiropractors right next door.

DES MOINES

WORLD PIPE-SMOKING CHAMPIONSHIP

30th Annual contest—to be held at Howard Johnson's Motor Lodge,
4800 Merle Hay Road, Des Moines, Iowa;
Aug. 4,5,6, 1978; free

Each contestant gets 3.3 grams of tobacco. At the call "Light your pipes," they have sixty seconds to get the tobacco burning, after which all matches and excess tobacco are removed. One or two hours later there will be only one man left puffing a lit pipe. He will be the World Champion Pipe Smoker. The idea is to keep that 3.3 grams of tobacco burning for as long as possible. The minute you can't produce a puff of smoke, you're out. The all-time record was set in 1975 by William Vargo, who kept his brier going for two hours, six minutes, thirty-nine seconds, smashing the twenty-one year record held by Max Igree of two hours, five minutes, and seven seconds. The 1977 defending champion is Paul Spaniola, who won with a time of seventy-six minutes, fifty-two seconds. He attributed the low score to the air-conditioning unit in the competition hall. "It created so much suction that the tobacco burned fast. Only three of us went over an hour." The second-place winner, though, was only thirty-nine seconds behind Spaniola, making this a neck-and-neck contest.

Pipe-smoking is not generally considered a spectator sport, but one visit to the world championship and you may find yourself hooked. Imagine the tension as a contestant senses his pipe is about to go out: He huffs, he puffs, he blows, he disassembles the pipe—all in hopes of fanning an ember. There are surprises, too, like a sudden sneeze fatefully extinguishing an otherwise well-cared for bowl, or a sudden plug of tobacco drawn into the stem, blocking the air drafts and calling for quick, sure extraction before the fire goes out.

There is plenty of action in the smoke-filled air; and as contestants drop out there is a tension not normally associated with the calm induced by puffing leisurely on a pipe. All this brierophilia is, in fact, practiced in the name of peace. The motto of the International Association of Pipe-Smoking Clubs is "Peace through pipe smoking." Head of the clubs, defending champion, and instructor in pipe smoking, Paul Spaniola told us "The Indians knew it long ago. They knew that the paper those treaties were written on wasn't worth a hoot. But smoking the pipe—that meant something. Believe me, if everybody smoked a pipe, there wouldn't be any wars."

INDIANOLA

U.S. NATIONAL HOT AIR BALLOON CHAMPIONSHIPS

Simpson College, N. Buxton St. & W. Clinton Ave., Indianola, Iowa; August 4–12, 1978 (Always 2nd week of August); free

There are over eight hundred racing balloons in the United States today—and that is a lot of hot air. Since the cost of one of these sixty-foot bags, fully equipped, can get as high as twelve thousand dollars, most balloonatics work through clubs. Each year the clubs congregate in Indianola to determine a national champion balloon racer.

Aeronauts (balloon pilots) compete in four events: Convergent Navigational Task, Predetermined Spot Landing, Elbow Task, and Hare and Hounds. The CNT requires the aeronaut to take his aerostat (balloon) over a fixed target, and drop something there to mark his proximity to the target. For the Predetermined Spot Landing, the aeronaut chooses a field five miles from the start and tries to get as close to it as the wind and his skill will allow. The object of the Elbow Task is to fly to a spot three miles away, then come back via a totally different course. Aeronauts are judged by the variance (more is better) between the outgoing and return trip. The Hare and Hounds is modeled after a fox hunt. The "Hare" is a lead balloon that all the "Hounds" (other balloons) try to follow. The winning Hound is the one that lands closest to the Hare.

Balloon-racing is not a sport that sets spectators' blood racing. Fliers still depend on an open flame to heat their air to lift-off temperature, and the prevailing winds determine how fast the aerostats can move. It is nonetheless one of the most graceful and quiet racing sports imaginable. You can watch it lying flat on your back.

LE GRAND

F. W. STICE'S CARVINGS

The Doll Museum, 409 E. Main St. (Rt. 30), Le Grand, Iowa;
May–Nov daily 7 AM–8 PM; donation

F. W. Stice was a tailor who died a few years ago at the age of ninety-six. During his retirement he carved tiny wooden figures and dressed them in scaled-to-size, hand-tailored outfits. His work is now on display in the back of a souvenir store run by Mrs. Gladys Stice. The small sign outside says simply "Doll Museum"—hardly a hint of the talent displayed within.

There are forty-five tableaux carved in wood. Each is about two feet across, and in front of the painted and carved backgrounds there are six-inch-tall people acting out scenes from Mr. Stice's imagination and memory. There is "The Quilting Bee," "The Square Dance in 1890," and "Skating Party." "Down in Mississippi" shows three black musicians in energetic poses, dressed in sports coats and bow ties, strumming guitars and singing. "The Square Dance" freezes a crowd of country people in the middle of their dos-à-dos.

They wear calico dresses, overalls and straw hats; the band is playing tiny carved instruments. Other scenes show soldiers, country bumpkins, Southerners, cowboys—all dressed in perfect miniature style, all engaged in their own special activities, all expressing on their faces a special enjoyment of their lives. Stice was a master carver. His work is expressive, energetic, and genuinely charming without being sentimental or overly cute. Ignore the touristy façade of this small store, and pay your donation to see Mr. Stice's work before some folk art museum or smart collector snaps it up.

NEWTON

MAYTAG HISTORICAL CENTER

300 W. 4th St., N., Newton, Iowa;
daily 8 AM–8 PM; free

It is easy to imagine what a Movietone newsreel crew from the early 1950s would have done with the Maytag Historical Center: "Here they are! *(trumpets blare)* Laundry . . . on the March!!" At this, the camera pulls back to show rows and rows of gleaming washtubs, lined up like the First Infantry, ready to march into the homes of America and do the wash of a mighty nation.

Today the Maytag approach is more folksy. They are the people who bring you "Ol' Lonely," the repairman in the TV commercial who never gets any calls, thanks to the sturdy build of the new machines. But a walk through the Historical Center recalls days when the washing machine was practically a revolutionary presence in the home, doing diapers by the dozen for growing families. The first Maytag was called the Pastime (1907). It's here along with the newer Gyrafoamers, the Master Wringers, and the fifteen millionth Maytag (produced in the early 1960s). Each is in mint condition, and is lined up for easy comparison and contrast. Above each machine, on the wall or next to it, the curators have placed newspapers, lamps, and other period bric-a-brac to set the mood.

Serious students of sanitation will be happy to know that the Maytag Historical Center includes dryers as well as washers, including the Halo-of-Heat model first offered to the public in 1957. There are dishwashers and disposals on display, too. For further research, we recommend a trip to Chicago's Museum of Science and Industry, where Maytag has built "The Tale of a Tub," featuring a see-through seven-hundred-gallon clothes agitator.

You may come home to realize that you own a museum piece.

STANTON

MRS. OLSON'S HOME TOWN—THE WORLD'S LARGEST COFFEE POT

Stanton, Iowa, Rt. 34 E. of Red Oak

Mrs. Olson is the kindly Swedish lady on television who rescues young couples from marital difficulties by showing them how to brew a decent cup of coffee. If Joe DiMaggio is "Mr. Coffee," she is the Queen of the Pot. The two of them together have probably produced more caffeine jitters than the Hills Brothers. Mrs. Olson's real name is Virginia Christine, and she hails from Stanton, Iowa, a town whose emblem is a giant coffee pot.

Stanton is the Swedish capital of Iowa, and they put up the pot as a symbol of hospitality. Like every single house in town, it is white with a floral design. It is a "percolator-style" pot, with a handle, a spout, a knob on top, and flames painted on the bottom. It rises 125 feet in the air and is lit at night. The big pot is said to hold 640,000 cups of coffee.

TAMA

WEIR'S MINIATURE CARNIVAL

1000 W. 13th St.; Tama, Iowa;
Memorial Day–Labor Day daily 9 AM–5:30 PM; 25¢

Ron Weir's idea of a good time is to go to a carnival with his wife and take measurements. "He constructed the Spitfire when we were dating," Mrs. Weir told us, "and I can't remember how many carnivals we've been to since then." The happy result of this hobby, which began in 1949, is a miniature carnival that occupies the back room of what would otherwise be a run-of-the-mill souvenir and gift shop.

But the minute you go through the doorway, you are transported into a land of midway thrills and blood-rushing excitement. In a space that seems hardly bigger than eight feet square, an entire miniature carnival is in full swing. Over five hundred tiny light bulbs—some no bigger than grains of wheat—light the rides, the midway, and the concessions. There are cotton-candy stands, spill-the-bottle games, shooting galleries, and a freak show. A boy is trying to impress his girl by slamming the hammer down on the Hi-Striker. In the snake wagon a miniature python writhes up and down on a hidden piston.

The scene is breathtaking. As if entering the midway of a real carnival, everything beckons for your attention. The hootchy-kootchy girls lure you one way. Death-defying acts are promised in the Spinaroo and Motordome. Princess Atasha—next to the Stage of Horror—threatens to turn from a woman into a gorilla. "Is She Human?" asks a miniature sign.

The walls of this room are covered with carnival posters. Perhaps the tight space and flickering lights add to the headiness of this scene. But it is a shock to leave and realize that you have only been in the back room of a small store that sells corny Indian pottery and junk jewelry.

A more mundane but in some ways stranger sight awaits the dedicated seeker of the unusual while in Tama, Iowa. There is a man in town who has the world's largest collection of different gas station oil rags—a total of over 1,300. They are stacked up in his basement, and he does not operate the collection as a tourist attraction. But serious collectors, potential donors, and dedicated aficionados are invited to ask directions in the town's general store. From there, you will be sent to the collection. It is a conceptual sight more than a physical wonder, but well worth the trip if you like bizarre collections, or have never seen a spotless oil rag.

WEST BEND

THE GROTTO OF THE REDEMPTION

Iowa 15 at the north end of West Bend, Iowa;
daily 8 AM–5 PM;
suggested donations: 50¢ adults, 25¢ children

The Grotto of the Redemption is the largest collection of petrifaction in any one spot in the world. Shells, fossils, and all manner of petrified plants and animals are encrusted all over what is known as the largest grotto in the world. Stones and minerals from every state and every continent give this place an estimated geological value of nearly three million dollars. For forty-two years Father Paul Dobberstein pressed rocks and minerals and petrified matter into concrete in order to tell the story of how Christ set out to redeem the world.

The grotto is actually composed of nine individual grottos, each portraying a scene from the life of Christ. Each is a cacophonous mosaic. At the Grotto of Gethsemane there is a replica of Michelangelo's "Pietà." It is placed at the top of a forty-foot mountain that is encrusted with shells and stones. Over one hundred carloads of rocks were used to build the cavelike Grotto of the Ten Commandments.

Next to the grottos is the Christmas Chapel, which contains Father Dobberstein's twenty-two-foot-high altar, carved from bird's-eye maple. The chapel also houses a three-hundred-pound Brazilian amethyst.

KANSAS

ABILENE

GREYHOUND HALL OF FAME

407 S. Buckeye, Abilene, Kan.;
April–Oct daily 9 AM–5 PM, Nov–March Fri, Sat & Sun 9 AM–5 PM; donation

Dog racing is like horse racing in that it is possible to love dogs and still have no affinity whatsoever for the sport at which they excel. Watching muzzled greyhounds race around a track has little in common with playing tug-of-war with your pet dog, or hunting with your retriever, or giving your poodle its weekly bouffant hairdo. And so we expected not to like the Greyhound Hall of Fame, dedicated as it is to professional racing dogs. But in the lobby sits Texas, a tall, slim, brindle-coated mascot who won our hearts and immediately erased any innate prejudice about skinny athletic dogs being high-strung. Texas is as even-tempered as can be as she greets visitors, flirts with photographers, feigns boredom, then finally falls into her "glamour" poses.

Texas does a good job of putting visitors in the right mood to bone up on her sport. Inside this luxurious, modern building is the story of greyhound racing from 5000 B.C., including a spectacular 160-foot-scale model dog track and plaques to honor the great greyhounds of history. There are slide shows, pictures, and narration. Of course, we would be happy to skip all this and spend the day in a museum that enshrined Cute Dogs of History, or Cavorting Canines. But for the dogtrack tout, this is the complete museum.

THE MICROZOO

S.E. 6th and Kuney, Abilene, Kan.;
March–Sept daily 10 AM–6 PM;
adults: $1, under 12: 55¢

Most of the animals in this zoo are not actually very cute, but some are quite beguiling. Take, for instance, the amoeba, who is microprojected onto the wall, wriggling and squirming about as happily as if he were in his natural habitat. The suctorian is a little devil, living as he does on the back of a snapping turtle. He's a sedentary type of guy who puts on the feedbag by paralyzing other microscopic animals, then sucking them dry. These are only two of the zoo's residents. Some are larger—like the horseshoe crab and the chicken embryo and the pseudoscorpion. A whole section of the zoo is reserved for molds and fungi, including live cultures of cheese and beverage molds, and even one jet-setter who thrives in the fuel tanks of airplanes. In the "Underseas World" you can observe a forty-one-inch man-eating clamshell (now domesticated). In "The World on a Turtle's Back" you will see the more than one thousand different animals that constitute a veritable microcivilization on the back of a tortoise.

In fact, the animals in this zoo are so weird that there is one on display about which the zookeepers ask "What is it? Does it live on earth or in outer space?" If you can guess what it is, you get into the zoo at a reduced price.

BONNER SPRINGS

AGRICULTURAL HALL OF FAME

Bonner Springs, Kan.;
Daily 9 AM–5 PM;
adults: $1.50; children: 50¢

The Agricultural Hall of Fame is a colossal place built to show off "the largest enterprise in America." It is housed in two buildings and an enormous field, and its exhibits include everything from a full-size, one-room schoolhouse to a collection of over three hundred different kinds of barbed wire. Outside there are antique cars, horsedrawn carriages, and a vast collection of farm machinery. Inside there is a see-through Allis-Chalmers gleaner combine with all operating parts visible. There is an old-time veterinarian's office with horrifying horse-sized operating tools, a fully equipped log cabin, a display of antique telephones, a blacksmith shop, a butter-churn collection, and several carved miniature farm scenes. Anything remotely associated with agriculture or farm life is here.

Every year on the last two Sundays in July the Agricultural Hall of Fame stages a threshing show at which a great deal of this old-time machinery is put to use. Steam engines, water wagons, a sawmill and scale-model steam trains all go into operation. Local farmers enter into the horse- and pony-pull contests, and there are country-music concerts in the evening.

Bonner Springs, incidentally, is within one hundred miles of the exact geographical center of the United States in Lebanon, Kansas.

CAWKER CITY

THE WORLD'S LARGEST (OR SECOND LARGEST) BALL OF TWINE

Wisconsin St. (Rt. 24), Cawker City, Kan.

In 1953 Frank Stoeber, a farmer from Cawker City, tripped over a piece of twine lying on the ground near his barn. He picked it up and rolled it into a ball, and vowed he wouldn't trip over twine again. To that end, he spent the next twenty years rolling up all the twine he could find. "The world's largest ball of twine" is now his legacy, and is on view by the side of the road in Cawker City.

The ball is kept under a parabolic hood shelter to protect it from the elements, and is illuminated at night. It has a circumference of twenty-nine feet, weighs 8,953 pounds, and contains over one and a half million feet of twine. It grew so large that toward the end of his project, Mr. Stoeber had to use a long stick with a hook at the end to work the string around in a circle. And, in order to keep it circular, he used a tractor and hook to rotate the ball. The Cawker City Community Club (now in charge of the ball of twine) says

77th ANNUAL
NATIONAL
Hobo Convention
Britt, Iowa
Saturday
August 6, 1977

The Hobo Convention, Britt, Iowa

*The Greyhound Hall of Fame,
Abilene, Kan.*

*The late Frank Stoeber with his Ball of Twine,
Cawker City, Kan.*

that if the ball were unrolled down U.S. Highway 24 eastward, it would reach Carrollton, Missouri. "We don't know how far west it would reach," they said, "because it is too heavy to roll uphill."

Travelers will want to compare Mr. Stoeber's ball of twine with Francis Johnson's in Minnesota. They look approximately the same size, although Johnson claims the greater weight. We do know that both men knew of each other's work, although neither saw the other's ball of twine. It seems fair to say that these roadside wonders are a testament to what free competition can inspire.

COFFEYVILLE

ORAL WATTS TELEPHONE MUSEUM

RR #1, Box 305, 3 1/2 mi. SW of Coffeyville, Kan.;
hours erratic; donation; (316) 251–5605

We have a friend named Michael who has a hobby of collecting names of people that reflect their work: Storm Field, the weatherman, Francine Prose the writer, and B. M. Harvard, the Boston proctologist. Oral Watts, curator of a telephone museum, is one of our favorite examples. His mother had no idea he would develop a fascination for telephones when she named him Oral, and the family name was Watts long before that marathon talker's favorite, the WATS-line, was invented.

Oral started collecting phones when a friend gifted him with an antique crank-model wall phone. He now has a collection of over 3,000 telephones and telephone parts, and most of them are on exhibit at his farm in Coffeyville. The phones are kept in a small building next to his home, and he is willing to show them off to interested passers-by. He has one that he says predates Alexander Graham Bell's by ten years. He also has a full line of touchtones and Princesses, as well as wall phones, desk phones, switchboards, wooden phones, and hundreds of phone photos. "Just stop in," Mr. Watts says. "There's no need to call."

GREENSBURG

THE BIG WELL

Sycamore St., 3 blocks S. of US 54, Greensburg, Kan.;
June–Sept daily 7 AM–9 PM, Oct–May 8:30 AM–6 PM;
free to look, 35¢ to walk down

A conversation overheard at the Big Well:

KID: "I decided not to go down. I'm scared."

FATHER: "Go! I paid 35¢. You wanted to go. Go!"

KID: "Do I have to?"

LADY SELLING SOUVENIRS: "It's educational."

The father joined his son and both descended into the world's largest hand-dug well, leaving Mom, along with us, peering down from above. What, exactly, is educational about walking down a narrow staircase into a hundred-and-nine-foot hole we cannot say. But we did watch father and son emerge victorious and leave with many souvenir ashtrays, bumper stickers, and plates by which to remember their journey.

A few years ago *The Wall Street Journal* published an amusing article about tourism in Kansas in which they used the Big Well as the butt of their jests about the state's eccentric attractions. There *is* something odd about attracting tourists by means of a hole in the ground, unless one wants to put the Big Well in the same class as the Grand Canyon. But the Big Well offers more: inside the souvenir shop there is "Space Wanderer," the world's largest pallasite meteorite. And the souvenir shop itself is a marvel, selling plates depicting all the presidents and their wives, mini-meteorites, and slides and post cards showing leggy cowgirls standing next to Space Wanderer and waving from atop the Big Well.

HARPER

ROSALEA˙'S HOTEL

121 W. Main St., Harper, Kan.;
May–Labor Day; no phone

Rosalea˙ (she spells it with the dot) feels that media coverage of her unique hotel has distorted the facts, so we quote from her own brochure: "If you can find inspiration in the vast flatness of the Kansas prairie and it's [sic] open skies; if you aren't afraid to pick a purple daisy blooming in a pile of fresh cow shit; or if listening to coyotes howling songs of love on a clear, starry night makes goose bumps slide down your spine—then you know Life intimately and you will have no difficulty understanding what Rosalea's Hotel is all about, for it is like that subtle beauty many cannot fathom. But if you are part of the 99.9 percent Americans who need 'plastic' commercialism in order to obtain pleasure, then I suggest you find another sleeping place more geared to your needs."

What's it like at Rosalea's? "The decor of the hotel is '1960s decadent' poorly integrated with '1950s bland.' It has one-socket lighting, artesian-type plumbing, mattresses that resemble a lumpy hammock, and water marks on the ceiling."

What about reservations? "There is no longer a telephone at Rosalea's Hotel. I wearied of hassling with a phone company that took much and gave little but rip-offs and empty promises . . . It's always nice for my head to know when 'company's coming,' but it certainly isn't necessary in order to secure a room . . . If you want a room and the front door is locked, ring the doorbell twice (so I will know you want a room and are not just a gawking tourist)."

But what about tourists and sightseers who want to look around but not stay? Rosalea offers a "Tourist and Sightseer Membership" for $2.50, "Good for a one-time, one hour visit . . . I will let you in if I am not busy."

What is there to see at Rosalea's? "Art on exhibit or . . . unscheduled activity such as reading, listening to music, working puzzles, or just relaxing." And there is Rosalea's "Hide Art," which consists of hundreds of 1 1/4 inch-square lithographs that she has put up all over the country in phone booths, libraries, art museums, supermarkets, and even the White House. They are hidden in these places with the inscription on the back: "This miniature piece of art was hidden by Rosalea for the finder's enjoyment; it is intended as a gentle reminder to purchase the work of living artists; for they get hungry, too!"

We don't know if there is any Hide Art in Rosalea's Hotel, "The Oasis of the Bible Belt—Since 1968." But we can guarantee that there is no hotel like this anywhere else in the country. Rosalea used to call it "The Hotel with a Happening." It still is.

LIBERAL

INTERNATIONAL PANCAKE DAY

Shrove Tuesday, Liberal, Kan.

For over five hundred years the women of Olney, England have been racing to church when they hear the bell on Shrove Tuesday. It is said that the custom began when a housewife, using up all her cooking fats (forbidden during Lent) by making a batch of pancakes, heard the shriving bell ring out. She ran to church so fast she forgot to remove her apron and, in fact, still had her skillet in her hand. Next year, the neighbors took to this method of arriving at church, and pretty soon they were all running at the sound of the bell, hoping to be the first to collect the "Kiss of Peace" from the bell-ringer.

In 1950, Liberal, Kansas joined the competition and now, every Shrove Tuesday, the two towns have a cross-continental competition, with winning scores over the 415-yard course compared by trans-Atlantic telephone. Entrants must wear housedresses, aprons, and headscarves, and have to flip their pancake twice during the run. The score now stands at 16–11 in favor of Liberal.

Both races begin exactly at 11:55 A.M., Kansas time.

LUCAS

THE GARDEN OF EDEN

2nd & Kansas St.; Lucas, Kan.;
Summer Daily 9:30 AM–5:30 PM, Winter Daily 10 AM–4 PM;
Adults: $1.50, Under 12: free

"This is my sign—GARDEN OF EDEN. I could hear so many, as they go by, sing out, 'What is this?' so I put this sign up." Those were the words of S. P. Dinsmoor, deceased, who created what he considered to be "the most unique home, for living or dead, on earth." Dinsmoor was a Civil War veteran who, at the age of eighty-one, married a twenty-year-old woman, moved to Lucas, Kansas, fathered a child, and began building the Garden of Eden.

In the center of the garden is Dinsmoor's "Cabin Home," made from stone cut to look exactly like logs. Here he and his young family lived while he created the garden outside. The garden tells the story of Cain and Abel, Adam and Eve, the soldier and the Indian, the dog and the fox, capital *vs.* labor, liberty *vs.* the trusts, and God *vs.* the Devil. Everything is made from concrete. Dinsmoor's statuary surrounds the home, climbs on concrete "trees," hangs from concrete lampposts. Above it all waves the world's largest concrete American flag. The statues are painted, and some of the scenes are bloody. It is a labyrinth of energetic figures—some sweet, some dignified, some ghastly —all forming a vast, primitive, private universe, the logic of which was known only to S. P. Dinsmoor.

Although he is dead, you can still see him when you visit the Garden of Eden. He had himself put in a glass coffin, which was placed in his stone mausoleum (along with a jug of water to carry below). Before his death he said "I have a will that none shall go in to see me for less than a dollar. I promise everyone that comes in to see me (they can look through the plate glass in the lid of my coffin and see my face) that if I see them dropping a dollar in the hands of the flunky, and I see the dollar, I will give them a smile." The price of admission to the Garden of Eden is now up to $1.50, and a peek at what's left of Dinsmoor is part of the tour.

MEDICINE LODGE

CARRY NATION HOME

211 W. Fowler (Hwy. 160), Medicine Lodge, Kan.;
Summer daily 9 AM–5 PM, Winter daily 1 PM–5 PM; 50¢

On June 6, 1900, Carry Nation rode from her home in Medicine Lodge to Kiowa, Kansas and there smashed up the town's saloons with her hatchet. Mrs. Nation was not by nature a violent or anarchic person, but if there was one thing that made this temperate, Christian woman mad it was booze. Her first husband had been a drunkard, and so she took it upon herself to become the "Loving Home Defender," as she is known today by the still-faithful W.C.T.U. Her home is now maintained as a peaceful memorial to her activities. There are pictures, articles, and historical mementos here documenting the life of a woman who was "loved and respected by her friends and feared by her enemies."

WICHITA

LEROY'S MOTORCYCLE MUSEUM

1441 S. Washington, Wichita, Kan.;
Saturday only 9 AM–4 PM
call in advance —(316) 262–2181; free

Leroy Hamilton and his wife remember the gypsy days of motorcycling, the way it was before *The Wild One* crystallized the equation of biker with hood. They now run a motorcycle museum in Wichita with exactly four exhibits— four of their retired bikes. What they lack in variety they make up for by a wealth of folklore and personal reminiscence about the days when cycling was a real adventure. "Mrs. Leroy," as Mrs. Hamilton calls herself, was once a "Motor Maid," the first (and perhaps only) road-riders club exclusively for women. Leroy himself has retired from biking, and now sells parts for pre-1968 BMW motorcycles.

Here is what their museum contains: a BMW they call "Rommel," which looks as if it was hauled across the Sahara during the war; a '59 BMW complete with sidecar; a '64 BMW fully loaded with every available accessory; and Mrs. Leroy's personal favorite, a blue late '50s BMW with 99,999 miles on the odometer.

There are stories that go with each mile chalked up by the motorvatin' Hamiltons. Also on display are motorcycle trophies they won, pictures of cycling "as it used to be," and scrapbooks of pictures and mementos from their gypsy tours.

WILSON

ED ROOT'S FARM GARDEN

N. out of Lucas on 232 past Lake Wilson to the 2nd dirt road on the right in Wilson, Kan.

Ed Root's home and much of his original sculpture garden is now at the bottom of man-made Lake Wilson. But before the flood, a significant portion of what he created was moved to his son's farm here in Wilson. Now John Root, Ed's son, is an old man himself, living in an archetypal Kansas farm-house, surrounded by a garden full of concrete and glass sculpture. The sculptures are arranged neatly in rows, almost as if they were an audience looking out over the land. Some are human forms, some are birds or turtles, and others are abstract. Into the concrete Root pressed bits of colored glass and mirror, or tiny pieces of china, wire, or colorful stones. On the human forms he hung hats or beads. One human shape that looks like a cutout doll holds a coffee pot in one hand.

John Root is pleased to have people look around this outdoor exhibit of his father's work. When you walk through the garden, you get a sense of Ed Root's whimsical sensibilities. A tiny china Donald Duck peeps out from under a concrete toadstool. One shiny construction of mirror and glass is built around a rubber three-way electrical plug—a shrine to electricity. Real antlers sprout from an expressionistic concrete moose head. Brush away some new foliage and you see the letters E-d-R-o-o-t sparkling out of the earth, where they were once planted in concrete and glass.

MICHIGAN

MURAL CITY

Downtown Bay City, Mich.

There was once a Scottish rock-and-roll group that needed a name. They stuck a pin into a map of the world, looking for a town to lend them one, and they wound up as the Bay City Rollers. But their popularity is not the only thing that has put Bay City on the map. The town is building a reputation as Mural City U.S.A.

It began as a bicentennial project to correct deterioration of the downtown area, and has now resulted in one of the most unusual looking business districts in America. There are fifty different murals painted on the walls of Bay City by artist Terry Dickensen. He has used a specially developed, long-lasting exterior paint to illustrate historic scenes. Other murals depict all the men whose faces appear on currency; a figure of blind Justice; an astronaut, and racing automobiles.

Dickerson started by painting houses, and then took a few courses in art at a local college. His first mural was for a local Pontiac dealership, and now the town is covered with his work. It is one of the most colorful downtown areas anywhere.

DEARBORN

THE WORLD'S LARGEST TIRE

W. of Oakwood Blvd. exit off I–94 Dearborn, Mich.

Akron, Ohio boasts that it is the rubber capital of America, but Dearborn Michigan has the largest tire. It is a whitewall outside the Uniroyal factory, clearly visible from the highway. We've heard rumors about a similar 100-foot-tall tire somewhere in the Akron area among the rubber works, but have seen neither the Ohio tire nor documented proof of its existence. So if you want to be sure of seeing a colossal tire, go to Dearborn.

DETROIT

THE MONEY MUSEUM

National Bank of Detroit, Tower 2, Renaissance Center Street level,
Detroit, Mich.;
Mon–Fri 9 AM–4:30 PM; free

You couldn't bring a boar's tusk to a teller at the Detroit National Bank and expect to change it for singles, but there is an exhibit here of "money" from around the world that includes boars' tusks, and cowrie shells, along with bars of silver, early coins, gold, and a $10,000 bill. Guided tours are available on request. No free samples.

FENTON

THE PAINTED BARNS OF FENTON, MICHIGAN

7200 US 23 & 10231 Parshallville Rd., Fenton, Mich.

"Ziggy Grabowski" is the alias of an artist who reproduces famous works of art on the sides of farmers' barns. One of his creations, belonging to Cornell Dexter, is at 7200 US 23. Here, painted in shades of black and white, is an exact copy of John Singleton Copley's study of Paul Revere, two stories tall. Nearby, on Robert Wakeman's barn, Ziggy has reproduced a sixteenth-century study of Baldassare Castiglione by Raphael. They are faithful reproductions of the original works of art, but somehow their magnification and their location in the middle of a rural landscape turn the contemplative portraits into exclamation marks. One expects both Paul Revere and Castiglione to be endorsing a soft drink or sun-tan lotion.

GRAND HAVEN

THE MUSICAL FOUNTAIN

Dewey Hill, Grand Haven, Mich.;
Memorial Day–June, one show nightly at 9:45,
July–Labor Day, one show nightly at 9:30 PM; free

• There are 1,875,352,500,000,000 possible musico-visual variations of this fountain.
• It would require twenty million years and four billion miles of tape to record all these different variations.
• There are over 20,000 feet of electrical wiring.

These statistics might not impress the folks at the Juillard School of Music, but the fountain in Grand Haven is in a class by itself. It is the largest of its kind; "its kind" being fountains that play in synchronization with music and colored lights that illuminate shooting jets of water. The repertoire is mostly pop, but anything is possible. The only disappointment is that Esther Williams never rises on a pedestal in the center of it all.

GRAYLING

THE FRED BEAR MUSEUM

RR #1, off Rt. 72, Grayling, Mich.;
daily 10 AM–6 PM; adults: $1, 6–12: 50¢

Fred Bear shot bear and just about every other creature that walks, runs, or flies—all with a bow and arrow. Very few people have honed their archery skills to the degree of accuracy, strength, and stealth required to hunt game, and this is the only museum we know specializing in bow-and-arrow trophies. Along with the stuffed animals, the bear museum has what is reputed to be the world's largest private collection of archery artifacts, including unusual bows and a fantastic collection of arrows from around the world. On the second floor of the museum you can see movies of Fred Bear in action, on some of his hunts.

The Fred Bear Museum also contains a pro shop, and cases filled with medals and awards won by archers who shoot at concentric targets instead of wild beasts.

THE HARTWICK PINES LUMBERING MUSEUM

Rt. 93, 7 mi. NE of Grayling, Mich.;
summer daily 8 AM–10 PM; free

We have always envied the legendary lumberjack; not so much for his robust life style as for the number of calories he is listed as needing in all the diet books. While we who spend the day sitting at a desk are allotted a few hundred calories to fuel our efforts, the mighty logger gets thousands of calories worth of flapjacks, oatmeal, and pork chops to start his day. The lumberman's two-fisted diet is typical of the heroic proportions he has assumed in American folklore.

The Hartwick Pines Lumbering Museum tells of the years that gave birth to these legends—the late 1800s, when Michigan produced more lumber than any other state. One hundred and sixty billion board feet of pine were cut between 1869 and 1897—enough to build ten million six-room houses or to floor the entire state of Michigan, with enough left over to cover Rhode Island. The dollar value of this wood was greater than all the gold mined in California during the same period. The museum displays the tools of these booming years in reproductions of lumber-camp buildings, and large dioramas depicting the logger's life. There are pictures of camps and old mills, and stories of strikes and treacherous logjams. But the nicest part of the museum is its location— in a stand of virgin white pines.

INDIAN RIVER

THE WORLD'S LARGEST CRUCIFIX

The Catholic Shrine in Burt Lake State Park, 1/2 block W. of I–75,
Indian River, Mich.

The World's Largest Crucifix is wood and bronze. The cross is constructed from California redwood. It is fifty-five feet high, twenty-two feet wide, and weighs seven tons. It is in a rustic setting at the Catholic Shrine, and on each side are the "Holy Stairs," "for those who wish to go to the cross on their knees." Each stair contains "a First-Class Relic." There are rows of pews in front of the cross for the various Masses that are said here daily.

Also on display at the shrine is a statue of Our Lady of the Highway carved from Carrera marble, and a display of dolls dressed as nuns, representing two hundred and seventeen religious orders, with meticulous attention to detail. The dolls are displayed in cases along the walls of a room that is also used for bingo games.

The shrine, which has one of the best-stocked souvenir stores in the Midwest, is situated in lovely woods, with paths to wander along. You can get everything from shrine jewelry to alligator-head "fanny-pinchers."

ISHPEMING

THE NATIONAL SKI HALL OF FAME

Mather Ave. and Poplar St., Ishpeming, Mich.;
Mid-June–Labor Day daily 10 AM–4 PM,
rest of year Wed–Sun 1 PM–4 PM donation

Skiing was introduced to America by Carl Tellefsen, a Norwegian who came to Michigan and became the first president of the National Ski Association (now called the United States Ski Association). The NSA was founded in 1904 in Ishpeming, Michigan, "the birthplace of organized skiing in the United States," and home of the National Ski Hall of Fame.

The building that houses the hall of fame is a simple two-story structure that you could almost mistake for a home or tavern. On the ground floor there are displays of skis, Olympic memorabilia, and a replica of the ancient arctic type of ski and pole, used 4000 years ago by Stone Age people to traverse the snowy north. Upstairs there are pictures of honored members of the hall of fame, selected from four categories: athletes (who have to be at least forty years old to be elected), ski-sport builders, athletes-of-the-year, and foreigners from any of the three categories.

Some of the skis here are beautiful, carved and painted with elaborate floral patterns. Others look like broomsticks. The most famous pair was pointed out to us: Oscar Gunderson's "yoompin' " skis, the ones he wore in 1909 for his record 138-foot jump.

Any questions you have about the sport as you look at the trophies, exhibits, and artifacts will be answered by the senior citizens who staff the hall of fame on a volunteer basis. They are local Ishpemingers, and more than likely have tumbled down a few slopes in their younger days.

LELAND

LUND'S SCENIC GARDENS

On M22 between Leland and Glen Arbor, Mich.;
Memorial Day–Oct 1, daily 8 AM–10 PM; donation

Lund's Scenic Gardens are a primitive tour de force created by two evangelical ministers, Mr. and Mrs. Lund. They were inspired to build their garden in 1938 while painting scenery for a church play. They relied on God's good will to provide the strength and money to finish their creation. Mrs. Lund battled blindness and a heart attack while working with her husband, but eventually the garden was finished, and it is now open for all to see.

It is like a Rousseau painting, but with a religious theme. It is most beautiful at night, when the thirty-six scenes depicting Christ's life are illuminated. The scenes are placed within sixteen wooded acres, and they are observed by slowly walking along a designated path. Each looks like a stage set, flatly two-dimensional, depth being created by placing one flat in front of another. Cut-out flowers, rocks, and stones are interspersed with real ones. All the angels, animals, and people are drawn with a charmingly naïve skill, and at night the illumination makes them resemble the figures you might see peeking through an ornate Easter egg. Our favorite scenes are the pastoral ones, populated with cattle, lambs, and shepherds, and profusely decorated with painted flora.

"Most art is carefully guarded in a building," Mrs. Lund says. "This is right out in the open woods, under the trees."

OSSINEKE

DINOSAUR GARDENS PREHISTORICAL ZOO

US 23 S. of Ossineke, Mich.;
daily May–Oct, park always open;
adults: $1, children: 50¢

The showpiece of Dinosaur Gardens is a sixty-thousand-pound, life-size brontosaurus. It has a staircase leading up into its rib cage, where there is a pink and white candy-stripe painted shrine to Jesus Christ, "the greatest heart." The brontosaurus is the only "walk-in" dinosaur here, but it is a good example of the very special nature of this prehistorical zoo. Surrounding the brontosaurus is a paradise of tall pine trees, wild flowers, shrubs, and swamps—populated by sculptures of other dinosaurs, and statues of early man battling pythons or looking for food. There is a scene of the La Brea tar pits that shows mastodons and wolves ankle-deep in prehistoric muck.

The statuary is in good condition, and the piny setting is lush and natural. There are a few hand-lettered signs explaining that this is a "dog-jawed reptile," and that is a "herbivorous dinosaur." Other signs warn "no flower-picking" or "no climbing on the animals." Aside from these few regulations, it is an Edenic place. It operates on the honor system when there is no one up front to take admission money.

We have seen folk-art books in which the sculptures here are described as examples of naïve artistry. The statue of the man and the python, in particular, displays more imagination and exuberance than faithfulness to archaeological facts. Each dino has personality, from the rascal-eyed sail-back dimetrodon to the furtive paleoscincus. Far from the "Taiwan tackiness" of so many other dinosaur parks, this prehistorical zoo is a very special place, where nature, prehistory and religion mesh together in an idyllic way.

REED CITY

THE OLD RUGGED CROSS

The Old Rugged Cross Park, 5 mi. N. of Reed City on US 31, Reed City, Mich.

Several years ago, NBC polled its listeners to determine the most popular hymn in the country. "The Old Rugged Cross" won hands down. It was written in 1913 by the Reverend George Bennard, an evangelical minister who preached in every state of the union except Utah and Louisiana. For many years he made his home in Reed City, Michigan. In 1954 the Reed City Chamber of Commerce erected an Old Rugged Cross in his honor. "The two greatest thrills in his life," Reed City proclaims, "were riding in the Rose Bowl Parade in Pasadena, California on the 'Old Rugged Cross' float which was thirty-five feet long and covered with a large variety of flowers; the other was when the Chamber of Commerce of Reed City erected the 'Old Rugged Cross.' "

MINNESOTA

BEMIDJI

PAUL BUNYAN AND BABE THE BLUE OX

Rt. 71, Bemidji, Minn.

Our immediate reaction upon seeing this statue of Paul B. and his ox was to speculate about what might happen if these two took on the mammoth statue of Hermann the German, also in Minnesota. For this duel of titans we would recruit Inoshiro Honda or one of the other great Japanese monster movie directors. There could be dozens of sequels, the monstrous stars of which could be drawn from Minnesota's burgeoning population of larger-than-life fauna. At last look these included a Prairie Chicken (Rothsay) a pelican (Pelican Rapids), a duck (Blackduck), a loon (Vergas), and a muskie (Nevis)—plus a Jolly Green Giant in LeSeur and Paul Bunyan's girl friend in a Brainerd amusement park.

This statue of Paul and Babe in Bemidji was the first of Minnesota's mutant monuments. They are rough-hewn giants, and loom near an information center that has on display Paul Bunyan's shoehorn and toothbrush, as well as a fireplace that has been built with stones from every state in the union, plus Canada.

CHISOLM

MINNESOTA MUSEUM OF MINING & HILL-RUST-MAHONING MINE

Community Park, Chisolm, Minn.;
June–Labor Day Daily 8 AM–5 PM;
Adults: $1, children 12–18: 75¢;
Hill-Rust-Mahoning Mine is N.W. of Hibbing; free

Hibbing, Minnesota is the Iron Ore Capital of the World, the birthplace of Bob Dylan, and the home of the Greyhound bus. We don't know of any local monuments to Dylan, but Hibbing's two other famous products are given their due at the Minnesota Museum of Mining. The museum is in Chisolm, six miles Northeast of Hibbing. Here you can take a guided tour of an underground mine and look at tools and exhibits that illustrate the last seventy years of mining history.

Also in the museum is an early Greyhound bus. It is an ancient ancestor of the modern Americruiser—the fleet-footed rival of the long-haul trucker. The gray dog-line has developed considerably since its founding in 1914 (an open car was the first "bus"), and we don't know of another museum where bus aficionados can glimpse a bit of "the hound's" past.

In Hibbing, you can stand on a platform that provides a view of "the Grand Canyon of Minnesota"—a name that must make environmentalists shudder, since this "Grand Canyon" is the world's largest strip mine—four miles long, two miles wide, and, in some places, as deep as five hundred feet.

COSMOS

COSMOS, MINNESOTA

Cosmos is a heavenly place. It was once a plain Jane of a town, called Nelsontown after a pioneer named O. K. Nelson, known for being a "helpful person." But Daniel Hoyt, an easterner who moved here in 1870, wasn't happy with the handle Nelsontown. He thought this place would be perfect for a university, but he knew that any university worth its salt would prefer to take up residence in a town with a cultured name. He prevailed upon the Nelsonites, and they agreed to change the name of name of Nelsontown.

Hoyt chose the name Cosmos, a Greek word referring to the universe. Universe . . . university—it made perfect sense. To Hoyt, Cosmos meant the whole universe of created things, and soon the newly named Cosmosians saw their town as a universal place. Reverend Thomas Smrcka suggested they follow the stars: all streets and avenues must be given celestial names.

Although the universal university never came to town, you can enter Cosmos on Astro Boulevard (Highway 7) or the Milky Way (Highway 4, named for the town creamery). East-West streets are named for constellations; North-South for planets. So if someone here tells you to meet them on Mars, or just the other side of Gemini, don't call the men in the white coats. Just hop in your car and drive across Cosmos.

DARWIN

FRANCIS JOHNSON'S MUSEUM AND BALL OF TWINE

U.S. 12, Darwin, Minn.; 50¢

Francis Johnson's five-ton ball of twine is probably the most famous ball of twine in America, having appeared on *I've Got a Secret* (with Francis, too) and in *Ripley's Believe It or Not*. It is certainly heavier than the other huge ball of twine—in Cawker City, Kansas; but whether it is bigger is hard to say, since nobody has really compared them side by side.

But even if Francis Johnson's ball of twine were only the second largest in America, his museum would be unique. He has a collection of five thousand pens and pencils, seventeen hundred carpenter's aprons, sixty-five jacks, one hundred and forty Seven-Up bottles, one thousand wrenches, five meat cutters, nine poppy-seed grinders, two hundred and eighty-four Steam Engine Show buttons, three hundred hammers and hatchets, twenty different kinds of plows, four kinds of rope makers, and a creamery-can-cover expander. And lots more.

Francis's favorite pencil is one given to him by Mickey Mantle's mother. It has the name of Mickey's bowling alley on it. A runner-up pencil is the one with a three-foot-long eraser, "for people who goof a lot," says Francis. His favorite pen is engraved "Sam Rayburn, Speaker of Congress."

The museum is housed in the inverted bottom of a Dassel railroad water tower. The twine is outside.

ELY

ELY SLED-DOG RACES

Behind the old depot, downtown Ely, Minn.;
Jan 21 & 22, 1978; free

In late January, you might think Ely was Alaska and Hollywood had descended upon the town to remake *Nanook of the North*. More than two hundred and fifty sled dogs, mostly Siberian huskies, show up in this northern town for the All-American Sled Dog Races. If you are a spectator and not a musher, you will learn that "mush!" is a command strictly for the likes of Sergeant Preston and other celluloid Northerners. A real musher calls out "hike!" to get his team started, "gee!" to get them to go right, "haw!" for left. You'll also find out about things like snowhooks, snub ropes, and swing dogs. But the real fun of this event is not the lingo. It is watching the stamina and coordination of men and dogs pushing through snow too deep to walk through.

Expect to find these arctic aficionados engaging in Sled Dog Beauty Contests, Sled Dog Breakfasts, and Sled Dog Dances during the two-day event. After all, they have to thaw out sometime.

EVELETH

UNITED STATES HOCKEY HALL OF FAME

Just off Hwy 53 on Hat Trick Ave., Eveleth, Minn.;
June 15–Labor Day Mon–Sat 9 AM–8 PM, Sun 10 AM–8 PM,
Winter Mon–Sat 9 AM–5 PM, Sun noon–5 PM;
Family rate: $6, Adults: $2, children 13–17: $1, 6–12: 75¢

Why is the one-million-dollar Hockey Hall of Fame situated in Eveleth, Minnesota, a town of less than five thousand people? Eveleth has sent eleven players to the National Hockey League, and is considered to be the amateur hockey capital of the United States. In fact, of the thirty-nine members of this hall of fame, most are "amateurs," and most played long before the days professional hockey became synonymous with the televised blood baths of today.

On the first floor of the hall of fame there is a theater and a slide show that tell something of the history of hockey since the 1890s. There are exhibits of skating equipment, different styles of pucks, and methods of facing-off and checking. Each hall-of-famer gets a pylon dedicated to him, upon which are indicated his vital statistics and claim to fame.

NEW ULM

HERMANN THE GERMAN

Hermann Heights Park, W. of New Ulm, Minn.;
Sun–Fri 9 AM–4 PM; 10¢

Hermann the German is a one-hundred-and-two-foot-tall statue whose name-sake, Hermann the Cheruscan, united the German tribes in 9 A.D. to defeat the Romans. Hermann now watches over the town of New Ulm, which was settled by a group of German immigrants, many of whom belonged to the Turner Society—an organization devoted to the development of a healthy body and a pure mind. Under Hermann's surveillance, the town has remained prosperous and spotless, a model planned community. You can see all of New Ulm and the Minnesota Valley below from a platform at the top of a staircase that winds up to the top of Hermann. Below, under the mighty Teuton's shadow, there is a lovely picnic area.

NISSWA

THE NISSWA TURTLE RACES

Nisswa, Minn.;
July & Aug. every Weds 2 PM

The turtle jockeys stand in a circle facing outward, waiting for the turtlemas-ter's cry. On command they drop their turtles, run to an outer circle, then pivot back toward the center to cheer their entry on. The first turtle to cross the outer circle is the winner. Races are run in heats of ten (sometimes there are 200 entrants), with 50¢ prizes for the preliminaries and a $3 grand prize daily.

The big problem in Nisswa is the racing-turtle shortage. Since a turtle's racing career is significantly less than that of a thoroughbred horse, as the summer wears on, the supply diminishes, and by August jockeys have to share turtles. So if you plan on coming to Nisswa, by all means bring your own stable of shelled creatures. One may become the new tortillian Seattle Slew. The local turtles know their way around the track by the end of the summer, but they are far from energetic about the whole racing game. A peppy, hard-shelled newcomer would have it all over these sore-flippered veterans.

ROCHESTER

MAYO MEDICAL MUSEUM

217 1st St. S.W. in Damon Bldg., Rochester, Minn.;
Mon–Fri 9 AM–9 PM, Sat 9 AM–5 PM, Sun 1 PM–5 PM; free

The Mayo Medical Museum is of course attached to the world-famous Mayo Clinic. It is a museum about the human body, with exhibits such as transparent men, different-sized fetuses, models of eyes, ears, and teeth, and even a few bones that visitors are invited to pick up and examine. The most dramatic exhibits are those that deal with illness and accident and their treatment.

Take the display called "Farm Accidents." It portrays the kinds of medical trouble a farmer might run into—losing a finger, or getting a third-degree burn. These moments are depicted by small dioramas, complete with grimacing mannequins.

For the urban museum-goer, too removed from the soil to appreciate farm accidents, there are wax models of stomach ulcers and inflamed gall bladders. For moms and dads there is a whole display case filled with objects that have been extracted from babies' stomachs: bottle caps, needles, razor blades, etc.

For the cineaste, there is a film called *Heart Attack*. This has all the thrills and suspense of a disaster film, and twice the impact, since the open-heart surgery at the end is no Hollywood mock-up.

The Mayo Museum is, in short, a mecca of hypochondria. It tells all about the human body and the myriad things that can go wrong with it. Even if you are well balanced when you walk in, you are sure to leave with visions of diseased organs and farm accidents dancing in your head.

VIOLA

THE GOPHER COUNT

Viola, Minn.;
3rd Thurs. in June; free

In Viola, Minnesota, a gopher's two front feet are worth 25¢, but only 10¢ if it is a striped gopher. A rat's tail brings 2¢, and a woodchuck's foot two bits. These values are in effect only the third Thursday in June, when Viola celebrates Gopher Day.

Mrs. Clair Smith, a local townswoman, told us that except for the Kentucky Derby, the Viola Gopher Count is the oldest continuous celebration in the United States. It began in 1874, when the town's farmers became worried that gophers were going to eat all their crops. So they set a bounty on gophers' feet, and have managed to turn their rodent extermination program into the town's biggest yearly festival. Residents wax poetic around this time, and gopheresque sonnets are published by local papers in homage to the pest that provides Viola with a chance to parade around every June. Incidentally, the town is so small that the parade must circle it twice to herald the morning of the big day.

YOUNG AMERICA

BED RACES

Main St., Young America, Minn.;
3rd Mon. in June; free

Pity the poor traveler who pulls wearily into this small Minnesota town the night of June 20th, looking for a nice, soft bed in a quiet motel. He will find the residents of Young America, along with neighbors from Cologne, Waconia, and Hamburg, racing wheeled beds down the main street of town. The beds are decorated with stuffed moose heads, streamers, fins, and ribbons; and bed-pushers often play polka music on concertinas as they pilot their vehicles toward the finish line.

Most of the entries in the bed races are sponsored by local bars like Bouncer's or El and Esther's ("We've been rolling for fifteen years"). There are five preliminary heats and a championship race; when the casters have cooled, there is street dancing to the music of the Polka Padre and his band.

MISSOURI

BRANSOM

KEWPIE DOLL FESTIVAL

Bransom, Mo.;
late April; free; for info. contact:
The Rose O'Neil Society, Box 668, Bransom, Mo. 65616

The Kewpie doll is that chubby-cheeked character with a hair-do that resembles the top of a soft ice cream cone. Like Shirley Temple or the Happy Face, Kewpie dolls once represented the epitome of cuteness, and were a national craze. Today you will find the Kewpie doll sitting on antique dealers' shelves, and costing a small fortune.

The Rose O'Neil Society is named after the Kewpie doll's creator, and today claims members from most of the fifty states and several foreign countries. Once a year they get together in Bransom—Rose O'Neil's home town—to talk Kewpie-talk, show off Kewpie memorabilia, swap and sell dolls, and generally reaffirm their belief in the adorableness of the little dip-top.

Nonmembers are welcome at the Society's annual gathering, so if you are traveling through Missouri in April and are starved for a heavy dose of the cutes, Bransom is the place to go.

FULTON

JESSE HOWARD'S HOUSE

West 2nd St., Fulton, Mo.

Jesse Howard was a railroad man. He befriended hobos, traveled the length of the country, and worked as a dishwasher and cook before he settled down in Fulton. When he did make a home for himself and his wife and five children, he was inspired to decorate it with hand-painted signs taken from Bible verses. The verses created a stir in Fulton, and the home was vandalized and became the subject of delinquents' pranks. But the more they threw things his way, the more Jesse Howard retaliated. He kept right on building signs, and now the house looks like a gigantic surreal typesetter's shop. Slogans, sayings, and prayers are everywhere—a primitive Gutenberg Bible in three dimensions.

His wife calls this work "a big mess." Folk-art museums have bought up some of it. As far as Jesse is concerned, he is following God's command. He is a fighter against sinners, Communists, the hoodlums who lurk around the borders of his imagination. There is a sign for all these people, telling them exactly where to go. Jesse Howard is ninety years old, and has only a sixth-grade education to draw on. He is a tough man to beat.

HANNIBAL

NATIONAL TOM SAWYER DAYS— NATIONAL FENCE-PAINTING CONTEST

Hannibal, Mo.;
July 4th; free to entrants ages 10–14

If Tom Sawyer were suddenly to materialize one wonders how he would fare in the National Fence-Painting Contest. Here is the "Authenticity Code," which all entrants must follow:

a. jeans cut off
b. patch on right rear pocket
c. patch on knee
d. suspenders
e. straw hat

f. light-colored shirt, sleeves rolled up
g. bare feet
h. handkerchief in pocket
i. freckles
j. weed in mouth

Contestants are encouraged to research further details so as to become even more authentic.

Once the Tom Sawyer facsimiles are ready, each boy is given a bucket of whitewash and a brush and stationed at a mock-up of the fence that Mark Twain described. They are judged on speed, accuracy, and resemblance to Tom. The oddest rule is that each contestant must do his own painting. No recruitment of outside help is permitted. What would the real Tom Sawyer think of that?

KANSAS CITY

THE OLDEST SHOPPING CENTER IN AMERICA
(COUNTRY CLUB PLAZA)

4629 Wornall Rd., Kansas City, Mo.

Here stands a monument as crucial to the nature of American life as Plymouth Rock, the first diner (in Worcester, Mass.), and Elvis Presley's boyhood home (in Tupelo, Miss.). It is the original shopping center. It was opened in 1922 by the C. J. Nichols Company, which had looked into the future and seen a suburban America filled with cars. The Country Club Plaza now occupies fifty-five acres and is host to one hundred and fifty stores. It has grown more cultured as it has aged, calling itself a "shopping city" and even publishing a monthly newsletter, the *Plaza Bulletin,* that details life in the not-so-mini-city. The "Country Club" is so couth, in fact, that a recently opened McDonald's in Seville Square (one especially classy part of the Plaza) sports Picasso prints on the wall, "marblelike" table tops, a vaulted brick ceiling, a fireplace, and a glass chandelier. At the entrance to this "Mac's" is a life-size bronze statue of a young man sitting on a rock, holding a book in one hand and a Big Mac in the other. It is entitled "Out to Lunch."

NEOSHO

HORNET GHOST LIGHT

Neosho, Mo.

The Hornet Ghost Light—alias the Tristate Spook Light—has been raising goose bumps for over seventy years. It stalks a backroad nicknamed "The Devil's Promenade." It appears as a luminous spot suspended in the air. Some say it looks like a bobbing lantern. Some have driven down the road for miles, following it, trying to get closer, but the light always stays ahead and finally disappears. Some even say that the light has attacked them, sneaking up behind their car as they were driving along, then flashing brightly into the back window.

No one has yet determined the cause of this light that appears near the shared border of Missouri, Oklahoma, and Kansas. Scientists have offered the explanation that it is "mine gas," but nobody in Neosho agrees with that. The Hornet Light seems to have a mind of its own—it can't be only a cloud of gas. Locals who ran from it as children now come back to the Devil's Promenade to show the old ghost to their grandchildren. It's almost a town mascot.

Here is how to see the Hornet Ghost Light. Take Rt. #86 out of Neosho. Cross #43. Continue to dead end. Turn right. Go two miles to second road on left. Turn and proceed 1/4 mile. You are now on the light's turf. Of course, it only appears at night.

ST. JOSEPH

THE PONY EXPRESS MUSEUM

914 Penn St., St. Joseph, Mo.;
May–Sept Mon–Sat 9 AM–5 PM, Sun 2 PM–5 PM; free

WANTED
Young skinny wiry fellows, not over eighteen.
Must be expert riders willing to risk death daily.
Orphans preferred. Wages $25 per week.
Apply Central Overland Express.

With ads like this, it is a wonder that anyone ever applied for the job. In fact, there are just four hundred registered riders of the pony express; the legendary mail service lasted only eighteen months—until October 24, 1861, when the telegraph put it out of business.

Here in St. Joe is where the riders set out for the West. The Pony Express Museum is located in the Pike's Peak Stables, where the westbound horses were kept. Here are displayed saddles, guns, horseshoes, maps, and portraits of some of the daredevil riders. It is a hair-raising look into the very Wild West.

ST. LOUIS

NATIONAL MUSEUM OF QUACKERY

St. Louis Medical Society Building, 3839 Lindell Blvd., St. Louis, Mo.;
daily 11 AM–4 PM; free

"Want to lose that flabby bulge around your middle?" "Want to sprout some hair on that 'chrome dome'?" Who hasn't seen come-ons like this in the backs of magazines and wondered, "Who'd ever fall for that?" Most people know that double chins and flat chests cannot be "cured" by sending $3.95 to a post-office box. Or do they? The National Museum of Medical Quackery displays dozens of devices, drugs, and potions that have been confiscated by the U. S. government as utterly worthless. Photographs demonstrate how some of the bogus items were supposed to be used or applied. Among the contraband are mechanical breast developers, air "purifiers" that do nothing, health foods with no nutritional value, and hormones to increase virility.

The Museum of Quackery shares space with twenty-five exhibits that demonstrate the contributions of St. Louis medical men to the health of the community. Included are dioramas depicting Dr. Evart Graham's "first successful removal of an entire lung" in 1932, Dr. E. C. Ernst's first X-ray room in the potato bin at Mullanphy Hospital, and the beginning of "sports medicine" in 1938, when Dr. Hyland started treating the St. Louis Cardinals. Other unusual exhibits include a history of X-rays, a collection of medical superstitions, and a replica of the first hospital west of the Alleghenies.

WARRENSBURG

DRUM THE BLOODHOUND MONUMENT

Courthouse Square, Warrensburg, Mo.

Old Drum was shot by his owner's neighbor. The owner sued the neighbor and won. The neighbor appealed the decision and had it reversed. The owner brought forth new evidence, but lost. He brought forth more evidence and finally won. By the time the case got to this point, it was being argued on both sides by U. S. representatives, senators, and a Missouri governor. Senator George Graham Vest successfully won a final judgment for Old Drum's owner by appealing to the emotions of the jury, telling them, "The one absolutely unselfish friend that a man can have in this selfish world, the one that never deserts him and the one that never proves ungrateful or treacherous is his dog." Vest's words, spoken on September 27, 1870, have gone down in history as "Eulogy to a Dog." They are inscribed on a monument beneath a likeness of the droopy hound in Courthouse Square.

NEBRASKA

BELLEVUE

STRATEGIC AEROSPACE MUSEUM

2510 Clay St., Bellevue, Neb.;
daily 8 AM–5 PM;
adults: $1.50, children: 50¢

If gun collections or that old piece of artillery in front of the V. F. W. hall tickles up a vicarious power fantasy in your secret soul, the S.A.C. Museum will send shock waves through your nervous system. At the entrance there is an eighty-two-foot-tall Atlas missile—not a mock-up; it's the real thing. Down the line is the B–17 Flying Fortress, which "helped destroy the Axis Powers in World War II, and stands now in mute testimony to that violent conflict." You can stand under the wing of the giant ten-engined B–36 Peacemaker, the plane that "provided the big stick during the angry days of the cold war." Altogether there are twenty-six aircraft—bombers, fighters, strategic support, trainers, and helicopters, as well as seven missiles, from Atlas to Titan. Prominently displayed at the S.A.C. Museum is a sign inscribed with their motto: "Peace is our profession."

CHADRON

THE MUSEUM OF THE FUR TRADE

3 mi. E. of Chadron, Neb., on U.S. 20;
June 1–Labor Day 8 AM–6 PM;
adults: 75¢, children free with parents, or 15¢ by themselves.
call (308) 432–3843 for app't other times of year

This is not just another Old West museum, but a serious, in-depth study of the fur trade, from colonial days to the present. Mink, badger, beaver, sea otter, buffalo, and wolf pelts are all on display, as are the weapons used to hunt and skin them. Objects frequently traded with Indians are shown, too. There are beads, kettles, and tomahawks, and a now almost extinct crop called Mandan tobacco—actually a type of midget corn. The museum houses a model trading post complete with sod roof and containing the kinds of western clothes and horse gear traders and trappers once needed. There is even a library with microfilm files for serious scholars of the skin. We only wish there were some documentation of modern fur trade, like "The Mink Stole Story," or "Fun Fur Futures."

GORDON

MARI SANDOZ'S ROOM

Chamberlin Furniture Store, 122 N. Main St., Gordon, Neb.,
Mon–Fri 8 AM–5:30 PM, Sat 8 AM–6 PM; free

The northwestern part of Nebraska is known as Mari Sandoz country, in honor of the woman who told the story of Indian–white man relations in books like *Cheyenne Autumn* and *The Buffalo Hunters*. Gordon was her home, and the Chamberlin furniture store celebrates the town's favorite daughter with a special room set aside to display her awards, scrapbooks, pictures, favorite possessions, and articles of clothing. The collection was put together by Mrs. Chamberlin with Mari Sandoz's sister, who still lives in town.

Twenty-one miles south of Gordon on Nebraska Route 27, there is a small building called the Mari Sandoz Museum, where an attempt has been made to approximate Mari Sandoz's Greenwich Village apartment. This vision of bohemian living quarters in the middle of the Great Plains is even more incongruous than finding a museum in one room of a furniture store. The nicest thing about this small museum, located in a rest area by the side of the road, is its proximity to the orchards planted long ago by Mari's father, "Old Jules," the subject of her first famous book. In the orchard just behind the museum is Mari Sandoz's grave.

MINDEN

CHEVYLAND, U.S.A.

Rt. 6, 1/2 mi. W. of Junction U.S. 6 & 10, Minden, Neb.;
April 1–Nov. 20 daily 11 AM–9:30 PM;
season pass: $2, Adults: $1.50, children 8–12: 50¢

Chevyland is a specialized automobile museum designed with logic and a sense of purpose. Most car museums are aimed at dilettantes, and offer up a random collection of antique autos, with no more than a general fascination with old cars as a guiding principle. At Chevyland—as at any great museum—there is a master plan of curatorship.

Here the novice automobilophile may survey the fields of historical development, model evolution, and genealogy within a single make of car. One can observe the Chevrolet style as it developed over the decades; notice refinements and radical alterations; study the progression from the primitive designs of the 1920s through classical (1940s to early '50s), mannerist (late '50s) and ultimately neoclassical forms. One can decide for oneself about the Corvette: anomaly, Darwinian mutation, or necessary expression of submerged alter ego? Chevyland has every Corvette model made, and provides a perfect opportunity to contemplate the meaning of the telling transition from "Corvette" to "Corvette Stingray."

But serious students of the Chevrolet, who have resolved these issues to their own satisfaction, will find material here for advanced research and study. What about the progressive use of chrome in models 110, 210, and Biscayne? Or the sudden undermining of the chrome dynasty with the introduction of the Super Sport line, marked as it was by smooth side panels and sport wheel covers? Here, too, is the bathos of the Bel-Air, once king of the line, now mere utility vehicle.

Sad to say, Chevyland is not complete. Where are the delightful fillips of Chevy history—the Nomad wagons or Apache pickup trucks? Where are the Corvairs? We miss the story of Chevrolet Tu-tone paint, and the rise and eclipse of the Chevy-bird hood ornament. Chevyland might score a coup if it had the full scoop on modern cross-hybridization with other General Motors cars, considering the national attention recently given to the Olds–Chevy engine switcheroo.

But for all these gaps in scholarship, Chevyland is still remarkable—and its collection of sports coupes from the 1950s is unsurpassed. Along with the Auburn–Cord–Duesenberg Museum in Indiana, it is a rare opportunity to study a meaningful exhibit of America's most popular art—automobile design.

HOME APPLIANCE BUILDING

Harold Warp's Pioneer Village, U.S. 6, Minden, Neb.;
daily 8 AM–sundown;
adults: $3, 6–15: $1

Harold Warp—for those who have not heard of his Pioneer Village—was a man who acquired over thirty thousand items during his life for the purpose of showing his children "man's progress since 1830," and the glories of the free-enterprise system. He arranged his collection in twenty-four buildings stretching across twenty acres. It's got everything, from old cars to old china to the oldest steam merry-go-round in the United States. It is the kind of museum that requires sturdy shoes and true grit from a visitor, and resignation to the fact that unless one spends a whole summer here, one will never see it all.

If you have less than three months to spend, we recommend you start with the Home Appliance Building. Here are enshrined washing machines, refrigerators, stoves, bathtubs, and an enormous array of kitchen utensils. Most are antiques, quainter than your home model Westinghouse or basement dryer. It is a bit ironic to see housewives on vacation staring in awe at Warp's parade of appliances. The vista of tubs and washing machines so formally displayed for thoughtful viewing is a sight that would make a Dada artist happy.

NEBRASKA CITY

J. STERLING MORTON'S GRAVE

Wyuka Cemetery, S. 19th St., Nebraska City, Neb.;
always viewable; free

There is a mansion in Nebraska City that was once the home of President Grover Cleveland's Secretary of Agriculture, J. Sterling Morton, and it can be visited throughout the summer. It's really only a nice big home, like many others, but J. Sterling Morton's grave is unique. Having invented Arbor Day, Morton thought that his grave ought to serve as a reminder of this feat to future generations. Instead of a tombstone, his plot is marked by a tall granite tree. There are smaller "stumps" nearby, and a concrete pseudowood fence runs around the graves of Morton and his family.

Apparently Morton's idea of a "personalized" tombstone shape inspired at least one other resident of the Wyuka Cemetery. Near Morton's grave, there is a large marker in the shape of a desk. We presume the departed was a writer.

OMAHA

NEBRASKA'S 500-MILE SCULPTURE GARDEN

Interstate 80 between Omaha and Sidney, Nebraska;
always viewable; free

Like the food served up at most highway rest areas, the scenery from one oasis to the next can be pretty monotonous—unless you happen to be driving through Nebraska. In 1975 as a bicentennial project the state decided to spruce up its rest areas by making them into a state-long sculpture garden. Not since the 1860s and its furious battles about where the state capitol was to be located has any issue in Nebraska history so polarized its population. The sculptures on display are modern, abstract shapes, the type of monument that inevitably results in endless eyewitness news interviews in which the local populace argues either that the abstract shape is a gigantic hoax and a put-on, or that it is a daring and meaningful visual statement. Debate over the project was fueled by the name of one work in particular, "Erma's Desire" (at the Grand Island rest area). It is a group of copper-colored spires that *could* be interpreted as an abstract rendering of a prone female body. Such an interpretation demands considerable stretching of the imagination, but the sculpture was, in fact, called obscene by some critics. Others called it a pile of junk. And still others saw it as magnificent expression of the human spirit. Artist John Raimondi said that he named it after his mother.

Whatever one's opinion about "Erma's Desire" or the nine other works on permanent exhibit by the side of the Interstate Highway, there can be no doubt that they go a long way to alleviate the anonymity of the Route 80 rest areas. Here's where they can be seen:

MEMORIAL TO THE AMERICAN BANDSTAND by Richard Field: Platte River eastbound rest area.

NEBRASKAN GATEWAY by Anthony Padovano: Brady westbound rest area.

UP/OVER by Linda Howard: Ogallala westbound rest area.

ARRIVAL by Paul Von Ringelheim: Blue River eastbound rest area.

CROSSING THE PLAINS by Bradford Graves: York westbound rest area.

NEBRASKA WIND SCULPTURE by George Baker: Kearney westbound rest area.

ROADWAY CONFLUENCE by Hans Van de Bovenkamp: Sidney westbound rest area.

ERMA'S DESIRE by John Raimondi: Grand Island eastbound rest area.

PLATTE RIVER RIBBON by Steve Urry: Cozad eastbound rest area.

SEED OF NEBRASKA by Jerry Rothman: Kimball eastbound rest area.

NORTH DAKOTA

BLANCHARD

THE WORLD'S TALLEST STRUCTURE

Blanchard, N.D.; Rt. 18 S. of Mayville

Fie on the World Trade Towers! Fie on Chicago's Sears Building and the Empire State! Here in North Dakota is the tallest thing made by man. It may not be as flashy as the twin towers in lower New York City, but it gets better reception.

Here are some facts:

If an ironworker dropped his wrench from the top of the tower, it would be traveling at a speed of 250 miles per hour when it hit the ground.

If a twenty-second commercial started at the same moment a baseball was dropped from the top of the tower, it would have ended nearly four seconds before the ball hit the ground.

If a hunter at the base of the tower shot at a goose flying near the top of the tower with a .45 caliber pistol, he would have to lead the goose by more than the length of a football field, approximately 335 feet.

These facts were given us by KTHI-TV, which broadcasts from the top of this 2,063-foot tower. We thank them, but have one question: Who conjures up these statistics? What a job!

JAMESTOWN

WORLD'S LARGEST CONCRETE BUFFALO

17th St. S.E.; Jamestown, N.D.

According to the brochure distributed by Frontier Village, a tourist attraction in Jamestown, The World's Largest Concrete Buffalo was a product of the combined "artistic genius" of Mr. Elmer Peterson and $2,000 donated by the city council. The original two grand was not enough, and eventually $9,000 more was added before the 26-foot, 60-ton behemoth was completed. We won't venture a judgment concerning the work's "artistic genius," but we can truly say that we have seen no concrete buffaloes that are larger.

PARSHALL

THE PAUL BROSTE ROCK MUSEUM

Hwy. 23, Parshall, N.D.;
Memorial Day–Labor Day, Mon–Sat 9 AM–7 PM, Sun 10 AM–7 PM;
Adults: $2, High School: $1, children 6–12: 50¢

Parshall, North Dakota is the last place we might have expected to find a perfect re-creation of atomic space. Atomic space, to clarify the term, is outer space as it was depicted during the 1950s. Its emblems include molecularly arranged Tinker Toys, fluorescent lights, and a Geiger counter. Such things once symbolized the future, and can still be spotted in the Westinghouse logo, Japanese monster movies, and reruns of *Science Fiction Theater*. The Mirror Room at the Broste Rock Museum affords a perfect view of anachronistic futurism. Curtis and Joanne Wittmayer, the curators since Mr. Broste's death, explain it:

"It is a room by itself, 17 feet by 17 feet with all four walls covered with mirrors. You don't actually see the mirrors, you see the reflections, a fantastic optical illusion. In the center of the room is a stand that is an abstract conception of space. It is made of solid iron rods bending and turning in such a way that it flows and twists wonderingly, aimlessly, suggesting the vastness of space. There is no beginning or end. It is infinity, cosmic space. Spheres represent the planets, consequently an astronomical cavalcade."

There is art and poetry at Broste's, in addition to atomic space. Mr. Broste's three books are for sale, along with "first-class oil paintings." The museum brochure describes it as "World Outstanding Museum . . . all a dream of Aesthetic Beauty."

THE LONGEST ROAD WITHOUT A CURVE

The longest road in the United States without a curve is North Dakota Route 46 between Route 81 (Interstate 29) and North Dakota Route 30, just South of Streeter. You get on this arrow-straight highway heading west about fifteen miles south of Fargo. From there, it's 110 miles until you've got to wake up and turn the wheel. It's a great place to test that new Porsche or Stingray; but you're on your own when you hear the sirens in the distance.

BAINBRIDGE

JOHN HARRIS DENTAL MUSEUM

U.S. 50, W. of Bainbridge, Ohio;
April 15–Nov 1, Fri–Wed 10 AM–5 PM; donation

Until John Harris moved to Bainbridge, Ohio in the 1820s, dentistry was learned only by apprenticeship, and procedures—whether in a doctor's office or a barber's chair—were hardly more sophisticated than yanking out the tooth that made your head swell up like a melon. In 1827 Harris placed an ad in the Chillicothe *Supporter and Gazette* offering instruction in medical techniques, and promising students a large supply of brand-new shiny instruments for the practice of dental surgery. "No student will be received," the ad noted, "who has not at least a first-rate English education." Tuition was described as "reasonable, depending on circumstances."

Today the small, white brick home in which John Harris lived, practiced, and taught is considered the "Cradle of Dentistry," for it was Harris's students who went on to found America's major dental schools in Baltimore and Cincinnati. The home is a dental museum, in which one can see some of the early tools of the profession. They look more like pearl-handled hedge trimmers and ivory pliers from a gardener's shack than the kind of equipment used today. At one time, however, they were the most sophisticated instruments available for drilling, poking, and tugging at troubled teeth. Also on display are portraits of some of the early "painless dentists" who pioneered the profession, and a large collection of false teeth.

BELLEFONTAINE

OLDEST CONCRETE STREET IN AMERICA

Columbus, Opera, Main & Court St., around the courthouse,
Bellefontaine, Ohio

In 1891 concrete was poured around the Bellefontaine courthouse in an eight-foot apron to cover the area where horses were hitched. The concrete proved to be so much easier to clean than bricks and so much more sanitary than dirt that the entire street was covered with it, and the four-block area around the courthouse became the first concrete street in America. There is a plaque commemorating this fact outside the courthouse, and the street is kept in excellent condition, with nary a pothole.

BROOK PARK

PARK PLACE, INC.

18975 Snow Rd., Brook Prk, Ohio (216) 362–1080

Bill Maloof is a clever man and a Monopoly player. He has combined recreation with business, and built what must be the most unusual public parking lot in the country. The lot is designed to look like a Monopoly game board. He felt that the number and letter systems used by most lots create confusion, and customers wind up wandering the ramps, cursing and searching for their car. But who could forget that they are parked on Ventnor Avenue, or St. Charles Place, or Boardwalk? Even the rest rooms here are called the Waterworks. Buses to take customers from suburban Park Place to the Cleveland airport are disguised as trains on the Reading Line. And when the lot is full, a sign points to a competitor's lot, saying "Go directly to jail."

BRYAN

ETCH-A-SKETCH

Ohio Art Co., 711 E. High St., Bryan, Ohio;
tours Weds & Thurs 10:15 AM & 1:15 PM by appointment 636–3141; free

Some toys are acknowledged playtime classics: Silly Putty, Mr. Potato Head, jacks, marbles, and Etch-a-Sketch. We can't remember how many Etch-a-Sketches we personally have bought. Loss, jealous siblings, and hammers to break them open and see what makes them work have all contributed to a quick and constant turnover. Fortunately, they are still made by the Ohio Art Company, which produces one and a half million a year. You can tour their factory to see how the magic TV-shaped drawing board is made, along with other toys like the Fli-back Paddle (another classic), Emenee Home Chord Organs, and basic metal pails that are *de rigueur* for a visit to the beach.

Ohio Art prefers groups, but allows a family or two to walk along with a prearranged tour. It is wise to call ahead. Unfortunately, children under eleven are not admitted.

CLEVELAND

THE PLIDCO PIPE LINE MUSEUM

1831 Columbus Rd., Cleveland, Ohio;
Mon–Fri 9 AM–4 PM; free

Until the monumental pipeline in Alaska came along, most of us were content to think of pipes as mere conduits. But at the Plidco Pipe Line Museum one sees "the recorded history of pipelines and the contributions they have made to civilizations all over the world," as told by Plidco, an acronym for the Pipe Line Development Company.

The museum is itself an historic place–a hundred-year-old stable in the "Flats" section of Cleveland, on the banks of the Cuyahoga. The idea of a pipeline museum was Joseph B. Smith's, who has been collecting pipeline memorabilia for over forty years. Among the rarer items on display here are an ancient wooden pipe, hand-carved wood mountings of pipeline logos, fittings, pumps, and road-crossing markers from companies around the world.

The pipeline, one learns, is as old as 4000 B.C., when the Chinese used hollow sections of bamboo to carry natural gas.

COLUMBUS

THE ACCOUNTING HALL OF FAME

University of Ohio, Hagerty Hall, 4th Floor, 1775 College Rd., Columbus, Ohio; Mon–Fri 8 AM–5 PM

This might be a good place to visit just before April 15th. Perhaps you will be inspired by the portraits of the thirty-eight most famous accountants of all time who are enshrined in this hall of fame. Men like John Queenan and Robert Trueblood (author of *The Trueblood Report*) are pictured here over plaques that describe their contributions to the world of accounting and to society at large.

FINDLAY

"DOWN BY THE OLD MILL STREAM"

Tell Taylor Memorial, 231 McManness Ave, Riverside Park, Findlay, Ohio

Tell Taylor's song "Down by the Old Mill Stream" is probably the most harmonized tune ever written. It has been the joy of barbershop quartets, vaudeville acts, and serenading sweethearts. Tell Taylor's hometown of Findlay has erected a charming memorial to their native son. It is in Riverside Park, down by an old mill stream. It consists of three smooth rocks, into which the song and a bas-relief of a mill have been carved, along with a short biography of the composer. There is a picnic area behind the rocks, a perfect place to eat lunch and relive the harmonious days in which Tell Taylor found his inspiration.

HINCKLEY

BUZZARD SUNDAY

Hinckley, Ohio;
1st Sunday after March 15

The buzzards of Hinckley
    Are back on their ledges
All ugly and wrinkly,
Their eyes glowing pinkly,
    They perch on the hedges,
Their feathers unruly,
Their beaks dripping cruelly,
Repulsive and drooly,
    Their claws bloody wedges
    With flesh on the edges . . .

These are the first lines of Cleveland columnist Joe Newman's ode to the notorious buzzards of Hinckley Ridge, who return every year on March 15 to this small town in Ohio. On exactly that date every year, for no scientifically determined reason, the sky overhead is dotted with dark birds flying toward their roost in Metropark. Throughout the summer they come and go, and almost any citizen of Hinckley can tell you a buzzard story, like the one about the bird who perched on the backyard apple tree every afternoon, eyeing a pet cat; or the hamburger snatched off the barbecue grill by a dive-bombing buzzard.

The bald-pated, black-winged creatures, although not nearly as pretty as Capistrano's swallows, have provided the citizens of Hinckley with a mascot, of sorts. At least the buzzards are something to celebrate. Townspeople have come up with black-frosted "buzzard cookies," T-shirts, and bumper stickers. They have elected several buzzard queens. Now that the birds are taken for granted as a natural phenomena, some of this celebratory spirit has flagged; it is reduced to the annual Buzzard Watch and a pancake-and-sausage breakfast held the Sunday after their arrival. Any day during the summer, though, visitors to Hinckley will find it easy to spot the buzzards—either in their roost in the rocks at the town park, or flying overhead looking for carrion.

LOVELAND

CHATEAU LAROCHE

12025 Shore Dr., Loveland, Ohio;
10 AM–10 PM; donation

Some people feel at home in an apartment or condominium. Others need the privacy of a house. A few can only be at home in a castle. Of course, if you are not a king or William Randolph Hearst, castles are difficult to come by, real-estate prices being what they are. Harry Andrews solved the problem by building his own. He began in 1929, when he and the twelve boys in the Sunday School class he was teaching decided there was too much sin in the world. They decided to build a castle and live like King Arthur, obeying the Ten Commandments and living as pure a life as possible. They become known as the Knights of the Golden Trail, now one hundred strong, and Chateau Laroche, Harry Andrews' home, is their castle.

Visitors are welcome at this monumental medieval fortress perched in the woods of Loveland. It is made of stone, with turrets, terraces, and tall, skinny glass windows. You will find initials and names carved into the stones—these are the signatures of the knights who have helped Harry build this five-decade project. Outside, on the terraces, Harry will show you his plants; these, along with knighthood, are his favorite hobby. He specializes in crossbreeding, and has developed a "Bullmoose potato" with eyes that stick out instead of in, for easy peeling. He has also crossed cucumbers with watermelons, and tomatoes with potatoes.

Work still continues inside the castle, which is more modern than the thoroughly archaic exterior might lead you to believe. There is electricity in every room, and most furnishings are less medieval than they are simply timeworn. There are plans for a meeting hall, in which Harry wants to install a Round Table for his knights.

His advice to visitors is this: "As you roam the castle, try to imagine it peopled with the spirits of those courageous men of might whose nobility, courage, and virtue saved (and will save again) mankind from total degradation and degeneration . . . Any man of high ideals who wishes to help save civilization is invited to become a member of the Knights of the Golden Trail . . ."

LUCAS

HUMPHREY BOGART, ERROL FLYNN, HEDY LAMARR, AND ALICE FAYE SLEPT HERE

Malabar Farm, Bromfield Road, Lucas, Ohio;
daily 9 AM–5 PM;
adults: $1.25, children: 60¢

They didn't all sleep here at once, but Bogie and Lauren Bacall did, on their wedding night. Malabar Farm was the home of writer Louis Bromfield. Bogart and Bacall were married here and spent their first connubial night in the guest bedroom. This fact is clearly pointed out by your guide to Malabar farm, as you are shown the very plain room, furnished only with a couple of cabinets, and two fourposter twin beds.

In addition to the above-mentioned celebrities, the guest room was occupied by James Cagney and Kay Francis (again, separately). There is a nice view of the farm from the windows of the bedroom, and if the indoor tour whets your appetite, you can tour the grounds on which Mr. Bromfield and his famous guests trod—an extra 50¢ buys a wagon ride around the outside.

NORWICH

THE NATIONAL ROAD— ZANE GREY MUSEUM

8850 E. Pike, Norwich, Ohio;
Mon–Fri 9:30 AM–5 PM, Sun 11 AM–5 PM;
adults: $1.25, under 12: free

The National Road once reached from Cumberland, Maryland to Vandalia, Illinois. It was the first major trail west, the national link between the east coast and the western frontier. On it traveled freight, pony-express riders, and thousands of homesteading families. It was dotted with tollhouses and roadside inns, and was the source of legends about highwaymen, muddy passes, and ornery toll-takers. With the coming of the railroad the road lost its primary importance as a vital artery, but as automobiles and bicycles became popular at the beginning of this century, the old National Road again took on importance. It became known as Route 40 in 1925. With the creation of the Interstate Highway (Rt. 70), its fortunes waned.

Noba Artificial Insemination, Tiffen, Ohio

The World's Largest Penny, Woodruff, Wis.

Here is the whole story of the road, told in dioramas, documents, historic signs and vehicles. The museum's showpiece is its 136-foot-long "chronology shelf," a diorama that depicts the buildings, vehicles, and human activities on the road from its initial construction to modern times. Other exhibits include a Conestoga wagon, a carriage, a bicycle, and antique autos. These are displayed on various roadbeds, such as gravel, brick, asphalt, and concrete.

The road shares billing at this museum with the man who fantasized about what lay at the westernmost end of it. Zane Grey is known as the father of the adult Western. There is a reconstruction here of his study, with a wax model of the author hard at work on a manuscript, devising the myths of the Wild West, in a museum that tells the real story of the trip out there.

RIO GRANDE

INTERNATIONAL CHICKEN-FLYING MEET

Bob Evans Farms, Rt. 35, Rio Grande, Ohio;
3rd week in May

Once a year, sportsbirds like Shake and Bake, Gregory Peck, and Chicken-Eval start flapping their wings to get in shape for the only chicken-flying meet in the country, or the "ICFM" as it is known to regular chicken jockeys.

It is common knowledge that chickens are lousy fliers. If they could get off the ground, they surely wouldn't spend their lives sitting around a yard clucking and waiting for the axe to fall. But the Bob Evans Farms are willing to stake $500 to prove that chicken-flying is a dynamite sport.

Chickens are placed in white, rural-style mailboxes. At the starting gun, the flaps are jerked open, and the chickens fly out of their coops. If they are sluggish, jockeys are permitted to nudge them with a bathroom plunger. Chickens and jockeys (or pilots, as some prefer to be called) have come to Rio Grande from as far away as the Netherlands for this match, that determines the undisputed world champion chicken. The record-holder is an English game hen who flew 163 feet nonstop before her mighty wing-power gave out. The sight of poultry pilots using chickenlike body language to keep their birds in the air is liable to leave you as weak from laughter as the birds are from trying to fly.

TIFFEN

NOBA ARTIFICIAL INSEMINATION

684 E. Perry St., E. of Tiffen, Ohio;
Mon–Fri 10 AM–3 PM; free

One Noba worker on his lunch break mused, "Buddy, if I had a bucket of the right semen, I could retire a rich man." Noba is a semen-gathering facility that handles the product of the country's best bulls. These animals can be as expensive as a Rolls Royce or a suburban home. They are bovine royalty. Once they are proven to have what it takes, their semen is used to father thousands of cattle across the country.

The big daddies are kept in ultraclean quarters and are watched over constantly. Some look sweet and docile. Others have fire in their eyes. They occasionally bellow, with a rumble that shakes the rafters. Each is known personally to the management. Some are noted for producing great milk cows. "Cezon" is known to be the sire of cattle with lean meat. "Milord" is known for calving ease, "Ajax" for growth. "This boy has a libido problem," we were told, as a sad-looking Brahmin was pointed out. "We have to be bull psychiatrists here."

There are no formal tours of Noba, but it is a personal enough operation to show visitors whatever it is they would like to see, except for the actual retrieval process, which would make the bulls too nervous. You meet the bulls and are shown the equipment used, including industrial-strength bull condoms and the freezers in which the valuable semen is stored.

The Noba brochure is inscribed "Where the hot ones are."

VANDALIA

TRAPSHOOTING HALL OF FAME

Route 40 at I–75, Vandalia, Ohio;
Mon–Fri 9 AM–4 PM; free

The best known shooter of them all was Annie Oakley, here enshrined with other old-timers such as Pop Heikes and Mrs. Plinky Topperwein. It is said that Annie Oakley fired over one million shots during her life. Her favorite trick was to lie on her back and have her husband throw six glass balls into the air at once. She would scatter all six before they hit the ground, by means of three double-barreled shotguns.

Annie Oakley was the most colorful shooter, but there were others, too, such as George Ligowsky, who invented glass pigeons that burst into flame and smoke when hit, and "Doc" Carver who, aside from being a crack shot, used to train horses and elks to do trick diving. Of course, all this is peripheral to the real business of the Trapshooting Hall of Fame, which is to honor the best shooters in history (47 have been elected so far). They have a complete collection of guns, traps, shells, glasses, clay targets, trophies and just about everything associated with the sport, including a complete shooting library.

Each year, the Grand American Tournament is held here during the second and third weeks of August. This determines the North American trapshooting champions from among 3,000 shooters. More than two million shells are fired and over twenty truckloads of targets are used during the event, which is held on the mile-long firing line just behind the Hall of Fame.

SOUTH DAKOTA

CUSTER

THE WORLD'S LARGEST SCULPTURE

4 mi. N. of Custer, S.D., on US 385;
hours vary; $4 per car

On June 3, 1948 Chief Henry Standing Bear touched off a dynamite blast on the side of Thunderhead Mountain. It was a groundbreaking ceremony of sorts. In the three decades since, sculptor Korczak Ziolkowski has been blasting, digging, and jack-hammering away at the mountain in order to turn it into the world's largest sculpture. It will be a likeness of the Sioux Chief Crazy Horse, to remind people that this was Indian land long before the four white men depicted on Mount Rushmore down the road were born.

Ziolkowski has moved an estimated 5.5 million tons of rock from the mountain. The sculpture, which shows Crazy Horse on his horse, pointing forward with his left arm, will be six hundred feet long and five hundred and sixty-three feet high—nine times as tall as Mount Rushmore. Ziolkowski says that a five-room house could be fitted into the nostril of Crazy Horse's horse.

Ziolkowski learned his craft by apprenticing himself to John Gutzon Borglum, the creator of Mount Rushmore. His life's work is not yet complete, but visitors are invited to come by and watch him bulldoze his sculpture into—

or out of—the mountain. There is a visitor's center and museum here, tended by the sculptor's second wife (his first left him shortly after he began the project) in which you can see displays of Indian lore and some of Korczak Ziolkowski's earlier and more manageable sculptures.

HURON

WORLD'S LARGEST PHEASANT

on U.S. 14 E. near Memorial Park, Huron, S.D.

Huron likes to think of itself as "The Pheasant Capital of the World," and for this reason they have erected a forty-foot high, twenty-two ton steel and fiberglass statue of one looming near Route 14, the highway that runs through town. It resembles the statuary placed outside certain burger places, but, alas, pheasantburgers are a fantasy that the people of Huron have yet to provide.

MITCHELL

THE CORN PALACE

6th Ave. & N. Main, Mitchell, S.D.

This bizarre piece of architectural Americana bills itself as "the world's only" corn palace. Built of basic brick, then augmented in 1937 with Moorish minarets and Cyrillic kiosks, the corn palace undergoes a complete face-lift every September for Corn Palace Week. Individual cobs of corn are sawed lengthwise, then arranged according to color in picture-panels along the sides of the building. Over ten thousand pounds of corncobs are used each year to create pointillistic murals showing subjects such as "Relaxation in South Dakota," "Mother Goose," or Salute to Agriculture." The cobs are augmented with grain and grasses, all in their natural colors, so that nearly the whole building seems plastered with agricultural products. In fact, all of Mitchell is corn-happy. Its radio station is KORN; its baseball team The Cobs; its basketball team The Kernels. The local nickname for the Corn Palace is "The Big Birdfeeder."

SPEARFISH

THE BLACK HILLS PASSION PLAY

The Amphitheater at 400 St. Joe Street, Spearfish, S.D.;
Early June–Early Sept.;
call (605) 642–2646 for tickets

Josef Meier has been playing the role of Jesus Christ in the Black Hills Passion Play every summer for thirty-eight consecutive years. Each winter he takes on the same role in the same play presented in Lake Wales, Florida. In Spearfish it is acted on a mammoth outdoor stage set before Lookout Mountain. Swirling around Josef Meier are pigeons, moneylenders, Arabian horses, Roman soldiers, camels, artificial Palestinian sunsets and moonrises—twenty-two scenes in all, from Jerusalem and Bethany to Golgotha and the Ascension. The play is Josef Meier's tour de force, a testament to his purposefulness. He has played the same role over six thousand times.

WALL

WALL DRUG

U.S. I–90 (Main St.), Wall, S.D.;
June–Aug Daily 5 AM–10 PM; Sept–May; hours vary

Wall Drug is a national and international joke. Like "Kilroy," the signs for this colossal bit of Bad Lands humor pop up all over the globe. Why Wall, South Dakota? Where else can you see an eighty-foot dinosaur or a six-foot real fur rabbit, or a genuine jackalope? Only here, at the store that got famous by giving away ice water forty years ago.

It is a practical joker's mecca. The jackalope is, of course, a rabbit with antelope horns stuck on—fools the city slicker every time . . . haw haw! You can see the original "ice-water well"; you can eat buffaloburgers; and on your way here you can read "see Wall Drug" signs at intervals as insistent as late-night TV commercials. Wall Drug persists and grows, an oddball landmark in the miles of nothingness that lead to it and beyond.

WISCONSIN

BARABOO

WORLD'S LARGEST COLLECTION OF CIRCUS WAGONS

Circus World Museum, 426 Water St., Baraboo, Wis.;
May–Sept daily 9:30 AM–5 PM;
adults: $3.75, children 5–11: $1.75

Long-haul truckers refer to any excessively gaudy rig as a "circus wagon," but there isn't an eighteen-wheeler anywhere that can compare to the real thing, no matter how much chrome and leopardskin the driver has employed.

There was a time when the luxuriousness of a circus wagon was an indication of the quality of the circus it represented. The wagons were paraded down Main Street when the circus came to town, and if they were spectacular enough, that meant the circus would be, too.

Here at the huge Circus World Museum are 152 of these rococo beauties. They are so ornate that after you have seen ten, your eyes might start to hurt. Our favorites are the silver-and-green "Black-Maned Nubian Lion," and the "Gladiator Telescoping Tableau"—a 7,880-pound monster wagon with gold carved figurines of people and animals that can be raised and lowered. The elaborate woodwork on these wagons represents a lost art.

BLOOMER

THE JUMP-ROPE CONTEST

Bloomer Junior High School, U.S. Highway 53, Bloomer, Wis.;
last Sat in Jan;
adults: $1.50, high school: 75¢, grade school: 50¢

There is a misconception that jumping rope is sissy stuff. One way to clear up this erroneous notion is to go to any gym where boxers train, and watch the many hours these mighty pugilists put in at the ropes, strengthening their legs and sharpening their reflexes. A slightly less sweaty way to appreciate great rope-jumping is to come to the Jump-Rope Contest held once a year in Bloomer. The contest began as a way of getting lazy school-agers off their rumps and on their toes, but it has expanded in the last seventeen years to rope-jumpers of all ages.

Although there are exhibitions of fancy and trick jumping between contests, the big events here are speed jumping, with individual meets arranged by age group. The current world record set by an eighth-grade student—is sixty-three skips in ten seconds!

BOSCOBEL

BIRTHPLACE OF THE GIDEON BIBLE

Hotel Boscobel, Wisconsin Ave., Boscobel, Wis. (608) 375-4111

Have you ever stopped in a hotel or motel in the United States and *not* found a Gideon Bible tucked into the drawer? They are everywhere, from high-and-mighty Hiltons to low-priced rendezvous. The Gideons' purpose is "A Gideon Bible in every guest room in every hotel in America."

This crusade began in 1898, when John H. Nicholson and Samuel Hill met in Room 19 of the Hotel Boscobel and with Mr. W. J. Knight, formed the Gideons. Eighty-five million Bibles later, they can't be too far from their goal.

You can stay in this historic room for $12 a night. It is just like all the others in the Hotel Boscobel—neat and simple. It was touched by history once more, in 1960, when John F. Kennedy stayed here during the Wisconsin primary campaign.

Herman Rusch and his Self-Portrait, The Prairie Moon Museum, Cochrane, Wis.

We were told that the Gideons don't mind if you take the Bible with you when you check out—just tell the management, so they can replace it.

COCHRANE

THE PRAIRIE MOON MUSEUM

Highway 35, 2 mi. S. of Cochrane, Wis.;
April–Nov daily
adults: $1, children: 50¢

There is no better way to spend a dollar than to visit the Prairie Moon Museum. Herman Rusch, the creator and curator, says there are two shows —one inside and one outside. But to those we add a third—Mr. Rusch himself. He is ninety-three-years-old, and until early 1976 was still toting ninety-pound sacks of the concrete he uses to construct his statuary. "When you get to be ninety-three years old and look into the future, what do you see?" he asked, with a sparkle in his crystal-clear blue eyes. We shrugged. "Heaven!" he exploded with a laugh as he clapped his hands and did a little shuffle of a dance step. Herman is full of jokes. "Folks pay seven dollars to hear Bob Hope and his sour jokes," he said. "I only charge a buck, and the jokes are better. Plus you get a museum to look at."

The museum is a wondrous place. Outside, there are several acres of beautifully landscaped property, populated by a phantasmagorical collection of animals—dinosaurs, polar bears, flamingos, and snakes. These are not your ordinary, tacky, down-in-the-mouth plaster constructions that fill decrepit roadside dino-lands. They are witty, streamlined creatures that perfectly express the energetic Scandinavian sensibilities of Herman Rusch. Surrounding the animals are ornamental spires and gates, neatly embedded with rocks and bits of glass. A spectacular arching fence runs parallel to the road. Everything expresses an impeccable sense of design and clarity at the root of Rusch's whimsical temperament. Even the flowers are arranged so that the morning glories form an Indian tepee, or make concentric circles of color. Overseeing this landscape is a bust of Herman Rusch himself, looking much as he does today only younger, and wearing a coat and tie instead of overalls. On the back of the bust is a handwritten legend explaining that he started the Prairie Moon Museum at seventy-one, because it was a "good way to kill old-age boredom."

The collection inside the museum consists of "anything that is good to look at." To Herman Rusch that means everything from his grandmother's old flour box (which he remembers raiding for a small bit of dough) to a hog back scratcher, a poster with a German song on it, a few stuffed animals, and some of his own creations. "Do you want to meet your uncle from outer space?" he asks, and then shows you a rock that looks as if it has a mouth and eyes. "Now this is a four-hundred-pound land turtle. You don't have these where you come from." He shows a large tree stump into which he has whittled a head and feet. A diseased tree trunk is labeled "The warthog of treedom." The show goes on until you can hardly walk another step or see another sight. The only one who isn't pooped is Mr. Herman Rusch, who is busy telling the story about the time he battled the Grim Reaper and won by throwing him headfirst into the trash barrel out back, or explaining how Communists lose all their hair, using the evolution from Karl Marx to Kruschev as his proof.

As you leave, Mr. Rusch walks back to the house trailer in which he lives behind the indoor museum. We figure that, dollar for dollar, the Prairie Moon Museum is America's best bargain. And Herman Rusch's jokes *do* beat Bob Hope's any day.

DICKEYVILLE

HOLY GHOST PARK

W. Main St., Dickeyville, Wis.;
May–Oct daily 8 AM–8 PM;
donation; guided tours June 1–Aug 31 10 AM–7 PM, on weekends in May, Sept, Oct.

"It is about five years now since this work was started. Many reasons urged me to put up 'Religion in Stone' and 'Patriotism in Stone.' The main reason it was done I could not reveal. The Last Day will tell you more about that."

These were the cryptic words of Father Mathias Wernerus, who spent his life creating an awesome monument next to his church in Dickeyville. It is a chapel and patriotic park of buildings and statuary, all of which look as if they were dipped in glue and rolled in a lapidary's tumbler filled with shiny pieces of rock and glass. Shrines, grottos, fences, altars, and gates are all encrusted with color and words that invoke patriotic or religious sentiments.

The main entrance to the park is flanked with tiled American flags. There are huge "flower pots" blanketed with stones and filled with stone "flowers." At the patriotic shrine there are stone American eagles and famous figures from history, including Christopher Columbus. The religious shrine, baroque though it is in design, offers straightforward church dogma, "the twelve fruits of the Holy Ghost," written in stone.

Father Wernerus saw his work as "God's wonderful material collected from all parts of the world . . . piled up in such a way that it appeals to rich and poor, to educated and uneducated, to men, women, and children alike."

FENIMORE

IGOR THE RAT

Outside the Fenimore Butter and Cheese Factory, Rt. 61, Fenimore, Wis.

"Hi there! . . . I'm Igor the Rat." This salutation is inscribed under the gray, whiskered symbol of the Fenimore Cheese Company. Wisconsin is "Dairyland, U.S.A.," and so it is little wonder that an eight-foot rat like Igor would be found here. He is actually a product of nearby Creative Display, Inc., which made him from fiberglass. They told us that Igor's presence has increased Fenimore's business by fifty percent. Perhaps the sight of a rat stimulates Wisconsonites' appetites.

Igor is nice to pose next to, being at least twice as tall as a man. He has bright blue eyes, curly lashes, long whiskers, and a scaly tail. He is noshing on a gigantic piece of Swiss cheese.

Inside the Fenimore Factory you can buy your own cheese to eat, as well as look through an observation window to see how it's made.

FOUR CORNERS

WEGNER'S GARDEN AND CHAPEL OF BROTHERHOOD

Rt. 71 just W. of Rt. 27 Junction, Four Corners, Wis.;
visible from road

"It was the Disneyland of its day," Don Wegner told us about the landscape his father constructed outside his house. "He wasn't interested in fishing when he retired, so he did this instead." It was in the 1930s that Paul Wegner constructed his elaborate Chapel of Brotherhood, a replica of the German ship *Bremen,* a gate that says "Home," and a great golden wedding cake. They are concrete, ornamented with glass.

"It was his way of trying to preserve certain facets of his life—his immigration here [on the *Bremen*], his golden anniversary, his American Legion affiliations," Don continued. "It's a shame that it isn't in the best shape. The town talked about raising money to preserve it, but it never quite happened."

Wegner's garden is overgrown now, and one has to push aside weeds to see some of the stonework he put into the ground. Much of it is crumbling and faded, but there is something especially touching about this work of folk artistry, perhaps because of the personal meaning that each structure has. It is like looking through the pages of a treasured scrapbook depicting a man's life, seeing those moments he best remembered. Each of these moments has been recalled by the carefully constructed souvenirs he has built in his yard.

GREENDALE

NATIONAL BOWLING HALL OF FAME AND MUSEUM

5301 S. 76th St., Greendale, Wis.;
Mon–Fri 9 AM–4 PM; free

The National Bowling Hall of Fame and Museum is located in "Bowling Headquarters," the home of the country's major bowling associations. They like to think of it as a "treasure house of historical splendor." It is a depiction of bowling's long and honorable past, and a celebration of its present-day heroes and heroines.

Here are the ancient ancestors of the sport, and its relatives from around the world: half-bowl, skittles, ninepins, five pins, candlepins, and duckpins. Wooden balls from the late 1800s, along with old bowling bags and shoes are displayed nostalgically. Even the infant days of the American Bowling Congress and the Women's International Bowling Congress are recaptured in pictures and memorabilia from early tournaments.

But not everything here is ancient history. The stars of the game are enshrined on the second floor of the Hall of Fame; here you can see all those athletes who have rolled their way to glory on the bowling circuit. The men get bronze plaques with portrait likenesses. The women get color pictures.

NEILLSVILLE

THE LARGEST CHEESE IN THE HISTORY OF MANKIND

1201 E. Division, Neillsville, Wis.; free

Although we love braggadocio as much as anyone, we did not dub this cheese "mankind's largest." It is displayed with this grandiose title which, in fact, may not be mere literary hyperbole. Who, in mankind's history, would have wanted a cheese this big? Wisconsin did, and so they built it and it now sits in the trailer of an eighteen-wheel semi-truck. One side of the trailer is glass, affording a look at the seventeen-ton Wisconsin cheddar. It is parked next to a combination cheese store–army recruiting station–beauty parlor. Here are the specs:

> Weight: 34,591 lbs.
> Length: 14 1/2 feet
> Width: 6 1/2 feet
> Height: 5 1/2 feet
> Milk used to produce cheese: 17,000 quarts
> Number of years it would take one cow to produce this much milk: 43

We peered closely at the cheese, and thought it looked pretty unappetizing, like a block of compressed burlap. We looked closer at the fact sheet: "This cheese was eaten in 1965 at a cheese convention." So the "Largest Cheese in the History of Mankind" is only a dummy.

Next to the Largest Piece of Cheeselike Burlap in the History of Mankind is a statue called Chatty Belle, the World's Largest Talking Holstein Cow. If you push her button she will tell you all about the dairy products of Wisconsin.

PHILLIPS

FRED SMITH'S CONCRETE PARK

Rt. 13, Phillips, Wis.

Fred Smith's concrete-and-glass sculpture garden has a larger population than many of the Wisconsin villages that surround it. He was certainly the most prolific of all the folk artists whose medium was concrete and glass. There are over two hundred figures here—people, horses, kings and queens, drunkards, soldiers, lions, and Fred Smith's friends and drinking companions. They're all busy doing something in the pine grove that stands next to what used to be Smith's tavern. There is one taking a picture; another swigs beer from a bottle; some ride horses; some of the horses are bucking, their back legs high in the air; others pull the famous Budweiser wagon. There are altogether over two hundred sculptures.

Most of these figures are made from concrete decorated with glass insulator knobs or broken beer bottles. Some wear concrete fedoras. Almost all have an identical expression: straight nose, straight mouth, straight-ahead-looking eyes. Some of the sculptures have begun to disintegrate, and real horse skulls peep through a couple of the horses' heads.

Concrete Park is a festive place. Some of the sculpture groups represent celebrations that Smith remembered or had heard about: a group showing two couples sitting in a wagon drinking beer celebrate a double wedding held in Phillips in 1900. Others show Smith's friends, including Hans Everson the wagon driver. Some show legends. There is an oversize Paul Bunyan, a pioneer couple, and the Lone Ranger's horse, Silver.

During his life Fred Smith refused to charge admission to the park, and refused to sell any of his sculpture to collectors. When he died recently, the park fell into disrepair until Wisconsin artists Don and Sharron Howlett got some grant money to put it back just the way it was. Now the population of Fred Smith's concrete universe appears very happy by the side of the road—drinking, riding horses, acting up, and generally showing off for visitors under the pine trees next to the bar Fred Smith used to own.

SPARTA

CREATIVE DISPLAY, INC.

431 Holtan St., Sparta, Wis.;
Mon–Fri 7 AM–5 PM, sometimes Sat AM; free (608) 269–6771

For the man who has everything, may we suggest the gift of a lawn ornament in the shape of a Black Angus bull? It is ten feet high, twenty-one feet long; it wears a plaid chef's hat and sunglasses, and is smoking a cigar. This Texas-size creation costs $750 at Creative Display, Inc., the country's major manufacturer of oversized cows, pigs, pink elephants, gorillas, lumberjacks and

Gasoline Alley, The Home of Frank King, Tomah, Wis.

Henkelmann's Museum, Woodruff, Wis.

other such roadside mascots. People order these fiberglass colossi to stick on top of restaurants, put onto miniature golf courses, tote on floats in parades, or otherwise advertise their product, their town, or themselves. The best known Creative Display sculpture is the Big Boy who stands over the popular fast-food burger joints.

Creative Display is a small organization, and they are happy to show people around, through the animal-packed grounds, and into the hangar-sized building in which Dave Oswald sculpts. Around here they consider Dave "the greatest sculptor in the world." He is an artist without formal training who makes molds from his original foam sculpture so that he can mass-produce his work. There is no doubt that the sculptures of Dave Oswald have been seen by more Americans than the work of any other living sculptor.

We asked Dave what he thought of pop art (an expensive form of what he does). He looked up from his nineteen-foot-long walleye pike. "What's that?" he asked. "You know," we said, "like Claes Oldenburg's giant lipstick that he sold to Yale." "How much did he charge?" Dave asked. "I bet I could do it bigger and for less money."

TOMAH

GASOLINE ALLEY—THE HOME OF FRANK KING

Tomah, Wis.

Skeezix was once the most famous character in the most popular cartoon strip of all time—Frank King's *Gasoline Alley*. If you walk the streets of Tomah, Wisconsin, you just may see Skeezix's inspiration. For it was in this small Wisconsin town that Frank King grew up. And you can bet that the town hasn't forgotten their famous native son. Everywhere you look in Tomah, you are reminded that this is the home of the man who created *Gasoline Alley*. Almost every lamppost in the business district tells you so; and there are exhibits of his work everywhere. A good place to start is the old pullman car that is parked on "Gasoline Alley" outside the chamber of commerce. Here they've got drawings, portraits, letters, cartoons, and other personal mementos. It was here we learned that Skeezix was the first comic-strip character to start out as a baby and grow to manhood day by day, right before the eyes of *Gasoline Alley*'s doting readers.

WOODRUFF

THREE MUSICAL BEARS AND TWISTING SQUIRRELS

Henkelmann's Museum, Hwy 70 East, 3 mi. N. of Woodruff, Wis.;
May–Oct 9 AM–9 PM; $2

Mr. and Mrs. Henry Henkelmann shot more kinds of animals than we have ever seen. They have bagged tayras, king crabs, trogons, albino porcupines, coypus, curassows, and jaguarundis. Most of these stuffed trophies are displayed in Henkelmann's museum in dioramas that replicate their natural habitat—designed to set hearts aflutter and trigger fingers itching among the sportspeople and nature lovers who visit.

To be honest, the sight of all these stuffed animals made us sad, and we realized that we are far from being the Great White Hunters that the Henkelmanns were. But there was one thing here that even we bleeding-heart animal lovers couldn't resist. It is a diorama of three stuffed bears. One has a harmonica, one a guitar, and the third an accordion. They have been rigged to "play" the instruments, and as they play, two couples of stuffed squirrels twirl around a dance floor to their music. Henkelmann's latest brochure says the squirrels are doing the twist, but to us it looked more like a waltz.

Incidentally, Henkelmann's has the only souvenir shop we found that keeps a full inventory of sea monkeys. Inspired by the Henkelmanns, we bought some of the little critters, and tried to grow them in hopes that one day we could set them loose, hunt them down, make a clean kill, and mount their heads over our fireplace.

THE WORLD'S LARGEST PENNY

3rd and Hemlock, Woodruff, Wis.

P. T. Barnum started it all. He once posted a sign reading "This way to the egress." People inside the already too-crowded circus tent rushed through the door under the sign expecting to see the egress on display. They didn't know that "egress" is a fancy latinate word for "exit."

We were driving through Woodruff and saw a sign pointing to "The World's Largest Penny." We veered off our route and drove in the signified direction. Like Barnum's suckers, we were fooled. Instead of a real "Abe," we saw a huge clay mock-up of a penny with a slightly distorted Lincoln profile across its front. Next to it a plaque explained about Dr. Kate Newcombe and her "Million-Penny Parade" to raise funds for the town hospital.

The World's Largest Penny commemorates her work, and although we were at first disappointed, the longer we stared at the slightly askew face of Honest Abe on this piece of small-town handiwork, the more we liked it.

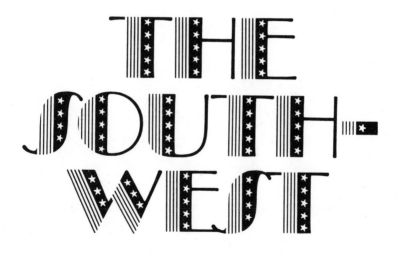

THE
SOUTH-
WEST

ARIZONA

THE RIDERLESS HORSE

7 mi. S. of Florence, Ariz. on Highway 80–89;
always visible; free

Travelers heading south toward Tucson on Highway 80–89 will notice a statue
of a riderless horse by the side of the road. The horse is "Tony," Tom Mix's
favorite mount. The statue marks the spot where the flamboyant cowboy died.

Mix was the original diamond-studded hero, right down to the horsehair
belt that announced in flowing script that its wearer was "Tom Mix, America's
Champion Cowboy." He loved luxury, including custom-made Rolls Royces.
But he was no sissy, either. Mix was known for doing all his own stunts and
trick riding, in the movies and later in the Sells Floto Circus.

His last ride was alone, heading out of Florence in his Rolls, skimming
across the prairie. A detour sign appeared. The car flipped over. There was no
time for a daring escape or trick jump. Tom Mix's neck was broken.

The statue of Tony is riderless to symbolize that no cowboy could ever take
the place of the original Good Guy who dressed all in white.

PHOENIX

HALL OF FLAME

110 N. Project Drive, Phoenix, Ariz.;
daily 9 AM–5 PM;
adults: $1.50, children 6–17: 50¢

Although it sounds more like a shrine to pyromania, the Hall of Flame aims to be the world's premier fire-fighting museum. It is operated by the National Historical Fire Foundation, whose 92-vehicle collection of fire-fighting apparatus is now being restored for display. There is a workshop on the premises that takes care of the ongoing restoration work, as well as providing displays for the museum of historical apparatus in action. The museum showroom now includes equipment from England, France, Japan, and the United States, including motorized, steam-powered, horse-drawn, and hand-operated machinery, some of which dates back to the seventeenth century. Also in the modern building is the Richard S. Fowler Fire Service Historical Research Library—over 4,000 books devoted to the subject of fire apparatus and fire fighting.

Plans for the future include the building of demonstration roadways outside in the Phoenix Activity Complex, the construction of a turn-of-the-century firehouse and the erection of an International Fire Fighter's Memorial Fountain.

To call the Hall of Flame, just dial (602) "ASK-FIRE."

TEMPE

BIG SURF

1500–1520 N. Hayden Rd., Tempe, Ariz.;
May–Sept, Tues–Sat, hours vary; $2.75;
(602) 947–2478

Big Surf is Arizona's ocean, a 2 1/2-acre body of water with custom-made waves to keep surfers happy when they are hundreds of miles from the real ocean. The waves come crashing in on Big Surf's sandy beach thanks to a very fancy hydraulic system that pumps water to a pre-arranged height in the reservoir and releases it through gates to break over an underwater baffle. Each wave, coming at regular intervals, is four to five feet high.

Surfboard riding periods at Big Surf alternate with other kinds of water sports. There are times allotted to swimming and rafting, and a shallow water area for small children. There is also a three-hundred-foot-long twisting water slide, down which you can either ride a raft or body surf. The architecture around Big Surf is Polynesian, with palm trees and cascading waterfalls creating the "Pacific Look." It looks real, the thrills are there; but you know that there is a master hand at the big board, regulating things in case of a wipe out. The biggest thrill of all is being able to enjoy a day at the ocean without leaving landlocked Arizona.

TOMBSTONE

THE WORLD'S LARGEST ROSEBUSH

The Rose Tree Inn, 4th and Toughnut Sts., Tombstone, Ariz.;
daily 9 AM–5 PM;
adults: $1, under 14: free

The world's largest rosebush is a white Lady Banksia. It was planted in 1885 by a Scottish girl who came to Tombstone as a young bride. Her family sent her a box of shrubs from Scotland, one of which she planted at the inn then known as the Arcade Hotel. The bush grew over the woodshed, and as the years went by the shed was torn down and a trellis built.

Today the Arcade Hotel is called the Rose Tree Inn, and the rosebush is over 8,000 square feet and still growing. Ripley's *Believe It or Not* and the *Guinness Book of Records* both conclude that it is the largest rosebush in the world. Every April it is covered with white blossoms.

In addition to the gigantic rosebush, the Rose Tree Inn has a small museum that includes a diorama of the gunfight at the O.K. corral, furnishings that once belonged to Wyatt Earp, "Boss" Tweed's bedroom set, and a collection of assaying equipment and minerals from local sites such as the Lucky Cuss Mine.

TUCSON

FARMER JOHN MURAL

1102 W. Grant St. (Clougherty Meat Packing Co.), Tucson, Ariz.

The Farmer John Mural in Tucson is one of the few spectacular urban wall paintings by Leslie Grimes, the same artist of the streets who painted the mural of "Piggies on the Rampage" in Vernon, California. His Tucson painting is more Western in concept. It is a panoramic scene of animals grazing across a landscape. A broad turquoise Arizona sky sweeps overhead, and fleecy clouds linger above the shadowless prairie. The scene is ringed in the far distance by the Sonora Mountains. The mural runs along Grant and State Streets.

YUMA

CHARLEY'S WORLD OF LOST ART

Sidewinder Rd. off Interstate 8, between Yuma, Ariz. & California border

Charles Caskin moved to Yuma from Arkansas about twenty years ago, and has been sculpting figures into the landscape around his mobile home all that time. He calls his creation Charley's World of Lost Art, and while it is hard to find, and truly "in the middle of nowhere," it is a world that shouldn't be missed.

Charley's World of Lost Art is populated by concrete figures of mythological animals, Biblical personalities, or historical characters as Charley remembers them. The carvings are soft-edged, tinted with delicate earth tones that impart a fading quality to the work and give it a wondrous historical authenticity.

There are Egyptian figures, caught in profile, looking as if they have just stepped down from a wall of hieroglyphs. There are sculpted prospectors and their mules, giant heads of wild beasts, astronauts, anthropomorphic alligators looking up from the ground, bears, bison, and small castles everywhere. The animals look like people, the people resemble animals. The consistency of his vision and Charley's use of natural materials such as rock and driftwood give his work the monumental qualities that characterize the best Eskimo and Indian carvings.

Charley himself, a weathered-looking desert man, is a fascinating sight. He will show you around if he isn't busy working on his Lost World.

YUMA TERRITORIAL PRISON

Yuma Territorial Prison State Historical Park, Interstate-8 in Yuma;
daily 8 AM–5:30 PM;
50¢ per single adult, $1 per car, under 14: free

The Yuma Prison was among the most notorious of the Old West. During its thirty-three years of operation, between 1876 and 1909, 3,040 men and 29 women served time here; 26 escaped; 8 died trying. Recaptured escapees got the iron ball and chain.

As infamous as the Yuma Prison was, it considered itself a "model" prison of its time. When they weren't making adobe bricks or building roads, convicts were allowed to make handcrafted items to be sold at public bazaars held at the prison on Sundays after church. One of the first public libraries in the territory was built here, and schooling was available to convicts who wanted it.

The territorial prison was moved to Florence in 1909, and Yuma became the site of the Union High School. Yuma High athletic teams still call themselves "the Criminals." When the high school moved out in 1914, the empty jail cells soon became known as "free lodging" for hobos during the 1920s and homeless families during the Depression.

Today you can still see the cellblock, made of granite and iron, and the "new yard"—twelve cells dug into the hillside in 1900 to relieve overcrowding. The "Dark Cell" is here too—a small, lightless room dug into the earth for the solitary confinement of unruly prisoners. There is also a museum built on the site of the old mess hall. It tells the whole grisly story of this "crowbar hotel."

NEW MEXICO

ACOMA

THE OLDEST CONTINUOUSLY
INHABITED TOWN IN THE UNITED STATES

Acoma, N.M., off NM 23

Today less than a dozen families live in Acoma year round, but the town has had residents continuously since 1075. Acoma is an Indian village 7,500 feet high in the mountains, with air as crisp as icicles, so quiet you can hear a piece of sagebrush roll down the street. The recorded history of Acoma began in the eleventh century when Indians living on nearby Enchanted Mesa were starved off after an earthquake. They called this new town Acoma, which means "close to heaven." If you come here, you will see adobe huts and townspeople who look like an Edward Curtis photo come to life.

ALBUQUERQUE

NATIONAL ATOMIC MUSEUM

Kirtland Air Force Base, entrance on Wyoming Blvd SE, Albuquerque, N.M.;
Mon–Fri 9 AM–5 PM, Sat & Sun noon–5 PM; free

This is a fascinating place that may give you nightmares. It is a plain, two-story stucco building on Kirtland Air Force Base that tells the story of atomic energy. Other such museums that we have visited concentrate on "the friendly atom" and show visitors how atomic power is nothing to be afraid of, how it works to create energy, light our homes, power factories, etc. There is a little bit of that at the National Atomic Museum, but the focus here is clearly on the use of atomic power in warfare. It tells the complete story of nuclear weapons, from the U. S. flag flown over Trinity (site of the world's first nuclear detonation) to the MIRV warhead.

There are regular screenings of a film called *Ten Seconds that Shook the World,* that shows how the "gun type 'little-boy' " bomb over Hiroshima and the implosion type "Fat Man" on Nagasaki "closed out" World War II, and set the stage for postwar stockpiling. Among the exhibits are a 280-millimeter canon, a Mark 17 early thermonuclear device, a Mark 91 penetration bomb, and one of the A-bombs recovered after the 1966 mid-air collision over Palomares, Spain. It is curious to see how bombs have changed aesthetically over the years. The early "nukes" were round and bulging things, painted a drab olive green. Newer styles are sleek and smaller, painted white with an occasional dab of trim.

Models and photographs illustrate weapons-delivery systems and different shapes of mushroom clouds. There are plans to put a B-52 bomber outside, along with several larger missile systems.

We don't know of another place where one can see a variety of real nuclear bombs on display. Of course, the working innards have been scooped out of these, but they are an awesome sight nonetheless. Whether this show of atomic muscle thrills and inspires you or sets your hair on end, there is no denying that the thermonuclear exhibits at the National Atomic Museum are of singular importance.

Kirtland Air Force Base outside is the field headquarters for U.S. weapons development and production—where yesterday's bombs took shape, and where the bombs of the future are being planned.

ANGEL FIRE

SHOVEL RACE CHAMPIONSHIPS

Angel Fire, New Mexico;
Washington's Birthday

The type of shovel most often used in a shovel race is the aluminum grain scoop. The racer places one "cheek" in each indentation with the handle between his legs and pointing down hill. He is then given a shove, and tries to slide down the slope of the Angel Fire ski slope faster than anyone else. Steering is accomplished by dragging either hand alongside. Rules dictate that the posterior of the racer must be in contact with the scoop portion of the shovel (although it may be padded) and that the scoop must remain in contact with the snow at all times during the run.

There are two categories of shovel race at Angel Fire—Modified and Production. In a Production Shovel Race the shovel must be exactly as it comes from the hardware store. In the Modified Class, add-ons are permitted. This might mean sails, skis, or tailfins—but no motors, spring drives, or mechanical power source. You've got to slide down all the way.

Other than on Washington's Birthday, Angel Fire is a ski resort, at which people hopefully slide down hills standing on skis, not sitting on their rears.

ARTESIA

THE ABO ELEMENTARY SCHOOL

18th & Center Sts., Artesia, N.M.;
late Aug–Late May Mon–Fri 9 AM–4 PM;
call (505) 748–2755; free

The Abo Elementary School was built in the early 1960s, just after the Cuban missile crisis. It is a school consisting of eighteen classes with thirty students per class, ranging from kindergarten to fifth grade. There are no windows in any of the classrooms. There are no windows because the Abo Elementary School is entirely underground. The building is radiation-proof.

From the outside all you see are three entryways—raised rectangles with double doors leading into a vestibule. The roof of the school, which is at ground level, serves as a playground. Enter one of the three rectangles and descend into the class area and you notice that there is a lot of wall decoration down here. All four walls of every classroom are used for blackboard space, teaching aids, and displays of children's projects. "You'll never find any of these kids staring out the window," one instructor said. "We've got no distractions here."

As a civil defense shelter, the Abo Elementary School says it is equipped to house and feed 2,000 persons for two weeks. But we seem to remember that it will take longer than two weeks for the radiation to dissipate after World War III, and so suggest that Abo revise its figures to read "two people for 2,000 weeks." That will give the two of us about 38 1/2 years until it's time to come out and pick up where we left off. The only trick is to make sure we're loitering at 18th and Center Streets in Artesia when the nukes start to fall.

MESCALERO

APACHE MAIDENS' PUBERTY RITES

Mescalero, N.M.; July 4th week;
price indefinite;
for more information, write Box 176, Mescalero, N.M.

Every year the Mescalero Indians perform a puberty rites ceremony for the thirteen-year-old girls of their tribe. Outsiders are allowed to watch the principal parts of these rites. Although much of the dancing, chanting, and symbolism of the Mescaleros is untranslatable, observers are provided a mimeographed explanation of the activities.

Over the course of the five-day ceremony, tribe members pitch teepees on the hillside of Mescalero and revert back to life as their ancestors knew it. The maidens wear ceremonial buckskins and are painted with sacred paints derived from special plants. They avoid any contact with water for the five days, drinking only through reeds, not washing, and not moving their face ("to avoid aging"). They are required to behave decorously, and not like the giggly teenagers they were before womanhood.

There are blessings by the medicine man, ritual dancing, and constant tribal activity—all of which creates an eerily accurate picture of what Apache culture must have been like before modern civilization intervened.

RUIDOSO

MULE-O-RAMA

Gateway Meadows, Ruidoso, N.M.;
2nd full weekend in Oct.;
adults: $2, under 10: free

Ruidoso is the home of the "All American," the race that is to the quarter horse what the Kentucky Derby is to the thoroughbred. A few Ruidosians started thinking that most of the quarter horses they saw on the track were priced more like thoroughbreds and less like the poor man's horse that originally inspired the running of the All American. So once a year, to get back to their roots, the people of Ruidoso stage a Mule-o-rama, where the poor man's animal is run for the roses.

A local fellow named Mr. Reed, who is himself a veteran mule racer, told us that the event is a real "equalizer." You never know when a mule is going to go into some new stubborn and frustrating antic. He said, "They start off when the flag goes down, and they're running along fine, and all of a sudden the woman in the bleachers with the flowered hat starts to wave that hat in the air. A horse—all he'll do is glance out the corner of his eye. But the mules —they'll turn at once and run off the track toward the grandstand." He added "That's when the giggling begins."

OKLAHOMA

BEAVER

COW-CHIP CAPITAL OF THE WORLD—
WORLD CHAMPIONSHIP COW-CHIP THROW

Beaver, Okla., at the Fair Grounds;
held the Saturday closest to April 22 (Oklahoma Day);
free

Here is a contest that city dwellers concerned with the urban blight of doggie do-do might well consider. Every year, the people of Beaver, Oklahoma get together and hold an "Organic Olympics." Practically everybody in town puts on their cow-chip T-shirts, which feature a portrait of smiling "King Cow Chip" (a cow pie with arms, legs and a face). Contestants line up in the chip-throwing arena and start slinging cow chips as far as they can. Winners receive gold trophies that look like cow chips.

The origins of cow-chip throwing stretch back to pioneer days when, each fall, families would take their wagon out to the fields and load it full of cow chips to use as fuel during the winter. It became an informal sport to determine

World Championship Cowchip Throw, Beaver, Okla.

Ralph Rector, town scatologist, Beaver, Okla.:
The Cowchip Capital of the World, Beaver, Okla.

who could throw chips into the wagon with the most accuracy. Today, at the annual contest, it is distance that is measured. Each contestant gets two chips, which must be selected from the official Cow-Chip Wagon, and may not be altered or streamlined in any way. The chip thrown the farthest is the one counted. In the case of a mid-air break in the chip, the piece going the farthest determines the measurement. The current record is held by Carl Engel of Odessa, Texas, who in 1973 sent his chip flying 165 feet, 8 inches.

Concurrent with the International Cow-Chip Throwing Contest, Beaver offers a free barbecue for all who attend.

Since Beaver is proud of its title as Cow-Chip Capital, and since it is the "Home of the Champion Slingers," cow chips are honored here year around. Ralph Rector, the Chamber of Commerce secretary and "town scatologist" spends a lot of time finding unusually large chips and making faces out of their natural creases and folds. He told us that Beaver cow chips have been sent around the world (by mail, not thrown) and that the Inspector General of the National Archives of France asked for—and received—a bulk shipment of chips. When you visit Beaver, stop in the Chamber of Commerce office and "talk chips" with Mr. Rector. There's nothing he likes better. And he has cow-chip bolo ties and T-shirts for sale, as well as gift-boxed chips to send to your friends.

The official Beaver Cow-Chip Wagon is viewable any time of year, parked at 7th and Douglas Streets.

CLAREMORE

WILL ROGERS MEMORIAL

1 mi. W. of Claremore, Okla., on OK Rt. 88;
daily 8 AM–5 PM; free

This is the ideal place for a complete immersion in the life and legend of Will Rogers. It is built on the land where he once planned a family home, overlooking the town of Claremore. Everything is here, from his "Dog-Iron" cattle brand to the things he had in his pockets the day he died.

The best place to begin a walk through Will Rogers' life is the Diorama Room, off the West Gallery, where thirteen scenes follow his life from his birthplace in Oolagah to the fatal plane crash near Point Barrow, Alaska. The West Gallery contains personal artifacts—the chaps and ropes he used in the Ziegfeld Follies, his own plain leather saddle, and his portable typewriter, its twisted keys showing the impact of the plane crash. The East Gallery contains the Saddle Room, with saddles and trappings from around the world, including Will's unique collection of miniature saddles. The North Gallery is designed to simulate a room in Will Rogers' Santa Monica home. It is uncluttered and quiet, with chairs for visitors, and a few original manuscripts on display. There are two major statues in the museum. One is equestrian, showing Will on "Soapsuds," his favorite mount, riding toward the west entrance of the building. It is called "Riding into Sunset." The other statue is Jo Davidson's famous bronze, the other copy of which now stands in the capital in Washington. Its toes have been rubbed gold by visitors. And outside in a sunken garden is the tomb containing the bodies of Will Rogers, his wife Betty, and their infant son, Fred.

Folks who have never actually seen Will Rogers can see a film here called *Ropin' Fool,* in which the cowboy-philosopher does some of his rope tricks. There is also a documentary of his life.

One of the fringe benefits about familiarizing oneself with Will Rogers is that he offers an appropriate thought or witticism for every occasion. In the context of this book, we offer these Will Rogers' words of wisdom: "There ought to be a law against anybody going to Europe until they had seen the things we have in this country."

DEWEY

THE TOM MIX MUSEUM

Delaware & Don Tyler Ave., Dewey, Okla.;
Tues–Fri 9 AM–5 PM, Sat & Sun 1 PM–5 PM, closed Mon & all major holidays; free

Tom Mix was the original good guy in the white hat. He was the "best-dressed in the west," the cowboy who created the fancy-fringed image later taken up by Roy Rogers and Gene Autrey. But Tom Mix was a hard-riding guy as well, serving as a wrangler for the British Army and later seeing action as a Texas ranger. He in fact captured the Shonts brothers, New Mexico's most notorious cattle rustlers.

Both sides of Tom Mix are on display in this museum, although it is difficult to draw the line between the man and the myth. His private life was anything but private. There are pictures here of his Beverly Hills Home, complete with English butler, swimming pool, and the initials "T. M." branded on the roof in lights. His famous $15,000 saddle is here, adorned with enough silver to make any horse swayback. He also owned the world's smallest silver saddle, silver bits, bridles, and belts—all of which are on display. In 1908 Tom Mix won the "World Champion Cowboy" award, shown here as a prized possession among the other memorabilia.

His philosophy of picture-making was simple: "I ride into a place owning my own horse, saddle, and bridle. It isn't my quarrel, but I get into trouble doing the right thing for somebody else. When it's all over, I never get any money reward. I may be made foreman of the ranch and I get the girl, but there is never a fervid love scene."

They don't make 'em like that any more.

MANGUM

MANGUM RATTLESNAKE DERBY

Downtown Mangum, Okla.; three days, late April;
for further info write Fang-master, Box 128, Mangum, or call (405) 782-2444

For three days every April it seems as if half the people of Mangum, Oklahoma, are walking around with bags full of snakes. They are participants in the annual Rattlesnake Derby. All contestants ride to the outskirts of town and capture rattlers. Prizes are given for the largest snake, the heaviest bag of snakes, the most snakes, the shortest snake, and specially marked snakes. After awards are given out, the snakes are taken to the butcher's where they are killed, skinned, and cut up. On Saturday night there is a barbecue, free to hunters. During the three days of the hunt, there is a "snake pit" where naturalists discuss safety measures and snakebite first aid, and give displays of venom extraction.

If rattlesnakes are not your idea of fun, you might try driving just outside of town to Bats Cove, where, in the late evening, it is said that thousands of bats may be seen doing whatever it is that bats do.

Mc ALESTER

STATE PENITENTIARY RODEO

Rodeo Arena, Oklahoma State Penitentiary, McAlester, Okla.;
Fri, Sat & Sun before Labor Day;
$4–6 per seat (in advance, order from P.O. Box 97, MCAlester, Okla 74501)

There is one rodeo event unique to the Oklahoma Penitentiary contest that captures the prevailing spirit of this "Largest Behind Walls Rodeo." It is called "Money the Hard Way," and this is how it works: The warden stands above a chute that contains a wild Brahma bull. He ties a Bull Durham sack containing a hundred-dollar bill to the horns of the animal, and lets the bull loose into the arena. Approximately two dozen convicts enter the arena after the bull, charging it and fighting off each other to try and grab the sack of money. This is the most popular event at the rodeo.

It is said that prison rodeos are the wildest of any, since participants feel they have little to lose, and since the rodeo offers them a break in the monotony of routine prison life. The audience at this rodeo is made up partly of relatives of inmate-cowboys and partly of people who come to watch men (and women, in some events) ride and scramble as if there is no tomorrow.

OKLAHOMA CITY

NATIONAL COWBOY HALL OF FAME AND WESTERN HERITAGE CENTER

1700 NE 63rd St., Oklahoma City, Okla.;
Memorial Day–Labor Day daily 8:30 AM–6 PM,
rest of year daily 9:30 AM–5:30 PM;
adults: $1.50, children: 50¢

"Cowboys and sod busters, trappers and traders, Indians and cavalry, rodeo champions and movie stars, bucking broncs and coyotes, a tent camp and a glowing fire! The entire west and all Westerners in one magnificent structure!" That is the way this Big Daddy of all Western museums describes itself. It has everything from Frederick Remington's most famous paintings, to an original chuckwagon, to a 32' by 48' relief map of the United States, to original Norman Rockwells of John Wayne and Walter Brennan. If big, expansive, gaudy overkill was an important part of the western spirit, the National Cowboy Hall of Fame captures it perfectly.

Downstairs they have the "West of Yesterday" exhibit, complete with life-size reconstructed (or in some cases original) saloon, gold mine, stagecoach, Indians (made of wax), sod house, nickelodeons, and raised wooden sidewalk. "Adventure tours" of this environment are available for conventions and school groups.

Because the appeal of the American West has always been concentrated more in its myths and legends than its realities, the Great Hall upstairs, which celebrates the legendary West, is our favorite part of the Cowboy Hall of Fame. Here you will find a giant map of the United States, with westward migrations shown by means of colored lights along the trails. Here also are the great collections of Western art, the Rodeo Hall of Fame, and the Hall of Great Westerners. And of course there is the best-known West, the West of William S. Hart, Roy Rogers and Dale Evans, Walter Brennan, Barbara Stanwyck, and "Duke" Wayne, creators of the Western epic in film and song, and honored in the Hall of Great Western Performers.

Joel McCrae, a Hall of Famer himself, says "The National Cowboy Hall of Fame is the greatest thing that has happened to the West in the last twenty-five years. It's the only institution that's preserving the great traditions of the West." Indeed, with history books and "anti-Western" films unearthing the "real" West, it does seem as if the National Cowboy Hall of Fame is one of the last outposts of that lonesome American folk hero, the cowboy.

NATIONAL SOFTBALL HALL OF FAME

2801 NE 50th, Oklahoma City, Okla.;
Mon–Fri 9 AM–5 PM, weekends noon–5 PM;
adults: 50¢, children: 25¢

In 1887, George Hancock, a Chicago board of trade reporter, was attending a Thanksgiving party at his boat club. He thought it would be a great idea to play a game that all party-goers could enjoy. He found a broomstick to use as a bat and wrapped up an old boxing glove to use as a ball. With these implements he and his friends played a slow and easy game of what they called "Indoor-Outdoor." Since 1887, the sport has been known as Kitten Ball, Playground Ball, Diamond Ball, and Mush Ball. Today, softball is one of America's largest participation sports. As it is played on a national level—slow pitch or fast—it is anything but a slow and easy game. As anyone who ever saw the Raybestos Brakettes or the Caterpillar Dieselettes or the Allmen Transfer play can tell you, softball is a hard-charging sport.

The National Softball Hall of Fame honors the game's best players—mostly from fast-pitch leagues, but in recent years from slow-pitch as well. Here are plaques to honor Harold "Shifty" Gears, who struck out exactly 13,244 batters in his lifetime, and had a career total of 866 wins and 115 losses! Here is the "Blonde Bomber," "Bullet Betty" Grayson, who pitched 115 consecutive scoreless innings in 1945. And how about Dot Wilkinson, the game's greatest catcher, who used a five-finger glove instead of a mitt, and caught 43 innings in one day during a national tournament in 1950?

Plaques honoring Hall of Famers are in one room of the National Ammateur Softball Association. Elsewhere in the building are exhibits of different balls, uniforms, explanations of softball around the world, and a softball archives and library.

PONCA CITY

PIONEER WOMAN MUSEUM

701 Monument Rd.; Highway 177 & 60 in Ponca City, Okla.;
May–Sept Mon–Sat 9 AM–7 PM, Sun 1 PM–7 PM, Oct–April Mon–Sat 9 AM–5 PM,
Sun 1 PM–5 PM; free

In the late 1920s, E. W. Marland, an Oklahoma oilman, held a competition for sculptors to see who could create the best statue symbolizing the spirit of pioneer women. Bryant Baker won with his "Confident," a dynamic full-length figure of a woman striding forward, the Bible clutched in her right hand, her young son holding on to her left. At the statue's dedication in 1930, Marland said "Women . . . became the unknown soldiers in the great battle for civilization and homesteads. They won. With this monument I hope to preserve for the children the story of our mothers' fight and toil and courage."

Today the statue stands in front of the Pioneer Woman Museum, built on land donated by Marland, who became Oklahoma's tenth governor. Inside the museum, one sees plenty of evidence of the toil of which he spoke. Household tools and equipment show the almost unbelievable amount of work that women had to do—as housekeepers, mothers, bakers, seamstresses, washerwomen, and paramedics. Most of the artifacts on display come from nearby log cabins or sod houses.

STILLWATER

NATIONAL WRESTLING HALL OF FAME

405 West Hall of Fame Ave., Stillwater, Okla.;
Mon–Fri 9:30 AM–4:30 PM;
adults: $1, high school age and under: 50¢

Don't come here expecting to see the Masked Marauder's mask or the Mendoza Midgets' sombreros. The kind of "professional" wrestling in which contestants wear blonde wigs and leopard-skin togas, attack "secret pressure points," and swing about the ring on the referee's microphone is *not* what is honored here. The National Wrestling Hall of Fame is devoted to amateur wrestling, the Olympic sport that goes back to the very civilized Greeks. In fact, the centerpiece in this modern, Georgian-style building is a replica of Cephisodotus's classic work, "The Wrestlers," sculpted over 2000 years ago. Other exhibits are as modern as the gold medals recently won by the U.S. Olympic wrestling team.

In addition to photos, uniforms, plaques, and memorabilia from America's top wrestlers, the hall now displays pictures of the great Watanabe of Japan and of the gold medal-winning Medved of the U.S.S.R. There is a hundred-foot "Wall of Champions" that lists individual winners from all eras of competitive tournament wrestling. There are now fourteen members of the Hall of Fame —collegiate players, coaches, and Olympic champs, some going back to the 1920s.

Amateur wrestling has never provided much financial reward or fame. The story is told here of Jack VanBebber, seven times the national champion, who in 1932 realized he was late for a gold medal match being held six miles away. He had no transportation and so set out on foot, arriving at the championship match only because a passing motorist gave him a ride. Perhaps that's why Chris Taylor, the four-hundred-pound-plus American champion who was flattened in the 1972 Olympics by Medved, has recently signed a deal to become the new terror of the lucrative "professional" wrestling arenas.

STROUD

INTERNATIONAL BRICK- AND ROLLING-PIN-THROWING CONTEST

Brick- & Rolling-Pin-Throw Finals: Stroud High School Stadium, Stroud, Okla.;
July 15, 1978, 7 PM; free,
Brick, Barbed Wire & Nail Collectors Convention:
High School Agriculture building;
July 15, 1978, all day; free

Each year Stroud, Oklahoma competes with the three other Strouds of the world—in Canada, England, and Australia—in an international contest to see who can throw a five-pound brick and a two-pound rolling pin the greatest distance. Competition involves a team of ten members from each Stroud in the brick-throw, and ten in the rolling-pin throw. Stroud, Oklahoma furnishes the official bricks to all other Strouds, and Stroud, Australia makes the rolling pins. The brick throw, which is open only to men, was dominated by an American champion, Jim Cantrell, from 1965 to 1971, when he was unseated by Englishman Robert Gardner, who now holds the current "Champion of Champions" title with a throw of 142' 6". The rolling-pin toss, open only to women, has been dominated by American champions since Sherri Salyer threw her pin 140' 4" in 1970. Team championships have been passed back and forth between England and America. There are mixed doubles contests, in which the men toss bricks and the women rolling pins. Strangely enough, although a "Miss Brick-Throw" is elected every year in all four Strouds, they have never to our knowledge considered selecting a "Mr. Rolling Pin."

During the Brick- and Rolling-Pin-Throw, brick collectors, barbed wire collectors, and dated nail collectors hold an annual convention and exhibit in downtown Stroud. Here you can delve into brick, wire, and nail history. We learned about a famous brick made between 1902 and 1923 and now found throughout the southwest that had "Don't Spit on Sidewalk" imprinted on it in an effort to wipe out tuberculosis. We also learned that most bricks have been "signed" by their makers. Signatures range from fingerprints found on bricks dating back to 2700 B.C., to printed town names that tell where nineteenth- and twentieth-century bricks are made— "Bartlesville," "Chandler," and—you guessed it—"Stroud."

WAYNOKA

WAYNOKA RATTLESNAKE HUNT

Hunt Headquarters: City Hall, Waynoka, Okla.;
1st Sat & Sun after Easter;
free to hunt; 50¢ admission to "snake pit" exhibition

Snake hunters in Waynoka fuel up for the Annual Rattlesnake Hunt activities at a "free beanfeed" which starts at 11:00 A.M., Saturday morning in the Saddle Club Building. Later that day, amateur snake hunters and informal groups scour the cliffs and gullies around town for snakes, which are brought into town and sold for $2 a pound to the Waynoka Saddle Club. The rattlers are turned into snake sandwiches, which are sold on Sunday.

Waynoka's information "for novices" includes the following suggestions: wear good walking boots, carry a gunnysack and a forked stick "at least six feet long," take your first-aid kit, and attend church before you leave for the hunt.

TEXAS

ALAMO

THE LIVE STEAM MUSEUM

2 mi. N. of Alamo, Tex. on FM 907;
Late Nov–April daily 8 AM–5 PM, Dec & March Sun, Jan & Feb Sat & Sun;
donation

This is the only museum of live steam in the world. It began as the hobby of
W. R. "Tommy" Tompkins, who noticed that the steam engine was becoming
a thing of the past. He wanted to preserve what he felt was the pivot of the
industrial revolution. He was worried that people would never be able to listen
to the action of live steam, smell the tallow oil, or hear the sound that only
a steam whistle can make.

This unique museum affords all these opportunities to visitors. Among the
engines on display are an 1896 portable steam engine and boiler, a 13-foot-high
Ford Vertical Engine, the gigantic Triple Expansion Marine Steam Engine
from the World War II ship *Liberty,* and a 15″-gauge railroad track and steam
locomotive.

If you get thirsty walking among all this puffing and tooting machinery, you
can belly up to the largest juice bar in Texas at the nearby Alamo Citrus
Center. This is the home of the ruby-red grapefruit, which you can pick
yourself from the trees. If you feel the need to steam-up and juice-up at the

same time, you can ride through the grapefruit orchards on the miniature locomotive.

AMARILLO

AMARILLO LIVESTOCK AUCTION

100 S. Manhattan St., Amarillo, Tex.;
always open (auction days are Mon, Tues, and sometimes Weds.); free

The Amarillo auction is the largest in the world. Eighteen thousand head of beef go past the auctioneer's gavel every week, and over one hundred million dollars change hands every year. The auction is of cattle only—no pigs, sheep, or goats.

Outside there are acres of pens. Cowboys and buyers walk overhead on skinny catwalks to have a look at the stock. Yes, an old cattleman told us, many have lost their footing and fallen in. There are occasional gorings, but usually all anyone gets is bruised and dirty. Visitors can obtain permission to traverse these overhead mazes or to sit inside the arena and watch the auctioneer spit out his rapid patter as one bucking and snorting animal follows another. Odd lots are sold in the morning, large lots in the afternoon.

Among the people working the cattle chutes were three booted and tight-jeaned cowgirls known here as "Charlie's Angels" because they work for a rancher named Charlie and are considered the best female cow-jockeys in the west. Between the "Angels" and the scores of tough-looking cowpokes around, the Amarillo auction is great food for fantasy, offering a heavy dose of the real West and the spirit of the Texas Panhandle.

CADILLAC RANCH

US 40 (formerly Route 66), 5 mi. W. of Amarillo, Tex., on S. side of highway;
always viewable; free

"What *is* that" asked the lady in raffia sun hat and harlequin glasses from the window of her Electra 225 with Florida plates.

"It's ten Cadillacs, buried face down," we explained.

"Why?" her daughter asked.

We shrugged. Cadillac Ranch can be described but not explained. It is a visual joke that loses its meaning if it has to be translated. Art critics have offered "the Decline of Automobile Culture," or "Detroit Decadence," or "Pop Art Whimsy" as explanatory titles of this creation by a group called Ant Farm on Stanley Marsh 3's ("3," not III, Marsh says) ranch. What it is is this: ten Cadillacs, ranging from a '49 fastback coupe to a 1960 Sedan de Ville, have been buried face down in a row—an informal history of the tail fin, from its modest introduction, through the flagrant '50s, to the fin's farewell. Like a great Detroit bumper crop they emerge from the dark, fertile earth as the only visual point of reference across the flat landscape.

If you wander close to the cars, away from the road, you become aware of a ghostly silence. The roadside joke looms like a lonely apocalyptic vision. Close up, you see that the cars have been scratched everywhere with graffiti, and are pockmarked by vandals' gunshots. Passers-by have expressed a savage anger at these cars buried upside down in the earth. "This is a national monument," one person has scratched. "Monument, my ass," replies another, punctuating the words with bullet holes.

INTERNATIONAL HELIUM TIME COLUMNS AND HELIUM PAVILION

110 N. Project Drive (I-40 at Nelson St.), Amarillo, Tex.;
daily 9 AM–6 PM; free

Among its other claims to fame, Amarillo is the Helium Capital of the World. Over 90 percent of the "free world's" helium is found in the ground within a 250-mile radius of town. To celebrate this fact, and the 100th anniversary of the discovery of helium, a monument and time column were erected by the Amarillo Helium Centennial Committee in 1968.

About four thousand items are sealed within its slim towers in an atmosphere of inert helium. Individual columns of the four-part monument are designated to be opened after twenty-five, fifty, one hundred, and a thousand years have passed. Inside the museum next to the monument are display cases showing what's sealed inside the columns. We saw a box of All detergent, bedroom slippers, roller skates, Corning ware, Elizabeth Arden skin cream, light bulbs, chewing tobacco, a pack of Kents, a Sears catalogue, and an 8-mm projector. We were told there is also a dehydrated apple pie, flower seeds, vegetable seeds, and a bank book for a $10 savings account. This last item is in the thousand-year column, and will be worth one quintillion dollars (at 4 percent interest) when the column is opened in 2968. Proceeds have been made payable to the U. S. Treasury.

The museum also tells the story of helium, from its discovery by Sir Joseph Lockyer as a solar substance to its current use in sophisticated microscopes and gyro systems. There are no free samples for balloon fill-ups, and no explanation of why helium makes everyone sound like Mickey Mouse if it is inhaled.

BEAUMONT

THE EYE OF THE WORLD

J. J. Steak House, 6685 N. Eleventh (Texas Freeway), Beaumont, Tex.;
Mon–Sat 6 AM–11 PM; free

The J. J. Steak House looks like any other reasonably priced Formica eatery that one finds on the outskirts of large cities. A fiberglass cow logo stands on the roof, and the menu inside offers basic "steaks and chops." Only a small window on the west wall hints that there is something unique here. Above the window, in small neon letters, are the words "Eye of the World." Look inside this window, and you get a god's-eye view of one man's cosmology.

Inside the restaurant, past the room where the Kiwanis meet, a door opens into the alcove that houses the vast landscape of all civilization that John N. Gavrelos created between 1923 and 1948. Working with bits of wood, cigar boxes, and a small knife, he created a microcosm of history, in his words, "the true story of world philosophy [sic]."

The landscape is terraced. Formal Greek temples with Corinthian columns have been stained with shellac until they glow. They overlook subsequent developments in the history of religion and politics. Among the pillars, columns, steps and archways, Plato speaks; Lady Liberty unfurls the American flag; the Declaration of Independence is signed. Inside a two-foot-tall church, people pray before a tiny illuminated altar. Small busts honor great composers, philosophers, writers, and politicians. The carvings sprawl on and on—too much to appreciate all at once.

Mr. Gavrelos's relatives run the J. J. Steak House now, and if they are not busy they will take you to see the Eye of the World, flipping on the switch that illuminates the miniature cosmos.

THE FRAGRANCE GARDEN

Tyrell Park, TX 124 SW, Beaumont, Tex.

The Fragrance Garden is designed for the blind and physically handicapped. It is an oval landscape in Tyrell Park, laid out with hard-surfaced walks for wheelchairs and thirty-foot-high handrails throughout the path system. Raised beds are planted with fragrantly scented plants, and there is an area set aside in which certain plants can be touched. Braille plaques are planned to explain the foliage. At this time the garden has a bird sanctuary, a waterfall and two pools, as well as dogwood, azaleas, roses, orange mint, dill, sweet woodruff, peppermint, and more. The Fragrance Garden is, of course, open to the sighted as well.

BUFFALO GAP

THE ERNIE WILSON MUSEUM

William and Elm Streets, Buffalo Gap, Tex.;
Sunday afternoons, "usually"; donation: 50¢

Our guide through the Ernie Wilson Museum commented to his grandmother, "Cissie, it smells like a dead person's in here." Granny reassured us, "It's only the stuffed bear." So it goes at this most personal and eccentric of all museums. The ten-year-old guide said that he was the great-great grandson of John Wesley Hardin, and his namesake as well. Granny, who came along on the tour, is "restoring" the museum and some old buildings across the street. The restoration is going very, very slowly, which is fine with us. We love the Ernie Wilson Museum just the way it is.

To begin with, there is a glass case inside with three original rubber "Froggy" statuettes—the very same Froggy who tortured Andy Devine on *Andy's Gang,* who used to pull on the tail of Midnight the Cat. These three Froggys share the showcase with a whole mess of other gnawed rubber kiddie toys. Then there is the room that smells of the bear. It is illuminated by one lightbulb. On display are a mid-1950s TV set without the knobs, a pile of dusty western books, and a set of steer horns. Upstairs, there are some gorgeous rodeo posters printed in France, a few stuffed heads, and a yard-high advertising statuette of a cowboy with his saddle slung over his shoulder. Other displays include a Snow White stove for kids, some branding irons, bits of barbed wire, and "I Like Ike" buttons, and some 78-r.p.m. records of old country-and-western tunes—a collector's dream.

The Salt House, Grand Saline, Tex.

Cadillac Ranch, Amarillo, Tex.

Outside another building on the grounds are two headless gargoyles holding upside-down guitars. This is the "Art and Music Annex," containing more *objects d'art,* including a one-of-a-kind collection of Roy Acuff souvenir plates. John Wesley told us that there is an old Edsel in another building. He also pointed proudly to bullet holes and bloodstains throughout the premises— reminders of when this was Taylor County's first jail.

The Ernie Wilson Museum is a dusty, unkempt place. Horses neigh and roosters crow across the street, and the front yard is liberally sprinkled with cow chips. But a visit here is wonderful—like wandering into a favorite uncle's attic that has been closed for decades.

CARTHAGE

JIM REEVES MEMORIAL

Memorial Park, 3 mi. E. of Carthage, Tex. on Highway 79;
always viewable; free

Jim Reeves was always considered one of the friendliest guys in country-western music, so much so that he was called "Gentleman Jim" Reeves throughout his career. He became nationally famous in 1955 with his song "Mexican Joe," and he remained at the top of the charts until his death in an airplane crash near Nashville in 1964. Jim was born in Carthage, Texas, and his grave is now marked by a life-size statue on top of a gracefully curving pedestal. A guitar-shaped walkway leads to the statue, with a disclike plaque at the center of the walkway that tells of his life. The memorial is in a beautiful park of pine and oak trees, just the kind of place that the singer of "Billy Bayou," "Four Walls," and "This Is It" would have loved.

CRYSTAL CITY

THE SPINACH CAPITAL OF THE WORLD

Crystal City, Tex.

Do you remember the Popeye cartoons in which the pugnacious sailor-hero mainlined cans of spinach, then beat the daylights out of his enemy, Bluto?

Popeye is practically synonymous with spinach-eating, and in honor of the venerable fighting gob the citizens of Crystal City have erected a statue of him outside the Crystal City Municipal Building on the main street of town. He is at least life-size, and is depicted with the familiar bulging forearms, a pipe stuck into his mouth over the bulbous jutting jaw. He has anchors tatooed on his arms, and looks ready to fight anybody who doesn't like spinach.

You see, a large portion of the population of Crystal City is employed by Del Monte Foods, which has a huge cannery on the northern edge of town, where freshly grown greenery is funneled into cans. The cannery was built in 1945, but Crystal City considered itself the Spinach Capital long before Del Monte came along. The statue of Popeye was erected in 1937.

DALLAS

TOLBERT'S CHILI PARLOR AND MUSEUM OF CHILI

802 Main, Dallas, Tex.;
weekdays: 11 AM–2 PM, Saturday: 7 PM–1 AM

Frank X. Tolbert is the author of *A Bowl of Red,* the book acknowledged by almost every serious chili eater to be the first and last word on the subject. Dining in this chili parlor operated by the grand sage of the pod is the gastronomic equivalent of learning math from Einstein or creative writing from Will Shakespeare. It has been called the last true chili parlor left in Texas (and therefore, inevitably, the world). But for our ravings about Tolbert's chow, please read our own *Roadfood* (David Obst/Random House, 1978).

Here we will rave about Tolbert's Museum of Chili. On the walls of his parlor are portraits of famous chili lovers, including Will Rogers and Will Rogers, Jr. There are photographs and trophies from the annual World Championship Chili Cook-off in Terlingua (which Tolbert was instrumental in founding), as well as posters by artist Bill Neale to announce the event. There are oil paintings of chili peppers and bowls of chili ready to be eaten. All around are indications of Tolbert's own prominence in the world of the pod. He has cooked chili everywhere, including "the northernmost town in the world," Honningsvåg, Norway, where he showed them how to make reindeer chili. A live band plays here on Saturday nights. Its name: Wally Wilson's Hot Sauce.

The best thing about Tolbert's museum is that it affords the visitor an opportunity to engage actively in chili culture, surrounded by fellow aficionados and connoisseurs, observing all-around exhibits and artifacts from the world of the pod. But of course the best exhibit is the one set down on your table—a twelve-ounce bowl of red and a few Lone Star "long necks." *That's* museum-going!

EAGLE LAKE

THE ATTWATER PRAIRIE-CHICKEN REFUGE

NE from Eagle Lake, Tex. on FM 3013 6 mi.;
free—call ahead (713) 234-3021

The prairie chicken, or *tympanuchus cupido attwateri,* was once the commonest of sights in the Texas–Louisiana prairies, but the species gradually diminished, becoming extinct in Louisiana in 1919. In 1965 it was estimated that there were less than 1,000 birds left in Texas. In 1972 the people of Eagle Lake got together with the World Wildlife Fund and the Nature Conservancy of Texas and bought an 5,600-acre refuge to preserve and rebuild the species. The preserve is composed of native grasses in which the bird lives, and "booming grounds" (areas with little ground cover) in which it mates.

The prairie chicken is a lot better-looking than the henhouse variety. It has turkeylike feathers, a tufted crown on its head, and two feathery puffs to the side of its neck.

In order to assure the most rapid recovery of the Attwater prairie chicken species, most of the refuge is closed to public use. During dry periods, however, when roads and trails are passable, it is opened up to birdwatchers, photographers, and casual nature observers. If you venture here it is possible you will also see the roseate spoonbill, the white-faced ibis, Sennett's white-tailed hawk, or a prairie falcon—all rare birds who have been found to share the refuge.

There is no camping, fishing, picnicking, or hunting.

EASTLAND

OLD RIP

Eastland Courthouse, Main St. between Seamon & Lamar, Eastland, Tex.;
always viewable; free

In 1897, when the cornerstone of the Eastland Courthouse was being dedicated, Justice of the Peace Ernest Wood noticed that his small son was playing with a horned toad. It occurred to Mr. Wood that he ought to place the little toad into the cornerstone.

By 1928 when the courthouse was about to be demolished to make way for a new one, all of Eastland knew about the toad that Mr. Woods had placed into the cornerstone. A crowd showed up at the demolition ceremony to see what had become of the amphibian, now known as "Old Rip." Judge Ed Pritchard removed some of the other things that had been placed into the cornerstone, including a Bible. Underneath it sat Old Rip. Eugene Day, a wealthy oilman, reached in and lifted up the dusty toad. He handed it to the town preacher, who handed it to Judge Pritchard, who held it up for all to see. Suddenly Old Rip started to shake and snapped back to life after a thirty-one-year nap. A legend was born.

Old Rip became an Eastland celebrity. He toured throughout the Southwest and the rest of the country, even paying a visit to President Calvin Coolidge. Old Rip died in 1929, and was embalmed for posterity. He now rests in a fancy coffin lined with red velvet and silk, especially made by the Abilene Casket Company. The coffin can always be seen through the glass door of the Eastland courthouse. A granite plaque outside marks Old Rip's final resting place.

If all this moves you to tears, the Old Rip Café a few blocks away on Route 80 will brace you with a good strong cup of coffee.

THE STAMP WINDOW

Eastland Post Office, Eastland, Tex.;
daily 6 AM–10 PM

Working between August 6, 1957 and July 11, 1968, Marlene Johnson Johnson of Eastland, Texas used 11,217 postage stamps to create a giant collage-mural for the lobby of the Eastland Post Office. She considered it a philatelist's gift to those interested in history and geography. Included in the stamp mural are portraits of Ben Franklin and Abraham Lincoln (made partially out of stamps that bear their own likenesses), a map of the state of Texas, and the flags of the United States, Texas, and the Confederate States of America. It is bordered by a lush red rose pattern made of stamps. The mural, which is six by ten feet, contains enough stamps to send the whole building anywhere in the country by first-class mail.

FINK

FINK DAYS

Fink, Tex. (FM 120 3 mi. N. out of Pottsboro);
June 23–26, 1978; free

Are you a fink? If so, please note the dates of National Fink Days this year. You will be expected to attend. If you are not a Fink, it is possible to attend anyway, just by becoming an honorary Fink for the four-day festival.

Fink happens to be a tiny Grayson County town seventy-eight miles north of Dallas. It was once a watering place for cowboys between the Red River and Pottsboro, but the railroads passed it by, and the population has hovered around nine ever since. Finkites looking for a way to bring recognition to their dwindling town noted that its name was rich in slang meanings. "Fink" can mean either strikebreaker or informer, but in popular parlance it has come to signify a nerd of the "what, me worry?" variety. Finkites called for festivities to celebrate the name and all who carry it. The fourth Thursday of June is Fink Day, and the Fink Day Celebration lasts through the weekend. Frank Tolbert reports that all this actually began as a "Be Kind to Finks" movement, encouraging people to "fink it over" before making a joke out of the next Fink they met.

However it began, the Fink Days celebration is firmly entrenched as an annual event. Attending the festivities are notable Finks such as O. L. Fink, poet laureate of all Finks and Fink Fiddle Maker, too, and people who spell their name Finke, Finque, Phink, Phinque, and even Finch. This latter group claims to be the original Finks from Germany, who changed their name to Fink when they came to America. Presiding over Fink Days is Mayor Robert Lattimore, who became mayor by purchasing the "town hall" (alias the Fink grocery) from the previous mayor, Mrs. Albright.

If you come to Fink Days expect to find people giving out Big Fink chewing gum, carving Fink toys for the kids, selling Fink golfballs for the Fink golf tournament, giving away free barbecue sandwiches from the grocery store, and reciting Fink philosophy and verse—the poetics of which demand that each end with the same last line. Examples:

> When dear Papa went up to Heaven,
> What grief Mama endured;

And yet that grief was softened,
For Papa he was insured.
          —FINK IT OVER

If the soup had been as hot as the claret;
If the claret had been as old as the bird;
and if the bird's breasts had been as full as the waitress's,
It would have been a very good dinner indeed.
          —FINK IT OVER

OK, so it's not T. S. Eliot or even Rod McKuen, but what do you want from a bunch of Finks?

FREDERICKSBURG

THE FREDERICKSBURG EASTER FIRES

Fredericksburg, Tex.;
Sat night before Easter

Every year the people of Fredericksburg put on their bunny costumes and prance about town. These are not the Hugh Hefner breed of bunny, but rather the traditional type, like Dr. Dentons with ears and a tail. The custom honors pioneer days, when the town was often surrounded by hostile Indians who communicated with each other by smoke signals. The story goes that the children of the town were scared by the smoke, and so the town's mothers soothed them by explaining that it was the Easter Bunny and his helpers in the hills, cooking up eggs and preparing dyes in large cauldrons.

Since pioneer days, this story has become a traditional Fredericksburg legend, and it has been told to generations of children, long after the hostile Indians were no longer a threat. Each year bonfires are lit and a hundred "rabbits" enact the egg-cooking and dyeing that are supposed to be taking place in the hills. The pageant is supplemented by the dancing of a floral ballet and the creation of a "living cross" by the Fredericksburg marching band.

We wonder what an unexpecting traveler might think if he drove into Fredericksburg the Saturday night before Easter and saw a hundred human-size rabbits dancing under the moonlight.

GRAND SALINE

THE SALT HOUSE

Rt. 80 (junction of Rt. 17), Grand Saline, Tex.;
always viewable; free

It is Texas tradition to make the most of natural salt—at "salt licks," over which animals run their tongues to help keep going in hot weather, and in the use of heavily salted food to counteract the sweat pouring down one's collar.

Here in the hot, dusty town of Grand Saline, right across from the used-car lot of Honest Bud Milam ("The Smiling Irishman") is the only house in America made entirely of salt blocks. These translucent blocks are grayish in color, and each is about two or three cubic feet. In front there is one block that has been partially crushed in order to show the familiar crystalline structure. Inside the house is a display of salt bricks, salt bags, salt shakers and every other salty thing Grand Saline could think of.

One question we forgot to ask: What happens to the house when it rains?

HALLETTSVILLE

TEXAS DOMINO TOURNAMENT

Knights of Columbus Hall, Highway 77, S. of Hallettsville, Tex.;
4th Sun in Jan. all day;
free to watch, $5 to play; players limited to men over 21

This is a "doubles only" tournament, with two out of three games determining the winning team. Play goes something like this: One partner sets a domino. This is called a "down." The player to his left makes the next play, trying to make a count, which must be a multiple of five. If a player has no domino to fit, he passes to the next player. If a player "calls for your tongue," that means he is playing so there are very few dominoes you can play. If he "cuts his water off," that means he is playing where he knows you have to play. If you've got a "tombstone," you're in trouble, because that's the domino without spots. And if you play your "big dog" (double six) right, you just might win. The player who plays all his dominoes first calls "domino," at which point he and his partner count the dominoes of their opponents and those on the table. The first team to reach 250 wins the game.

Domino players are in general an ornery, hard-fighting group of sportsmen. Tournament organizers tell us they must provide ashtrays, spittoons, and plenty of barbecue, enough to satisfy "the average tobacco-chewing, smoking, and snuff-dipping Texan." Nearly four hundred people compete, with $100 and a plaque going to the winning team. One attraction for spectators, aside from the competition, is the first-rate food, prepared by the Werner Brothers, "Big Shot" and "Cudlum." They serve Texas beef, cowboy stew and bohemian sauerkraut, along with beer from the breweries of Lavaca, which is proud of never once having closed during Prohibition.

HEREFORD

NATIONAL COWGIRL HALL OF FAME

211 E. 4th (in the basement of the Deaf Smith County Library); Hereford, Tex.
Mon–Fri 9 AM–noon, 1 PM–5 PM, Sat 10 AM–noon;
free (806) 364–5252

The National Cowgirl Hall of Fame pays tribute to the women who won the West and to women actively involved in preserving western heritage. Among the modern women selected for the Hall of Fame are the country's top rodeo stars. They are enshrined in the tiny facility that is temporarily located in the basement of the county library. There are plans for a bigger building. As it is now, there is barely enough room for this ambitious project, the stated aims of which are to "honor the pioneer spirit of all women, everywhere."

Each of the fourteen women who have been selected for the Hall of Fame has been asked to contribute a memento of her accomplishments, so that among the examples of art and sculpture by women artists are trophies, saddles, belt buckles, and fancy leather handbags won or owned by the champs. One of the prized possessions is the painting of 1977 inductee Sydna Yokely Woodyard, showing her and her horse. She is now deceased; her parents donated the painting along with her white leather chaps and saddle. Among the mementos are action photographs of the annual all-girls rodeo held in Hereford every May.

HOUSTON

INDETERMINATE FAÇADE

Best Products Co., Almeda-Genoa Shopping Center, Kingsport & Kleckley St.,
Houston, Tex.;
always viewable; free

Indeterminate Façade is a spectacular example of radical architecture. It is
in the middle of a run-of-the-mill shopping center in Houston, and houses
a run-of-the-mill catalogue showroom. It was built by the architectural
group known as SITE (Sculpture in the Environment). This SITE is indeed a sight!

It looks like a building that has survived a severe bombing. The white-brick
façade has taken a crashing blow in front, where a tumble of bricks cascades
onto an "awning" that shelters the entryway. The rest of the building's walls
are an undulating profile of destruction. There are no more brick piles, but the
roof line is a jagged pattern of apparent disaster, what looks like a war-torn
fragment of a wall that once was.

SITE has designed similar "deconstructions" around the country, so if you
are driving along and see what appears to be an omen of the final apocalypse
by the side of the road, you'd best do a double take. It may be just another
SITE.

HUNTSVILLE

HUNTSVILLE PRISON

12th St., Huntsville, Tex.

If one had to choose a maximum security calaboose in which to spend some
time, Huntsville might be a good choice. There are more activities here than
on a cruise ship.

Huntsville annually stages the Texas Prison Rodeo, "the roughest behind
bars." Held every October, with seats going for $4 and up, the rodeo "at the
walls" is a bloodcurdling exhibition of courage and/or foolishness. Take a
group of men and women who have been cooped up all year, take a few
truckloads of angry bulls and wild horses, put the two together and you've got
yourself one hell of a rodeo. It has been held annually since 1933, and is among
the most popular rodeos in the state.

If prisoners don't like the idea of hard money, rodeo-style, they can pick up brush and palette and prepare some canvases for the Inmate Fine Arts Festival, held the first week of every May. Art ranges from silly sad-eyed puppies to energetic, primitive expressions of convicts' sensibilities. And there are sketches, watercolors, and ceramics that are just plain pretty. At last year's festival there were performances by an inmate country-and-western band and the "Goree Girls" modern dance group. The agenda has not been set for next year's festival, but it is a sure thing that most of the artists will be back.

Finally, one can visit the Inmate Craft Store (year round; Weds–Sun 9 AM–5 PM). The nicest work here includes Western saddles and leatherwork. The range of talent is far-reaching, from outdated psychedelic to first-rate craftsmanship. It all depends on who is in the clink at the time.

JUNCTION

THE DEERHORN TREE

U.S. 377 in Junction, Tex.

Junction is not only the wool and mohair center of the country, it is a game hunter's paradise, with squirrels, wild turkeys, and deer visible in abundance at the bead end of one's rifle. In honor of the deer who died to make Junction so popular, the Business and Professional Women's Club erected a tree made out of deer horns. It is well over six feet tall and shaped like a Douglas fir, except that, since it's all antlers, it's pointier.

KILGORE

THE WORLD'S RICHEST ACRE

Bus Rt. 135 at Main and Commerce Sts., Kilgore, Tex.

Kilgore, Texas is known as the home of the Kilgore Rangerettes, the most gorgeous group of synchronized females ever to twirl batons. They are like several dozen Farah Fawcett-Majors all in a row—except that they are ten years younger and as pink-cheeked as cactus roses.

But there is more to do in Kilgore than keeping your eyes peeled for roaming Rangerettes. Kilgore has the world's richest acre. It was once the site of

Huntsville Prison Rodeo, Huntsville, Tex.

Indeterminate Façade, Houston, Tex.

twenty-four oil derricks, the highest concentration of oil ever pumped from the ground. There was so much black gold gushing around Kilgore that they even drilled through the marble floor of the Kilgore bank to set up one of the wells. Today only one derrick remains, at Main and Commerce Streets, where there is a plaque to tell the whole story.

LAPORTE

THE 3/5 WHITE HOUSE

515 Bay Ridge Rd., LaPorte, Tex.;
always viewable; free

This White House is an exact replica of the one at 1600 Pennsylvania Avenue in Washington, except that it is three-fifths the size, and it lacks a famous tenant. Actually, only the side that faces the water replicates the original. It can be seen by boat from Galveston Bay, or by walking around from the front. As you drive along Bay Ridge Road, it looks like any other ordinary Texas millionaire's home.

The LaPorte White House is the brainchild of former Texas Governor Ross Sterling who, fifty years ago, decided he wanted a distinctive home. Nothing his architect showed him matched his visions of grandeur. He reached into his wallet and handed the designer a crisp twenty-dollar bill. "Make it look like that," he drawled, pointing to the White House on the back of the bill.

Paul Barkley bought the White House in 1961, and is accustomed to passers-by taking "gag" photos of themselves near the rear façade of his home. He is now trying to sell the misplaced executive mansion, but it seems as if the White House is now a white elephant. Barkley sat on the south portico and rhetorically asked "Who in the hell wants 21,000 square feet, fifteen tile bathrooms, and three kitchens?" The presidential runner-up, maybe?

LULING

LULING WATERMELON THUMP

Luling, Tex. (N. of I-10, 58 mi. E. of San Antonio);
3rd week in June; free

382 ★ THE SOUTHWEST

Luling is the watermelon capital of Texas, and for the last twenty-five years they have been celebrating their production of the sweet and festive "August ham" with an annual Thump. The Thump is a four-day festival that starts on Thursday and continues through the weekend. There is, of course, a watermelon-eating contest, as well as a Champion Melon Auction and the selection of a Watermelon Thump Queen. Saturday's activities culminate in a championship watermelon-seed spit-off. Sunday is reserved for golf and bowling tournaments.

We asked around Luling to find out why they call their annual celebration a "Thump." "This is Texas," we were told. "We grow some thumping big melons in these parts."

MEMPHIS

TURKEY, TEXAS, THE HOME OF BOB WILLS

Rt. 70 & 86, W. of Memphis, Tex.

Fans of western swing music need no introduction to Turkey, Texas, the town immortalized in the song "Down in Turkey, Texas." Turkey is the home of Bob Wills, the "King of Western Swing," and as it says in the song, not a whole lot happens here. It is, however, the best place in the world to be on the last Saturday in April. That's Bob Wills Day Celebration. It begins with a parade and a big Texas-style barbecue, followed by a Texas fiddlers' contest and a western swing concert with guest bands like The Original Texas Playboys or the Country Impressions. At night you put on your best Stetson, polish up your alligator boots, and high-step over to the Bob Wills Community Center for the all-night western dance.

If you're passing through Turkey at any other time of year, you might just hear the sweet strains of "San Antonio Rose" wafting through the air. The tune will be coming from the Bob Wills Monument on Highway 86—a pink-granite beauty with a rotating fiddle on top that continuously plays Bob Wills tunes. Etched into the side of the monument is the story of the fiddle player from Turkey who became the "King of Western Swing." At the other end of town is the tiny Bob Wills Museum (open 1 PM–5 PM Tues–Sat; free). Here you can see several of his fiddles, his belt buckle, his watch, his clothes, his army gear, and his diamond rings. You can also buy Bob Wills post cards, ashtrays, bumper stickers and memorial coins, the proceeds from which go to improving the Bob Wills Day Celebration, the Bob Wills Community Center, and the Bob Wills Museum.

MULESHOE

THE NATIONAL MULE MEMORIAL

Intersection of US 70 and 84, Muleshoe, Tex.

When the residents of Muleshoe decided years ago that there were entirely too few mules around, they decided to build a monument to the stubborn creature after which their town had been named. They started to solicit contributions in the mule's honor, and it quickly became evident that mules have a loyal following throughout the country. They even received twenty-one cents from a mule driver in Uzbekistan, U.S.S.R.

You can see this noble-looking mule statue on display in the town center.

ODESSA

THE PRESIDENTIAL MUSEUM

622 N. Lee St., Odessa, Tex.;
Mon–Sat 9 AM–5 PM; free

The Presidential Museum was conceived after the assassination of J.F.K. as a memorial to all of America's presidents. Its purpose is to create a better understanding of the office of the presidency, and to that end, the compact, two-room museum in the lower level of the Ector County Library houses over 35,000 artifacts.

The core of the museum is the Ben Shepperd, Jr., Library, with 3,000 first editions, autographed books, pamphlets, and other documents by or about presidents. The art on display includes portraits of each president and first lady, portraits of all the vice presidents, wood mosaics depicting the presidents made from sixteen million pieces of natural wood, and a collection of pastels called "Pets of the White House" that includes Abraham Lincoln's turkey, Jack—designated for the Thanksgiving table, but given a reprieve by the Great Emancipator.

There are displays of campaign memorabilia and political cartoons, as well as a large collection of personal belongings, including F.D.R.'s red silk parasol and L.B.J.'s Stetson. There are busts of the presidents, and "first-lady dolls" wearing exact reproductions of their inaugural gowns. One fascinating collection is the set of charcoal drawings called "The Gallery of Also-Rans," depicting the four runners-up for each election. The 1968 picture reminds us that not only Hubert Humphrey and George Wallace lost, but so did Dick Gregory and Eldridge Cleaver.

A place in the main gallery is reserved for a large oil portrait of the current president. We remember the peacock-shaded Nixon portrait, about which museum curator Glenda Morgan explained, "[the artist] always saw Mr. Nixon in terms of black and white until he met him in person and sketched him. Then he realized that he reflected more of the renaissance colors."

THE WORLD'S LARGEST JACK RABBIT

400 Block, N. Lincoln St., Odessa, Tex.

Nothing could be more typically Texan than a long-eared, stringy jack rabbit hopping across the brushy plains. To honor the creature that provided many a settler his meal and many a fox a good chase, a huge "jack" adorned with a bronze plaque has been erected in the center of Odessa.

QUITMAN

THE MISS IMA HOGG MUSEUM

518 S. Main St. in Governor Hogg State Park, Quitman, Tex.;
Thurs–Mon 8 AM–noon and 1 PM–5 PM;
free (admission to Honeymoon Cottage: 50¢)

For years we had heard stories about Big Jim Hogg, the flamboyant governor of Texas who named his daughters Ima Hogg, Ura Hogg, and Wera Hogg. It was not until we came to this museum in Texas that the bubble broke and we learned that there was only one Hogg daughter—Ima. Rumors about the other daughters began during Hogg's campaigns for governor.

Ima Hogg survived her name to become a well-loved philanthropist and favorite daughter of the Lone Star State. The Ima Hogg Museum in the Governor Hogg State Park shows the history of Northeast Texas and artifacts relating to the Hogg era. There is a life-size silhouette of Big Jim against which one can measure one's own girth.

Next to the Ima Hogg Museum is Governor Hogg's honeymoon cottage, moved to the park and restored in 1952. Some of Mrs. Hogg's handmade quilts are on display here, as well as personal items that belonged to the whole Hogg family.

The museum and cottage are surrounded by twenty-seven acres of lovely woods and picnic areas.

ROCKSPRINGS

THE ANGORA GOAT-BREEDERS ASSOCIATION MUSEUM

Austin St., Rocksprings, Tex.;
Mon–Fri 9 AM–noon, 1:30 PM–4:30 PM; free

This is the only museum in America devoted to goats, and the only official Angora goat registry. It is operated more as a service to goat breeders than as a tourist attraction for the general public, but the modest displays will show you the history of the goat and the goat-breeding industry, as well as giving a genealogical record of the breed. The Angora goat is the one that produces those gorgeous soft woolens that cost a small fortune.

SAN ANTONIO

THE ALAMO MURAL

The Alamo, Alamo Plaza, San Antonio, Tex.;
Mon–Sat 9:30 AM–5 PM, Sun 10 AM–5:30 PM; free

The Alamo itself is too familiar a sight to mention here, but we can't resist pointing out one of its lesser-known features. It is the full-color mural painted on the wall within the archaic structure, showing Jim Bowie, Davey Crockett, and William Travis fighting off the Mexican Army. These three real, historical heroes appear to have the faces of John Wayne, Richard Widmark, and Laurence Harvey, the movie stars of *The Alamo*. We can't figure out if this is a case of life following art, art following art, or art following life.

THE BUCKHORN HALL OF HORNS

Lone Star Brewery, 600 Lone Star Blvd., San Antonio, Tex.;
daily 9:30 AM–5:30 PM;
adults: $1, 6–12 and servicemen in uniform: 50¢

Lone Star calls itself the world's most beautiful brewery, and boasts of having the world's largest collection of horns and antlers. The Buckhorn Hall of Horns is actually five separate halls, cataloging horned animals from all over the globe and displaying the stuffed heads or horns of most of them. Of course, it wouldn't do for a Texas Hall of Horns not to have the world's largest set of longhorn steer horns, so here they are, once mounted on the mighty head of Old Tex. The horns measure 105 inches across, a bullfighter's nightmare. Another seeming record are the antlers from a 78-point buck, looking like they were taken from a deer who got a bramble bush caught on his noggin. There are hundreds more horns of all shapes and sizes. The only animals missing are a jackalope, a unicorn, and a horned toad.

SAN MARCOS

THE CHILYMPIAD

Hays Civic Center off I-35, San Marcos, Tex.;
2nd week in Sept.; (512) 392–2495

Senator Barry Goldwater once said that Texans don't know their chili from leavings in a corral. His comment is an indication of the kind of inflamed rhetoric that accompanies chili cook-offs throughout the Southwest. The Chilympiad is the state cook-off of Texas, chief competition to the notoriously rowdy (and now, therefore, allegedly extinct) annual Terlingua uprisings.

The rules of the Chilympiad are a constant source of dispute. In recent years "chililibbers" have objected to the traditional "men only" regulation, claiming that it doesn't take a man to make that bowl of red sing. Some were alleged to have thrown their bras into a male chauvinist chef's pot.

Ever since Chief Fulton Battise of the Alabama–Coushatta tribes in Livingston took the Champion Chili Pot in 1971, there has been an intense rivalry between Indian and white cooks. One white man claimed the Indian chili was so hot that it blinded the judges. The Indian called the whites' chili "a bowl of watery bouillon."

One needn't concern oneself with internecine invective in order to enjoy the Chilympiad. The legendary chili chef Wick Fowler once said that no mouth should go through life without tasting a good bowl of red, and the Chilympiad provides plenty for all spectators. In recent years over a hundred chefs have lined up at the chili pots, and up to 100,000 people have come to watch them huff, puff and whisper incantations in order to charm their chili to perfection.

It is said that the championship chili from the first Chilympiad in 1970 is enshrined, uneaten, on the mantelpiece of one chili-mad Texan's ranch.

VERNON

R. L. MORE, SR., BIRD EGG COLLECTION

1905 W. Wilbarger St. (2nd floor), Vernon, Tex.;
April–Sept Mon–Fri 9 AM–noon, 1 PM–5 PM, Sat 9 AM–noon

A few years back, the American Egg Producers Association started a television ad campaign to promote "the incredible edible egg." Other than this commercial recognition, and the presence of Edy "the Egg Lady" in John Waters' film *Pink Flamingoes,* we have seen only one cultural expression of the uniqueness of eggs. It is the R. L. More, Sr., Bird Egg Collection, devoted not to eggs that one eats, but to eggs that birds lay. There are over ten thousand different types on display, from little jelly beans to eggs big enough to make an omelette that would feed the cast of *Aïda.* Some are flimsy, others look as if they'd resist a sledge hammer. A few eggs date back to 1888, when Mr. More began his collection.

There are some fine examples of taxidermy here, as well as the eggs, but nothing can compete with the imposing sight of ten thousand birds that never were.

WACO

TEXAS RANGER HALL OF FAME

Fort Fisher Park, where I-35 meets the Brazos River, Waco, Tex.;
daily Sept 1–May 31 10 AM–5 PM, June 1–Aug 31 9 AM–6 PM;
adults: $2, 6–12: $1

There are few groups in American history with as romantic an image as the Texas Rangers. They were the flower of Western manhood, the bravest, straight-shootingest, most heroic of lawmen. Twenty rangers are enshrined here as the most courageous of them all.

Besides honoring the top twenty, the Texas Ranger Hall of Fame depicts the 150-year history of the elite corps in a film called *Tradition of Courage*. The film is accompanied by slides and sound equipment that create a multimedia bombardment of law-enforcement glory. In addition, there are dioramas, life-size, three-dimensional wax figures, and displays of western art. There is a Moody Texas Ranger Memorial Library here, with a large collection of books, documents, photographs, and manuscripts for those who wish to research Ranger history.

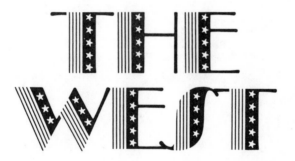

CALIFORNIA

ANGELS CAMP

CALAVERAS JUMPING FROG JUBILEE

The Fairgrounds, Angels Camp, Calif.;
3rd full weekend in May;
adult pass for all four days: $8.50, children: $4 (includes fair rides)

It was the California gold rush that first put Calaveras County on the maps. About this time, Mark Twain wrote a story called "The Celebrated Jumping Frog of Calaveras County." In 1928 the citizens of Angels Camp reenacted the Twain story as a means of celebrating the paving of their city streets. Since that time, Angels Camp's annual celebration of the Jumping Frog Jubilee has turned Calaveras County into the Frog-Jumping Capital of the World.

Local folks breed their own limber-legged entries for the contest, but for out-of-towners or froggie dilettantes the jubilee offers a Rent-a-Frog service:

For the small sum of $2.00 a hardy leaper from Frogtown's stable of famous jumpers will be available for you to jump. Or if preferred, a trained Frog Jockey will jump the leggy amphibian for you. You need not be present, as all results are promptly sent to all out-of-town and out-of-state entries who wish to enter a frog but who are unable to attend.

A word of warning to amateurs who bring "pet" frogs: this is the big league of frogdom, and the stars of the jumping world are usually in attendance—from Rayne, Louisiana, from Croaker College in Sacramento, from semifinals in states across the country. A $1,200 prize is awarded to a frog if it sets a new world's record, $300 for placing first. The current world record of 20'3" is held by a frog from Santa Clara named E. Davy Croakett.

The international finals are held on Sunday afternoon.

CALIPATRIA

CALIPATRIA, CALIFORNIA—
THE LOWEST TOWN IN THE WESTERN HEMISPHERE

Rt. 115, N. of El Centro

If you are feeling "low down," you might want to take up temporary residence in Calipatria. There is no place lower on this side of the earth. The town's American flag flies at sea level, but only because it is at the top of a 180-foot flagpole.

CARMEL

GALLERY OF FINE COMIC ART

Mission and 7th St., Carmel, Calif.;
daily 10 AM–5 PM; free

The Gallery of Fine Comic Art is a tasteful gallery housed in a single room at street level in the very refined town of Carmel. Here the cartoon is accorded all the respect and honor normally reserved for highbrow art. Not only is the aspiring classicism of *Fantasia* represented here, but so are Elmer Fudd, Dudley DoRight, and the Seven Dwarfs. Displays consist of original artwork from animated shorts and feature-length films, as well as classic newspaper comic strips such as *Pogo* and *Prince Valiant*. There is also a whole collection of ceramic bisque figurines representing the Walt Disney menagerie.

The original artwork for cartoon films are called "cels." Hundreds of thou-

Croaker College, Sacramento, Calif.

The Mystery Spot, Santa Cruz, Calif.

sands of them are made for a single film. The Gallery of Fine Comic Art sells cels for prices ranging from $30 to over $1000, depending on the complexity of the work and the "greatness" of the cartoon.

DEATH VALLEY JUNCTION

AMARGOSA OPERA HOUSE

Calif. 127 & Calif. 190, Death Valley Junction, Calif. (29 mi. SE of Furnace Creek);
Oct 15–April 30 Fri, Sat & Mon, May & Sept 1–Oct 14 Sat only;
doors open 7:45, curtain: 8:15; sugg. donation: $2.50

The Met it isn't. If you yearn for the spine-tingling arias of a Beverly Sills or the glitter of the sable-coat crowd, forget it. Because what goes on in this opera house in the middle of the blast furnace of the California desert isn't really opera at all. According to its creator the Amargosa Opera House offers the experience of "sitting inside a painting and watching a dance performance by the painter."

It all began about fifteen years ago when Marta Becket and her husband Tom Williams were driving across Death Valley. Their car had a flat; while Tom fixed the tire, Marta explored the ruins of a town called Death Valley Junction. She found an abandoned movie theater, and realized that here she could realize her artistic dream: to perfect a unique art combining classical ballet and pantomime with painting. In 1968 she began painting a vast mural across the interior of the opera house. She painted a back wall filled with a king, a queen, and ladies and gentlemen of the court. In the balconies she created monks, nuns, cupids, gypsies, and ordinary spectators. To date, 260 diamond-studded operagoers have been created in the two-dimensional gilt-edged balconies that surround the folding chairs in the theater where Marta's living audience is invited to sit.

Marta Becket's performances are elaborate, one-woman shows. In each of three programs in her repertoire she portrays over a dozen characters—a tour de force of acting, dancing, and mime that gives the illusion of a full company. As Marta performs, Tom serves as M.C., ticket-taker, and stage crew. We are told that the show here goes on even if the house is empty. Death Valley is, after all, the loneliest place on earth. During the peak winter "season," reservations are recommended. Just call telephone number 8 in Death Valley Junction.

EL CENTRO

EL CENTRO, CALIFORNIA— THE MOST AIR-CONDITIONED CITY IN THE U.S.

El Centro is the largest town below sea level in the country. It is in the heart of the Imperial Valley, California's marketplace. Because it is also hotter than just about anywhere else, except perhaps Death Valley and Yuma, El Centrans went about air-conditioning every place in town long before anybody heard of an energy crisis. They advertised El Centro as "The Most Air-Conditioned City in the U.S.," and every place we've been in El Centro has been a pleasant refuge from the burning sun outside, so we have no reason to doubt the town's claim. The only inconvenience is going from building to building or building to car. Outside, the sun still rules.

ESCONDIDO

LAWRENCE WELK'S COUNTRY CLUB VILLAGE MOTEL

8868 Champagne Blvd., Escondido, Calif.;
(714) 746–3000

If Lawrence Welk is your glass of bubbly, you'll be happy to know that the Music Maker runs a motel, mobile-home park, and country club in Escondido. The rates at the motel are similar to those of the large chain motels, but only at Lawrence Welk's can you enjoy the champagne atmosphere of dining, gift-buying, and golfing among the permanent residents of the 204 mobile-home spaces that make this a community infused with the spirit of a perpetual bubble machine.

GARDEN GROVE

CALIFORNIA'S DRIVE-IN CHURCH

121–41 Lewis, Garden Grove, Calif.;
(714) 750–7000

"We are so glad Dr. Schuller has touched our lives."
—Mr. and Mrs. Jerry Lewis
"His ministry has caused miracles to happen in my life."
—Rhonda Fleming
"I like the Reverend Dr. Schuller . . ."
—John Wayne

These Hollywood stars are talking about America's foremost "televangelist," Reverend Robert Schuller, the inventor of "possibility thinking." Dr. Schuller has raised a few hackles in the theological community with his show-biz approach to religion, based on what he calls the "sperm-to-worm" principle, which means caring for his flock from conception to when they meet their maker.

The best way to do this, Dr. Schuller believes, is to sell religion. This he does from the Garden Grove Community Church, which he calls a "22-acre Shopping Center for God, part of the service industry." Over two thousand people attend his Sunday services, and those who can't get inside tune in to his words on their car radios or portable battery-operated TV sets. He attributes his success to five principles: "Accessibility, service, visibility, possibility thinking, and excess parking."

Plans are now underway to move the ministry to an even bigger building, the all-new Crystal Cathedral, for which Dr. Schuller is now soliciting donations. It will cost $10 million, be 124-feet high, and constructed completely of glass "so that there will be brightness and joy everywhere." Each of the cathedral's ten thousand windows will be inscribed with the name of a donor.

From the present location in Garden Grove, parishioners parked in the right spot are afforded a good view of Disneyland's "Matterhorn" in the distance.

HIDDEN VALLEY

TEAKETTLE JUNCTION

20 mi. S. of Ubehebe Crater, toward Hidden Valley;
always viewable; free

Today there is a sign for Teakettle Junction, last seen topped with four of five varieties of teakettles and one electric coffee maker—all the gifts of an inspired tourist, no doubt.

Years ago there was no sign here, just an abandoned teakettle lying under a creosote bush. The kettle served as a guidepost—"left at the kettle" to go into the Cottonwood Mountains, "straight at the kettle" took you to Hidden Valley and Ulida Flat. The area was so desolate that the kettle stayed in the same spot for years, slowly disintegrating. Eventually the "Teakettle Junction" sign was put up, and soon people hung a few new kettles on it. Teakettle Junction is still as bleak as a bleached skull, but the sign is a bit of whimsy in the midst of Death Valley's vast emptiness.

HOLLYWOOD

FREDERICK'S OF HOLLYWOOD

6608 Hollywood Blvd., Hollywood, Calif.;
Tues,Weds,Thurs & Sat 10 AM–6 PM, Mon & Fri 10 AM–9 PM

"Don't get caught with nothing to wear! Stock up now with lots of new, smart Hollywood originals! Styles that will bring you Hollywood Glamour and Allure, Many Flattering Compliments, Thrilling New Romance, Dreams Come True!" Frederick's of Hollywood has been in the mail-order seduction business since 1947, redesigning the female form, changing sagging bosoms into pneumatic thrusts, skinny gams into upholstered drumsticks, and inadequate derrières into plump, pinchable pillows. The Frederick's promise of Glamour, Allure, Compliments, Romance, and Dreams-Come-True has been available to the plainest women simply by clipping the coupon in the back of whichever ladies' magazine they read and sending for the catalogue—a hope chest for the under-endowed.

In recent years, however, the feminine ideal has changed considerably, from "Movie Date" and "Hollywood Polka" styles to mod jump suits and fruit-flavored body lotions. Frederick's ads have become harder to find and some-how they don't seem quite as outrageous. So for a dose of Frederick's sexuality "in the raw" one must go to the source—6608 Hollywood Boulevard.

You can't miss the building. It is a shade of lavender unique to Southern California, with the familiar "Frederick's of Hollywood" lettering over the door. Inside is a fantasyland of torrid panties, feathered baby-doll P.J.'s, and vinyl jump suits with provocative zippers. Of course, there are sex stores with clothing and accessories that go much further than those you'll find here. But none offers the salon atmosphere of Frederick's and none offers so much opportunity to tease and titillate in the old-fashioned way. It is definitely a store for the girl who is naughty but nice. And there is no doubt that if you are planning to become a Total Woman, Frederick's of Hollywood is the place to start.

INDIO

"THE ROMANCE AND SEX LIFE OF A DATE"

Shields Date Gardens, 80–225 Hwy III, Indio, Calif.;
daily 8 AM–6 PM, free

"The Romance and Sex Life of a Date" is not a how-to manual, nor does it have anything to do with blind dates, first dates, hot dates, or double dates. It is rather a film all about those sweet and succulent dates that grow profusely in this part of California. After seeing this G-rated "sex" flick, you can stroll around in Shields Gardens and observe the dates *au naturel* on date palms that grow near citrus trees. Finish off your tour with some black date ice cream, and take home recipes for date crystal peanut butter chews and date crystal chutney.

KELSO

TOWN WITHOUT TELEVISION

It is surprising that antitelevision sociologists haven't descended on the tiny town of Kelso to use its children as proof of how the boob tube has eroded the brain of the average American child. Of the fourteen children who attend school in this one-hundred-person town, not one watches television. Kelso is too far out-of-the-way to receive TV signals, so its population must listen to the radio, talk, play games, and otherwise relate to each other.

There are no telephones either, nor movie theaters, nor gas stations, nor stores. One daily newspaper is sent in by mail and placed in the school, where townsfolk can stop in to read it.

Every adult male in Kelso except the schoolteacher and postmaster is an employee of the Union Pacific Line, which established the town in order to provide extra "helper" locomotives to pull trains up the nearby Cima grade. The town's twenty hotel rooms are all reserved for railroad personnel, but for passers-by there is a restaurant in the station that serves meals twenty-four hours a day.

For the person who wants to get away from Farrah Fawcett-Majors and her Bionic Bulkhead, or the person who just doesn't like TV, Kelso is heaven—except for its location, which is in "the Devil's Playground," where temperatures sometimes hit 115 degrees.

LOS ANGELES

THE WATTS TOWERS

1765 E. 107th St., E. of Harbor Freeway in Watts, Los Angeles, Calif.;
daily 10 AM–dusk; 50¢

Simon Rodia's Watts Towers are probably the best-known work of folk sculpture in America. Since the 1960s they have come to symbolize the spirit of the people of Watts.

Their builder emigrated to the United States from Italy when he was eleven years old. He worked as a telephone repairman and tile setter, and devoted himself to building the Watts Towers between 1921 and 1954. He apparently had no specific plans as he worked—old photographs show that some structures were built, then torn down as the major towers inched skyward.

As the thin twists of concrete and glass grew, Simon Rodia became more reclusive. His wood-frame house (now destroyed) virtually disappeared behind the mosaic wall, and beneath the pillars and archways. In 1954 he gave the property to a neighbor and moved out of town, his work complete.

Since that time the towers have been threatened with demolition several times. They lean like the tower of Pisa, and were once thought to be hazardously unsound—a suspicion disproven by city building inspectors. It was not until the late 1960s that people began to realize that Simon Rodia's towers were not only unique, but possibly Southern California's most distinctive architectural landmark.

The Watts Towers are certainly the tallest thing around. They spiral upward like tall mosaic cages, or primitive twin Eiffel Towers. Below the two major spires are several smaller ones, two or three fountains, a thronelike entrance pavilion, a bejewelled concrete ship, and a serendipitous scalloped wall that runs along the street. Everything seems connected to everything else, making the whole environment into a great enclosing web, sparkling with shells, glass, pottery, and tile. Etched into the wall by the main gate are the words "Nuestro Pueblo," which can mean "Our Town" or "Our People." It is Rodia's enigmatic name for his very personal work, which has now been adopted by his neighbors as a symbol of community spirit.

MILL VALLEY

THE UNKNOWN MUSEUM

39 Corte Madera Ave., Mill Valley, Calif.;
no set hours, but usually open on weekend afternoons; free

Car Art is a form of expression admired and practiced throughout America. There are thousands of museums devoted to antique autos, and a few choice shrines to the modern car, like Cadillac Ranch in Texas and Lemon Grove (Edsel Park) in Pennsylvania. The Unknown Museum is the only place we know with an exhibit of that most personal form of Car Art—customizing.

They have on display what is, in fact, the most customized car of all time, a 1961 Ford Falcon that has been covered with thousands of trinkets, souvenirs, and miscellaneous doodads. At first glance it looks as if the artists took a Falcon, covered it with Elmer's Glue, got drunk, and careened through a flea market. But a closer look reveals a sense of artistry underneath the apparent madness. Shoe soles have been affixed in patterned rows along the fenders and doors. Mosaic tiles run the length of the car where chrome once shone. And from one hubcap sprouts a rainbow of feathers. Emerging through the roof of the ex-two-door sedan is a mosaic-encrusted "passenger," wearing what looks like horns or an Indian headdress. The passenger is surrounded by the figures of Donald Duck, Mickey Mouse, dozens of less famous character-dolls, and a few cacti.

Other than this permanent exhibit (which is always being added to by artists Dickens Bascom, Larry Fuente, Lois Anderson, Mickey McGowan, "and others"), the curators of the Unknown Museum tell us that they are seeking to display other objets d'art, as well as "oddities and curiosities from around the globe."

POPE VALLEY

LITTO DAMONTE'S PLACE

Pope Valley Road near the Pope Valley Garage, Pope Valley, Calif.
call first: (707) 965-2342

If the address above seems confusing, don't worry. Litto doesn't think he has a street number. But it would be impossible to miss his house by the side of

Pope Valley Road. In the spot where most people keep their mailbox, Litto has three automobile tires standing up, each painted white, two with the word "Litto" written across them. A surfboard stands between two of the tires. On this he has written "Damonte." Around the surfboard and tires, there is a conglomeration of hubcaps, deer antlers, spoked wheels, birdhouses, shiny pipes, and rocks.

This roadside display of orchestrated junk is itself worth a look, but if you call Litto in advance, there is more to see. He will show you around his yard, filled with over two hundred individually designed birdhouses—in rows, on posts, propped up on discarded toilets, interspersed with a cattle skull here, a road sign there, a crèche, a flower pot, a lantern. The walls of Litto's barn are decorated with hubcaps, and not just ordinary hubcaps. There are sleek "baby moons" everywhere, alternating with vintage 'caps from Buicks and Plymouths, all tastefully arranged in symmetrical patterns, with rectangular TV-dinner plates, license-plate holders, and oval foreign markers to add variety and interest. What is remarkable about Litto Damonte's place is that for all the junk he has here, it doesn't look the least bit junky. Reigning over the clutter is Litto's elaborate but infallible sense of design.

SACRAMENTO

CROAKER COLLEGE

430 Park Fair Dr., Sacramento, Calif.;
by app't: (916) 489–2521

Croaker College is the brainchild of Bill Steed, Professor Emeritus of Frogdom and Doctor of Frog Psychology (Dfp). Under his tutelage, frogs are transformed from neurotic do-nothings into superamphibian overachievers. His alumni are owned by the likes of Johnny Cash, Dinah Shore, and Glen Campbell. Croaker frogs are the nation's elite, most often seen decked out in custom-made suits, showing off their education by giving weight-lifting exhibitions, concerts, or equestrian shows.

Visitors are welcome but only by appointment, since the daily training schedule does not allow for casual interruptions. Frogs begin their day with vibrating massages. Professor Steed then dips them into a tiny whirlpool bath, after which they are given a special diet designed to eliminate any poor nutritional habits they may have picked up before enrollment. Once the frogs are relaxed, Professor Steed will ask any visitors to stand back and be very quiet

—intensive training is about to begin. He flips the frogs over and hypnotizes them by rubbing their bellies. He then stands over them and speaks in a strange dialect that somehow penetrates the learning centers of the sleeping frogs' brains. They are then snapped out of their trances.

All this might seem a bit silly, but there is no disputing the performances given by Croaker-trained frogs on the Johnny Carson, Merv Griffin, and Dinah Shore shows, to name only a few. In fact, we don't know of another academic institution with as high a job-placement rate. Steed's pupils are encouraged to specialize. Some become cowboy frogs, and learn to wear vests and chaps and ten-gallon hats. They are taught to leap onto the back of a toy horse. Other frogs are groomed for the pop singing scene, and cultivate the eccentric dress and mannerisms of Elton John, or the hip gyrations of the late Elvis Presley. A few frogs delve into physical culture, and learn weight lifting. Croaker College is especially strong in bench press instruction.

Steed is the country's major supplier of professional racing and jumping frogs. You will see a Croaker College entry at just about any major Frog Jump in America. His own prize competitor now is one Buffalo Bob, a big bruiser of a toad that has never been beaten.

When you call to visit Croaker College, do not be surprised if the reception-ist goes out of her way to tell you that Croaker is *not* a regular university for humans. She has been beset by out-of-work academics who send Professor Steed their résumés in hopes of a job. Steed says he loves to see their expres-sions when they arrive for an interview and are confronted with rows of frogs draped in terry-cloth exercise suits, loosening up for their morning lesson.

NOTCH PROJECT

Best Products Co., Inc., 1901 Arden Way, Arden Fair Shopping Mall, Sacramento, Calif.;
always viewable; free

Most people are accustomed to entering and leaving a building through a door. A group of writers, designers, and architects calling themselves SITE have discarded that simpletonian notion in exchange for what has to be one of the most amazing buildings in America.

The Best Products showroom is a fairly standard-looking rectangular ma-sonry structure, except that the entryway is at the corner of the rectangle. Here you see a jagged section of the building that has apparently been torn off by King Kong and pushed several yards away. It appears to be a miracle that the building still stands with this chunk ripped off its corner. On closer look, you see that the large crevice between the torn-off chunk and the building is an entryway. The chunk is on rails, and slides away from the building at opening time. At night, it slides back, literally closing the rectangle.

SITE's aesthetic philosophy is worth a book-length explanation, but it is really quite simple. The front page of their brochure quotes Marcel Duchamp: "Have fun, if not you'll bore us."

SAN FRANCISCO

THE AUTOMATIC HUMAN JUKEBOX STREET MUSIC SYSTEM

Beach Street near Victorian Park, San Francisco, Calif.;
summers daily approx. 10 AM–7 PM, winters irregular; donation

Grimes Posnikov, alias the Human Jukebox, is a fixture of the San Francisco streets. For the last seven years he has sat inside a crudely constructed, multicolored box, a jukebox of sorts, with slogans, buttons, song titles, and slots covering the outside. If you put some money in the slot, Grimes Posnikov plays a tune.

The Human Jukebox used to be a regular at Yippie conventions, operating his American Lobotomy Machine outside the convention halls in Miami and Chicago. When he settled in San Francisco he founded the Society for Advancement of Non-Verbal Communication and teamed up with a woman named Miss Harmony, a trick roper.

"I get asked to play 'I Left My Heart in San Francisco' and 'When the Saints Go Marching In' more than anything else," he told us, but there is a slot in his box for tunes other than the regular repertoire listed on the side. If he doesn't know a tune, just hum it for him and he will improvise. If you are a piker, however, and deposit only a nickel, all you get is a kazoo rendition of your song. More generous donations are rewarded with long-playing trumpet performances.

You may, of course, listen to someone else's song, but Grimes doesn't like you to photograph him on someone else's money. Miss Harmony stands outside and collects a "photo tax" from offenders. The box itself is worth a long look. It is like a Flash Gordon rocket ship made by Red Grooms, a festival of gizmos and dials. There are slogans about the recession, inflation, and the Rockefeller trust, and occasionally Grimes Posnikov will discourse on his personal political platform—presidential elections every week, the lowering of the voting age to five. He is one of the most politically minded jukeboxes we have met, and is serious about his brand of street theater. He sees himself on a peace-keeping mission: "Put this box in the Middle East, and it will eliminate all armed conflict."

WINE MUSEUM OF SAN FRANCISCO

633 Beach St., San Francisco, Calif.;
Tues–Sat 11 AM–5 PM, Sun noon–5 PM; free

There are wine museums around the country that trace the way wine is produced, from grape to bottle, but the Wine Museum of San Francisco is unique because it strives to show the ways in which wine has been portrayed and admired by artists and connoisseurs throughout history. It sees itself as a "ceremonial environment where people can come to enjoy and appreciate the efforts of others who have attempted to perpetuate the story of wine and the richness of life."

Outside, a grapevine sculpture supports a sign announcing "The Wine Museum of San Francisco." Inside the museum is a seven-foot-tall vine sculpture carved from Douglas fir, growing out of a textured wooden base which symbolizes the earth. Behind the "vine" is a painting of the sun, while in the other direction there is a picture window looking out on a fountain. The vine, earth, sun, and water—these are the basic elements essential to wine production.

Inside the museum there are overhead beams on which are written quotations from Shakespeare, Li T'ai-po and the like, all in praise of wine. There are porcelains, drawings, prints and sculptures all selected to show the mythology of the grape and the vintner. Two "picto-walls" contain 40,000 words and 250 illustrations showing the "story of wine and civilization," and the history of California wine.

The museum also offers a reference room filled with books on wine, some as early as the sixteenth century—in six languages. This is reserved for use only by serious scholars of the grape.

SAN JOSE

THE WINCHESTER MYSTERY HOUSE

525 S. Winchester Blvd., San Jose, Calif.;
daily summer 9 AM–6 PM, winter 9 AM–4:30 PM;
adults: $3.75, children: $2.25

If a person were obsessed with the idea that eternal building would give them eternal life, and that person had the money to put the belief into practice, what would be the result? The answer is the Winchester House—a bizarre and intriguing Victorian monument to the terror felt by Sarah Winchester, heiress to the rifle fortune.

After a barrage of deaths in her family, the tiny, 95-pound woman turned to a spiritual adviser. He told her that the ghosts of all the people killed by Winchester rifles were out to get her, and the only way to escape was to move from Connecticut to the West, buy a house, and stay one step ahead of the ghosts by continuously enlarging and complicating it. If she added room after room, chimneys and staircases and closets galore, she might confuse the spirits enough to escape them. Since she had millions of dollars, she soon hired 20 servants, 20 gardeners, and 20 carpenters and set them to work. Twenty-four hours a day for thirty-eight years the Winchester House and its 160-acre site were filled with the sounds of saws, hammers, and landscaping tools. Mrs. Winchester died in her sleep in 1922, aged 85.

Wherever possible, Mrs. Winchester used the number 13 in her construction. Each closet has 13 coat hooks; rooms have 13 windows, staircases have 13 steps, chandeliers have 13 candles . . . The house is filled with stairs that lead nowhere, doors that open onto blank walls, trap doors, and escape hatches. Today, as in any self-respecting haunted house, guards report hearing weird sounds and footsteps when no one else is around.

SAN LUIS OBISPO

THE MADONNA INN

100 Madonna Rd., San Luis Obispo, Calif.;
rates from $30 up; call (805) 543–3000

If you are tired of staying in motel rooms that look alike whether they're in Butte, Montana or the Bronx, spend a night at the Madonna Inn. It was designed by Alex Madonna, perhaps as competition for San Simeon, just to the north. It is a design so eclectic that one cannot employ any of the usual categories of taste by which to judge it. Its towers and rocks are brightly lit from the outside with spotlights of red, green, and yellow. Inside, every room is different—but *really* different. The Tack Room is hung with a painting of pink horses, and is decorated completely in red. The Carin Room, for honeymooners, sports a suspended golden cherub above the king-size bed. The little fellow hangs from the purple ceiling on a golden chain. Some rooms look like dormitories, others like Tahitian swimming holes. A series of three is called Ren-dez-vous.

The Madonna Inn is just the opposite of the Holiday Inn philosophy of "no surprises." When a cuckoo clock chirps the time in the middle of the night, or a water wheel spins little men and animals in circles around your bathroom, or you discover your bedspread to be made of leather, you know that your stay here is not going to be just another night in another anonymous motel. For all its eccentricity, the Madonna Inn is a clean and well-run establishment, a delightfully wacky place for the adventurous traveler.

SAN QUENTIN

DINNER TOUR OF SAN QUENTIN PRISON

San Quentin, Calif., Sat nights, March–Oct.;
Limited "primarily" to students of criminal justice and law enforcement personnel;
no ex-felons; no handbags; no blue or black jeans; no cameras; no weapons
(including pocketknives); no narcotics; no alcoholic beverages.
Visitors are urged to have as few metal objects in their possession as possible. No tipping.
By appointment only in advance, call Margie Pometta, Warden's Secretary (415) 454–1460, ext. 201; $4 (includes dinner)

Visitors to the prison gather in the Inspectoscope area, then pass through the metal detector to the front witness room of the gas chamber. Here you are stamped with fluorescent ink. Each tour is broken up into groups containing approximately thirty people, each led by an inmate tour guide.

The tour proceeds through the yard, down the roadway past the dungeon, and into the furniture factory and maintenance vocational building. You then are escorted through the vocational landscape area, the laundry, and the gymnasium. A walk through the west cell block follows. All inmates have been removed prior to the tour's arrival. After the cell block, it's time for dinner.

After dinner, guests repair to the multipurpose room for a light entertainment of not more than three acts, utilizing the talents of not more than twenty inmate performers. There are questions and answers afterward in the Catholic chapel, presided over by the officer of the day. Visitors are then counted out; each one first passes his hands (with the fluorescent stamp on them) under the ultraviolet light.

Per Section 3304 of the Rules and Regulations of the Director of Corrections, "Hostages will not be recognized for bargaining purposes."

SANTA CRUZ

THE MYSTERY SPOT

1953 Branciforte Drive, Santa Cruz, Calif.;
daily 9:30 AM–5 PM;
adults: $1.50, children: 75¢

UFO fans have been trying for years to tell us that there are magnetic cones buried deep in the earth to serve as navigational reference points for flying saucers. Scientists have not been able to offer any better explanation for the strange phenomena that occur within the 150-foot diameter area known as "The Mystery Spot."

A guide ushers you into a one-room shack among the redwood trees of the Santa Cruz Mountains. You will begin to feel the powers at work. No animals come near this spot. Trees grow in twisted, corkscrew fashion. Balls roll uphill. Compasses go kaflooey. Try to stand up straight—you'll find yourself leaning over at a precipitous angle. You may even feel faint from the force of the unseen power.

The Mystery Spot is not the only one of its kind around. There are others in America and Europe—all hidden vortices of power that have never been explained. Albert Einstein himself once visited this Mystery Spot and speculated that a piece of a star was buried deep in the earth, giving off magnetic signals. The question is: How did it get there?

SANTA MONICA

GOLD'S GYM

1452 2nd St., Santa Monica, Calif.;
Mon–Fri 6 AM–9 PM, Sat 8 AM–6 PM, Sun 10 AM–4 PM; free

Gold's has long been the west coast mecca for devotees of physical culture. It is a hang-out for the country's (and sometimes the world's) best body-builders. You will see more muscle inside Gold's on Saturday than you could find in a whole summer scouting the shores of Long Island. Visitors are welcome in this sanctum of pumped-up musculature, and even if you don't spot favorite heroes such as Arnold Schwartzenegger or Franco Columbo, you are sure to see pec's pop, delt's develop, and glutei maximi magnify. Some body-builders claim that when they're really pumping iron, they can *hear* their muscles expanding. All we heard at Gold's were groans and moans as the weights were lifted, and an occasional cry of "What a hunk!" from a spectator.

The only drawback about a visit to Gold's is the way one might feel passing a mirror on the way out.

SANTA SUSANA

GRANDMA PRISBREY'S BOTTLE VILLAGE

4595 Cochran, Santa Susana, Calif. (Simi Valley);
daily, open except when Grandma Prisbrey is eating lunch;
adults: $1, teens: 50¢, kids: 25¢ shoes must be worn.

Grandma Prisbrey began building the Bottle Village in 1955, when she was sixty-two years old. She and her husband had moved their trailer onto a site 40 by 300 feet, and Grandma needed a place to keep her pencil collection. She had about 4,000 pencils then, including one from the governor of North Dakota, her home state. Since there was no money left for construction materials, Grandma Prisbrey drove her Studebaker pickup truck to the town dump and came back with a truck full of bottles. She used the bottles as bricks and built a room to keep her pencils. Since then she has built thirteen more buildings out of glass, ten other structures, and a mosaic sidewalk throughout the one-third of an acre "Village." Her pencil collection has increased to 17,000, now mostly housed in the Pencil House attached to the Round House, which is attached to the Shell House.

Pencils hang in the Pencil House like Spanish moss from a cypress. They are arranged in aesthetic patterns, hanging from the ceiling and decorating the walls, tables, and floor. Some patterns are circular, with all pencils forming spokes of a wheel. Some form patterns of endless horizontal bars, some are hearts, many are carefully planned abstracts. Great blocks of pencils are stuck into Styrofoam. Around the pencils are scraps of taffeta, organdy, and tile. Behind them are the glass walls. It is said that Grandma Prisbrey used one million bottles in her "Village"—each one salvaged from the dump that she went to every single day for nearly twenty years.

From the Pencil Room, Grandma Prisbrey may lead you to Cleopatra's bedroom, its door surrounded by horseshoes, its walls a crowd of brown-neck beer bottles. Here is Grandma's "Monument to Show Biz." Brick steps lead to an ornate bed on which two dolls recline. An altar of kitschy plant containers filled with cactus stands before the bed. Stuffed animals, jars, mirrors, more pencils, and statuettes crowd the tiny space. Of course, the sun shines through the walls of all Grandma's buildings, filtered through brown and green glass, and bottles that Grandma Prisbrey has painted when she could get the paint.

Outside, at the end of the wishing well, there is a five-foot-high pyramid made from automobile headlights, and encrusted at the top with bottles and with 150 gold lipstick cases. "Shades of Cleopatra!" Grandma Prisbrey says.

Other buildings and monuments include the Doll House, which is crammed with dolls in stages of disrepair, seated on chairs, hanging from nails, frighteningly frozen in space. There is one wall made entirely from blue milk of magnesia bottles, another constructed of TV tubes.

Grandma Prisbrey loves taking people through her village, and showing off her work. She has a cat that occasionally gives birth to kittens. Grandma dyes the kittens different colors, and tells the story of the time one man asked her how her kitten got pink. "I fed her mother pink cat food!" was the reply. "I talk a lot," Grandma Prisbrey says, "and people get all excited."

The Bottle Village is the expression of an almost unbelievably creative will, a constant force in existence from the time Grandma Prisbrey hid the wheels on their trailer so they would have to settle down to the present day when, at eighty-five, this grande doyenne of Bottle Art is still on hand to show people her creation. Grandma Prisbrey recently wrote us "I had 5 men from London England, they have quite a brogue. And 2 weeks ago I had 6 Frenchman that couldn't even talk English but they had a lady along who done the talking. I guess you would call I'm famous now." Has Grandma Prisbrey allowed fame to slow her down? Hardly. "I would like to trade shelled English walnuts," she wrote. "Will trade for pencils or dolls. If anyone is interested, please write me . . ."

The Unknown Museum, Mill Valley, Calif.

Roy Rogers, Dale Evans and Trigger, Victorville, Calif.

VERNON

FARMER JOHN MURAL

Clougherty Meat Packing Co., Vernon, Soto, and Bandini Streets, Vernon, Calif.;
always viewable; free

Leslie Grimes had a checkered career as an artist, having painted scenery for 20th Century-Fox, stallions on Mae West's beach house, and palm trees for Vic Tanny's gym. He also worked as a professional wrestler. Today Leslie Grimes is remembered by art historians as the man who painted the Farmer John mural on the side of a meat-packing company in Vernon. Michelangelo Antonioni used it as a backdrop in his film *Zabriskie Point.* It is still there, viewable any time of night or day.

It is a long, long painting of railroad cars with slatted sides. Inside the cars there are dozens of fat pink-and-black hogs. Some have escaped the cars and are seen running along the top of the train, chased by railroad workers with sticks. Behind the train are billowing clouds against a blue sky, lush hills and grass plains. It is a winsome and funny fantasy, with porkers climbing, running, and looking mischievously back at their pursuers.

We learned that Grimes was a man who never planned his work. He painted spontaneously, with the energy of his other profession, wrestling. He died in 1968 when he fell from a scaffold. The Farmer John mural is the best remaining example of the work of this artist of the streets.

VICTORVILLE

ROY ROGERS–DALE EVANS MUSEUM

15650 Seneca Rd, Victorville, Calif.;
daily 9 AM–5 PM;
adults: $1.50, juniors: $1.00, children: 50¢

The Roy Rogers–Dale Evans Museum is best known for having Roy's horse, Trigger, stuffed and on display. Trigger is only one small part of this remarkable shrine to the most popular cowboy and cowgirl team ever to ride the silver screen. Flanking the once-faithful palomino are Dale's horse, Buttermilk, and the family dog, Bullet. Trigger is the most impressive of the three, wearing his silver saddle and bridle, rearing up on his hind legs before a painted western sky. The animals are honored with a poem: "Oh, put my spurs upon my breast/My rope and saddletree./And while the boys lay me to rest,/Go turn my horses free."

There is more than stuffed animals. The museum contains Nellybelle (Pat Brady's gray jeep from the TV series), Hoot Gibson's boots, William S. Hart's easy chair, and Tom Mix's hat. There are scale models of old-time Western vehicles, and Roy's own Pontiac Bonneville, festooned with horns, pistols, silver dollars, and plenty of cowboy-style high-fashion hand-tooling.

"This is our life," the sign at the entranceway says. Most of the exhibits here are very personal. There is "Angel Corner," a shrine to the three Rogers-Evans children who died before adulthood. There are life-size dioramas depicting "typical scenes" from Roy and Dale's home life, including their fabulous Western clothing (some designed by Nudie of Hollywood). In addition to the usual trinkets, the gift shop sells books and records by Roy and Dale, including the best seller *Angel Unaware*.

"Howdy, folks," the happy trails couple says, "Welcome to our museum. We sincerely hope you will enjoy your visit with our families and friends." They call their collection of vintage Americana "The Museum with a Heart."

WEST CAMBRIA PINES

ART BEAL'S HOUSE

Nitwitt Ridge, off Main St., West Cambria Pines, Calif.

Art Beal is an individualist in true California style. He has lived all of his eighty-plus years on the west coast, and he has been busy for the last fifty building his home on Nitwitt Ridge out of found materials. The house is built 250 feet up the side of a cliff, and is a huge meandering structure with nine levels connecting the free-form rooms. Construction materials include rocks, wood, seashells, beer cans, and spare tires—all things that Art Beal, alias "Captain Nitwitt," picked up during his life.

Growing from the house are outcroppings of sculpture, weather vanes, deer antlers, gates, and nameless things that twirl and spin in a breeze. If you visit here, you will most likely find Art working, transforming some new cast-off object into a part of his never-finished environment. He will talk to you about his philosophy of life, and of his antipathy toward the concrete jungles in which many people grow up.

To find his house, just follow the signs pointing to Nitwitt Ridge.

YERMO

POSSOM TROT

Calico Ghost Town Rd., Yermo, Calif.; free

"Free to See. Inside we have the most beautiful dolls U Ever saw . . . hand-carved . . . some can sing." This is one of the hand-lettered signs that welcomes visitors to Possom Trot, an environment inhabited by Ruby Black and fifty dolls. The dolls were carved by her husband Calvin, who also built the trains, structures, and artificial scenery that make up the anthropomorphic landscape of Possom Trot.

The Blacks' creation is in the middle of the California desert, surrounded by ghost towns—the kind of place where the air is so still you can hear a lizard puff out its sac. In this elemental world, Calvin and Ruby created a wooden family for themselves. Each doll is named. There is Hellen, Weird Rhoda, Gizelle, June, Lizie, and Silvia. Each has a stark wooden face. Each wears a dress and wig. They appear to be a strange hybrid cross between an Indian kachina doll and a department-store mannequin. Calvin carved them, Ruby dressed and named them. Most were created to do things. Some are set up on bicycles, some are on a stage, where they dance and kick up their feet. Others skate, a few ride a merry-go-round. In the last few years, Ruby Black has stopped putting on the elaborate shows that once filled the air of Possom Trot with the wooden click of animated beings, but visitors are still welcome to look in at the handiwork, and walk through the Blacks' fantasy world.

Outside, Possom Trot looks like a sketch for a carnival drawn by a child. Dolls are perched on top of buildings or on benches. Some, like "Often Seen Jim and his Limb" appear to oversee the others with a look of wry amusement. There are wooden trains, windmills, and colorful toys—an energetic, whimsical world into which Ruby Black welcomes all who pass by.

COLORADO

BOULDER

ALFERD PACKER MEMORIAL GRILL

University of Colorado, Boulder, Colo.

Everyone complains about college food tasting bad. Here is an example of college food served in bad taste. Alferd Packer, after whom this eatery was named, was convicted of cannibalism in 1886 after spending sixty days in a snowed-in mining camp with nothing to eat—except for five dead men. The judge who sentenced him declared, "There were only six Democrats in all of Hinsdale County, and you, you S.O.B., you ate five of them."

University of Colorado students named their grill after Packer in 1968, and have been trying to make Alferd Packer Day into a nationally recognized event. You can eat a Packerburger in the grill, even though Packer reportedly became a vegetarian after being paroled from prison in 1903.

Packer Clubs around the country (composed mostly of U. of Colorado alumni) have adopted the motto "Serving his fellow man since 1874" (the year Packer invented the Packerburger).

CRIPPLE CREEK

THE OLD HOMESTEAD

353 E. Myers Ave., Cripple Creek, Colo.;
Memorial Day–Mid-Oct daily 11 AM–5 PM;
adults: $1, children 10–12: 50¢, under 10: free

Carrie Nation once called the town of Cripple Creek "a foul cesspool" because of the drinking, gambling, and carrying on for which it was known. East Myers Avenue was once the red-light district of this notorious gold-mining camp, and the Old Homestead was its best-known "Parlor House." Although town records now list names like "Dirty Neck Dell" and "Bilious Bessie" on the 1890s census, it is unlikely that such people ever found their way into the Old Homestead—for this was the classiest bordello in town. Its employees dressed in Parisian gowns and leghorn hats; and its customers were strictly the *nouveau riche*. Under the madamship of Pearl Devere, the Old Homestead achieved a renown equal to the Trois Moulins house of pleasure in Paris.

You can tour the Old Homestead and see from the office the three parlors where Madame Devere's girls once displayed their wares and bargained with customers. Mannequins sit or stand among the cupid-backed chairs, listening to an old Edison phonograph, or beckoning to customers. It is an elegant place, and grand soirées were once its trademark. Among the artifacts displayed are a gambling table (from Johnny Nolan's Saloon, another of Cripple Creek's dens of iniquity), a "fainting couch," and of course, the beds.

Just outside of town, in the Mount Pisgah Cemetery, you can see Pearl Devere's grave—marked with a heart-shaped tombstone.

GOLDEN

BUFFALO BILL'S GRAVE AND MUSEUM

Rt. 5 Golden, Colo. (Lookout Mountain Road, 3 mi. N. of I–70);
Oct 1–April 30 daily 10 AM–5 PM, May 1–Sept 30: 9 AM–7 PM; free

Buffalo Bill was so flamboyant a figure during his life that today, over sixty years after his death, there are monuments, museums, and celebrations in his honor all over the West. Buffalo Bill has come to symbolize the Mythical West —the American epic that had little to do with actual historical fact, but signified instead a spirit and a state of mind. Of all the Buffalo Bill memorabilia around, the memorial museum and grave are among the most interesting—because here is the personal story of the man who brought the Wild West back to the tenderfeet.

The museum highlights his boyhood in Iowa and Kansas, his work for the Pony Express (where he made one of the longest rides on record at age 15), buffalo hunting, scouting for the army, and his debut in show business in Ned Buntline's play "Scouts of the Prairie."

All these experiences were mere preludes to Buffalo Bill's Wild West Show. Here are displayed Buffalo Bill's saddle, costume, and Colt "Peacemaker." Also shown are posters used to advertise the show, artifacts and clothing worn by the Indians, Sitting Bull's .44 Winchester repeater, and exhibits that tell the stories of Annie Oakley and Buck Taylor.

Next to the museum, and encircled by a white picket fence, is Buffalo Bill's grave—a simple marker made of stone over which flies the American flag.

MONUMENT

THE NATIONAL CARVERS' MUSEUM

14960 Woodcarver Rd., Monument, Colo. (Exit 72 off I–25);
Mon–Sat 9 AM–6 PM, Sun 10:30 AM–6 PM (closed at 5 PM Oct–March);
adults: $1, under 14: free with adult.

It's not too often that one drives down the street and sees folks sitting on their porches, lazily whittling a piece of wood. But people still do it, and evidence of the variety and strength of this craft is on display here—the only museum in the country devoted exclusively to whittling and wood carving. It is a large modern building filled with hundreds of displays, ranging from the simplest, charming examples of folk carving to elaborate sculptures.

Some of the most impressive works are those by "Uncle John" Findley, pocketknife artist of the Ozarks, who carves tiny mechanized works inside of bottles. On the other end of the spectrum is George A. Clark's 87-foot chain, carved over several years from ponderosa pine. In the "Baseball Diamond" display are a collection of Louisville Slugger bats, autographed and carved with the faces of famous players. The Boy Scout display shows hundreds of neckerchief slides; and "Carving in a Nutshell" shows seven lucky gods carved into a ginkgo nut. Other exhibits display hand tools and power tools used by craftsmen to "bring out" a piece of wood's flowing lines or grain coloration.

There are memorial displays, with works by great woodcarvers of the past, patriotic displays of Americana, aquarium and aviary displays, religious displays, and "how-to" displays showing the step-by-step evolution from block of wood to finished sculpture.

Woodcarvers-in-residence are often invited here to display their work, demonstrate techniques, and answer questions. And there is a wide selection of instructional books and whittling tools for visitors who find themselves inspired.

GRANGEVILLE

RAY HOLES SADDLE COMPANY

213 W. Main St., Grangeville, Idaho;
Mon–Sat 8:30 AM–5:30 PM; free

A few decades back, any cowboy star would have been considered half-dressed without an ornate saddle on which to rest his hard-ridin' rear. Modern cowboys have streamlined their image since the halcyon days of Gene Autry and Roy Rogers, but it is nice to know that the making of fancy saddles is not a lost art.

Forty-two years ago Ray Holes founded this company, which used to make saddles for the most famous rodeo riders around. Today it is run by his son Gerald Ray Holes, who supplies custom leather products for horses and pack mules to customers around the world. The front of the building is filled with Western wear and tack, but visitors are invited to follow the heady fragrance of good leather toward the back, where Jerry Holes or Bob Kelly will be found, swiftly and steadily turning plain leather into custom dress saddles. They use tools designed by Ray Holes to create "Copper Rose," "Golden Poppy," or "Egabbac Flower" designs. Jerry will tell you that most people have never even seen real hand-carved leather. Most leather labeled as such is made with machine-stamps and precut patterns. No two Ray Holes leather products are alike.

Basic saddles begin at $500 and run up to several thousand for a dude's delight. We know a filmmaker who retired from horseback riding several years ago. He keeps his Ray Holes saddle in his living room for visitors to admire as a work of art, or to sit on and fantasize.

MOSCOW

THE APPALOOSA HORSE MUSEUM

State Highway 8, 1 mi. west of Moscow, Idaho;
Mon–Fri 8 AM–5 PM, weekends by appointment (208) 882–5578; free

The Appaloosa first gained fame as the war-horse of the Nez Percé Indians. They valued it for its speed, stamina, intelligence, level disposition, and distinctive markings. Most people are familiar with the horse's spotted coat—sometimes the spots cover the whole body, and almost always appear over the hindquarters. Other distinctive features are an eye circled with white like a human's, a mottled black-and-white spotting around the nostrils, and vertical black-and-white stripes on the hoofs.

In 1938 there were few pure Appaloosas left, and it was then that the Appaloosa Horse Club was founded. The sponsors of the club took the best descendants of the Nez Percé horses and built a breed that today numbers over a quarter of a million. The Appaloosa Horse Club headquarters are here in Moscow, Idaho, near the original home of the Nez Percé horse. Here are kept the stud books, registration facilities, and a museum devoted to a history of the speckle-rumped horse.

The breed was named for the Palouse River, home of the Nez Percé Indians, but the museum traces the history of the spotted horse as far back at prehistoric times, when cave-dwellers drew them on walls. The American Indians bred them to have enough stamina for mountain life, and yet be quiet enough to keep around a camp. The museum tells the history of the Nez Percé, and of the mountain men, miners, and cattlemen—all of whom played important roles in the evolution of the breed. Saddles, blankets, and other horse gear are displayed, along with a large contour map that traces the routes of the Indians and cavalry during the Nez Percé War, pinpointing important campsites and battlefields.

Visitors with a special interest in the breed can consult the museum's collection of publications and documents, and the established standards for registration. But even the casual visitor looking for a sense of the Old West or an equestrian view of history will have a field day at this museum.

TWIN FALLS

NIGHTCRAWLER AND ANGLEWORM BAKE-OFF

Northern Bait and Ecology Farms, 270 Falls Ave. W., Twin Falls, Idaho;
contest held in March, visitors welcome year round; free

Irene Stockman won last year's bake-off with her special recipe for worm cake. Runners-up included wiggle biscuits, chocolate worm delight, and "Mexican bean casserole mucho wormo." One contestant entered her family's favorite —worm egg salad, but the judges found it a bit bland.

Northern Bait and Ecology Farms want to show the world that worms can be delicious. They are a great cheap source of protein, and most people could harvest enough for "dinner for two" just by raking through their lawn after a good rain. The trick is to beat the early birds. So far the Farms haven't had much success in convincing the general public to replace ground round with mashed nightcrawlers, so most of their worm stock is used for bait and bird-feed. If you come here during the month of March for the bake-off you might be able to coax the people at the Farms into letting you be one of the judges. The only compensation is a T-shirt—plus all you can eat. A plate of spaghetti may never look the same again.

WEISER

THE FIDDLERS' HALL OF FAME

44 West Commercial St., Weiser, Idaho;
Daily 10 AM–5 PM; free;
for specific info call Weiser Chamber of Commerce (208) 549–0452

Weiser has hosted fiddle contests since as far back as 1915. They were discontinued during the war, but in 1953 Blaine Stubblefield, "the Idaho fiddlers' friend," resurrected the contests. Now each year in late June, Weiser hosts the National Fiddlers' contest. It's the biggest old-time fiddling jamboree in the West, complete with beard-growing contests, parades, and staged "vigilante" activities.

For a more sedate look at the world of old-time fiddling, we recommend a visit to the Fiddlers' Hall of Fame. It's a fledgling operation, but they've got some jim-dandy exhibits. It's actually divided into two sections—the Hall of Fame and the Fiddlers' Museum. The Hall of Fame has pictures of grand champions, music, books, and records of the contest back to its beginnings. The museum has famous fiddles, more pictures, mementos, and one piece that steals the show. It is a fiddle made entirely from matchsticks, rarer than a Stradivarius.

MONTANA

ANACONDA

THE WORLD'S LARGEST SMELTER

E. End of Anaconda, Mont.;
tours begin at main gate at 9:45 AM & 1:15 PM, Mon–Fri, June 1–Aug 31; free

A tour of the Anaconda Smelter is an awesome experience, like a dream scripted by Ayn Rand. The "Big Stack" is 585 feet tall, with an outside diameter of 86 feet. 2,466,392 "large bricks"—the equivalent of 6,672,214 common house bricks—were required to construct the twenty-four-ton behemoth. Smoke first belched forth in 1919. To the north of the smelter is a pile of slag that almost dwarfs the Big Stack. Inside, in the copper-casting department, molten metal is poured into molds to produce 465-pound anodes that are 99.5 percent pure copper. We don't know of another tour that is as forcefully expressive of raw industrial might.

Anaconda itself is a copper town from way back. Marcus Daly first called it Copperopolis, and tried to make it the state capital during the "Copper Wars" of the 1890s. Helena, Montana won out, but Anaconda has the biggest smelter. The townspeople still celebrate Smelterman's Day every August 8th, in honor of the industry that put them on the map.

BUTTE

LUIGI'S ONE-MAN BAND AND DANCING DOLLS

1826 Harrison Ave., Butte, Mont.;
Mon–Sat 8 AM–2 AM

Luigi's is a bar in Butte, Montana, but that no more explains this place than describing the Grand Canyon as a hole in the ground in Arizona. Luigi's is like no other place in the world. It is a madhouse, a kaleidoscopic tunnel of fun, a musical menagerie created and presided over by one of the oddest characters in America—Luigi. He is bartender, puppeteer, musician, magician, and master of ceremonies.

Luigi's is best at night. Sit down. Have a drink. Don't mind the stuffed monkey that dangles from the ceiling, about to snatch your glass. Pay no attention to the stuffed sea hawk gliding overhead or the B-52 bomber sailing past on strings. Imbibe some of the décor: pictures of the Kennedys, a four-foot replica of the space needle, decorative toilet plungers, balloons, fish tanks, fluorescent snakes, and Day-Glo rubber spiders. A little dizzy? Go into the bathroom to throw cold water on your face. Here you will see Luigi's mannequin. Put a nickel in her cup and she falls into a million pieces. Best return to your seat. The show hasn't yet begun.

At about 9:30 each night, Luigi himself steps onto a small stage. He begins with lousy jokes and malapropisms, and punch lines that are lost in his thick Slovakian accent. Luigi tells you he is the "Bob Hope of Butte."

He is also the "World's Largest One-Man Band," and when he begins to play "Tiny Bubbles" on the accordion, iridescent bubbles—which Luigi swears are "square"—cascade down over the stage. Then suddenly the whole bar is alive. The stuffed hawks and monkeys begin a phantasmagorical dance in which everything in the bar starts to move. There is no such thing here as an inanimate object. The walls seem to walk with climbing puppets, stuffed toys crashing cymbals, and gyrating dolls. Luigi and his one-man band are now going full blast, and most everything in the room is literally spinning.

If you have been taking Luigi's advice and drinking his special "Tequila Nightmares" (six shots of tequila, six shots of brandy, peppermint schnapps, and orange juice), you will probably think that the whole scene is a marvelous hallucination. But Luigi's bizarre show can be enjoyed cold sober. It is an event to amaze the person who thinks he has seen everything. Luigi is something else.

HAMILTON

RICKETTS MEMORIAL MUSEUM

Off Rt. 93 NW of Hamilton, Mont.;
June 15–Aug 15, Mon–Sat 10 AM–4 PM; free

"From these ticks we will make a vaccine." Above these words is a diorama depicting three men inspecting a tick-infested guinea pig. They are R. A. Cooley, R. R. Parker, and R. R. Spencer, who in 1923 set out to find a cure for Rocky Mountain spotted fever. The diorama is one exhibit in the Ricketts Museum, which is itself located in the small, simple schoolhouse building in which the early tick research was carried on. According to William L. Jellison, the founder and curator, it is the only museum in the United States devoted to the history of a disease.

The Ricketts Museum was named after Dr. H. T. Ricketts, who came west from Chicago in 1906 to study spotted fever. He determined that it was transmitted by wood ticks, and after his discovery went to Mexico to study typhus fever. He contracted the disease himself and died in 1910, aged thirty. Errol Flynn played the heroic doctor in the film *Green Light,* and today the museum remains a monument to Ricketts and others "who worked with highly infectious diseases, knowing full well the hazards of their profession."

In addition to the diorama, the small museum has a collection of documents relating to the history of disease research, and portraits of contributors to good health such as Dr. Ricketts, other researchers, and even Clarence Birdseye, the inventor of frozen vegetables.

MILES CITY

KYUS-TV—CHANNEL 3

Miles City, Mont.

"We have the smallest and most unique TV station in the world," says KYUS-

TV station manager David Rivenes. He and his wife Ella, both in their sixties, serve as programming executives, newscasters, secretaries, talk-show hosts, and entertainers. The only thing they don't do is operate the video equipment. That is handled by three recently graduated engineers. The Rivenes put in seven days a week, seventeen hours a day to beam KYUS-TV into the homes of their Miles City audience.

A sample of KYUS-TV's action-style programming would go something like this: a local rancher's car breaks down near Billings. He calls home to tell his wife he'll be late for dinner, but the line is busy. So he calls Ella at Channel 3 and tells her that his Missus is going to be mighty worried, because he said he would be home by six. Ella tells David, and the information is run as the lead story on the evening news. The other news items are feature stories, human interest, and assorted pleasantries. "If the people want the bad news," David Rivenes said, "they can get it somewhere else. There are too many good things to report."

Other than weather and news, the Rivenes produce a puppet show for kids. David, sitting behind a partition, is the puppeteer; Ella sits in front and talks with the puppet. They've got a talk show, too, on which they interview interesting people from the Miles City area, or folks just passing through. In fact, if you are driving through town or staying in a local motel, give them a call (232–3540). David says "We are almost always able to involve tourists in one of our local live shows. They enjoy it, we enjoy it."

You might even want to have your own show this fall. A "Class A" thirty-minute show goes for $80. Commercial time is available for as little as $8.75 for a ten-second spot.

There are 208 TV stations in the United States. KYUS-TV is 208th in the ratings, with fewer viewers than any other. But where else do the TV programmers know each of their viewers personally?

MISSOULA

SMOKE-JUMPERS' SCHOOL

U.S. Highway 10 E. of Missoula, Mont.;
Mon–Fri, tours start at 3:30, 7 days a week July 4–Labor Day; free

Smoke jumpers are men trained to parachute into forest fires where land transportation cannot reach. Their dormitory and take-off field are seven miles outside Missoula. The public is welcome to come here and see how these steel-nerved firefighters are trained and examine tools they use to extinguish otherwise inaccessible fires.

The first thing one sees is the Exhibit Hall, which explains the origin of most fires (lightning and human carelessness), and displays firefighting tools of the past. In the early 1900s there were only hand tools—axes, shovels, picks—and fires were approached only on horseback. Aerial detection and attack have been in use since the 1940s. Films are shown to give visitors a smoke-jumper's-eye view of a blaze, to show how a fire line is built and maintained, and to explain the work of forest-fire spotters in their lookouts on mountain peaks.

Tours are given throughout the summer, showing the parachute loft, fire lab, warehouse, loading ramp, retardant plant, and training area. The best time to come is during June, since that is when new smoke-jumpers undergo intensive training and conditioning courses. The only thing visitors cannot see is their final exam—seven parachute jumps into the mountain forests.

CARSON CITY

NEVADA STATE PRISON STORE

Fifth St., Carson City, Nev.;
daily 8 AM–7:45 PM

Here's a good place to know about if you are heading through Nevada and need to pick up a birthday or Christmas present for the person who has almost everything. It is one of the most unusual stores in the West—the Nevada State Prison Store, staffed by inmates, situated just outside the prison's main gate. The store sells painting, jewelry, and crafts all made by prisoners. If you don't see what you like, you can special-order it—providing there is an inmate serving time with the appropriate skills. We have seen everything here from repaired saddles (for local ranchers) to hand-lettered wedding invitations. Some cons can even knit a respectable muffler or pair of socks.

Of course, not all work is of outstanding quality. But according to one inmate who told us he has seen his share of hoosegows, the merchandise here rates among the very best.

ELKO

NATIONAL BASQUE FESTIVAL

Elko, Nev., in the City Park, armory, and downtown;
admission varies depending on events; hotel reservations necessary;
1st July weekend

Nevada has become the center for Basques who have come to the mountain country of the West, and Elko is their capital. Every July Fourth, they come from Boise, Winnemucca, Ely, and the surrounding sheepherding country to celebrate their unique culture in a series of dances, contests, and banquets.

The festival begins on Saturday with the playing of "Guernicako Arbola" (the Basque national anthem). Then the bar opens, drinks are served, and spicy chorizo sausages are eaten like hot dogs. Contests include a Walking Weight Carry, in which entrants walk as far as they can with a 104-pound weight in each hand (last year's winner went 988 feet); the Granite Ball lift, in which entrants lift a 225-pound ball to their shoulder, circle it around their neck, let it to the ground, and then do it again—as many times as possible; and other traditional events like the Soka Tira (a Basque tug-of-war), sheepherder's bread-baking contest, and barehanded handball. Saturday's activities are followed by a big dance.

It is well to work up an appetite watching (or participating in) Saturday's contests and dance, because Sunday afternoon is the Basque Festival Feed, and if there is one thing these people know how to do well, it is feast—with plenty of lamb or steak, good breads, stews, wine and brandy. This puts Basques in the right mood for the Irrintzi Contest later that afternoon. "Irrintzi" is a Basque warcry, a cross between a wavering yell, a laugh, a shriek, and a horse's neigh. It provides a fitting end to a wild and colorful festival.

IMLAY

CHIEF ROLLING MOUNTAIN THUNDER'S MONUMENT

Off I-80 in Thunder Mountain, Nev. (near Imlay);
open daily—call (702) 538–7530; donation

Chief Rolling Mountain Thunder's daughter wrote us:

The sculptor of THE MONUMENT (dedicated to the West's Earliest Peoples) is Rolling Mountain Thunder, Medicine Chief. In 1969 Chief Thunder commenced his sculpture in the arid prairie contiguous to I-80 on a piece of geography that was considered valueless, not lived on by contemporary or ancient man.

With the aid of a vintage Chevy p/u truck he put in roads, hauled water, rocks, collected junk items from immigrant days to now, and started his sculptures. Within five years sculptors from several points of the globe declared it to be the "greatest sculpture the world has known."

Chief Thunder is now seventy years old, and lives with his young wife and three children in this desolate part of the Nevada desert. He says he has many other children scattered through Nevada, including "an executive in Reno." He runs a school at Thunder Mountain to teach people how to survive, how to live the Indian way. Visitors are welcome to his monument, for a donation dropped into the box marked "Improve your Image and our Spirits."

Chief Thunder's Monument is three stories high, with walls made from flint, opal, Nevada Wonder Stone, turquoise, onyx, cement, marble, and "thunder eggs." It looks like a festive stone wedding cake that has stayed in the blazing sun to the point where it all began to melt together. It is heavily garnished with carved figures representing American Indian leaders, spirits, and early immigrants.

The top story of the monument is a bedroom with a wall made of bottles. The second story is the Thunder Mountain Library, with a bottle wall and rock arches supporting the ceiling. The ground floor holds the display room and shrine. Massive rock columns and arches support the upper rooms and the mighty sculptures that merge the inside with the outside walls. The shrine holds artifacts of the Hokan-Sioux tribe, and evidence of ancient man's existence in California.

The Monument is a very personal crazy quilt that merges architecture, archaeology, and religion with a desert-pack-rat sensibility. In the Nevada desert it is a powerful counterbalance to the neon seas of Las Vegas or Reno.

LAS VEGAS

THE MINT CASINO—BEHIND THE SCENES

Mint Hotel, 100 E. Fremont St., Las Vegas, Nev.;
daily 11 AM–6 PM (tour leaves every 40 min.);
free; over 21 only

Here is an opportunity to observe gambling from the house's point of view. Del Webb's Mint Hotel and Casino offers tours that allow visitors to peep through the "Eye in the Sky" one-way mirrors and see gamblers in action from a security guard's perspective. The tour also goes through the coin-counting room, where proceeds from the one-arm bandits are piled up higher than Scrooge McDuck's personal treasury. A glass elevator takes tourists to the top of the hotel for a view of Las Vegas. And down below, there is a "school for gamblers" that teaches you everything you need to know about casino games —except how to win.

RENO

THE MOST BEAUTIFUL CAR IN AMERICA

Harrah's Automobile Collection, 2nd St., E. of downtown Reno, Nev.;
Daily June-Sept 9 AM–10 PM, rest of year to 6 PM;
adults: $3.25, teens: $1.75 6–12: $1.25

If Baudelaire had designed cars, the 1938 Phantom Corsair Coupe might have been his crowning achievement. It is an awesome, evil-looking beauty next to which elegant Rolls or Cords or Duesenbergs look positively plain. The Phantom Corsair is a complete custom job; it was designed in 1938 by Rust (57 Varieties) Heinz to be the ultimate in aerodynamic engineering. The front seat has room for four, the back seat faces rear, and the instrument panel features a barometer, compass, and altimeter.

Don't think though that this is a flashy James Bond–mobile that you can't help but love because it spits tacks out on the road to pop the bad guys' tires. The futuristic gizmology here is only a fringe benefit. It is looks that make the Phantom Corsair Number One.

It is jet black, swooping low to the ground. Its wheels are fully covered and its tiny windows are darkened so that none may gaze inside. It is rounded and streamlined, a front sweep of chrome bumper the only flash in the glossy blackness. It appears to have an expression, like a fierce and inscrutable warrior, and rearing back on its haunches, coiled, ready to spring. It looks as though it hardly needs a human driver to come to life. The doors are flush and invisible. The tiny windshield is like two lidded eyes.

At Harrah's Automobile Collection, you can compare the Phantom Corsair with the best—including two Bugatti Royales, a '57 Eldorado Brougham, and Lana Turner's Chrysler Newport. There are over 1,100 vehicles in this glorious collection, but none gives the Phaeton Corsair a run for its money.

RHYOLITE

MRS. HEISLER'S MUSEUM

Rt. 58, Rhyolite, Nev.;
hours vary; admission cost "depends"

Rhyolite is a wonderful crumble of a town, ghostly except for a few hardy souls who tenaciously cling to their homes in the midst of Death Valley.

Mrs. Heisler is one of the survivors; she is originally from Georgia, but here long enough to remember when Rhyolite had fifty-six saloons. She lives in what was once the railroad station. The one-foot-thick stone walls keep out the silver heat of the sun. She uses the front room of the depot as a museum and curio shop open to the few people who are passing through.

On display in Mrs. Heisler's museum are trinkets and artifacts from the heyday of Rhyolite, picks carried by miners during famous strikes, and some of the possessions of Shorty Harris, the "single blanket jackass prospector," once a personal friend of Mrs. Heisler, who lies buried nearby. She says that "all of Europe" has visited her tiny collection of mementos, rocks, and faded photographs.

Mrs. Heisler is a Death Valley character who should not be missed. You'll know how much she likes you by what you are charged to get into the museum. Admission price seems to depend on how she sizes you up.

TOMMY THOMPSON'S BOTTLE HOUSE

Rt. 58, Rhyolite, Nev.;
always viewable; donations

Tommy Thompson died last year, and his bottle house is now maintained by his son. Thompson was a musician who played his accordian in the saloons of Rhyolite when it was a boom town. That was back in 1905, the year that

Tom Kelly, a saloon owner, constructed a house out of 51,000 bottles. When the boom went bust, Tom Kelly moved out and Tommy Thompson moved in. He stayed in the bottle house with his pet dogs and a collection of ancient curios from the wilder days of Rhyolite. The Bottle House is today open to the public, and is just a stone's throw from Mrs. Heisler's Museum.

OREGON

WORLD CHAMPIONSHIP TIMBER CARNIVAL

Timber Linn Memorial Park, Albany, Ore.;
July 4th weekend;
adults: $3 for the weekend, children 6–12: $2 for the weekend.

The Timber Carnival is like a rodeo, only here instead of cowboy *vs.* beast it is logger *vs.* tree. Each contest pits the world's best loggers against each other. The skills measured are things like log-rolling, speed-climbing, tree-topping, double-bucking, and the horizontal chop. At the end of the weekend, an All-Around Logger is crowned, and contestants return to their homes, some of which are as far away as Tasmania and Australia.

A look back over the record books tells how intense modern competition is. In 1941 the top tree-topper was Jack Tienhaara of Washington, with a time of six minutes, twenty-four seconds. Tree-topping means you must climb to the top of a pole forty inches in circumference and a hundred feet tall, and saw through its width. Time is measured from the moment you leave the ground

to when your cut hits the ground. The 1974 winner still holds the world record
—one minute, eighteen seconds! Speed-climbing (up and down a one hundred-
foot pole) has been honed from a 1946 time of one minute, nine seconds to
thirty-three seconds in 1972. Our favorite event is the awesome power-saw
championship, in which contestants mow through a thirty-inch diameter log
with a buzz saw. Top time here is seven and four-tenths seconds.

As at a rodeo, there are fun events, too, like the men's and women's log
rolling contests, in which the field of contestants is narrowed down by giving
them thinner and thinner logs, until only one is left above water, rolling
furiously. There is a horse-pulling contest, a lumber parade, and clown acts
on top of spar poles.

PORT ORFORD

PREHISTORIC GARDENS

Highway 101 between Port Orford and Gold Beach, Ore.;
daily 8 AM–dark; adults: $2, students: $1.50

Mr. and Mrs. E. V. Nelson don't just run a dinosaur park. Prehistoric Gardens
is a shrine to the animals they love, a veritable dinosaur fan club. "We've got
a whole woods full here," Mrs. Nelson told us. "Every one is an exact model.
My husband made sure of that." The Nelsons have been here since 1955,
building and tending their *Triceratops, Brachiosaurus,* and others. Each dino
has an individual plaque, explaining how it fits into the evolutionary scheme,
favorite foods, and "leisure-time activities." We are not qualified to judge the
scientific accuracy of the Nelsons' efforts, but we can say that these dinosaurs
are real beauties—in perfect condition, freshly painted and well-maintained,
with none of the plaster-of-Paris patchwork, tubular distension, or old-age
decay that besets dinosaur parks with less enthusiastic or less able proprietors.

Prehistoric Gardens is set in a gorgeous coastal rain forest, as much an
attraction as the cold-blooded beasts who inhabit it. The Nelsons' property
goes all the way to the ocean, although the Gardens' walkways don't afford
a view of the water. It is audible, though, and the sound of the waves in the
distance adds just the right note of elemental significance to Prehistoric Gardens' primeval scenes.

ROGUE RIVER

NATIONAL ROOSTER-CROWING CONTEST

Downtown Rogue River, Ore. (just outside of Grants Pass off Highway 99);
last Saturday in June; free

Beetlebaum is the Babe Ruth of rooster crowing. He has 109 crows to his credit, a record set in 1953, the first year of the annual contest. Since that date, cocky fowls with names like Guber, Drum Stick, and T-Bird have tried to crow their way close to Old Beet's record, but none has even topped a hundred.

For some strange reason, the contest begins at two-thirty in the afternoon rather than at dawn, when one would expect the birds to be most loquacious. Rooster handlers get thirty minutes to coax cackles and squawks from their entries. The one who crows the most wins. There are additional prizes for the most unusual rooster cage and for the rooster who came the farthest to enter the contest.

The National Rooster Crow also includes a parade in which Riley, the eight-foot fiberglass rooster, rides up and down the street, selection of a Rooster Queen, an official photography session with the winning bird, and a barbecue (all beef).

SAND LAKE

WIBB WARD'S BEARS

2 mi. past Sand Lake Store on Galloway Rd, turn left Sand Lake, Ore.;
always viewable; free

Wibb Ward is an ex-logger who loves to work with wood. He lives in a grove of trees, and all around him in his clearing are animals he has carved. Most of them are bears of various sizes, some black and some brown. The bears all have rounded bodies and faces that resemble those of expressive dogs. Some are naked, as in nature, others wear Smokey-style hats, and a few are dressed in pants. There is a bear "couple" that looks like man and wife, a bear standing at a podium delivering a lecture, a small group of bears sitting together having a pow-wow, and one vagabond bear, with his belongings slung over his shoulder and carried on a stick.

There are other animals, too, including a duck with a tiny stovepipe hat, a jack rabbit with gigantic ears, and a green tortoise, who is apparently challenging the rabbit to a race. Wibb told us he was working on a "bigfoot" sculpture, but we weren't sure whether he meant a sculpture of a big foot, or of the legendary Bigfoot.

He began carving in 1964, and has sold some of his works to local people as lawn ornaments or for home decoration. But he much prefers to keep his creations in the woods around his house—where they look very much at home.

UTAH

MONUMENT VALLEY

GOULDING'S TOURS OF MONUMENT VALLEY

Goulding's Lodge, off Route 163, Monument Valley, Utah;
tours March 15–Nov 1, 9 AM to 5 PM (lunch included);
$25–$30 per person, depending on number of persons & exact tour; reservations:
(801) 727-3231

Goulding's began as a lodge and trading post in Monument Valley in 1923, when the West was still pretty wild. In 1939 John Ford brought his cast and crew here to film *Stagecoach*. Since that time, Monument Valley has become part of the American Western mythology, and Goulding's has become a first-class, air-conditioned facility for tourists who want to see "John Ford Country" for themselves.

Tours from Goulding's are conducted in large four-wheel-drive station wagons, for three to six people at a time. It is an all-day adventure, conducted by bilingual Navajo guides who show you through ancient Indian camps and the ruins of long-gone Valley civilizations, point out fossil prints of prehistoric animals, hidden canyons, Indian cornfields, and flocks of sheep and goat—while traveling through what is surely the most spectacular natural landscape in America. It is easy to see how John Ford was able to use this setting as a heroic backdrop for his epic vision, but even if you've never seen a John Ford Western you will find a visit to Gouldings an awe-inspiring experience.

OPHIR—PARIA

THE GHOST TOWNS OF OPHIR AND PARIA

Ophir: 20 mi. SSE of Tooele; Paria: on the Paria River, 40 mi. NE of Kanab, Utah

Selecting the right ghost town to visit can be as difficult as choosing the country's essential dinosaur parks or outstanding halls of fame. There many ghost towns scattered across Utah, Nevada, and California; some have completely disintegrated and are only sites of former towns; others are mere piles of wood; still others have been turned into tourist attractions, and are anything but ghostly. Unless one has the time and energy to explore all of these, Ophir and Paria, in Utah, are our nominations for the two places to go. They are sufficiently decrepit and depopulated as to give the feeling of time's sands trickling down; and yet they retain enough character to suggest what they were like during the boom.

In fact, some folks still live in Ophir. The few dozen who remain inhabit the comfortable old homes shaded by immense locust trees. The Utah Travel Council warns "Please use discretion when entering a dwelling; it may be a private home!!!" Much of Ophir is falling apart, but it is still a beautiful place. It was built into a narrow canyon during the 1860s to house the men working the gold, silver, copper, zinc, and lead mines in the surrounding hills. The brothels, dance halls, saloons and earthen sidewalks are still there, and if you try very hard you may be able to hear the wild spirits of the boomers who flocked here from Nevada and California.

Paria is completely dead. It was settled as a farming community in 1868 by the Mormons. Floods kept chasing the settlers out, and gold-mining companies tried to pan the waters, but got flooded out themselves. What remains today are those implements and structures that have been impervious to the flood waters: a few cabins and remnants of sluice boxes, some farming tools, and a cemetery.

WASHINGTON

THE WORLD'S LARGEST BUILDING

Boeing 747 Division Plant, 25 mi. N. of Seattle on State Highway 526 near Everett,
Wash.;
June-Sept Mon–Fri 9 AM & 1 PM, Oct–May at 1 PM only;
no children under 12; by reservation only (206) 342–4801

This is not a vertical behemoth like the Sears Tower or the World Trade
Center, but rather the building with the most interior space. It is large enough
to accommodate six 747 jumbo jets in the making—205 million cubic feet laid
out across fifty-three acres.

Boeing Company tours of this 747 assembly building begin with a film, then
proceed along a specially constructed viewing platform high up in the eleven-
story building, from which viewers can see the "assembly line" in action.
Unlike Detroit, things here move quite slowly, and one is impressed more by
the colossal nature of the enterprise than by speed or efficiency. The line moves
ahead every fourteen days, in between which you can see workers riveting in

the sub-assembly and assembly sections. "Primary manufacturing" and "final operations" on the planes take place elsewhere in the 780-acre Boeing complex in Everett.

The tour of the world's largest building, including the film, lasts just over an hour. Reservations are essential.

GARDINER

LOBOLAND

Route 101 in Gardiner, Wash. (28 mi. E. of Port Angeles);
daily 10 AM–dusk;
adults: $2, children: $1

Loboland has the last of the buffalo wolves, a breed that got its name as a result of the wolves' habit of following the buffalo herds. As the buffalo disappeared, so did the wolves, until Dr. E. H. McCreary rounded up the few remaining specimens he could find and tried to keep them in a close-to-natural habitat in Pennsylvania. In 1971 McCreary moved his brood of wolves to Washington, where they are now tended and nurtured by Jack and Marjorie Lynch.

Between 10:00 A.M. and dusk every day you can walk through Loboland (escorted, of course) and see these magnificent animals running relatively free in large, natural enclosures. The *Canis lupus nubilus* is the largest of wolves —reaching two hundred pounds at maturity and standing as tall as a full-grown mastiff. The wolves have small ears with a sort of "rainbow curve" that looks like a dog's "rose ear." They are almost completely silent and travel in pairs. A Loboland tour takes visitors close to the wolves, but, for obvious reasons, there is no petting allowed. Some of them look as gentle as a family dog. Others are skittish and maintain a distance.

Loboland has other species of wolves, too, mostly for comparison's sake. There are little Mexican desert wolves, the Siberian wolf, and usually a litter of buffalo wolf puppies. Loboland has almost a hundred and fifty wolves altogether, and it is a beautiful place to observe them—overlooking Discovery Bay just off Route 101.

MARYHILL

AMERICAN STONEHENGE

Rt. 14 near junction of US 830 & US 97, 2 mi. NE of Maryhill, Wash.

The building of the original Stonehenge, that awesome calendarium in Wilt-shire, England has been attributed to everyone from Druids to men from Mars. The origins of America's Stonehenge are a bit clearer. Samuel Hill, a pacifist, wanted to build a monument to commemorate World War I and the soldiers who died in it. He figured that since the original Stonehenge has an altar stone in the center that was supposed to have been used to make sacrifices to the god of war, an exact duplicate might serve as his own offering, and might stand as a reminder of the losses suffered in the Great War.

So here it is in Maryhill, Washington—forty stones, each nine feet high, surrounded by thirty stones each sixteen feet high, five pairs of trilithons rising up to twenty-eight feet, and in the center a great altar stone. On the outer slabs are engraved the names of local men who lost their lives during the war.

The major difference between this and the original Stonehenge is that Amer-ica's version is, of course, comparatively brand-new, with none of the runic mystery that has drawn tourists to the ancient Stonehenge. But perhaps people four thousand years hence will discover Samuel Hill's monument and wonder over its archaeological eccentricity and astronomical accuracy. His creation isn't exactly "original," but it is the only exact, life-sized duplicate of Stone-henge in the world.

SHELTON

SIMPSON TIMBER COMPANY

Main gate on Railroad Avenue, Shelton, Wash.;
Mid June-Mid Sept, two tours: 10 AM & 1 PM;
no children under 12; free

Shelton, Washington calls itself Christmas Town in honor of the evergreens that grow all around and the number of trees processed by the Simpson Timber Company. Every summer Simpson offers tours showing how majestic trees are converted into planks and boards. Tours go through the plywood plant, where one sees logs come out of the water and through the voracious debarking machines. In addition to the plywood plant, visitors see the logs cut down by various cut-off saws, headsaws, edger saws, and trim saws. Visitors should expect to view this mighty display of heavy machinery from a minuscule catwalk up above. Fresh-cut wood everywhere makes this the best-smelling tour in the Northwest.

SPOKANE

THE CROSBYANA ROOM

Upper floor of the Crosby Library, Gonzaga University, East 502 Boone Ave., Spokane, Wash.;
Mon–Fri 8 AM–5 PM by appointment (Library open year-round);
free (donations accepted)

West magazine once published a cartoon of a man sprawled out on his face under the gate of Gonzaga University. He has just been given "the bum's rush" by three priestly silhouettes, who are depicted in the distance marching militantly back toward the campus. The caption reads "He talked against Bing Crosby in Spokane." It's hardly a joke, for Spokane and more specifically, Gonzaga University is a small island of Bing-o-mania. Bing himself was a classmate of Father Francis Corkery, the nineteenth president of Gonzaga, and over the years he contributed generously to the university. In return for his charity, Gonzaga U. established the Crosby Library and reserved a very special section to commemorate the life and work of "der Bingle." It is called the Crosbyana Room, and is generally used for conferences. But when it's free, make an appointment to take a look. It is a fascinating shrine.

The walls of the Crosbyana Room are lined with glass cases containing over three thousand pieces of Crosby family memorabilia, including genealogy records, citations, awards, and photographs. There are twenty gold records, from still-remembered hits such as "White Christmas" and "Too-Ra-Loo-Ra-Loo-Ra" to "Galway Bay" and "Pistol Packin' Mama." There is a platinum plaque of "White Christmas" commemorating Bing's sales of over two hundred million records. There is Bing's Academy Award for *Going My Way,* and a sketch of the award done by Father Vachon. There are awards and mementos from all over the world, including a citation from Mysore City, India, electing Bing Crosby as "The Most Emotional Hero of 1944."

WYOMING

CODY

BUFFALO BILL HISTORICAL CENTER

Sheridan Ave. & 8th St., Cody, Wyo.;
June, July, Aug daily 7 AM–10 PM, May & Sept daily 8 AM–5 PM, Oct, Nov, Mar,
April Tues, Thurs, Sat, Sun 1 PM–5 PM
Adults: $1.50, 6–15: 75¢, under 6: free

The Buffalo Bill Historical Center is four museums in one—The Plains Indian
Museum, the Whitney Gallery of Western Art, the Winchester Museum, and
the Buffalo Bill Museum. It is the complete museum of the Old West—as it
really was, and as it was in art and legend.

The Plains Indian Museum displays material telling of the Sioux, Cheyenne,
Shoshoni, Crow, Arapaho, and Blackfeet tribes, including personal belongings
of their chiefs—ceremonial pipes, headdresses, beadwork, and weapons. One
learns that most Indian beads were imported from Venice until 1850, when
white men started trading French and Czech beads to the Indians. The museum also informs us that scalping was a custom unknown to most of the Plains
tribes until white scalp-hunters came around.

The Whitney Gallery of Western Art has works by Remington, Bierstadt, Catlin, Russell, Moran, Bodmer, and others—paintings, prints, and sculptures documenting the real West and the fantasy-land of the Wild West.

Across from the Art Wing are the Winchester Collection and the Buffalo Bill Museum. In the Winchester Museum there are over five thousand projectile arms—the complete story of American firearms, from matchlock through Gatling gun to modern weapons. The collection was begun in 1860 by Oliver Winchester, and moved from Winchester Arms in Connecticut in 1975. It is considered the most complete firearms collection in the country.

In the Buffalo Bill Museum you will find guns, saddles, clothing, trophies, posters, uniforms, and Bowie knives—a vast collection representing the life and career of Colonel Cody. There are faded photos of Annie Oakley, Kit Carson, General Custer, and Crazy Horse. There is a scalp and war bonnet allegedly taken by Cody from Cheyenne Chief Yellow Hand after Cody killed him with a single shot. There is even an Indian bone necklace, supposedly made from the trigger fingers of Custer's men.

The best time to see the Buffalo Bill Historical Center is over the Fourth of July weekend, when the town of Cody hosts a "stampede" that brings cowboys in from all the nearby towns to whoop it up, Old-West style.

THE HOTEL IRMA

1192 Sheridan Ave., Cody, Wyo.,

If you come to Cody for the stampede or for a look at the Buffalo Bill Historical Center, make sure you spend the night at the Hotel Irma. It was built by Buffalo Bill in 1902, and named for his youngest daughter. For the last seventy-five years it has been a gathering place for cattlemen, oilmen, and the wool-growers of Wyoming.

Although the Irma has air conditioning, TV, and other modern facilities, it has preserved its Victorian look. The walls are hung with period pictures. The rooms have washbowls and basins, and vintage furniture is still the favorite. There are suites named after famous Westerners, like the Jimmy Tuff Suite (he rode horses better than anyone else), the Simon Snyder Suite (he was an early dude rancher), and five others, including Buffalo Bill's own.

The bar at the Irma is famous in its own right. It is solid cherrywood and valued at over $100,000, a gift to Buffalo Bill from Queen Victoria in return for the command performance of the Wild West Show he put on in England.

The bar was made in France, shipped to New York by steamer, sent by rail to Red Lodge, Montana, then taken to Wyoming by horse-drawn freight. It is an ornate piece, heavily carved with turrets and finials, and looking perfectly at home in this remaining piece of Old-West history.

DOUGLAS

THE JACKALOPE CAPITAL OF THE WORLD

Douglas, Wyo.

On Center Street in the small town of Douglas, Wyoming, there stands an eight-foot statue of a jackalope. Outside of town on Interstate 25 a sign warns motorists to "Watch out for jackalopes." The Chamber of Commerce of Douglas issues jackalope hunting permits. And almost every saloon in town has at least one jackalope head mounted on its wall. There is nothing extraordinary about this, except that there are some people who claim that there is no such thing (in nature) as a jackalope.

These doubters will tell you that the jackalope was a mythical animal created in 1934 by local taxidermist Ralph Herrick along with his brother Douglas. They "invented" the animal by mounting deer antlers on a jack rabbit's head. They sold their trophy to a local tavern keeper as a tourist attraction. Since 1934 the Herricks and others have sold nearly 3,500 jackalope trophies to tourists, at about fifty dollars apiece.

We personally have never seen a living jackalope and, indeed, the jackalope trophies do look a lot like a rabbit with deer's antlers. But Douglas people explain that the jackalope is a real "sportin' animal," and the only reason we've never seen one is that "the jackalope is perhaps the rarest animal in North America." (These words are taken from the Jackalope hunting license.)

One thing is sure. If you don't see any live jackalope when you travel to Douglas, you can stock up on jackalope heads, bumper stickers, post cards, and canned jackalope milk. You may even learn to distinguish the lonesome wail of the jackalope under the starry Wyoming sky.

Locals explain that Douglas is also a good place in which to hunt fur-bearing trout.

FORT BRIDGER

EYE-GOUGING AND EAR-BITING CONTESTS

Fort Bridger Muzzle-Loading Rendezvous, Fort Bridger, Wyo. on highway 30.;
Labor Day weekend

What is your romantic ideal? To some, it is standing decked-out in whites and a captain's hat at the wheel of a yare schooner, the sea wind in their hair. Others fantasize a grand promenade in ante-bellum Natchez, Mississippi, living the life of Scarlett and Rhett. But a handful of men and women live out their romantic ideal by dressing in fringed buckskins, dining on buffalo stew, sleeping in a lean-to at night, and spending the day gouging each other's eyes and trying to bite off other people's ears. These are the "mountain folks" who band together every Labor Day weekend at Fort Bridger to shoot, trade, and tell tall tales.

The rest of the year they are architects, truckers, postmen, etc., but when it is time for the Muzzle-Loading Rendezvous, they return to more primitive styles of work and fun. Of course, the eye-gouging and ear-biting contests are now governed by rules to prevent severe bodily damage, as are the whip fights and shooting challenges. There is rattlesnake wrestling, knife- and tomahawk throwing, flint and steel fire-building races, Indian wrestling, and other appropriate mountain-style fun. While the men fight it out, the women husk corn or chew on leather to soften it for moccasins. Participants refer to each other by names like "Leg Shot" Highbee, Jim "Big Red Ramrod" Giles or "Broken Hand" Helms instead of plebian first names like Irving or Fred.

The occasion for this gathering is the annual celebration of the Great River Rendezvous held over 150 years ago at Fort Bridger. If you come to the Rendezvous, be sure to look inside the fort. They've got "Liver Eatin'" Johnson's rifle on display. Johnson was the man portrayed by Robert Redford in the film *Jeremiah Johnson*. Of course, what the film didn't show was how the famous mountain man got his name: eating the fresh-plucked livers of people he didn't like.

As far as we know, there are no liver eatin' contests at the Fort Bridger Muzzle-Loading Rendezvous. Events are limited to more civilized activities.

JACKSON

BUFFALO JERKY

Jackson Cold Storage and Distributors, 125 S. King, Jackson, Wyo.;
8 AM–6 PM Mon–Sat; free

Jackson Cold Storage and Distributors is one of the few places around that specializes in buffalo meat. Cattle aficionados are probably aware of "beefalo" (the cow-buffalo cross that is supposed to be easier to raise), and almost everyone knows that you can go to Wall Drug and similar "Old-West" eateries and get buffalo burgers. But how many people have had a chance to sample buffalo jerky, buffalo salami, or buffalo thuringer?

"Why buffalo?" you ask. The Jackson Cold Storage people explain: "Buffalo meat is high in protein, low in cholesterol and saturated fats and is nonallergenic. Because buffalo thrive on nature's ingredients alone, they do not need the drugs or antibiotics that are usually given to beef cattle; the meat is wholesome, pure, natural, nutritious food. The taste is similar to beef, but, we believe, better than beef; it is sweet, tender, juicy, and fine-grained."

Free samples are available in the Cold Storage store, along with "gourmet paks" of assorted products and recipes for hors d'oeuvres such as buffalo pinwheels and buffalo rolls. If you are expecially interested, you can be shown through the Cold Storage plant at no charge. And a catalogue of buffalo products is available by writing "Box A" in Jackson.

GENERAL INDEX

SUBJECT INDEX

Animals

Albert the Bull, 263
Amarillo Livestock Auction, 365
American Pet Motel, 254
American Work Horse Museum, The, 231
Angora Goat-Breeders Association Museum, 385
Annual World Chicken-Pluckin' Contest, 157
Appaloosa Horse Museum, The, 419
Arabian Horse Museum, 74
Aspen Hill Pet Cemetery, 81
Attwater Prairie-Chicken Refuge, The, 372
Big Duck, The, 95
Buzzard Sunday, 318
Calaveras Jumping Frog Jubilee, 391
Chinatown Chickens, 102
Clydesdale Hamlet, 49
Coon-Dog Barking Contest, 205
Coon Dog Memorial Park, 137
Croaker College, 401
Dinosaur Gardens Prehistorical Zoo, 290
Dog Mart, The, 229
Drum the Bloodhound Monument, 304
Eel Institute, The, 5
Ely Sled-Dog Races, 295
Fred Bear Museum, The, 286
Fred the Horse, 203
Frog Festival, 187
Goldfish Farm, The, 78
Gopher Count, The, 297
Governor's Annual Frog-Jumping Contest, 216
Greyhound Hall of Fame, 273
Hall of Fame of the Trotter, 96
Handsome Dan, 12
Hermit Tree Crab Race and Beauty Pageant, 88
Igor the Rat, 333
International Chicken-Flying Meet, 322
International Worm-Fiddling Contest, 148
I.Q. Zoo, 145
Jackson Laboratory, The, 20
Loboland, 440
Lucy the Elephant, 86
Mangum Rattlesnake Derby, 357
Microzoo, The, 274
Montfort Reptile Institute, 111
Morse Museum, The, 52
Mount Desert Oceanarium, The, 30
Mule Day, 163
Mule Days Celebration, 199
Mule-o-rama, 352
Nash-ional Dinoland, 41
National Hard Crab Derby, The, 77
National Mule Memorial, The, 383
National Muskrat-Skinning Contest, 76
National Rooster-Crowing Contest, 435
New Jersey Pheasant Farm, The, 85
Nightcrawler and Angleworm Bake-Off, 420
Nisswa Turtle Races, 296
Noba Artificial Insemination, 323
Old Rip, 372
Petrified Creatures Museum, 115
Prehistoric Gardens, 434
Purple Martin Festival, 215

Rattlesnake Roundup and International Gopher Race, 154
Red Hen Monument, 54
R. L. More, Sr., Bird Egg Collection, 387
Sea-Turtle Watch, 151
South Georgia Horse Auctions, 168
Spider Museum, The, 235
Stonewall Jackson's Stuffed Horse, 232
Three Musical Bears and Twisting Squirrels, 339
Trackmaster, 47
Traveller's Grave, 233
University of Vermont Morgan Horse Farm, 64
Warfield Quail Farm, 189
Wibb Ward's Bears, 435
World Championship Duck-Calling Contest, 147
World's Largest Concrete Buffalo, 312
World's Largest Jack Rabbit, 384
World's Largest Lobster Trap, 27
World's Largest Pheasant, 326
Waynoka Rattlesnake Hunt, 352

Architecture

Abo Elementary School, The, 350
Art Beal's House, 412
Big Duck, The, 95
Chateau Laroche, 319
Chief Rolling Mountain Thunder's Monument, 428
Coal House, The, 241
Coral Castle, 150
Corn Palace, The, 326
"Creek" Charlie Fields' Polka-Dot House, 231
Eddie Martin's Home, 161
Everett Knowlton's Town, 30
Fox Theater, The, 161
Fred Burns's House, 21
Gingerbread House, The, 237
Grandma Prisbrey's Bottle Village, 408
Indeterminate Façade, 378
Little House at Ellwood Park, The, 248
Lucy the Elephant, 86
Madonna Inn, The, 405
Mammy's Cupboard Restaurant, 192
Mrs. Quigley's Castle, 144
Notch Project, 402
Paper House, The, 39
Salt House, The, 376
3/5 White House, The, 381
Tommy Thompson's Bottle House, 431
Willie Owsley's House, 175
Winchester Mystery House, The, 405
World's Largest Building, 439

Birthplaces

Babe Ruth Birthplace Shrine and Museum, 73
Billy Graham's Birthplace, 200
Birthplace of the Gideon Bible, 329
Birthplace of Miniature Golf, The, 221
Birthplace of the Women's Christian Temperance Union, 249
Elvis Presley Birthplace, 195

Music

Natural Phenomena

ABOUT THE AUTHORS

JANE and MICHAEL STERN live in a pink house in southern Connecticut. When not at home they can be found watching movies, searching for a good restaurant, or walking their bull terrier, Spud. Michael is completing his doctoral thesis on films of the 1950s. Jane graduated from Yale with a Fine Arts degree. For the last five years, the Sterns have spent much of their time traveling America's highways researching long-haul truckers, small-town cafés, and the country's most unusual places to visit.

YOU'LL NEVER
HAVE TO EAT
PLASTIC FOOD AGAIN!

ROADFOOD

Hunger-struck on the highway? No need to settle for plastic food. A copy of ROADFOOD by Jane and Michael Stern will clue you in to the best of America's down-home regional cuisine—and at prices which will please your purse as well as your palate! From catfish parlors in Georgia to seaside stands featuring the best lobster rolls in Maine to seventy-two ounce Texas steaks and the best barbecue in the Western world, the over 400 great restaurants in ROADFOOD—each within ten miles of a major highway—will whet the appetites of all adventurous and budget-minded travelers.

A Random House/David Obst Book
$6.95